Sensory Marketing

What is sensory marketing and why does it matter? This book offers a global view of the use of senses in marketing strategy based on consumers' perception and behavior.

Integrating the company constraints and classical approaches of branding and communication, the author presents sensory marketing as an emergent marketing paradigm in theory and practice.

With a comprehensive historical introduction, this book will be an important contribution that will provide useful reading for marketing scholars and consumer psychologists across the world.

Bertil Hultén is Professor of Marketing at Linnaeus University, Sweden.

Routledge Interpretive Marketing Research

Edited by Stephen Brown *University of Ulster, Northern Ireland*

Recent years have witnessed an 'interpretive turn' in marketing and consumer research. Methodologies from the humanities are taking their place alongside those drawn from the traditional social sciences.

Qualitative and literary modes of marketing discourse are growing in popularity. Art and aesthetics are increasingly firing the marketing imagination.

This series brings together the most innovative work in the burgeoning interpretive marketing research tradition. It ranges across the methodological spectrum from grounded theory to personal introspection, covers all aspects of the postmodern marketing 'mix,' from advertising to product development, and embraces marketing's principal subdisciplines.

1 **The Why of Consumption**
   Edited by S. Ratneshwar, David Glen Mick and Cynthia Huffman

2 **Imagining Marketing**
   Art, Aesthetics and the Avant-garde
   Edited by Stephen Brown and Anthony Patterson

3 **Marketing and Social Construction**
   Exploring the Rhetorics of Managed Consumption
   By Chris Hackley

4 **Visual Consumption**
   By Jonathan Schroeder

5 **Consuming Books**
   The Marketing and Consumption of Literature
   Edited by Stephen Brown

6 **The Undermining of Beliefs in the Autonomy and Rationality of Consumers**
   By John O'Shaughnessy and Nicholas Jackson O'Shaughnessy

7 **Marketing Discourse**
   A Critical Perspective
   By Per Skålén, Markus Fellesson and Martin Fougère

8 **Explorations in Consumer Culture Theory**
   Edited by John F. Sherry Jr. and Eileen Fischer

9 **Interpretation in Social Life, Social Science, and Marketing**
   By John O'Shaughnessy

10 **Interpreting Consumer Choice**
   The Behavioral Perspective Model
   By Gordon R. Foxall

11 **Managing Service Firms**
   The Power of Managerial Marketing
   By Per Skålén

12 **Interactive Marketing**
   Revolution or Rhetoric?
   By Christopher Miles

13 **Beyond the Consumption Bubble**
   Karin M. Ekström and Kay Glans

14 **Music, Movies, Meanings, and Markets**
Cinemajazzamatazz
By Morris B. Holbrook

15 **Generation Y in Consumer and Labour Markets**
By Anders Parment

16 **Consumption and Spirituality**
Edited by Diego Rinallo, Linda Scott, and Pauline Maclaran

17 **Contemporary Perspectives on Corporate Marketing**
Contemplating Corporate Branding, Marketing and Communications in the 21st Century
Edited by John M.T. Balmer, Laura Illia and Almudena González del Valle Brena

18 **Motherhood, Markets and Consumption**
The Making of Mothers in Contemporary Western Cultures
Edited by Stephanie O'Donohoe, Margaret Hogg, Pauline Maclaran, Lydia Martens and Lorna Stevens

19 **Brands**
Interdisciplinary Perspectives
Edited by Jonathan E. Shroeder

20 **Analyzing Music in Advertising**
Television Commercials and Consumer Choice
Nicolai Graakjær

21 **Sensory Marketing**
Theoretical and Empirical Grounds
Bertil Hultén

Also available in the Routledge Interpretive Marketing Research series:

Representing Consumers: Voices, views and visions
Edited by Barbara B. Stern

Romancing the Market
Edited by Stephen Brown, Anne Marie Doherty and Bill Clarke

Consumer Value: A framework for analysis and research
Edited by Morris B. Holbrook

Marketing and Feminism: Current issues and research
Edited by Miriam Catterall, Pauline Maclaran and Lorna Stevens

Sensory Marketing
Theoretical and Empirical Grounds

Bertil Hultén

NEW YORK AND LONDON

First published 2015
by Routledge
711 Third Avenue, New York, NY 10017

and by Routledge
2 Park Square, Milton Park, Abingdon, Oxon OX14 4RN

*Routledge is an imprint of the Taylor & Francis Group,
an informa business*

© 2015 Taylor & Francis

The right of Bertil Hultén to be identified as author of this work has been asserted in accordance with sections 77 and 78 of the Copyright, Designs and Patents Act 1988.

All rights reserved. No part of this book may be reprinted or reproduced or utilised in any form or by any electronic, mechanical, or other means, now known or hereafter invented, including photocopying and recording, or in any information storage or retrieval system, without permission in writing from the publishers.

Trademark Notice: Product or corporate names may be trademarks or registered trademarks, and are used only for identification and explanation without intent to infringe.

Library of Congress Cataloging-in-Publication Data
A catalog record for this book has been requested

ISBN: 978-1-138-91462-9 (hbk)
ISBN: 978-1-315-69068-1 (ebk)

Typeset in Sabon
by Apex CoVantage, LLC

Printed and bound in Great Britain by
TJ International Ltd, Padstow, Cornwall

Contents

List of Tables and Figures   ix
Preface   xi

1 History of Consumer Marketing   1

2 The Marketing Dynamics   57

3 Sensory Marketing   88

4 The Brain and the Five Senses   128

5 The Sense of Sight   172

6 The Sense of Sound   221

7 The Sense of Smell   261

8 The Sense of Touch   304

9 The Sense of Taste   338

10 Multi-Sensory Brand-Experience   369

11 Sensory Marketing in the Future   394

Index   401

Tables and Figures

Tables

1.1	Producers' Distribution and Marketing, 1870–1930	5
1.2	Institutions and Distribution Methods, 1870–1930	8
1.3	Service Logic and Goods Logic—A Comparison	35
1.4	Assumptions about Received and Emergent Paradigm	53
2.1	Characteristics of Different Stages of Societies	60
2.2	The Main Characteristics of Fordism and Post-Fordism	63
2.3	Materialist/Postmaterialist Dimensions in Fifteen Countries	67
2.4	Culture of Society and Value System in a Global Marketing Environment	71
2.5	Values among Generations X, Y, and Z	76
3.1	TM, RM, and SM—A Comparison	102
3.2	Senses, Sensory Stimuli, and Sensations	112
5.1	A Classification of Stimuli in a Service Environment	194
7.1	Cultural Associations of Smells in Low and High Emotional Contexts	277
7.2	Associated Scent Experiment	284
7.3	Examples of Impact of Scents	287

Figures

1.1	Significant Stages in the Development of Consumer Marketing in Theory and Practice	3
1.2	Exchange and Relationship Perspectives in Marketing	27
1.3	The Howard and Sheth Model of Buyer Behaviour	37
1.4	Consumers Decision-Making	43
3.1	Individualization as Lifestyle	93
3.2	A Conceptual Model of Sensory Marketing	106
3.3	The Five Senses, the Firm, and the Individual	107
3.4	The Five Senses and the Sensory Experience	109

3.5	Sensory Marketing as Explanatory Model	120
3.6	The SEB-Model	123
4.1	Brain Areas and Structures	133
4.2	Left and Right Cerebral Hemisphere	135
4.3	The Perceptual Process	140
4.4	The Location of the Senses in the Human Brain	141
4.5	The Brain's Memory System	143
5.1	The Function and Structure of Vision	177
5.2	The Sense of Sight and the SEB-Model	184
5.3	Mehrabian-Russell-Model	193
5.4	Different Types of Brands	218
6.1	The Structure of the Ear	224
6.2	The Sense of Sound and the SEB-Model	232
7.1	The Structure of the Smell Sense	265
7.2	The Sense of Smell and the SEB-model	270
8.1	The Structure of the Skin	307
8.2	The Sense of Touch and the SEB-Model	312
9.1	The Concept of Taste	339
9.2	The Structure of the Tongue	343
9.3	The Sense of Smell and the SEB-Model	348
10.1	The Function of the Human Senses Externally and Internally	370
10.2	Sensory Reception, Processing, and Integration	373
11.1	The Five Senses and Their Impact Factors	396
11.2	A Framework for Sensory Branding	397

Preface

INTRODUCTION

Over the past five years, research in sensory marketing has expanded and spread on a global scale in a most significant way. From previously having been an unknown conference topic at the large annual scientific marketing conferences, such as the European Marketing Academy (EMAC), the Academy of Marketing Science, and the American Marketing Association (AMA), today sensory marketing has come to be recognized as an independent, scientific research area, compared with areas such as advertising, relationship marketing, or branding. Many researchers believe that sensory marketing will become more significant in the future and will establish itself as an important area for both academicians and practitioners.

In today's research, sensory stimuli, or sensory input, is addressed in connection with a place, a brand, or an environment where a service is offered and about how it looks, sounds, smells, feels, and tastes are perceived and influence consumers. It may relate to the impact on both consumers' product evaluation and choice of a product or as consumers' affections, cognitions, and actual behaviors regarding, for example, how much time is spent in a store or how much money is spent on the purchase of a certain brand.

The starting point in my research is to first understand how businesses, using the five senses, develop sensory experiences for consumers based on various sensory strategies and sensory stimuli. In the Swedish book *Sinnesmarknadsföring*, which was published in its first edition in 2008 and its second edition in 2011, how companies use the five senses to create long-term and sustained marketing is presented. The book *Sensory Marketing* was published in English in 2009 and has since been translated into Korean and Polish. It should also be mentioned that in 2014, the book was published in Chinese in Shanghai.

The interest in my research has always been great, and I have experienced strong support with many positive comments, from both colleagues in academia and practitioners in the business world. Without a doubt, this great interest has spurred me and helped me to develop this book.

The idea for this book arose in connection with the Swedish book, written together with my coauthors, Niklas Broweus and Marcus van Dijk, which received the Marketing Book of the Year in 2008. In connection with a seminar at HUI Research in Stockholm, Professor Sven-Olof Daunfeldt addressed the question of what the theoretical and empirical starting points might be to lay the foundation for sensory marketing. Thanks to this discussion, the work began to try to answer this question, which is this book's main purpose.

In recent years, I have presented my research at various scientific conferences and seminars in Denmark, China, Portugal, Sweden, Germany, and the United States. Furthermore, I have continuously published scientific articles in journals such as the *European Business Review*, *International Journal of Retail and Distribution Management*, and *Marketing Intelligence and Planning*, where both conceptual and empirical contributions have been presented. Recently, I have also written a chapter, together with Clarinda Rodrigues, PhD at Porto University, published in the book *Novos Horizontes Do Marketing*, which was released in Portugal in 2014. The book includes various scientific contributions from researchers in Brazil and Portugal on the current state of marketing and its development.

My research is conducted at the School of Business and Economics, Linnaeus University, Kalmar, Sweden, in a research group within sensory marketing at the Center for International Business Studies on Emerging Markets (CIBEM) together with colleagues and graduate students. The research is particularly focused on sensory marketing and branding, which receives increasing attention in the international research arena. This research is conducted at the national level in collaboration with Swedish companies such as Ikea and Volvo Cars. The research is also conducted at the international level, in collaboration with Porto University, Portugal; Zheijang University, China; the University of South Florida (USF) as well as the University of Northern Florida (UNF) in the United States.

CONTENT AND STRUCTURE

In this book, sensory marketing is treated on the basis of different theoretical and empirical starting points based on what is known today in research and literature. My desire has been to both on a broad level and a detailed level discuss and present what sensory marketing means and is characterized by, as a new emerging paradigm. This means that the book is based on different concepts, models, and theories that have been drawn from disciplines and research areas, such as consumer behavior, consumer psychology, marketing, neuroscience, sociology, and branding to name a few of the most common.

Using an eclectic approach as a marketing researcher, I have the ambition, with the help of these concepts, models, and theories, to offer an understanding of sensory marketing, which goes beyond today's notions

Preface xiii

of what marketing is all about in a global marketing environment and consumer culture. Then, mass marketing and relationship marketing as well as branding constituted the foundation to which sensory marketing must be related to in order to create a new understanding and knowledge of sensory marketing as an emergent marketing paradigm.

The first chapter presents the *historical development of consumer marketing*, as a theoretical discipline and practice. The theoretical ideas that are established in the form of transaction marketing, relationship marketing, and service logic are addressed in detail. Various concepts and models within consumer behavior, consumer culture theory, and branding are discussed further to lay the foundation for the continued development of consumer marketing.

The second chapter presents *the two forces of change*, in the form of the cultural value shift and the digital technology, which is most prominent in a global marketing environment and consumer culture. These two forces of change influence and give rise to new consumer values, behavior, and consumption patterns of consumers, as new strategies for dialogue, communication, and value creation in corporate marketing.

The third chapter presents *sensory marketing* (SM) as an emerging paradigm and approach in consumer marketing. Initially, a number of theoretical starting points are discussed with a postmodern approach, which lays the foundation for a better understanding of sensory marketing. In particular, the importance of service processes, sensory experiences, and sensory strategies are discussed with respect to consumer value, consumer experience, and brand as image. Finally, the significance of sensory marketing and a multi-sensory brand-experience are presented.

The fourth chapter presents *the human brain* as the center of the five senses. Different concepts of the brain's organization and structure as well as the role of the senses in the brain are covered in depth. In addition, the differences between a male and a female brain are discussed with regard to organizational, emotional, and sensory differences. Finally, the emergence of neuromarketing and its relevance to sensory marketers is discussed.

The fifth chapter presents *the sense of sight*, which is considered to be one of the strongest senses regarding sensory stimuli and sensory perception. The fundamental role of the sense of sight is addressed with respect to both physiological characteristics and psychological aspects. Thereafter, the importance of the societal culture, service environment, and brands is discussed with regard to stimuli, perception, and symbolism as well as their impact on an individual's affections, cognitions, and the actual behavior in the different buying and consumption processes.

The sixth chapter presents *the sense of sound*, which is considered to be one of the most intimate of a human's five senses. Various scientific ideas about the fundamental role of the sense of sound are addressed with respect to both physiological characteristics and psychological aspects. Thereafter, the importance of the societal culture, service environment, and brands are discussed with regard to stimuli, perception, and symbolism as well as their impact on an individual's affections, cognitions, and the actual behavior in the different buying and consumption processes.

The seventh chapter presents *the sense of smell*, which is considered to be strongly associated with both emotional and cognitive reactions of a human. Various scientific ideas about the fundamental role of the sense of smell are discussed with respect to physiological characteristics and psychological aspects, as well as the importance of a scent's effects. Thereafter, the importance of the societal culture, service environment, and brands is discussed with regard to stimuli, perception, and symbolism as well as their impact on an individual's affections, cognitions, and the actual behavior in the different buying and consumption processes.

The eighth chapter presents *the sense of touch*, which is considered to be strongly associated with both emotional and cognitive reactions of a human. Various scientific ideas about the fundamental role of the sense of touch are discussed with respect to physiological characteristics and psychological aspects, as well as the importance of touch and feeling. Thereafter, the importance of the societal culture, service environment, and brands is discussed with regard to stimuli, perception, and symbolism as well as their impact on an individual's affections, cognitions, and the actual behavior in the different buying and consumption processes.

The ninth chapter presents *the sense of taste*, which is considered to be one of the strongest emotional senses of a human's five senses. Various scientific ideas about the fundamental role of the sense of taste are discussed with respect to both physiological characteristics and psychological aspects. Thereafter, the importance of the societal culture, service environment, and brands is discussed with regard to stimuli, perception, and symbolism as well as their impact on an individual's affections, cognitions, and the actual behavior in the different buying and consumption processes.

The tenth chapter presents the *multi-sensory brand-experience*, which refers to the interaction between two or more senses for the individuals' perceptions and sensory experiences of the service environments and brands. Different ideas about the importance of the multi-sensory interactions are highlighted by means of studies. Thereafter, the different types of multi-sensory interactions and how these contribute to creating a multi-sensory brand-experience are discussed.

The final chapter discusses the book's main *conclusions* and suggestions are made for further research and development of sensory marketing in theory and practice.

THANKS

I would like to thank those people who contributed with knowledge, comments, and constructive suggestions to the book's various chapters.

During the book project, Gentiana Qavolli, my research assistant at Linnaeus University, searched through existing literature for the work on the chapters on the five senses. I would especially like to thank Gentiana for her great accuracy and theoretical sensitivity for different concepts and theories regarding the five senses. In relation to Chapter 7 about the sense of smell, Gentiana is a coauthor. Her great interest in scent marketing and her deep knowledge of the subject led to the chapter becoming as rich as it is.

My previous coauthor Niklas Broweus has in a very insightful way contributed with improvements, which I greatly appreciate. Furthermore, my colleges Hans Allmér, Kjell Arvidsson, and Åsa Devine, senior lecturers at the School of Business and Economics, have provided comments on the various chapters during the writing process.

I especially want to thank Professor Hans Jansson and Professor Stefan Lagrosen, both of whom, on their own initiative, contributed with constructive comments during the preparation of the book. Furthermore, I also want to thank my two PhD students, Andreas Eklund and Miralem Helmefalk, for the interesting comments and inspiring discussions regarding the book's various chapters.

Thanks to Meena Stromqvist, Stockholm, for the excellent work with the translation of the Swedish version of this book. It was a great experience to take part in the translation process from Swedish to English.

I also want to thank David Varley, Brianna Ascher and Autumn Spalding from Routledge, New York, for their assistance and support during the process with finalizing this book.

Last, but not least, thanks to my wife, Eva, for your inspiration and your support in my work to finish writing this book.

For those of you who want to get in contact with me, I can be reached at bertil.hulten@lnu.se.

Herreberga Farm, Blentarp, Sweden, Spring 2015

Bertil Hultén

1 History of Consumer Marketing

This chapter analyzes and discusses the historical development of marketing as a theoretical discipline as well as management practice with a focus on consumers. The dominating theoretical ideas established in the research and literature, namely transaction marketing, relationship marketing, and service logic, are addressed in depth. In particular, the differences between these approaches with respect to the relevant concepts, models, and theories are discussed to understand the development of consumer marketing in theory and practice.

Furthermore, how consumer marketing has evolved over different epochs with respect to various changes in society is emphasized. The economic, organizational, and social conditions that characterize a society during different periods have affected the development of consumer marketing, both theoretically and practically. Finally, the current situation of consumer marketing is analyzed and discussed based on the new theoretical frameworks that are emerging and being established.

THE MODERN MARKETING

The Importance of Consumption and the Freedom of Choice

The idea of free consumption and free personal choice for all individuals has influenced the emergence of the modern industrial society as the current global consumer society during the last three centuries. During this time, the industry's most important role in society has been to produce goods and services for personal consumption. This has been the case historically, and private consumption today plays a crucial role in a country's economic development and prosperity.

Already in the late 1700s, the economist Adam Smith suggested an economic system that was based on the personal self-interest, and the individual's utility maximization was accepted as prerequisites for a society's economic and social development. Further, giving all people in a society access to the goods and services that were produced emphasized the importance of free personal choice.

A voluntary and competitive exchange of goods and services, which emanated from both the sellers' and the buyers' personal self-interest, could lead to economic prosperity in society. Thus the principles for administering and building an economic system had been organized by the market—*the invisible hand*—and the possibility to satisfy the personal self-interest was established for both the producers and the consumers.

Ever since man first came to the realization that it is possible to meet one's own personal satisfaction through consumption, marketing, as a function and process, has existed and developed, which Baker (2000, p. 19, op. cit.) expressed as:

An insight which was to lead to acceptance of task specialization and exchange as the foundation for increased productivity and higher standards of living.

The principle of consumer sovereignty has been the basis for the theory of free personal choice, which came to constitute marketing—one's philosophical roots. Therefore, marketing has, in practice, come to express the economic principles, which have emanated from the personal self-interest. Historically, these principles of social welfare development as well as individuals' consumption and choice have formed the basis for the practical application of marketing. The time line that follows shows some of the key events that have affected marketing development, both theoretically and practically, with mainly American starting points (Figure 1.1).

For centuries, the fundamental starting point in a society was that sellers and buyers of goods and services met to exchange ideas and information and conduct business with each other. But from one social epoch to another, the methods and approaches have varied and changed, based on the new conditions that existed. But a meeting between the parties has always taken place by either the buyer going to the seller or vice versa.

> *"Even before Jesus's time, the classic market-place, where buyers and sellers meet to do business, was of central importance for the exchange of goods."*

Until the mid-1700s, the business life as a cultural element was regarded by most people as almost a criminal phenomenon. Before the introduction of the market economy, there were no established distribution or financial systems and both manufacturing and transportation were primitively developed areas. Furthermore, the majority of the population lived in rural areas and accounted for their livelihood through self-manufacturing and production. Thus there was no gap to be overcome between production and consumption. It is estimated that among the population, there was between

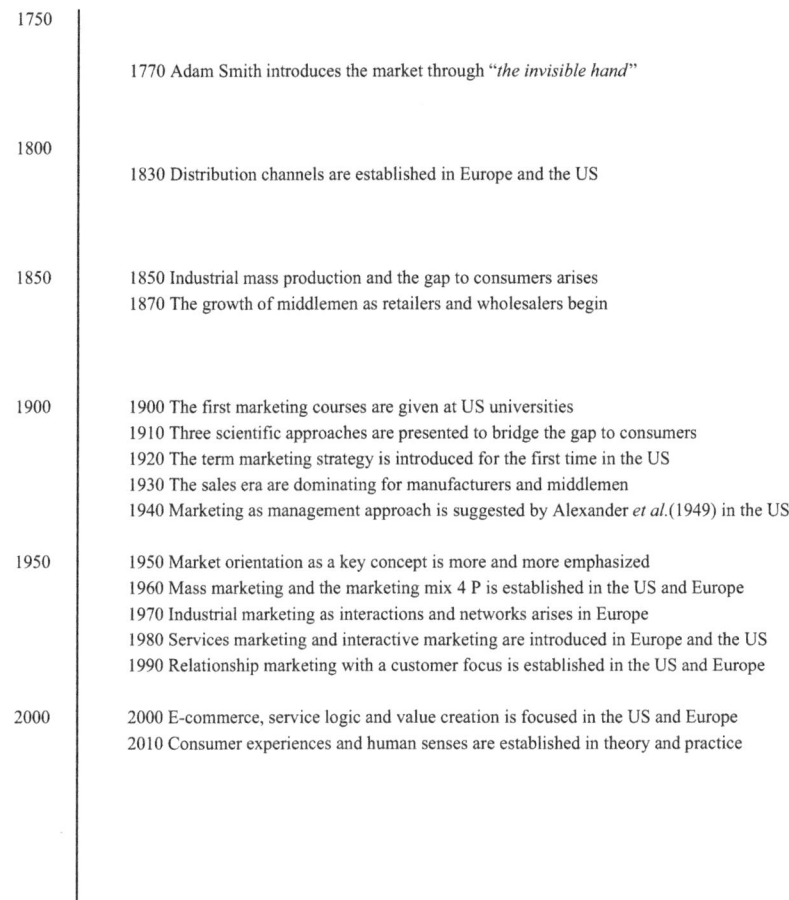

Figure 1.1 Significant Stages in the Development of Consumer Marketing in Theory and Practice

75 and 90 percent who were totally dependent on their own livelihood, whereas influential religious, political, and social forces opposed an increase in consumption, which at that time was very low.

Any monetary economies did not exist either, but it was common with barter. The most common meeting place for producers, merchants, and consumers was the local market, and contemporary businessmen—tradesmen and merchants—lacked the economic, organizational, and technological possibilities to be able to develop mass markets, i.e., markets that were not local but regional or nationwide.

It was, thus, natural to create and develop key institutions at the local level, such as stores, wholesale operations, warehouses, or a traveling salesman, to name a few typical examples. Eventually, financial institutions such as banks and formal credit facilities as well as paper money began to be created and developed, which offered new opportunities for buyers and sellers to do more businesses.

The Institutional Development as the Foundation

The historical development of the market can be traced back to Great Britain in the mid-1700s, followed by Germany about a decade later, and the United States around 1830. This first era, until the mid-1800s, was marked by a breakthrough of the market economy, among other things, to be able to meet and better stimulate the demand for goods and services that existed in society at that time. The Industrial Revolution, through the new cutting-edge innovations, such as production in factories and transport by rail and steamship, created the conditions for what later came to be mass markets. At the same time, the first urbanization processes began, which involved the relocation of many people from rural to urban areas. This created new economic opportunities for sales, purchasing, and distribution, and the importance of these activities for the development of society was great.

The functional and organizational development of marketing in society has meant a gradual establishment of the modern marketing, as illustrated in Figure 1.1. This has enabled an economic development in which production and consumption have come to be the focus for achieving higher standards of living, quality of life, and welfare for the general public. This development is considered to have started in Great Britain in the mid-1800s, then came to Germany, and then the United States two decades later and lasted until the early 1930s.

Mass production had its breakthrough during this time and led to a concentration of manufacturing and a powerful stimulus for demand. A geographical distance between the producers and buyers arose, as more and more goods started to be produced in factories. This meant that it became necessary for most manufacturers to have access to various institutions in marketing to be able to reach out to a local or regional market. This required that one should be able to distribute and disseminate information about their goods and services to the general public, who were also seen as potential customers.

For that reason, advertising, intermediaries, physical distribution, and market research, to name a few examples, were required, which Fullerton (1988, p.122, op. cit.) expressed as follows:

> *The new institutions and practices helped make marketing a major element of daily life for most of the population; descendants of self-sufficient peasant were consumers in the modern sense.*

The institutions and the methods that were established and developed during this period are shown in Table 1.1.

Table 1.1 Producers' Distribution and Marketing, 1870–1930 (Fullerton, 1988, p. 114–116)

Producer activities	Examples	Source
Branding, use of trademarks—before 1870, increase after	Pear's Soap (UK)—around 1860. Sapolio cleanser (USA)—from 1869 showed power of branding. Henkel's Soda (Germany)—1876.	Redlich (1935) Wilson (1954)
Packaging—to identify brand to appeal and protect—paper, board, pottery, glass, cans, and foil in use around 1900.	Dr. Lyon's Tooth Powder (USA)—1874. Lever introduced first laundry soap carton in 1880 (UK). Canned asparagus—several popular brands in Germany.	Davis (1967) Minchinton (1982) Wilson (1954)
Segmentation—widely practiced by producers, also mass producers. Many products intended for specific segments.	General Motors, "a car for every purse and purpose." Parker Pen & Co.—40 pens from USD 1.50–20.00 in 1899 catalog.	Lawrence (1977) Fullerton (1985)
Market analysis—study of competition, market potential, customer needs. Some American firms had established market Research departments around 1920.	Velhagen and Klasing analyzed demographics of customer lists in the 1880s. U.S. Rubber & Co., Swift & Co., Curtis Publishing Co., 1910–1920. General Motors tied production to short-run sales forecasts in the 1920s.	Egbert, Holbrook and Aldrich (1931) Fullerton (1985) Shaw (1916) Sloan (1965) Simmons (1924)
Producer-owned "branch houses" with wholesale functions allowed direct distribution to retailers.	Big meat packers like Armour, Cudahy, Swift and Wilson each had 400–500.	Breyer (1931) Ivey (1921)
Producer-owned retail stores, producer-franchised retail stores allowed direct sales to consumers.	Pioneered by Singer in mid-1800s. Clothing and shoe manufacturers and sporting firm A.G. Spalding 1920.	Egbert, Holbrook and Aldrich (1931)
Producer-dominated cartels established to ensure channel domination, e.g., Germany.	Exchange Union of German Booksellers controlled distribution and powerful department stores 1880–1890.	Hirsch (1925)

(Continued)

6 *History of Consumer Marketing*

Table 1.1 (Continued)

Producer activities	Examples	Source
Producer-operated direct sale to consumers, door-to-door sales, and mail order.	Used to open U.S. market for typewriters, cooking stoves, sewing machines, electric irons, washing machines, and kitchen cabinets.	Converse (1930) Nieschlag (1939)
Increased contact with independent retailers and chain stores.	Increased cooperation through sales training, window displays, advertising, and demonstrations.	Converse (1930)
Manufacturer-supported consumer credit for costly items as cars, appliances spread in the United States to circumvent banks' conservatism.	Pioneered by Singer around 1850. Willys-Overland and other auto firms around 1915 and General Motors 1919.	Hounshell (1984) Sloan (1965)
Advertising by producers expanded, including direct mail and cooperative advertising.	McCormick built part of its success on heavy advertising of its farm implements in the United States from 1850. Soap firms like Lever and Pears, United Kingdom, Procter & Gamble, United States, and Henkel, Germany, advertised heavily from 1870. The U.S. automobile industry was the heaviest advertising spender of any industry by 1915.	Fullerton and Nevett (1986) Presbrey (1929) Redlich (1935)

One can see from the summary that different groups of customer groups were at the center of the manufacturer's marketing already in the late 1800s and early 1900s. Noteworthy, segmentation, which is considered one of modern marketing's most important theoretical points, had already begun to be practiced then. This shows the leading manufacturer's early awareness that just one product could not generate satisfaction among all the buyers. The question of being able to distinguish the buyers from each other, based on needs and satisfaction, has been regarded as the very essence of modern marketing theory.

History of Consumer Marketing

> "Segmentation came to be applied early on by the producers as a fundamental principle in consumer goods marketing."

It also appears that the producers were active early on in creating and developing effective distribution channels, and the intermediary's role and importance was emphasized. This has been the basis for the claim that production and distribution have gone hand in hand when it comes to marketing's institutional development. The function of wholesaling, in this context, contributed to the emergence of a more comprehensive physical distribution at both the national and regional levels, whereas the retail operations contributed to the physical goods becoming exposed and available to the general public. It should be added that advertising agencies contributed in different ways to create awareness and interest in the goods, with the help of direct mail and interaction with the market.

Finally, it should be said that the creation of the new institutions also contributed to the emergence of competition between the institutions, which came to further stimulate the demand that existed at that time. An efficient and effective management function was considered to be of importance in the new institutions to succeed in the competitive situation that had arisen. Thanks to the new institutions that were founded and established in the late 1800s and early 1900s, there were conditions that producers needed in order to be able to introduce and implement their comprehensive marketing program, as shown in Table 1.2.

One conclusion is that in the historical development of modern marketing, the intermediaries, through the formation of institutions such as independent retailers, wholesalers, and franchises made it possible for the emergence and establishment of large-scale producers. With this, both the producers and intermediaries have contributed to marketing as an emerging scientific discipline from the early 1900s.

EPOCHS AND STAGES OF DEVELOPMENT

A Producer-Oriented Approach

Generally, the modern marketing development is analyzed and discussed based on a number of different epochs and stages of development in a society, through concepts such as production orientation, product orientation, sales orientation, and market orientation. Until the 1930s, wide distribution coverage and high production efficiency were the focus of what is called the production orientation. Thereafter, the product organization, as well as various sales and advocacy activities, came to be the focus of marketing in the 1940s, 1950s, and 1960s.

Table 1.2 Institutions and Distribution Methods, 1870–1930 (Fullerton, 1988, pp. 118–120)

Advertising agencies—*media analysis and creative work.*	*In the United States and Britain agencies were marketing consultants around 1900. They did research for clients, designed products and packages. They also did "scientific research in the psychology of advertising and promotion.*	Boss (1886) Fox (1984) Pope (1983) Redlich (1935)
Cash-and-carry—*sales for cash only, allowing lower prices and faster service.*	*Adopted by most chain grocery stores in the United States around 1908*	Converse (1930)
One-price selling—*items sold at the same price for efficient retailing.*	*Used by chain stores and department stores, as well as independent retailers*	Beable (1925) Ivey (1921)
Self-service—*customer served self, increased importance of advertising, packaging, and store display.*	*Adopted by U.S. grocery chains and independent retailers around 1916 and maybe earlier*	Converse (1930)
Mail order—*stimulated demand, enabled entrepreneurs to compete with passive retailers.*	*Started with parcel post around the 1870s and had some decline in the United States when the rural population declined and stores could be reached by car*	Ivey (1921) Nieschlag (1939) Worthy (1984)
Chain stores—*standardized operations, location, inventory control, displays, employee training, and sale as specialists.*	*Established from the mid-1800s with a huge expansion in the United States during the 1920s but also in the United Kingdom and Germany*	Converse (1930) Nieschlag (1959) Worthy (1984)
Department store—*pioneer institution of modern retailing, created modern "shopping" behavior, direct buying from manufacturers, popularized "customer is always right" philosophy.*	*Expanded around 1910–1920 in the United States and Europe to maintain high-value image through downtown palaces*	Beable (1925) Converse (1930) Nieschlag (1959)

An increased focus on consumer needs, integrated marketing, and profit through customer satisfaction meant that market orientation, as a concept, had an even greater importance from the late 1960s. During the past three decades, from the mid-1980s, customer orientation has emerged as a concept, which has come to focus on the importance of interactions, long-term relationships, and value creation between a company and its customers, regardless of whether the customer is a company or a consumer.

> *"For many decades, production orientation was the main focus of marketing."*

The importance that commodity production received in many companies, known as the term "production orientation," has been highlighted in an article by Keith (1960) to explain the evolutionary development of marketing. It describes how the marketing function by a producer, namely, the Pillsbury Company in the United States, had developed during the 1800s and 1900s. It appears that the production epoch has been regarded as covering the period from the late 1860s to the 1930s. Thereafter began the selling epoch, with a focus on advertising, market research, and personal selling, which lasted until the 1950s. This epoch was replaced by a marketing epoch, with a focus on a more sophisticated marketing with elements of segmentation, positioning, and target-audience thinking.

On the basis of this article, the Pillsbury Company, as a producer of consumer goods, has been considered to be representative of how the American producers developed their marketing during the 1900s. This case, thus, came to build the foundation for the early form of modern marketing's historical development through the different epochs and stages of development in the American textbooks. But Fullerton (1988) asked the question "How generalizable is Pillsbury's experience?" and found that no alternative interpretations were suggested in the American literature. Other researchers, however, have expressed how companies in the distribution channels, such as wholesalers and retailers, also developed evolutionarily for a long time.

It is noted that in comparison with production and distribution, modern marketing is a relatively late and new phenomenon. Sometimes it has been argued that marketing was regarded as an unnecessary and anachronistic activity and function in a company, often expressed as "a good product sells itself," which gives a different view of its importance.

For most American writers, the production epoch has been thought to cover the period before the Industrial Revolution in Western Europe and the United States between 1870 and 1930. With production orientation, it has then meant that producers focused on the manufacturing, and wholesalers and retailers handled the distribution. At this time, it was common that the demand exceeded the supply of goods, which often sold out quickly, so it was not regarded as important to take any great consideration for different consumer needs.

Furthermore, there was a relatively weak competitive situation in many commodity markets, because there were only a few producers and there often arose monopoly-like situations. A similar situation existed in many distribution channels, and various intermediaries, such as wholesalers and retailers, did not need to make an effort in marketing when the goods often sold themselves, which Fullerton (1988, p. 108, op. cit.) expressed as follows:

> *In sum, "firms gave little thought to marketing" (Bagozzi, 1986, p. 16), and little in the way of sophisticated and purposeful marketing practice developed until much more recently.*

Several American and European researchers have questioned the producer-oriented approach. Instead, it has been argued that this approach departs from historical data and facts, which instead pointed to the importance of factors such as intense competition, uncertain demand, and overproduction. The importance of macroeconomic decisions and actions regarding demand stimulus and government regulations, which affected commodity production in bad times, has not been taken into consideration either. Furthermore, the producers of different marketing activities are not emphasized sufficiently, and the producer-oriented view has also forgotten the dynamic development of the new institutions without producer sphere.

"*Historically, the primary buyers of consumer goods were for the first time women.*"

When it comes to private consumption, it has been affected by the scale of migration and urbanization in Western Europe and the United States, which changed the demographic and social environment. This meant that the new consumers—often called the masses—were seen as critical and smart. This was evident in that consumer tastes could change quickly, and this was done without the businessmen's control. There also occurred both depressions and recessions over several time periods, and in good times, demand was uncertain, which in various ways affected the consumption of both goods and services.

Importance of Marketing

Many have questioned the producer-oriented approach, and one of the main arguments has been that during the Industrial Revolution, production and marketing worked side by side, in tandem. In the American economist Gilboy's classic works *Facts and Factors in Economic History* from 1932, the author points out how a company's conscious efforts, for example, through various marketing programs, can explain the increasing demand. These programs have been considered to be as significant as the Industrial Revolution in the creation and development of the modern industrial society.

Fullerton (1988, p. 112, op. cit.) argues that the question is not whether marketing existed or if it had less importance, which is expressed in the following way:

> *Making more products available would have no effect on people who did not want them. However, in societies where there was mobility within and between classes, energetic, rational, and purposeful activity by merchants and entrepreneurs could stimulate demand, which in turn stimulated production. Production and marketing activities worked in tandem. They achieved results together that neither could have achieved alone, according to Gilboy.*

Therefore, it is argued that the marketing activities and the marketing programs that producers as well as merchants and entrepreneurs have carried out to develop the demand in the modern industrial society is not highlighted with a producer-oriented approach. Here the importance of the development that the *supermarket* and *consumer engineering* has had for marketing in the 1930s can be mentioned. In the United States, the first supermarkets opened around 1930, with an immediate success; however, it was only after the Second World War that this innovative new retail format was established in Europe.

> "The first Swedish supermarket was opened in 1940 by Stockholm Konsum, even if the big breakthrough for self-service first came in the 1950s."

The term *consumer engineering* meant that to meet new consumer needs, producers could design and develop both existing products and new products (Sheldon and Ahrens, 1932). The method came to be practiced and developed in both the United States and the United Kingdom as well as in Germany and has been identified and recognized by many historians.

One consequence of the dominating producer-oriented approach in the marketing literature has been that producers in the earlier decades did not emphasize the importance of marketing. This has, at the same time, led to them devaluing their own needs for marketing activities and marketing programs. A further consequence has been that a producer-oriented approach has neglected the establishment and the emergence of the leading institutions in the modern marketing development, particularly wholesale and retail businesses, as well as chains. In many industries, these businesses have integrated and developed traditional manufacturing, wholesale, and retail functions, resulting in a shift of power from the manufacturing line to the retail line during the last two decades.

The market orientation epoch known as the *marketing concept*, which, according to many writers began during the 1950s and 1960s, represents one of the most important steps in the development of modern marketing. In this way, marketing has influenced and developed through different eras and stages in the development of society. There has been an interaction, which has meant that marketing, as a practical phenomenon, has adapted and undergone a gradual development, which Fullerton (1988, p. 121, op. cit.) expressed as follows:

> *Its great virtue is to highlight the existence and intelligence of past marketing. . Saying that the roots of modern marketing go back in time for a century and more does not mean that marketing in 1886 was identical to that in 1986; it means only that some practices used in 1986 represented **further development** of those used a century before . . . At any point in the past, therefore, marketing was different from what it is today; the farther back in the past, the greater the differences are likely to have been.*

MARKETING AS A SCIENTIFIC DISCIPLINE

A Macro Perspective

The modern marketing thinking emerged in the early 1900s, as a result of the ideas presented then. The term marketing was initially launched to represent these ideas, which laid the foundation for what marketing was all about in theory and practice. Various explanations in the economic theory of how markets behave and how trade worked had until then been treated almost exclusively from a macro perspective. Therefore, there was a gap in the theoretical explanations that existed when the economic and social conditions for trading and distribution were based on assumptions about how markets worked from a macroeconomic point of view. This was no longer enough to explain how businesses and consumers behaved and worked, regarding production, distribution, and consumption.

Within organization theory, scientific studies of practical business management had been implemented at this time and came to emphasize both general economic issues as well as more private ones. Studies of private businesses have become accepted and more common, which then took place from a micro perspective, unlike a macro perspective. One problem that arose was that the study of distribution and distribution activities did not appear within organization theory. Thus there arose a need for scientific principles with application in trade and distribution in order to analyze and interpret economic activities, which Bartels (1970, p. 33, op. cit.) expressed as:

> Marketing was a discovery since "marketing" is recognized as an idea and not just as an activity . . . Before the idea was created to which the term "marketing" was applied, the simple task had just been called "trade," "distribution," or "exchange."

The first knowledge of the development of modern marketing thinking took place between 1900 and 1910 by Americans Edward D. Jones, George M. Fish, and James E. Hagerty. Previously, marketing was considered exclusively as a practical matter without a scientific, theoretical basis with related formal concepts, models, or theories. Between the years 1902 and 1905, the first courses were given at the American Universities in Illinois, California, Michigan, and Ohio for educational purposes. The courses addressed descriptions of different marketing methods for goods, classifications, use brands, as well as wholesale and retail businesses.

> "Initially the course The Distributive Regulative Industries of the US was offered in 1902 at the University of Michigan with Edward D. Jones as the originator."

Marketing, as a term, came into use in American university courses around the year 1905, but was previously unknown. The term is intended for an aggregated, integrated, or collective phenomenon regarding retail, wholesale trade, market research, or sales management. It should be noted that before 1910, there were no books or magazines that dealt with these areas, so there has been a pronounced need for new knowledge relating to distribution and trade based on the methods and principles that occurred in practice.

It is between the years 1910 and 1920 that the first exploratory concepts were established and developed in marketing thinking, especially with an emphasis on marketing as a new term. At this point, marketing elements and features were also emphasized, resulting in an integrative development of marketing thinking.

Three Scientific Approaches

Three different scientific approaches were developed at this time to analyze marketing from a theoretical and practical point of view, from a macro perspective. The first has been called the *functional approach* and has studied the intermediary's various functions and approaches in marketing relating to, for example, finance, packaging, sale, purchase, or transport. This has been compared with studying how production in a factory is organized and implemented.

American Arch W. Shaw was the originator of the functional approach through his hypothesis concerning the functions and roles of the different intermediaries in marketing. These hypotheses were first published in 1912 and are regarded by Bartels (1970, p. 35) as "a landmark in the development of science in marketing." The intermediary's functions and roles were the starting points for the hypothesis, and the functional approach has been regarded as a scientific approach to studying marketing from a micro-economic perspective.

In the functional approach, it is assumed that marketing functions have their roots in the activities or tasks that wholesalers or retailers, for example, perform in order to distribute a product from a producer to a consumer in a distribution channel. How these tasks are distributed between the different intermediaries or businesses is assumed to be based on either the profit interests of the business in question or what may yield the greatest profit to the consumer; therefore, the distribution is assumed to take place in various ways. An important assumption is that if a business sees an opportunity to be able to increase its profits, the allocation of functions within the business is changed. If the distribution of tasks leads to the desired result, then the structure and functions of the distribution channel can also change, and the way its members perform various roles can change as well.

Thereafter, Bucklin (1966) proposed a general theory about the structure and organization of the distribution channel based on the number of members and functions. Furthermore, Alderson (1954) proposed the concept of matching, when it concerned trying to analyze the different segments of demand and supply through what has come to be divided into shaping (production), sorting (wholesale), and fitting (retail).

The second scientific approach has been called the *institutional approach* and has studied the intermediary's role in the distribution of goods in marketing. In the early 1900s, the role of wholesalers was studied as intermediaries in the distribution of agricultural products, where particular methods and how the goods were marketed were analyzed in more detail (Weld, 1917). This type of study focused on the efficiency in the performance of the services and often put forward suggestions for different types of efficiency improvements.

In the institutional approach, distribution channels have traditionally been considered on the basis of how production and consumption occurred considering the exchanges of goods and services that have occurred in combination with or as a result of the business that had taken part in the exchange. It is also assumed that different stakeholders, such as intermediaries, can be regarded as a loose association of the business, instead of being regarded as allies and interconnected companies. Against this background, the intermediaries' existence, generally, has been motivated primarily by economic motives, as it is assumed that these contribute to create

> "Nordiska Kompaniet and Åhlens were among the first Swedish department stores that started in the early 1900s."

different types of benefits, such as the benefit of time by having goods in stock.

In this way, this approach has also come to focus on how effectively the exchange of various goods and services occurs in the distribution channels, also taking into account the degree of distribution services. One of the first contributions to the retail institution was presented by Nystrom (1915). He analyzed the history and content of the retail business in comparison with the foreign and US retail businesses.

The third scientific approach has been called the *commodity-based approach* and has studied marketing of commodities in industry and agriculture. There were many practical issues in these areas, but the studies that were conducted were often merely descriptive in nature. However, already at that time, it was suggested that the commodities could be divided into groups, namely, consumer goods and industrial goods. This was further developed by Copeland (1923) and resulted in a new division for consumer goods in the form of goods intended for "convenience, shopping, and emergency." Copeland suggested later that even specialty items should be included in the proposed division.

In the marketing literature, various utility concepts were also suggested, which emanated from the various benefits that marketing could conceivably contribute. Thus concepts such as benefits of space and time emerged to illustrate the economic importance that marketing created. Ownership advantage was also added later to these concepts, which would illustrate a general embodiment of marketing as an idea in the form of a general exchange of goods for money on the market. These three concepts became prominent in modern marketing when it came to demonstrate its economic rationality and logic.

Finally, it should be said that marketing as a scientific discipline, with its three scientific approaches, gradually came to be widely accepted in a wider circle of researchers and practitioners, thus ended this pioneer period, which laid the foundation for the establishment and further development of modern marketing thinking.

Marketing's New Principles

There was an integration and generalization of the marketing principles that were established and developed within the scientific part of marketing in the 1920s. The principles intended to make it possible to classify different forms of marketing thinking, as well as to establish logical cause and effect relationships, which made it possible to generalize by means of concepts and terms. A number of rules of thumb, from actual practice, had received scientific credibility, so that they could be proposed as alternative marketing actions. This helped to increase the confidence in marketing as a scientific discipline, which came to shape and influence the modern marketing development in both theory and practice in the coming decades.

The concepts, models, and approaches that had developed were now integrated in a macroanalysis of marketing. With the help of this analysis, marketing was considered to be an economic activity, which was influenced by various economic, organizational, social, or technological conditions on the market. It was considered to cover the execution of basic functions in terms of the distribution of goods, and it was run by businessmen and executives, who worked under social and political control by administrative decisions and controls. Bartels (1970) expressed the essence of the marketing concept as "all of those activities involved in the distribution of goods from producers to consumers and in the transfer of title thereto" (p. 41, op. cit.).

During this period, important advances occurred in retail thinking that were a result of the potential of research that began to emerge. Several books were published with an aim to improve and develop practical retail management, where an application of scientific methods could help contribute with different solutions to current retail problems. During this time, a scientific analysis and description were also applied for the first time to the wholesale agent. Of particular interest was to analyze the practical and theoretical differences between retail activities on the one hand and on the other hand, the wholesale business.

> "The term marketing strategy was first launched in the United States during the 1920s."

Furthermore, in the 1920s, the term "marketing strategy" was introduced for the first time, which was derived from the strategy and leadership area. With strategy, campaigns or smaller programs were intended, which could be regarded as actions and instruments to connect with a military strategic reasoning. As part of a campaign or program, instruments such as advertisements, salesmen, credit terms, prices, or other types of instruments could be used and insights that emerged through the various instruments were used for actions. Other military concepts were also introduced in the sales management theory, and American Leverett suggested the term *marketing manager*, which later became *marketing management*.

History of Consumer Marketing 17

At this time, sales activities in a company were highlighted and these came to be associated more tightly with the sales organization and broad marketing objectives than had been the case previously. It resulted in sales management and sales efforts being regarded more seriously, and sales management came to be regarded as a key function of marketing. It was believed that a company's success was largely dependent on the sales volume of the company. New ideas and thoughts within sales management began to be introduced that were drawn from organization theory and Taylor's principles of management, because general principles about the executive's role in marketing were missing.

In the emerging marketing thinking, there now arose an interest in market research and markets, which did not occur during the pioneer times. At that time, the interest was instead more focused on news than methodological issues and scientific applications. Therefore, an interest in the general methodology and survey questions arose, which resulted in questionnaires being developed and coming into use. This enabled various descriptions and analyses, which, in turn, contributed to the development of marketing as a scientific discipline.

A Micro-Economic Approach

Marketing thinking was now structured around the three previously mentioned scientific approaches, together with methodical practices using a variety of survey techniques. This provided opportunities for the continued establishment and development of modern marketing, both in theory and practice.

During the 1930s, the structure and approach to marketing thinking were not significantly affected by the recessions in Western Europe and the United States. On the other hand, savings and low prices became the focus from an economic perspective, as a result of the depression. This laid the foundation for a consumer movement with active and conscious consumers, at the same time as urbanization increased. Gradually, as the new marketing concepts, models, and approaches were introduced, a growing competition between companies in the distribution area developed. In light of the increasing consumer interest and the new values, a more large-scale retail infrastructure developed at this time, as well as the number of new voluntary and cooperative organizations.

> "An increased interest in scientific studies with a quantitative focus arose to measure the efficiency and costs of distribution."

An important element of marketing thinking was the quantitative focus, which increased the interest in scientific studies of distribution costs and sales quotas. Furthermore, an interest in the efficiency and the size of the market developed, which led to the scientific study of distribution channels being a focus. These studies were based on a micro-economic perspective and did not take into consideration other leadership, organizational, or social perspectives.

Numerous studies of the distribution channels, based on the micro-economic starting point, have assumed that an intermediary in a distribution channel may have the ability to perform an activity (or a function) at a cost that is lower than someone else's cost. It was revealed through studies that intermediaries could perform activities and functions at a cost that was lower than the producers' cost. One conclusion was that the maximum operational efficiency for a producer could be achieved with low costs that arise through the use of various intermediaries.

TRANSACTION-ORIENTED MARKETING

Marketing as a Management Approach

The first signs that the established marketing thinking began to be questioned, mainly the functional and institutional approaches, came in the late 1930s and early 1940s. The main reason was that the two approaches come to be regarded as universal knowledge, for which there was no consensus among the different researchers. An ongoing shift toward considering marketing as a management approach could be noted through the book *Marketing* by Alexander et al. (1949).

The main message of the book was based on an extension of the established notions and principles of what marketing means. The message was regarded by peers as more or less revolutionary and contained notions of marketing that had full impact during the following decade. In particular, the authors focused on the management marketing functions of a company as opposed to just the functions of a distribution channel. This meant that the planning and control of the marketing activities and programs became important with regard to marketing budgets and market research, with the result that market descriptions were of secondary importance from a management point of view.

This laid the foundation for a new marketing thinking, because in the 1950s, it was considered that there was no real marketing theory or some more identifiable theories in marketing.

The scientific approaches that developed were thought to be insufficient, because there should have been different schools of thought in modern marketing discipline. The former marketing thinking had not been focused on business and management issues with regard to leadership, control, and monitoring, but was of a more technical nature with descriptions focused on *"how to do it."* Furthermore, marketing thinking had been of a broader nature, focusing on descriptions of the market's behavior, mechanisms, and structure from a macro perspective.

> *"A new management approach called 'marketing management' came to light and marketing by a producer began from the consumer's needs."*

Instead, the new management approach came to focus on how marketing management should be pursued and developed in a company, which laid the foundation for what is commonly called *marketing management*. With this concept, Howard (1957) referred to the decision-making required in a company regarding, for example, goods, brands, selections, prices, distribution networks, localization, and various forms of influence. Furthermore, the consumer's needs were regarded as a fundamental starting point for the analysis, planning, and control in the follow-up of marketing; this is what the expression the *marketing concept* refers to.

One of the main reasons for the emergence of a new management approach was the increasing competition in Western Europe and the United States during the 1950s and 1960s. The excess demand that had existed since the late 1940s had slowly, gradually, as the standard of living and welfare increased, moved to excess supply. For most producers, this meant that a short-term, tactical marketing, regarding marketing campaigns and programs, could be successful. But from a long-term perspective, it came to place demands on an integrated strategic vision, which the new management approach was to focus on. Then marketing came to be increasingly considered as a strategic management philosophy with an increased emphasis on analysis, planning, control, and monitoring.

The Emergence of Mass Marketing

From a historical perspective, the business community has had its foundation in personal relationships between the customers and the suppliers. An important consequence of the creation and development of the modern industrial society has been that the personal relationships between the producers and consumers have lost their meaning, as a result of the industrial process and the emergence of the self-service system in marketing.

Marketing as a practical phenomenon occurred almost exclusively at the local level, where the goods and services produced were intended for individuals' and families' daily needs and everyday life. For the vast majority of people, it was crucial to be able to have access to food, such as fresh produce and groceries, clothes, shoes, as well as other practical necessities for everyday use.

The development that characterized the modern industrial society has meant major changes in several areas for producers,' wholesalers,' and retailers' marketing, as well as consumer consumption. Industrialization led to new production methods, including not only an increased mechanization but also the emergence of an increased scale in the new factories, which laid the foundation for the mass production of goods. This, in comparison with the old agricultural society, was a new groundbreaking phenomenon, which also came to influence the modern marketing.

The introduction of the new production methods made it possible for producers to manufacture goods for a national or a regional market, which both geographically and in terms of volume was greater than the local market. This meant a total transformation of how the marketing should be implemented and developed. In addition to the economies of scale that had already arisen in production, it was now possible to achieve the same advantages in distribution and marketing, which had not been the case previously.

For many producers, it also became possible to produce goods and mass produce without customer orders. This meant that it became more common to manufacture goods first and then sell them afterward, as shown by the increased importance of advertising in the late 1800s and early 1900s. But the most crucial was that the personal relationships, which were characterized by the direct contact between the producers and the consumers, now had less and less importance and eventually threatened to cease completely, which Frankelius (1997, p. 44, op. cit.) chose to describe as follows:

> When the shoemaker worked on a small scale and sold his self-produced footwear to consumers—often someone he knew in the immediate area—he could explain the benefits of the product and had no need for advertising help, in the sense of ads or similar. The manufacturers lost this opportunity and in this vacuum arose modern advertising. The producers, in this situation, theoretically had several options. They could refrain from advertising, they could invest in mass advertising to an "anonymous market," or they could invest in trying to create direct contacts and relationships with end customers despite the increased distance and more customers, i.e., find new forms of direct contact.

Instead, personal relationships with various intermediaries, such as merchants, retailers, or wholesalers, became increasingly important in marketing. The latter bought the goods in large quantities from the producers and goods were then sold to retail stores in urban and rural areas. Retailers and merchants then sold the goods to consumers, which meant that manufacturers, in most cases, had lost personal relations and direct contacts with consumers.

The breakthrough of mass production also led to the breakthrough of mass marketing, which has characterized the development of modern marketing from the 1950s. One of the reasons for this development was also the fact that most markets for consumer goods were in a period of growth in Western Europe and the United States. Historically, the major difference was that in previous decades and centuries there had been a general lack of demand, which had been fundamental and essential for both producers and consumers. This did not require cost-effective mass production and mass distribution, which, however, was the case in the modern industrial society.

It is against this backdrop that the modern marketing concepts and theories shall be understood, with its roots in the marketing of consumer goods in the United States. This has come to be the standard model and dominated marketing as a scientific discipline for a long time. Additionally, this theory has also had a large influence on the marketing of the producers' goods and services.

Transaction Marketing as a Model

A fundamental theoretical basis of marketing as a scientific discipline has been the business exchange between the sellers and the buyers when it has related to a physical product or a service in exchange for money. Producers have therefore been focused on planning and implementing their marketing to create a business exchange of products for money. It is against this background that the scientific discipline has intended to develop general theoretical concepts, models, and approaches to be able to analyze, explain, and predict this exchange.

In modern marketing, producers in the factories' manufacturing processes have created the products that are distributed to consumers in different exchange processes. However, these processes are no longer based on direct contacts in the relationships between the producers and the consumers, as was the case previously. Therefore, to be able to allocate the mass produced goods on the market, the producers resorted to various marketing activities and programs.

These have contributed to the goods being distributed and delivered, resulting in the exchange that was desired and providing value to the producers and the intermediaries as well as to the consumers.

> *"The famous 4 P model with different means of competition got its breakthrough in theory and practice."*

The so-called exchange phenomenon was studied scientifically by producers of consumer goods in the US manufacturing sector during the 1950s and 1960s. They utilized a competitiveness approach and the famous 4 P model with competitive tools, such as product, price, place, and promotion, as the central elements (Howard, 1957; McCarthy, 1960; Kotler, 2000). This approach has been based on how producers have designed the competitive tools in their mass marketing, and it has also come to be called the *marketing mix theory*.

Furthermore, the theoretical point of view assumes that individual consumers are anonymous in mass markets and that consumers are considered to belong to a particular segment of the market. It is an important starting point that consumers exhibit similarities in behavior, demographic characteristics, or lifestyles for a particular segment.

Another prominent theoretical point is that producers influence consumers to purchase by selecting a particular combination of competitive tools by applying a certain amount of resources. The core of the approach, therefore, is considered to be the management of the different competitive tools with links to other prominent factors in a company's marketing, such as marketing planning, segmentation, positioning, determining the target group, market research, as well as the company's business plan, goals, strategies, and organizational structure.

In addition to a theoretical point of view, this approach is based on regarding marketing as a function of the producers, next to functions such as manufacturing, distribution, logistics, product development, finance, or personnel. This means that marketing is regarded as any other function and not as a strategic management task at a company's executive level.

In the marketing literature, the competitiveness approach has come to be called transaction marketing (TM), which I have chosen to call *transaction-oriented perspective*. This form of perspective has focused on leading to occasional exchanges through purchases and transactions through various marketing activities and programs aimed at the mass markets. In this regard, transaction marketing can also be regarded as being synonymous with mass marketing.

One of the goals of transaction marketing has been to get consumers to choose a particular brand over another, in competition with other brands. It has then been regarded as natural that consumers are able to make independent choices between a number of competing brands, which is why the design for various means of competition has become of great importance for producers.

This also means that there has been a competitive relationship between the producer of brand A and the producer of brand B. This has meant that consumers have come to be regarded as someone "the marketer does something **to**, instead of does something **for**" (Grönroos, 2000, p. 25, op. cit.).

As a result, many researchers have come to the conclusion that there has been a general conflict of interest in the transaction marketing between the consumers and the producers, which is thought to have led to the conclusion that consumers have not been interested in purchasing the producers' goods[0]. Then the producers have instead assumed that the consumers must be influenced and persuaded through mass marketing, which Gummesson (1999, p. 231, op. cit.) has expressed as:

> *In practice, however, the 4P approach has led to a manipulative attitude to people. If we just select the right measures in the right combination and with the right intensity, the consumer will buy; it is a matter of*

putting pressure on the consumer. The consumer is a locked black box, maybe with a tiny peep-hole. We often know little what is in the mind of consumers, how they think and feel and what their motives are. It is more of a stimulus-response model, it is similar to the fisherman's relationship to the fish. If we improve the bait, the fish will bite and it is hooked. The supplier and its salespeople are the active party. Sometimes the consumer is pig-headed and rejects an offering. Conclusions: we used the wrong bait.

It is against this background that mass marketing has been considered to be false and manipulative, especially in the advertising context. This can be partly explained by consumers having come to be regarded as competitors to the producers in the competition for the brand, as consumers generally only choose one brand at a time during purchase.

Marketing has become so dominated by campaigns and activities that the goal of most producers has become solely to offer goods and services for sale in the short-term. Often the price has been the main theme of advertising and promotional campaigns and considered to be the only way to try to win new customers in the short-term, time after time, regardless of whether they bought the brand in the past or not. But it should also be said that many campaigns have also had as a goal to convey a message of an image to facilitate the purchase rather than marketing with long-term focus.

> "Campaigns and activities in mass marketing focused on consumers lay the foundation for recruiting new customers."

In this context, it has been argued that transaction marketing in certain situations, such as recruiting new customers, may work well. On the other hand, it seems that more and more companies today have realized the importance of being able to retain their customers rather than having to acquire new customers. Thus to start with an approach that has recruiting new customers as a primary focus does not seem to be particularly effective or appropriate.

When it comes to the marketing of consumer goods, there has for a long time been a fundamental dilemma, which has meant that mass marketing has been a given for the development of modern marketing. The importance that regional, national, and international markets has come to have for producers of global brands has led to a lack of opportunities for direct contact and personal relationships between the producers and the consumers. Therefore, there has been no other option for producers than to make use of marketing campaigns and programs aimed at the anonymous mass markets.

Finally, it should be said that for a long time it has been almost impossible to identify individual consumers as buyers, which has meant that the vast majority of buyers has remained anonymous for most producers. With this in mind, the transactional-oriented marketing, as an approach, has emerged and established itself in the modern marketing of consumer goods.

The Marketing Disciplines Crisis

Criticism was made in the early 1980s that marketing as a theoretical discipline had not managed to include marketing strategy in the marketing thinking to create a broader perspective. Among researchers and scientists, it was expressed that the marketing discipline had reached a stage in its development, which was characterized by discontinuity, despite the existence of the *marketing concept* and market orientation as a philosophy. Even among practitioners, objections to the marketing discipline were raised, and the well-known consulting firm McKinsey noted in a report in 1993 that marketing underwent its midlife crisis.

The conclusion was that the marketing discipline lacked the strategic perspective from both a theoretical and practical point of view. Authors such as Wind and Robertson (1983, p. 13) discussed in detail what the focus of a management perspective rather than a marketing strategy perspective had meant for the development of the marketing discipline in terms of a number of limitations, namely:

- A fixation with the brand as a unit of analysis,
- The interdisciplinary isolation of marketing,
- The failure to examine synergy in the design of the marketing program,
- Marketing's short-run orientation,
- The lack of rigorous competitive analysis,
- The lack of an international orientation, and
- The lack of an integrated strategic framework.

It was stated that the competitiveness approach with its basis to manipulate various parameters in a marketing mix in the short-term was inadequate for firms when it came to being able to respond to local, national, and international competition in the short-term. Instead, it was suggested that it should be considered necessary for a firm to integrate and coordinate the various parameters in a marketing mix with a broader strategic approach to be successful in the long-term.

The tactical marketing, which the competitiveness approach was based on, was also considered to not be sufficiently adequate to meet the new competitive situation that had arisen, primarily in Western Europe and the United States. The former national excess in demand had increasingly come to evolve into an excess in supply, which increased competition for consumers. This placed new demands on the producers' marketing, and in this context, criticism arose against transaction marketing, which was not considered as being able to meet the new demands placed in a more and more globalized world economy.

RELATIONSHIP-ORIENTED MARKETING

Buyer and Seller Interactions

In northern Europe and Scandinavia, a new direction of marketing thinking developed during the 1970s and 1980s, which was not based on a transaction-oriented perspective. The research within industrial marketing and purchasing by IMP Group (Industrial Marketing and Purchasing Group) in Uppsala, Sweden, and within services marketing by the Nordic School of Services, Helsinki, Finland, and Stockholm, Sweden, had generated new concepts and approaches to what characterized modern marketing. These new ideas were pioneering in nature and received international acceptance, which meant that they had strong scientific support from various sides.

> "The IM group in Uppsala and the Nordic School of Services develops and proposes new concepts and models for marketing."

From a scientific, theoretical perspective, this new train of thought meant that marketing in industrial markets and service markets—unlike the consumer goods markets—were characterized by buyer and seller interactions. These could occur between the suppliers and service providers and sometimes their industrial customers, often companies, and other times consumers. These interactions have affected both the sellers' and customers' behavior over time, which has come to influence the nature of the relationships.

The most important theoretical starting point was that the limitations of the consumer goods markets, when it came to the lack of direct, personal contacts between the manufacturers and the producers and the users, did not exist in industrial markets or services markets. Instead, it was exactly the opposite in these markets, and an exchange of business often required a deeper interaction between the buyers and the sellers in order for the business exchange to take place. In these contexts, a transaction-oriented mass marketing was not enough to explain how the marketing was conducted and designed in the industrial markets and services markets.

Historically, the business exchange between consumers, merchants, and producers, during the different social stages, has been based on relationships between the buyers and sellers who have been influenced by the personal contacts. These direct contacts have characterized the personal relationships between the local merchants and producers and peasants and craftsmen and consumers for a long time. Without a doubt, relationships have played a pivotal role in marketing, and the relationship-orientation that has occurred "is probably as old as the history of trade and commerce" (Grönroos, 2000, p. 23, op. cit.).

One of the main conclusions of the new concepts is that buyer and seller interactions, on a discrete or continuous basis, have come to constitute the relationships between the parties. This has meant that marketing has not focused on the exchange of business, but that this exchange has instead been seen as something that has occurred in the context of ongoing relationships. Grönroos (2000, p. 22, op. cit.) has expressed this as follows:

> *Thus, according to this view,* **relationships between parties** *are considered the core phenomenon in marketing. Continuous purchases and cross-sales opportunities, exchanges or transactions, follow from well-managed relationships. This is called a* **relationship perspective**, *in contrast to the* **exchange perspective**. *Singular transactions are not seen as most important in marketing; rather, relationships which are considered to facilitate and support exchanges or transactions are most important.*

A relationship-oriented perspective has come to show the possibilities of getting away from the limitations of transaction marketing, namely, the physical and psychological gaps between the producers and the consumers.

> "*A relationship-oriented perspective builds on dialogue, personal meetings, and two-way communication.*"

Instead, one has come to focus on how the buyer and seller interactions can influence the form of marketing, in ways other than through the traditional competitive advantages, such as product, price, place, and promotion.

A theoretical basis for a relationship-oriented perspective has been that different suppliers, customers, and other partners have been integrated with a company's marketing activities and infrastructure. It has generally occurred through mutual dialogue, personal meetings, and two-way communication, where interactions between the parties have been the central element. This has been one of the major differences between a transaction-oriented perspective and relationship-oriented perspective, which Sheth and Parvatiyar (1995) have illustrated in Figure 1.2.

The main theoretical difference between a transaction-oriented and relationship-oriented perspective has been the emphasis on interactive and close relationships in the latter. It has been seen that from a relationship

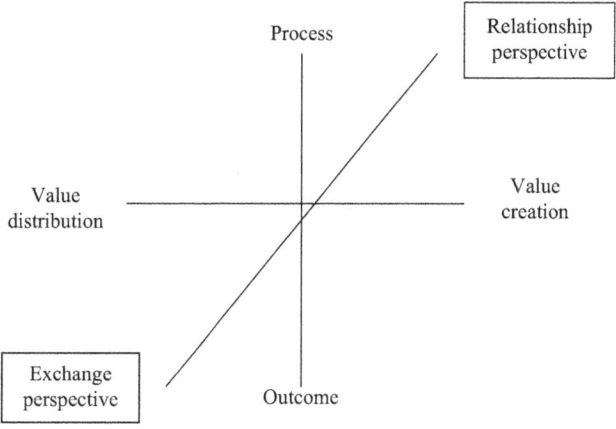

Figure 1.2 Exchange and Relationship Perspectives in Marketing

perspective, value has been created in the value-creating processes that have been going on between the buyers and the sellers and not just in the products manufactured by the manufacturers' factories from an exchange perspective. This has instead emphasized how the producers' goods have become mass marketed and mass distributed to consumers, but it has not happened through various interactions and the "moment of truth" in the value creation processes between the parties, which is considered to be the big difference.

A New Relationship Perspective

From a theoretical point of view, a relationship perspective points to two essential concepts, namely, the processes and value creation. In the processes of marketing that are built on interactions and cooperation, it has created and developed value for both the buyers and the sellers. This value has been achieved within the framework of the relationships that have existed between the parties, which then contribute to processes being carried out and value being created. Value for a seller has meant profitability or profit, whereas the value for a buyer has meant satisfaction of needs, availability, or self-fulfillment.

In micro-economic theory, profit maximization has traditionally been considered one of the company's main goals, and this, in competition with other companies, has been achieved by using various competitive advantages. Both the advantages of competition and profit have long been considered to be the main driving forces behind the ability to create value in a company, which the transaction marketing (TM) model is based on.

From a relationship perspective, these assumptions have come to be questioned, and, instead, the importance of interdependence and mutual cooperation between the buyers and the sellers has been emphasized when it relates to creating value. The value has then been generated by the interactions that have occurred in the relationships between the buyers and the sellers, where the supplier's main task has been to promote and support the customers' buying and consumption processes.

In the marketing literature, this form of marketing has become known as relationship marketing (RM). This term was introduced by Berry (1983) and has become widely recognized. Within the framework of relationship marketing, as an expression of a relationship perspective, one of the aims of this view has been to contribute to a better profitability and productivity of a company. The interactions one has had with customers and the closeness that they have shared have been able to contribute to particularly deep and long relationships over time. This has been able to create a competitive advantage, and it was thought to be essential to retain current customers and being able to avoid having to recruit new ones.

> *"Proximity to customers helps to create deep and lasting relationships between companies and customers over time."*

A relationship perspective has also come to affect the perception regarding which functions in a company should have a dialogue and interaction with the customers. Traditionally, the marketing function (or department) at a producer's company has been responsible for marketing the products that have been manufactured, but this has been questioned from a relationship perspective. Instead, the traditional borders have increasingly been questioned, and in practice this has meant that more and more functions (or departments) at suppliers have become part of the value-creating process.

In practice, this has been expressed through partnerships between suppliers and customers regarding joint marketing, research and development, or through strategic alliances. With this, both suppliers and customers are involved in higher value creation through personal interactions and processes that take place.

In relationship marketing, the meaning of customers' long-term needs and desires has also been emphasized more and more. It was viewed as important for a producer, a retailer, or a service provider to understand how a customer relationship has been developed, based on the assumption that a product has been regarded as part of an overall service offering. Thus it has meant being considerate and working from the customer's desires to be able to develop a relationship and not just focus on a single transaction, which a transaction-oriented perspective generally has been based on. Grönroos (2000, p. 28, op. cit. df) has expressed this in more detail:

Customers do not only look for goods or services, they demand a much more holistic service offering including everything from information of how to best use a product, to delivering, installing, updating, repairing, maintaining, and correcting solutions they have bought. And they demand all this, and much more, to be delivered in a friendly, trustworthy, and timely manner.

In relationship marketing, the overall service offering has come to regard the physical product as a fundamental and included component. It is no longer believed that it is just the physical product that will be in focus, which has implications for how a company has come to define its product offering. Customers are not just demanding the core product—in the form of the physical product—but have come to ask for a complete service offering that includes goods as well as service components.

In order to create a complete offering to customers, the components beyond the product itself, which may be able to contribute to this, such as knowledge, human resources, technologies, and time, to name a few, are therefore emphasized in relationship marketing, unlike in mass marketing. This has come to emphasize the importance of value creation management processes of a producer and not just activities and functions of a distribution channel, which had previously been the case.

Relationship Marketing as a Model

In marketing's scientific discipline, relationship marketing was established in the 1990s to explain what characterizes the relationships between the buyers and the sellers in both consumer markets (*Business-to-Consumers*, B2C) and organizational markets (*Business-to-Business*, B2B). The RM model has come to represent a general, overall marketing context (conceptual model) and has become an accepted marketing model for all types of transactions relating to goods, services, or products for consumers or industries.

There has been a clear transition from traditional mass marketing, targeted to anonymous customers, to the establishment and development of strategic competitive advantage when it has been necessary for a company to manage individual relationships. This has occurred despite the fact that relationship marketing has essentially become identified with marketing for services, which has had a clear focus on interactive marketing. It has therefore been suggested that the RM-concept is of importance for both consumer markets and industrial markets.

> "Relationship marketing is seen as a way to create relationships also for classical consumer goods."

For a long time, it has been considered obvious among many researchers that a transaction-oriented perspective has not been optimal to handle the forces of change that influence the development of the current society. Without doubt, the complexity and diversity of a company's global and local marketing environment has placed demands on other marketing methods than the traditional ones. It has been considered to be important for a company to establish and maintain relationships with the customers as a way to meet the ever-increasing complexity when it comes to new behavior patterns, new competitors, new brands, or new values.

Accordingly, the RM model has become an appropriate strategy even when it relates to consumer goods intended for the mass markets. The main reason has been that the TM model has taken its theoretical basis from short-term, financial transactions, often linked to quantitative methods and measurements. Furthermore, proven product strategies in many cases have not proved to work as well as before, which is why the transaction marketing's focus on individual business exchanges have not been enough.

Another important argument from a theoretical point of view has been that it is no longer possible for a company to establish a strategic competitive advantage only by means of product characteristics. Instead, the argument has been to consider a company's profitability in relation to existing and satisfied customers. Against this background, the development of a "relationship" has been regarded as a competitive advantage, which has been difficult for many competitors to copy. Thus a relationship-oriented perspective has been about building unique relationships, which has become an effective way for companies to differentiate themselves and differentiate their offerings from each other.

The RM model, with its broader business orientation, through its relationship perspective, has helped to focus on the importance of superior customer value. In order to deliver customer value, it has been found necessary for a company to develop strategic competitive advantages based on how a relationship has portrayed itself regarding its form, content, and development potential.

This has been in stark contrast to mass marketing and the importance that a marketing mix has had in transaction-oriented marketing. The TM model has therefore not been considered to be sufficient when it relates to a company being able to deliver customer value. Against this background, the RM model has become an increasingly important strategic approach in modern marketing.

Relationships and Networks

Within the marketing discipline's different areas, such as supply chain management, business or industrial marketing, consumer goods marketing, and services marketing, a paradigm shift has taken place over the past three

History of Consumer Marketing

decades. This paradigm shift has meant a shift from marketing to mass markets with anonymous customers to establish and develop relationships with previously more or less known customers.

A fundamental theoretical basis of the RM model has focused on the customer and supplier relationship. The increased awareness of the importance of the supplier's (and not merely the seller's) cooperation and co-production with the customer to achieve value creation has highlighted the customer and supplier relationship. One reason has been that traditional mass marketing has been too shortsighted and only focused on attracting and recruiting new customers. This has created the conditions for a relational perspective to gain ground, especially since both suppliers and customers have been able to create and obtain value through mutual cooperation and exchange.

Another theoretical basis of the RM model has been the dual focus of relationship-oriented marketing, which has meant both retaining customers and recruiting new customers. In the context of a relationship-oriented perspective, this has been expressed by terms such as aggressive strategies and defensive strategies with the aim of minimizing a company's customer turnover (Storbacka et al., 1994).

Furthermore, it has been deemed that the RM model has demanded a stronger customer orientation in combination with a market-oriented operation of a company. This combination has come to be regarded as an iterative process, where the design of the marketing strategies has been created in collaboration with the buyer's behavior and desires or needs. This has also meant that one regards the goods and services together, as part of a holistic, ongoing customer value proposition.

It has become increasingly common for manufacturers to look for new nonvisible elements to be able to support and develop their customer value propositions. Similarly, service providers have created and developed visible elements to make their value propositions more attractive and appealing. It has therefore been suggested that the traditional division of goods and services should be eliminated to allow suppliers to regard themselves as a services company.

In a relationship-oriented perspective, customers have come to be viewed as valuable partners of a company. This has meant a focus on what a company can do *for* and *with* their customers to create and ensure customer satisfaction. This has become increasingly important with respect to long-term relationships that have been built on customer loyalty through quality products and services.

> *"In 2008, the Swedish grocery chain ICA introduced one of its largest investments ever, where ICA offers its loyal customers discount offers based on customer purchase history."*

To achieve this, the RM model has pointed to the importance of integrative business processes between a supplier and its customers. In this context, there have existed both nonpersonal and personal interactions, where information and communication technology have been important elements in order to implement these business processes. It has therefore been suggested that companies, which are part of the RM model, should learn more about their individual customers through the development of knowledge-based systems. Companies have often used customer databases as their starting points and used methods that store data and manipulate the stored data in order to develop relationships with customers.

In practice, various useful marketing methods have developed, such as customer databases and direct marketing, as well as customer relationship management, often expressed through the concept of CRM (*customer relationship management*). The main purpose of these methods has been to build, strengthen, and maintain already existing customer relationships, which have come to be known as various customer and loyalty programs. The criticism made against these methods has been that they are based more on a short-term, tactical manipulation of data rather than to establish and develop long-term relationship strategies.

Furthermore, it has been suggested that the RM model shall be considered as including "the whole series of relationships, networks and interactions," which are part of the company's business and marketing environment and not just the dyadic relationship between the customer and the supplier (Gummesson, 1999). This means that all relationships, networks, and interactions a company has with its external and internal environment shall be emphasized in the context of a relationship-oriented perspective.

SERVICE LOGIC AS A MARKETING PARADIGM

Meanings and Ideas

From the mid-1970s until the early 2000s, service-based concepts and models have developed in services marketing and relationship marketing. Various authors have discussed the ability and aptitude of these theories to develop marketing, both theoretically and practically. In the Nordic School of Services, an important theoretical assumption has been that one should consider offerings and services as a starting point for a company's service logic, which previously differentiated itself from transaction marketing in terms of its goods logic (Gummesson, 1979, 1991).

In an article in the *Journal of Marketing*, the American marketing scholars Vargo and Lusch (2004) suggested that a service-dominated logic, as a new paradigm, should replace the dominant goods logic that has long dominated marketing thinking in both the United States and Europe. The main argument was that the exchange shifted from visible goods to intangible services, such as knowledge, processes, and skills. The new service-dominant logic, therefore, has come to challenge the traditional goods logic, where the customer perspective has often been neglected. It is obvious that a customer perspective is of vital importance in a service-dominant logic, as well as in services and relationship marketing where the customer's value creation is an important part of redefining markets based on traditional ideas.

The starting point in a service-dominant logic is that the service is the common denominator in the exchange processes and not any particular form of exchange. This means that customer needs and satisfaction are all about service, i.e., the intangible value and not the material value, with the result that everything is about service. Thus it is assumed that customer value and customer value creation processes are based on a vendor's ability to learn and to understand how customer value creation can be supported. Through this assumption, a service-dominant logic can be said to be more integrative in nature compared with goods logic, where the good itself is the starting point.

In the Nordic School of Services, service logic is based on customers participating in various purchasing and consumption processes, which can be considered as service processes. However, they do not go so far as to regard products as a service, i.e., the actual consumption of goods. In such situations, it is assumed that service logic works better than goods logic, which is consistent with the reasoning that Vargo and Lusch presented on a service-dominant logic. Instead, the service-like process is emphasized as the service that customers consume, which Grönroos (2006, p. 320, op. cit.) expressed as follows:

A customer does not consume a drill as a service, but the process of using the drill together with, for example, information about the drill and knowledge about drilling, in order to make a hole in the wall. This process is the service. The drill is not a transmitter of service, rather it is one resource needed to make a service process and service consumption possible.

A common notion in the literature is that service logic is considered by customers as co-producers of service processes. For companies, it is about them seeing themselves as value creators in accordance with the notions about *value-in-use*, which assumes that the value for the customers is created when they use products or services (Normann, 2001; Woodruff and Gardial, 1996).

Gummesson (1999) drives the argument so far and believes that "value creation is only possible when a product or service is consumed." It is also considered that the service logic assumes that all types of resources, including goods and services are used by customers as services to give them value and in that way supports the customers' value-generating processes; thus the service processes are deemed to be integrative in nature.

Furthermore, it is thought that the service logic is based on a supplier starting with an understanding of how the customer value creation process works and subsequently analyzing which process the supplier is able to support. In this way, a company can be seen as a value promoter or a *solution provider* by offering different kinds of resources to customers' consumption and value-creating processes. It has even been suggested that a company shall use its interactions with customers to influence their value creation processes. In this way, a company can support customers in their daily activities and processes by offering goods, services, hidden services, information and so on, as long as this generates value for the customers.

> "Customers shall be seen as co-producers and creators of value when they use goods or services."

It seems that the notion of value creation has become dominant in the service logic and is based on the idea that value is created for the customers in their value-creating processes on a daily basis. Grönroos (2008a, 2008b) makes a further distinction, which means that it is the customers who are the value creators and the suppliers should be considered as merely value promoters, developing value propositions. In this way, the customers are seen as the sole creator of value, and it is the suppliers' task to create the resources that can contribute to the customers' value creation on their own in their value-generating processes.

Service Perspective as a Process

A *service logic* assumes that a company shall help to promote the creation of value in the customer's daily activities and processes by contributing in various ways to facilitate these processes. When customers are involved in various interactive processes, both as a user and as a resource, the company and the customers create a service process together that leads to a common value.

With service logic as a starting point, it is therefore assumed that a service perspective is based on a process "where a set of resources interact with each other and with the customer in order to support customer processes in a way that creates value" (Grönroos, 2008b, p. 66). Table 1.3 summarizes the main differences between a service logic and a goods logic.

A *service perspective* assumes that a company complements its core products—regardless of whether it is a physical good or a service—with different types of services, with the objective to surpass the competition. It may be, for example, different types of hidden services, which, with its potential, can create new competitive advantages for the company. This may be regarded as particularly appropriate in situations where a core product with

Table 1.3 Service Logic and Goods Logic—A Comparison (Grönroos, 2008b)

	Service logic	Goods logic
The offering	Value supporting process.	Value supporting resource.
Perspective	A process with a set of resources interacting with customers in supporting their processes in a value-creating way.	A resource customers use, eventually together with other resources, with the purpose to create value for themselves.
Business logic	To facilitate the processes that support customers' value creation.	To do goods as resources available for customers' use.
Customer's role	Co-producer and co-creator of value.	Sole creator of value.
Company's role	Provide a service process and together with the customer produce and create value in the customer's consumption process.	Provide customers with goods as a resource and solely produce this resource.
Value creator	Experiences are the primary.	Need satisfaction is in focus.
Buying process	Consumption is the purpose.	Purchase is the purpose.

the same quality features and price dominates the market. Then new competitive advantages cannot be based on either new technological innovations or a lower price, which is increasingly common in homogeneous and mature market segments in many industries.

If a service perspective is to be introduced in a company, it requires a *service strategy*, which means that the company's employees must be involved. This, in turn, requires a different type of corporate culture, in comparison with a brand logic, called *service culture*, where it is considered natural and obvious for those employees to provide customers with good service.

A service culture, therefore, assumes that a company should be service-oriented, with common attitudes and values, so that the service that customers receive is perceived to contribute to a good quality of service and to strengthen the relationships with the company in question.

In conclusion, it should be said that a service perspective requires a redefinition of a company's business concept, where the starting point is to provide customers with various kinds of support for their service processes to contribute to value generation and value creation. This can be done through supplies, products, billing, technical solutions, customer training, advice, complaint handling, and so on. It is done through a flow of activities in a service process, which is continuously ongoing as support for customers' daily value-generating processes.

CONSUMER BEHAVIOR AND BUYING BEHAVIOR

Consumer Needs and Wishes

Since ancient times, the exchange of goods and services between buyers and sellers built on the goods and services offered corresponded to the buyers' needs, expectations, and desires. It has been considered self-evident for consumers to have the freedom to choose and thus be able to accept or reject the offers that sellers have provided.

Consumer choice situation has traditionally consisted of two different decisions: to buy or not to buy a particular product or service and which seller one would like to buy from. This is based on consumers' freedom of choice, which varies depending on how advanced a society's economic, organizational, and social development is with respect to prosperity and welfare.

In the marketing literature, for a long time, an important theoretical basis has been that the modern marketing should be consumer oriented and based on consumer needs and desires through the expression the *marketing concept*, as mentioned earlier. In light of this, marketers for a long time wondered how the consumer's behavior, as a buyer, could be explained and understood.

Buying behavior has been studied in research with economic as well as psychological and sociological vantage points since the late 1800s. Originally, buying behaviors were explained using utility theory in economics, where both the concepts marginal utility and total utility and equations for utility maximization developed.

Then, buying behavior was studied using the stimulus-response theories in psychology, where behavior could be easily explained with the help of stimulus and response, rewards and punishments, as well as signals and driving forces. On the other hand, complex and important concepts, such as attitudes, motivation, and values, were omitted in this context. During the 1950s, therefore, a psychoanalytically oriented motivational research was introduced with great interest to try to understand both conscious and unconscious motivation of consumers as buyers. Regarding personality theories, Freud's theories and psychoanalytical orientation were represented in consumers' behaviors for a long time.

Models of Buying Behavior

In the late 1950s, mainly quantitative, mathematical models were applied to understand the buying behavior, which laid the foundation for what later came to be research in behaviors of consumers (*consumer behavior*) in the United States. Again, psychological concepts and theories, through stochastic learning models, came to be adapted for the study of consumer behavior, which would later be followed by flow models, cognitive models, and computer simulation models.

> "The Howard-Sheth model is the most famous model for consumer behavior."

One of the most prominent and well-known models of consumer behavior was developed by Howard and Sheth (1969), and the model is a further development of a model originally conceived by John Howard. The Howard-Sheth model is considered one of the most discussed and useful models of consumer behavior and has also been the basis for Sheth's later model of organizational buying behavior (Sheth, 1973).

The Howard-Sheth model shows the variables and processes that influence an individual's behavior before and during a purchase, especially when the four variables of importance are: 1) stimuli, 2) perception, 3) learning, and 4) attitudes output (Figure 1.3). The model is intended to explain how consumers as buyers choose a product that is consistent with their wishes. It is further assumed that consumers learn about products by actively searching for information, which is then used to compare different brands based on the selection criteria of the consumer.

The model shows that an individual perceives a stimulus, which may be either a social or commercial stimuli. Learning takes place and results in the output, such as a purchase. Among the exogenous variables that influence both perception and learning, there are a number of social and psychological characteristics, such as culture, social class, personality traits, social context, time constraints, and economic status.

The Howard-Sheth model has the primary objective to show how exogenous variables affecting perception and learning processes explain the significance of these variables. The exogenous variables are always present and are assumed to change over time as a result of new learning, which is why the model is dynamic in nature and is based on changes in both the individual as well as societal conditions.

Furthermore, the model is considered to be a learning model, which is based on stimulus-response theory, where the notion of satisfaction was later given a prominent role. In the model, the researchers assumed that

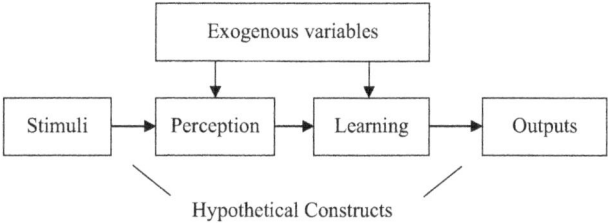

Figure 1.3 The Howard and Sheth Model of Buyer Behaviour (Zaltman and Wallendorf, 1979)

consumers' attitudes and selection criteria were influenced by the degree of satisfaction. It was further assumed that consumers learn to make brand choices by experience and perceptions (*experience*), which are based on what is called the *simplified psychology*. This is expressed through three different stages of a learning curve referred to as *extended problem solving*, *limited problem solving*, and *routine behavior*.

It is assumed in the theory that a consumer is actively seeking more information when *extended problem solving*, typically when you start to buy a new product family and generalize on the basis of past experiences rather than discriminating between brands. When a buyer has more experience, he/she reduces the information search and instead begins to discriminate between alternatives with the higher probability to choose one of these options; this is considered to characterize *limited problem solving*. Finally, when a buyer habitually chooses a particular brand, there is no information seeking at all, and it is considered to be a more *routine behavior*.

It is generally considered that the model has very much contributed to the study of consumer behavior. In particular, the model's ability to integrate different concepts and variables into a single model has been crucial, despite the fact that the relationships between them have not been precisely specified. Previously, these concepts and variables instead had been regarded as loose pieces or fragments without any interrelationships.

One of the model's strengths is that it has been empirically tested for consumers' decision-making, although not all relationships and propositions in the model have been confirmed. This should be compared with other models of consumer behavior, which have not been further investigated empirically and therefore are considered to be more tentative.

Among the weaknesses of the models, it may be mentioned that it is more about individual buying behavior than collective decision-making, like for example, within a family or an organization. Neither does it deal with interaction between buyers and sellers in a dyad; the model only deals with the buyer's part. This means that the model omits the social impact that may exist with respect to consumer decision-making.

Beyond the Howard-Sheth model, which is based on learning, Nicosia (1966) has proposed a more precise model based on a cognitive theory of decision-making. In this model, it is assumed that consumer behavior can be viewed as sequential decision-making, and using mathematical techniques and simulation, it is believed to be possible to predict a consumer's decision.

Furthermore, a model was developed, based on cognitive theory, in which the consumer is assumed to make decisions on grounds other than learning. Instead, it considered decisions to be based on an individual's cognitive structures, where information acquisition and processing are key concepts.

Concepts within Buying Behavior

Based on psychological and sociological theories, a number of different concepts have emerged to analyze and explain consumer behavior. These areas deal with aspects and issues related to consumer behavior with respect to factors based on the individual level (psychological factors) and the group level (sociological factors), as well as societal culture (socio-cultural factors).

Perception and Learning

In order to understand consumers' decision-making, concepts regarding perception, sometimes called views, and learning are of the highest importance, as they can explain what a consumer may perceive in their immediate surroundings.

> *"Most individuals perceive what he or she wants to perceive and nothing else, and what it is depends on the preferences and values."*

It is widely believed that perception may be affected by two types of factors, namely, stimulus factors and personal factors. When it comes to stimulus factors, it affects the views of an individual by how the sensory stimuli of sight, sound, smell, touch, or taste can be perceived and interpreted. When it comes to personal factors, the concept of *selective perception* is of importance, which means that an individual perceives what he or she wants to hear. Thus it is the individual's needs, moods, memories, experiences, or values that determine what he or she perceives in a message in his or her surroundings.

For an individual, different perceptions of things depend mostly on the particular values and preferences. It turns out that consumers often buy a product because of its symbolic content, because many consumers perceive a brand in a highly personal way.

Learning, as a cognitive concept, generally relates to how an individual's behavior can be explained as learned, and it is generally considered that an individual learns by repetition, by responding to stimuli, or by problem solving. With regard to stimulus-response theories, they assumed that all forms of learning is based on a chain of responses in the form of rewards or punishments for an individual in respect to a particular behavior, according to researchers like Pavlov and Skinner.

When it comes to cognitive theories, it considers that all learning is not based on stimulus-response but rather on memory capacity, expectations, and goals of a particular individual. A common notion is that individuals make use of their obtained insights, practice problem solving and thinking to acquire a certain behavior through learning and not just because of stimulus-response.

Field theory refers to the individual's behavior as related to the context and the situation that exists when a particular behavior occurs. In this manner, planning, thinking, purchasing, and consumption relate to the psychological field that consists of the individual and his/her surroundings.

Motivation and Personality

Generally, it is believed that an individual's motivation and personality are linked. Motivation is all about satisfying, protecting, or enhancing the self, and the way it is done defines an individual's personality.

The concept of motivation has its origin in both physiological needs and psychological needs. Physiological needs such as food, sex, or sleep are controlled by the body's biological needs to survive. When it comes to psychological needs, these are related to the social environment and the surroundings. The most famous hierarchy of needs, proposed by Maslow in 1943, includes physiological needs, safety needs, need for love, need for appreciation, and need for self-actualization.

The concept of personality is used by psychologists to explain how an individual reacts to different types of stimuli. Generally, behavior is controlled by how a stimulus is immediately perceived, which can be illustrated by a person who feels threatened, which may result in the person fleeing, hiding, crying for help, or asking for mercy.

Early focus was also a theoretical direction on lifestyles in the form of various psychographic factors to which psychographic analysis came to be applied both theoretically and practically. It is about trying to find segments of groups based on individuals' attitudes, interests, beliefs, values, and demographic characteristics, which the modern segmentation theory assumes in transaction marketing.

Beliefs and Attitudes

The term *belief* refers to what a person "knows" about things, and as a rule the ideas that an individual's beliefs are based on are true and real for that particular individual. There does not even need to be a correlation between an individual's beliefs and objective facts.

> *"Many consumers think they "know" how things fit together and work, but it is often a qualified truth."*

As a generic term, belief is often defined as knowledge, perceptions, and convictions an individual holds about things. If the term belief relates to what a person is considered to "know," then an attitude is deemed to be the emotional or motivational aspects of cognition, that is, understanding and thinking.

A common understanding within social psychology and other sciences is that the term "attitude" accounts for an individual's enduring attitude toward an object (attitude object). This attitude has been built through experiences and occurrences, and the vast majority of phenomena in a society's culture become the subject of attitudes. In market research, attitudes are often measured, for example, a brand's function, quality, or price.

Furthermore, an attitude is considered to consist of affective (emotional), cognitive, or intentional components, which in different ways express what an individual thinks about a particular object. An affective (or emotional) component relates to how strongly a person takes a stand for or against an attitude object and its various features, for example, in terms of positive or negative. A cognitive component refers to what an individual knows or believes about a certain object and its effects and impact on, for example, other people and society. An intentional component relates to the intent an individual has to act in terms of the attitude object, for example, to do something or refrain from doing something.

Attitudes differ in strength and can be strongly negative to strongly positive regarding valence, which often occurs in connection with the evaluation of a particular phenomenon or object. Often this is clear from statements about the phenomenon or object, such as "I hate it," "I love it," or "I avoid it." It is believed that attitudes can contribute to strengthening one's own self-perception, and it shows the attitude that an individual has to a phenomena or objects that are important and central in life.

In research, there are a number of different schools of thought and theories about the importance of attitudes and attitude changes, such as structural approach, functional approach, cognitive consistency, and cognitive dissonance. When it comes to measuring attitudes, there are a number of scales; the most famous are the Likert scale (1932) and the Osgood scale (1957).

Social processes

Thus far, the presented models and concepts have regarded the individual as a consumer, as a psychological entity. But all individuals are dependent on other people in their immediate environment and interact with others and are influenced by them, which results in a certain type of response that occurs in different individuals. The interactions that take place can be anything from an individual's interaction with a close friend to formal groups or large organizations.

A number of individuals who have a certain interaction over time with each other, and establish social relationships, are considered to be the basis for the concept of group. Add to this the fact that each member of a group feels that other members are part of the group in order for the group to exist and exert influence on the members.

In this context, the term "reference group" is the group that an individual mostly uses when it comes to asserting an opinion, a belief, and a behavior. An individual may have multiple reference groups that he or she either looks up to and wants to follow as a social model or wants to avoid because they have a negative behavior. When it comes to formal groups, most individuals belong to those that are governed by organizational structures and functions in business, government, community agencies, or other organizations.

> *"It is common to use reference groups to decide whether to buy the latest smartphone."*

Informal groups include, for example, colleagues, golfing friends, teenage gangs, or workout buddies, who often get together to pursue common social activities during leisure time. Although the structure and functions of these groups may be of minor importance, compared with formal groups, the informal groups are, without doubt, significant and important in the social processes.

In research, there are a number of theories about social processes, such as role theory, socialization processes, and group conformity, which deal with the interaction between individuals and groups in social processes.

Consumers' Buying Process

In accordance with the previously reported model by Howard and Sheth, consumers' decision-making in connection with a purchase has long been viewed with a cognitive and rational basis, where information collection and evaluation of a product should lead to a decision on the choice of product. An assumption has been that this rational decision-making process has been based on what is called the *economics of information*, which has meant that consumers will gather all the information needed to arrive at the right decision. When the benefit of additional information is considered less than the cost of the additional information, consumers no longer look for more information.

Figure 1.4 reproduces the five stages found in the consumer buying process regarding decision-making. It is also assumed that different types of problem solving, such as *enhanced problem solving, limited problem solving*, and *routine behavior*, which were previously mentioned in connection with the Howard and Sheth model, affect the process that consumers go through.

History of Consumer Marketing 43

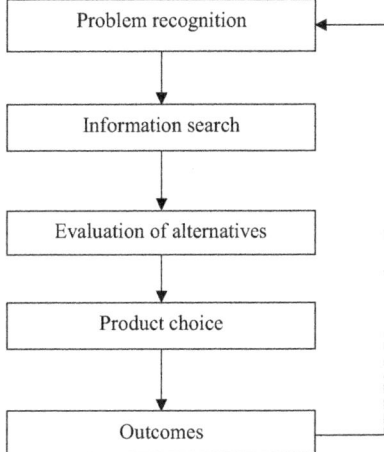

Figure 1.4 Consumers Decision-Making

With problem identification, a consumer discovers a problem in one of two ways, either that a product is missing or that a product is desired, which increases satisfaction. Often, the latter occurs when consumers pay attention to advertising messages of new products or products that are qualitatively better in comparison with those that one has.

Information gathering arises after a problem has been identified. This means that consumers go through a process where information is collected and processed to lead to a later decision on product selection. In the literature, both search before purchase and ongoing search are mentioned as two ways for consumers to act.

With regard to the evaluation of alternatives, it is considered to be due to the nature of the problem that consumers face. The more complex the problem, the more resources spent on evaluation, and the opposite is thought to apply to routine behavior. Often there are a smaller number of options depending on which products are already in memory.

When it comes to choice of product, this decision is influenced by past experience, partly the information that is gathered and partly the attitudes that consumers have toward the product in question. It is believed that consumers use different evaluation criteria for comparing competing alternatives, including what differentiates one product from another. Furthermore, it is believed that consumers have a number of decided product features that they choose between, which correspond to the product advantages that influence the final choice. The last phase of the process relates to the product that is ultimately purchased by consumers.

The criticism of this model is that consumers' decisions cannot only be explained on the basis of logical and rational grounds. Rather, it is that decisions regarding, for example, art, literature, or destinations emphasize the importance of emotions and feelings.

Consumers' Selective Perception Process

In previous sections, consumers' perceptions or views have been discussed from a general starting point without taking into account individual differences. Because information from one's surroundings, either through advertisements or good friends, can determine the final choice of a product, consumers are affected by different stimuli through the five senses. These are considered as sensory input and are stored in the sensory memory in the brain, which I will return to in the fourth chapter of the book.

The interpretations that a consumer makes of different stimuli are based on the attitudes, knowledge, and feelings that exist on the individual level, where both the expectations and the experiences play a major role in the final product choice in the form of a response.

The Concept of Consumption

From a sociological context, the analysis of the modern industrial society is based on the emergence of the importance that the consumption of goods and services have had. Historically, the economic importance of consumption in society came to be in focus by Adam Smith's work in the late 1700s, as mentioned earlier. Other scholars, such as Hegel and Marx, did not object to this later, but Marx pointed out in his writings that consumption should be spread more equally in a society.

In Sweden, during the 1900s, mass consumption took hold in earnest after the First World War, beginning with consumption for a certain lifestyle. This was facilitated by rapid urbanization, at the same time as the modern society began to emphasize the importance of democracy and individual freedom. During the 1950s and 1960s, this development was reinforced further, as industrially manufactured cars, ready-made clothing products, and home electronics began to be readily accepted. This laid the foundation for a more widespread hedonistic lifestyle, which, instead of emphasizing work ethic, came to be directed toward the consumption of entertainment experiences.

When the modern industrial society was formed and grew during the 1900s, the economists began early to scientifically show interest in the concept of benefit, which assumed that consumers sought the benefit of the goods and services as consumers. Sociologists, on the other hand, began to study why and how people consume in the transition from an agricultural society to an industrial society, with particular interest in how this affects ethics and morals.

From one perspective, it was suggested that consumption was a free and active action for consumers, which meant that one analyzed consumption as a communication action. It is argued that the Industrial Revolution in England, from the mid-1700s, was intimately associated with individuals' dreams, fantasies, and desires for change. This, together with the fact that there was a demand for new products and new inventions, created fertile ground for mass consumption.

> "There is no doubt that consumption plays a major role in consumers' self-fulfillment and image."

Another prominent perspective has been that the driving force of consumption has been based on people wanting to highlight social differentiation. Veblen presented the hypothesis of *conspicuous consumption* and stated that this explained the interest in consumption, because the lower strata of society wants to follow the society's elite, who showed their power and status through their consumption of expensive luxury goods. Other researchers, however, analyzed consumption as a system in which distinctions in taste and choices in consumption are the foundation of consumption, which is available for those who can understand the signals.

There are also theories that assume that consumption is characterized by manipulation, where a production perspective is prominent in the analysis. This starting point, which is often presented by Marxists, involves a cultural conservative approach and is based on the notion that consumers do not actually need certain goods but are persuaded to consume them. The American consumer culture has been analyzed as a phenomenon where citizens have been imposed a business system by producers, where advertising and promotional campaigns are included as a way to persuade consumers to purchase various goods and services through manipulation.

Generally, consumption has been thought to contribute to economic, social, and cultural changes in a society's development, which I will return to. Furthermore, it is believed that consumption fulfills a number of important social functions, where consumption in terms of demand, from an economic perspective, is believed to stimulate economic growth and affects a country's GDP. In this context, consumption, both nationally and individually, can be regarded as signs of success and prosperity.

Another influence relates to consumers from a sociological perspective, regarding what they consume as types of goods and services, which directly affects different individuals' quality of life and lifestyles. Both individual consumption and group consumption therefore are considered to have been one of the most important ways for many individuals to create an image of themselves, of others, and of society itself, to achieve the creation of identity and self-realization.

It is also considered, from a cultural perspective, that consumption is a form of collection of objects, because many people collect the artifacts that constitute the very foundation of a social culture. Hereby, consumption contributes in different ways to change both the societal culture and various sub-cultures, which was not the case earlier.

Consumer Culture Theory

In the 1980s, a *consumer culture theory* (CCT) developed in the United States, which was an approach to understanding consumer behavior, and not just buying behavior; and it had its first theoretical starting points in terms such as aesthetics and symbolism, as well as semiotics. Among the concepts and themes that came to be introduced were the value of structuralism, symbolic interactionism, semiotic perspective, critical macro perspective, and cultural, anthropological approaches. Different methods for the interpretation of consumers' behaviors with respect to the texts were developed, and there was an emphasis on the content and meaning of symbolism, with respect to both goods and advertisements in the form of communication in marketing.

Thereafter, in the 1990s, there formed a number of European research specializations within consumer culture theory in Denmark, France, Italy, and the United Kingdom, where British scientists developed a highly critical tradition in marketing. The Danish focus was culturally influenced, and it early on came to focus on understanding cultural differences in communication to consumers in different cultures. Among the French researchers, the interpretations of consumer behavior and studies of consumption experiences were in focus, along with the postmodernist idea, which I will return to. Furthermore, the French sociological research tradition played an important role by contributing to an approach that had a critical view of marketing.

This development resulted in the research field in traditional consumer research expanding in terms of both theoretical and methodological issues, and it was considered necessary to further study consumers' experiences of consumption and the personal significance of owning products. It was no longer about just understanding consumers' buying behavior, through theoretical assumptions of micro-economics and cognitive psychology, based on deduction and quantitative methods. Instead, consumer culture theory was viewed as a way to develop knowledge of consumers' behaviors with a humanistic and experience-based starting point.

> *"Consumers started to be regarded as creative and emotional individuals and no longer anonymous objects."*

In this way, consumers were regarded as creative, emotional, and inwardly focused individuals who were looking for self-fulfillment experiences, which were considered to be based on deeper meaning, strengthening for the body and soul, as well as authentic. These ontological premises violated the established perception of consumers, who maximize their benefit—and accumulate information—to be rational decision makers. The new approach came instead to focus on the importance of emotional spontaneity, the meaning of consumption, and its content in different contexts, which stood in stark contrast to theories of information gathering and processes.

Consumers' Behaviors

Within the new approach, the consumer's role as an individual in the culture of a society was also considered, and it was believed that social norms and rules affected consumer's behaviors. In this context, the advertisements and social media, as ideologies, came to influence consumers' behaviors, in an often contradictory way, in their quest to help individuals achieve their personal goals.

It should be added that aesthetic, symbolic, and experience-based aspects of personal consumption has also meant that the consumer, as a subject, has been considered as the basic unit of analysis from a methodological starting point.

In accordance with this assumption, several studies in the consumer culture theory have considered a societal culture as a symbolic supermarket, where independent consumers have made their choices, developed their identities, and built up their personalities by using and owning different material goods. It is in this context that consumption experiences form the basis of how individuals act and behave in a particular societal culture at a particular time.

Today, the philosophical roots of the consumer culture theory originate, for the most part, from a European research tradition, where a critical view of marketing is emphasized. Furthermore, the roots are considered to be applied and to be based on a consumer research that previously followed the American tradition rather than the present European. At the same time, cultural theory is considered to be a minority in consumer behavior research and a relatively marginal part of the marketing discipline; but on the other hand, this research has provided important contributions to the understanding of consumer behavior.

One of the most important concepts in consumer culture theory is symbolic interactionism, which emphasizes the importance of relationships with other people when it comes to shaping one's self and one's own identity. It is assumed that consumers, as individuals, surround themselves with different symbols in the environment and that these symbols give meaning and purpose in every situation. As an individual, one also learns the significance and meaning that symbols have in a societal culture. It is further assumed that the individuals who have a weak self-image and identity use different symbols through their own consumption in order to get a more complete self-image and identity.

Symbols are usually different owned goods that become part of what is called the individual's extended self-image (*extended self*). External objects can be included among the goods, such as different owned objects; persons, such as children or partners; and places or parts of the body, which an individual regards as "theirs." This means that different symbols become part of an individual, which one has control and power over. In this way, all purchases are considered to be an extension of one's self-image, which lays the foundation for identity and self-image among consumers.

The symbols contained in a particular societal culture help to create a meaningful system that consumers or groups of consumers use. It helps to create meaning and gives many people a sense of identity, where various consumer products, like brands, become culture-specific and have a certain cultural meaning. In this way, many brands are consumed not only for their material benefit, but also largely because of their symbolic meaning found in the image that consumers have of these brands.

Brands and Branding

As indicated, the brand, as a symbol, constitutes a way for many individuals to form their own self and create a positive self-image. Consumers often use brands to create meaning, which may also contribute to developing long-term relationships with a particular brand. Against this background, brands and branding are of importance for understanding consumers' affections, cognitions, and actual behaviors in the buying and consumption processes.

Brands and branding have been around for centuries and are not a new phenomenon in marketing. The English word *brand* is basically to brand or stamp a product to make it possible to recognize, which was done on the calves in Texas during the 1800s. The term *maverick*, which means individualist or rebel, was originally used by the American Samuel Augustus Maverick, who decided not to brand his calves, because all the other calves were branded. It became the characteristic feature of his calves and a way to distinguish them from other calves.

In connection with the emergence of mass marketing in the late 1800s, the *brand* came to be a necessary element in the mass production of many consumer goods. The

> "Lyle's Golden Syrup is considered to be Britain's oldest brand, characterized by its green and golden packaging, which has remained unchanged since 1885."

fact that the local production moved to factories meant that the goods lost their local identity if they did not have a name or logo on the packaging that could tell where the goods came from. The question for the manufacturers then became how to create confidence in a product that was not produced locally, because customers were not aware of it.

For this reason, the manufacturers needed to convince the markets that they could have confidence in a national product in the same way as for a local product. It was necessary then to introduce a brand for the goods as a way to increase consumer familiarity with the products. Among the companies that first introduced this were Campbell Soup, Coca-Cola, Juicy Fruit Gum, and Quaker Oats in the United States.

Around 1900, the American James Walter Thompson published an advertisement where brand advertising was explained, and this was considered to be the earliest commercial explanation of what is now known as brand building. This was then followed by a rapid development over the decades, with more and more companies making use of jingles, mascots, and slogans in marketing, mainly in radio and early television.

During the 1940s and 1950s, the producers of consumer goods began to identify how consumers developed relationships with their brands with social, psychological, and anthropological perspectives. This was the starting point for how the producers quickly learned to build a brand's identity and personality, for example, fun, luxurious, and youthful. What today is known as brand building assumes that consumers buy the brand rather than the product.

The Brand's Identity and its Personality

The literature defines a brand as the identity of a specific product, service, or business, and it can take many different forms. It may comprise, for example, a name, a shape, a color, a symbol, or a character, as well as a combination thereof. It should be said that a brand name, as part of the identity, aims to create a link between the brand's personality and the actual product or service, as perceived by the target audience. A brand name should be easy to remember, have positive connotations, and be associated with a trend.

The concept of brand identity is defined as a number of unique brand associations that a company creates and how it is supposed that consumers will perceive the brand. It has been suggested that a brand identity should be either functionally or symbolically oriented to fit into the consumer's functional and symbolic needs. This would make it possible for consumers to understand what a brand stands for in terms of solving practical needs problems, to contribute to one's own self-image, and to create social identification.

The brand's function and symbolism are different concepts in consumer consciousness, and it is assumed that consumers will not have any difficulties to embrace both functional and symbolic aspects. It is also considered that these associations can be concrete and emotional/symbolic or a combination of these.

> *"Owners of Harley-Davidson motorcycles often say that their motorcycle is not just a means of transport but a lifestyle, an experience, and a way to express who you are."*

When it comes to the brand's personality, the concept for the expression of the identity that a brand possesses has been widely accepted among academics and practitioners for a long time. A brand's personality is usually defined as a number of human characteristics that can be connected to a brand. This creates the opportunity for brand associations of a psychological nature in consumers based on the attitudes, fantasies, feelings, thoughts, or visions that fill a symbolic or self-expression function.

It is considered that consumers can readily put human characteristics on brands and that they can think of these as, for example, celebrities, famous historical figures, or just human characters. It is also considered that a strong brand personality can increase consumers' preferences for and use of a brand as well as their trust and loyalty.

Brand Relationships

To consider brand relationships as a natural part of the interaction between businesses and consumers is a fundamental basis in relationship marketing, as previously discussed. The literature reveals that brand relationships, as an extension of the brand's personality, are considered as a long-term, interactive process between a consumer and a brand.

Fournier (1998) suggested a relationship-oriented perspective, which assumed that a brand could be seen as an active, enthusiastic, and productive relationship partner to consumers. In this context, a brand is perceived as something that gives substance and meaning to consumers' daily lives and lays the foundation for a two-way communication to create interactions and relational bonds. It is worth noting that a brand, as an expression of interpersonal relationships, can help to create a sense of commitment and togetherness. This is considered to bind consumers to the brand through more high-quality relationships and develop a stronger image of the actual brand.

A common perception is that the emotional relationship that consumers build to a brand creates value of the brand, which occurs in various value-creating processes. Strong, positive consumer values occur in the close brand relationships, which facilitate the identification of the brand and in turn leads to consumers regarding the brand as part of their lives.

Some of the most emotional factors to enhance brand relationships deal with intimacy and personal greeting of consumers. It is considered that consumers first establish mental images or ideas about the brand, as a relationship partner, before a more intimate relationship is established with it.

Brand Experiences and Image

The emotional connection between a brand and consumers are considered to be important when it comes to building strong brands. It is also considered that consumers no longer buy products and services without looking for emotional experiences (Brembeck and Ekström, 2004). It proves to be especially prominent in terms of experience-based consumption, where contextual symbolic and nonfunctional aspects play a major role in the brand experience itself.

Brand experience as a concept has recently been defined in the literature as "subjective, internal consumer reactions (sensations, emotions, and cognitions) and behavioral reactions that are awakened by brand-related stimuli, which is part of a brand's design and identity, packaging, communication, and environment" (Brakus et al., 2009, p. 59). Furthermore, four different brand dimensions have been identified, namely, sensory, emotional, intellectual, and behavioral, which are related to the stimuli that consumers are exposed to when they are looking for or consuming the brand.

A common perception is that different brand experiences differ and affect memory to different degrees, which means that quite a few experiences are possible to revive and result in word of mouth. Furthermore, it is considered that consumers become increasingly skeptical of advertising as stimuli, the accuracy of which can only be confirmed through real experiences of the actual brand.

Brands with preferably hedonistic and experience-based contexts, in comparison with functional contexts, have shown to result in stronger attitudes in consumers for different brands. One result of this is that the relationship between the brand attitudes and purchase intentions seems to be strongest for holistic-minded consumers, compared with consumers who are just functionally oriented.

The starting point for the brand experience is all the contact points a consumer has with a brand. It can have a positive impact on the consumer's satisfaction, loyalty, and brand association, and consumers might be willing to receive additional stimulus if the experience is seen as positive, because a brand experience engages both body and soul.

> *"Consumers are involved in building a brand when their experience of the brand reinforces the positive image."*

In this context, brand image, as a concept, is the mental image that consumers have of a certain brand based on their experiences and perceptions of this brand in reality. The feelings and thoughts that exist about the product or a service help to create this mental image, which is then synonymous with the actual brand (Grönroos, 2008b).

The concept of brand awareness means consumers' ability to remember and recognize a brand and connect the brand to a name, a logo, a jingle, and so on in special memory associations. The degree of brand awareness determines the extent to which consumers consider a particular brand in connection with their decision-making or if they are aware of that particular brand or not.

Finally, it should be said that the concept of *consumer-based brand equity* has been used for a long time to explain how consumers perceive, relate to, and experience brands. A common view is that the concept has a consumer-based focus and involves what the brand means in reality for consumers. Consumer-based brand equity exists when the brand is familiar and consumers have gotten unique and strong brand associations, which they can remember. Furthermore, factors such as brand personality, brand relationships, and brand experiences are considered to lay the foundation for consumer-based brand equity.

Present Situation of Consumer Marketing

Consumer marketing as a discipline today covers a variety of areas, which together put the consumer at the center, regardless of whether it relates to mass marketing, relationship marketing, service logic, consumer behavior, or branding. The development that has taken place over the last few decades has increasingly come to focus on a theoretical and conceptual development, where leading concepts such as interactions, relationships, and value creation are highlighted.

When it comes to finding new theories and concepts to analyze and explain consumer marketing's future development, Achrol and Kotler (2012) have discussed the emergence of a new marketing paradigm. They believe that for a long time, marketing has evolved from a functionalist paradigm to a management paradigm and an exchange paradigm, where the classic manufacturing company has been the starting point.

But this exchange paradigm has since gradually come to include both interorganizational relationships between companies in the distribution channels and such interactions and relationships in the network, in the form of a networking paradigm. In the context of marketing exchanges, this has included not only goods, services, and money, but has also come to include ideas, places, symbols, emotions, and time. Similarly, the paradigm has come to cover consumers, employees, suppliers, and competitors, as well as all types of organizations, both for-profit and nonprofit.

In a new framework based on emerging shifts in the theoretical and empirical development of marketing, three new fields for a new marketing paradigm are presented. This is based on a compilation of a number of trends in research and literature, some of which have been around for some time and others that are of recent years, which have been condensed by the authors to create a future frame of reference.

The proposed frame of reference deals with the three new emerging fields that belong to the new marketing paradigm and consist of 1) consumer experiences, 2) network, and 3) sustained marketing (Table 1.4). This also links to the new emerging service logic, as previously discussed.

The first emerging field is about consumer experiences and takes as its starting point that consumption is the fundamental process in marketing. Furthermore, consumption is related to concepts such as benefit, satisfaction, and value, leading to the conclusion that the consumer's *perceptions*

Table 1.4 Assumptions about Received and Emergent Paradigm (Achrol and Kotler 2012, p. 36)

Received paradigm	Emergent paradigm
Consumer satisfaction	Consumer sensations and sense-making
Cognitive psychology of behavior products as "delivered services"	Neurophysiology of consumer behavior and sensory experiences Products and services as sensory experiences
Massive-scale manufacturing by contract manufacturers (phase one networks); early phase two innovation networks	Small-scale distributed, production-consumption networks products built atom by atom. Customer co-creation and co-production (phase three networks)
Dominant technologies: digitization and computer-controlled system	Dominant technologies: biotechnology and nanotechnology
Management as internal coordination of finance, marketing, production, R&D, and personnel in the firm	Management as customer care and network development-interorganizational coordination of finance, innovation, and production
Core competence: usually technology	Core competence: focal firm-marketing and network
Management priorities: growth, customer lifetime value, targeting middle and upper class growth	Management priorities: sustainable marketing, from lower-middle and base-of-the-pyramid market
Dyad as unit of analysis: hierarchical control, power and dependence, early relationship marketing, social norms of behavior	Multilevel networks as units of analysis: bottom-up networks, relational management of economic and ecological "commons," and social engagement
Corporate social responsibility	Proactive corporate strategies in ecology and development
Public policy: laissez-faire capitalism	Public policy: regulated capitalism

and *experiences* are particularly prominent in a consumer culture with the presence of digital technology and knowledge products.

That satisfaction of needs that consumers are seeking through consumption is filtered through the five human senses, namely, sight, sound, smell, touch, and taste. The senses are the tools that enable consumers to experience the world, and "It is the primary domain within consumer behavior theory and research" (Achrol and Kotler, 2012, p. 37).

When it comes to marketing and the five senses, as a phenomenon, the authors argue that too little research and attention has been directed toward sensations and implications of consumer experiences. For this reason, there has been a gap in academic research, because the five senses have been forgotten for decades. This has created a void when it comes to understanding the reality of consumers experiences and among the theories about the interplay between body and soul, as well as the interaction between emotion and consciousness.

> "A person's five senses have been forgotten in marketing research and more research is needed on their importance."

Furthermore, it is argued that today's societal culture provides consumers with stimuli that are easier to relate to and respond to. In this context, the importance of the haptic age and the presence of haptic sensations in computers, gaming systems, and cyberspace are discussed. This leads to the opportunity to separate the body and mind, and consumers can experience the body's need through virtual projections on the intellectual level.

Against this background, the digital world provides endless possibilities to create experiences or perceptions, which at the same time means that the physical world, as another world, will lose its importance for many individuals. In this context, the perceptions from virtual experiences become prime and help to create new opportunities for marketing.

Thereafter, the authors discuss neurophysiology and marketing, as phenomena, where the importance of analyzing and understanding how the human brain responds to different stimuli are the focus. Using different methods and technologies in cognitive neurophysiology, such as magnetic resonance imaging (MRI), it is possible to determine which neural activities occur in different areas of the brain to understand how consumer experiences are created. It is considered that future research in consumer behavior and consumption perceptions are totally dependent on neurophysiology or neuromarketing.

Thereafter, marketing and nanotechnology, as a phenomenon, are discussed, where the importance of materials, tools, and systems with new characteristics can help to enhance the consumption experience or perception of a product. It is emphasized that the application of new nanotechnology is about to change many consumer products, such as cars, computers, tires, sunglasses, and tennis rackets, to name a few recent examples. Furthermore, it is presented that nanotechnology will be able to develop tools that will directly be able to influence our taste buds and taste sensations as well as create new scent sensors and provide fragrance sensations.

Finally, the authors claim that there is a radical paradigm shift regarding how consumer products are created, delivered, and consumed. The experience that consumers have with products and services, which they get through the five senses, requires that marketing develop a better understanding of how consumer experiences and sensations are created in theory and practice.

REFERENCES

Achrol, R.S. and Kotler, P. (2012), "Frontiers of the marketing paradigm in the third millennium," *Journal of the Academy of Marketing Science*, 40, 1:35–52.
Alderson, W. (1954), "Factors governing development of marketing channels." I: Clewett, R.M. (ed.) *Marketing channels for manufactured goods*, Homewood, IL: Richard D. Irwin, p. 41–49.
Alexander, R.S., Surface, R.F. and Alderson, W. (1949), *Marketing*, New York: Ginn & Co.
Baker, M. (2000), *Marketing strategy and management*, 3rd ed., London: Macmillan Press, Ltd.
Bartels, R. (1970), *Marketing theory and metatheory*, Richard D. Homewood, IL: Irwin.
Berry, L.L. (1983), *Relationship marketing*, American Marketing Association's Services Marketing Conference, paper.
Brakus, J., Schmitt, B. and Zarantonello, L. (2009), "Brand experience: what is it? How is it measured? Does it affect loyalty?" *Journal of Marketing*, 73, 3:52–68.
Brembeck, H. and Ekström, K. (2004), *Elusive consumption*, Oxford: Berg Publishers.
Bucklin, L.P. (1966), *A theory of distribution channel structure*, Berkeley, CA: IBER Special Publications.
Copeland, M.T. (1923), "Relation of consumers' buying habits to marketing methods," *Harvard Business Review*, 1:282–289.
Fournier, S. (1998), "Consumers and their brands: developing relationship theory in consumer research," *Journal of Consumer Research*, 24, 4:343–373.
Frankelius, P. (1997), *Kirurgisk marknadsföring* (Surgical Marketing), Malmö: Liber Ekonomi.
Fullerton, R.A. (1988), "How modern is modern marketing? Marketing's evolution and the myth of the production era," *Journal of Marketing*, 1:108–125.
Gilboy, E.W. (1932), "Demand as a factor in the industrial revolution." I: *Facts and factors in economic history*, Cambridge, MA: Harvard University Press.
Grönroos, C. (2000), *Service management and marketing—a customer relationship management approach*, Chichester: John Wiley & Sons.
Grönroos, C. (2006), "Adapting a service logic for marketing," *Marketing Theory*, 6, 3:317–333.
Grönroos, C. (2008a), "Service logic revisited: who creates value? And who co-creates?" *European Business Review*, 20, 4:298–314.

Grönroos, C. (2008b), *Service management and marketing*, Malmö: Liber.
Gummesson, E. (1979), "The marketing of professional services—an organizational dilemma," *European Journal of Marketing*, 13, 5:308–318.
Gummesson, E. (1991), "Marketing revisited: the crucial role of the part-time marketer," *European Journal of Marketing*, 25, 2:60–67.
Gummesson, E. (1999), *Total relationship marketing: rethinking marketing management from 4Ps to 30Rs*, Oxford: Butterworth Heinemann.
Howard, J. (1957), *Marketing management, operating, strategic and administrative*, Homewood, IL: Richard D. Irwin.
Howard, J.A. and Sheth, J.N. (1969), *The theory of buyer behavior*, New York: John Wiley & Sons.
Keith, R.J. (1960), "The marketing revolution," *Journal of Marketing*, 24, 3:35–38.
Kotler, P. (2000), *Marketing management, analysis, planning and control*, The millennium edition, New York: Prentice-Hall.
McCarthy, J. (1960), *Basic marketing*, Homewood, IL: Richard D. Irwin.
Nicosia, F.M. (1966), *Consumer Decision Processes; Marketing and Advertising Implications*; Englewood Cliffs, NJ: Prentice-Hall.
Normann, R. (2001), *När kartan förändrar affärslandskapet [Reframing business: When the map changes the landscape]*, Malmö: Liber.
Nystrom, P.H. (1915), *The economics of retailing*, New York: The Ronald Press Company.
Sheldon, R. and Ahrens, E. (1932), *Consumer engineering: a new technique for prosperity*, New York and London: Harper.
Sheth, J.N. (1973), "A model of industrial buyer behavior," *Journal of Marketing*, 37, 4:50–56.
Sheth, J.N. and Parvatiyar, A. (1995), "Relationship marketing in consumer markets: antecedents and consequences," *Journal of the Academy of Marketing Science*, 23, 4:397–418.
Storbacka, K., Strandvik, T. and Grönroos, C. (1994), "Managing customer relations for profit: the dynamics of relationship quality," *International Journal of Service Industry Management*, 5, 5:21–38.
Vargo, S. and Lusch, R. (2004), "Evolving to a new dominant logic in marketing," *Journal of Marketing*, 68, 1:1–17.
Weld, L. (1917), "Marketing functions and mercantile organization," *The American Economic Review*, 7, 2:306–318.
Wind, J. and Robertson, T. (1983), "Marketing strategy: new directions of theory and research," *Journal of Marketing*, 47, 2:12–25.
Woodruff, R.B. and Gardial, S. (1996), *Know your customers—new approaches to understanding customer value and satisfaction*, Oxford: Blackwell.
Zaltman, G. and Wallendorf, M. (1979), *Consumer behavior: basic findings and management implications*, New York: John Wiley & Sons.

2 The Marketing Dynamics

This chapter presents the two forces of change—in the form of cultural value shift and digital technology—that are most prominent in today's global marketing environment and consumer culture. These two forces of change influence and give rise to new values, behavior, and consumption patterns of consumers, as new strategies for dialogue, communication, and value creation in consumer marketing.

Initially, various processes of change in the development of society are discussed, including the criticisms against the modern industrial society, the emergence of the cultural value shift, and the importance of societal culture. Furthermore, the values that are typical for the X, Y, and Z generations are addressed to create an understanding of their impact on marketing and consumption. Finally, the breakthrough of digital technology, including social media and its significance in the exchange of information and communication between both businesses and consumers and between consumers, is discussed.

BRAND EXPERIENCE IN FOCUS

A Global Marketing Environment

Today's global marketing environment is considered to be a consumer culture, where various activities, products, places, or brands are constantly bought and consumed in a highly individual and personal basis. This assumes the meaning that the selected products or brands have for a person's life, which means that it is possible to distinguish different types of consumer activities. Because experiences, dreams, and hopes steer consumers' buying decisions, the symbolic content of various goods, services, and products are crucial to a brand experience during consumption.

In a global consumer culture, marketing, on the one hand, and consumption, on the other hand, are intimately associated with individuals' experiences, image building, and self-fulfillment. This emphasizes the importance of the emotional element as different from a purely functional (rational) element as the basis for a brand experience. Therefore, marketing and consumption are built on both elements, putting the brand experience in focus.

The significance of the symbolic content in a brand experience is constantly increasing and leads to a consumption based on both fictitious as well as real self-images and experiences. This is a way to find and create meaning in the lives of many people (Fromm, 1976). Using postmodern concepts, it is assumed that consumption does not occur mainly due to material values but because of the symbolic content of the goods or services consumed. This I believe is the basis for an experience-based consumption as opposed to just a tangible good and/or services consumption.

Against this background, consumption has a key role in what people's everyday lives looks like and contributes to various experiences of a brand. Furthermore, consumption contributes to create meaning and is seen as a process of existential choice and has become increasingly linked to the individual's need for individualization and increased degree of self-fulfillment (Elliott, 1997). This leads to a purchase behavior based on creating self-images and experiences related to the self.

Today's young generation often view traditional advertising media, such as advertising and television commercials, as inspirational and entertaining, unlike before. Previously, the channels primary task was to inform and influence people to buy the products and services that were offered. If a company today manages to create commitment and inspiration through a brand, it means that the company has managed to establish an emotional relationship as the basis to continue building a relationship with the customer.

> "24/7 means that every individual, twenty-four hours a day, seven days a week—real or virtual–can create new sensory experiences for their own consumption."

Consumer goods and services, as brands, then become not only exchange items but can be thought of as "goods to think with, goods to talk with" (Fiske, 1989). These brands then form the basis of the image–or self-image– which individuals create, whereby goods or services are considered to be "brands." Some researchers argue that this has created a symbolic society, where symbolic characters in and of themselves constitute the basis for creating, maintaining, and communicating identity and social meaning in marketing and consumption.

The Symbolic World

In a symbolic society, based on a pure global consumer culture, different kinds of brands represent a link or a bridge to the symbolic world and the experiences that an individual's consumption gives rise to. It can mean a visit to a mall, a purchase of a good, or a meal at a restaurant. The total experience of an activity, a product, or a brand is more important for the individual than the product or service itself, which means that both the functional and the emotional factors are crucial for the brand experience.

The example that follows shows how Swedish consumers choose to spend their income on consumption of various goods and services with the purpose of obtaining experiences.

> *In a study, the consulting firm Kairos Future in 2013 asked 2,200 Swedes about their consumption habits. It appears that they spend almost a quarter of their monthly income, equivalent to 4,500 SEK, for the consumption of pleasure. It consists primarily of clothing, food, travel, and eating out, followed by movies, books, concerts, and theater visits. One conclusion of the study is that consumers expect to find an entertainment aspect in more and more consumption activities and that it should be fun and enjoyable.*

Researchers such as Jensen (1999, p. 3, op. cit.) have expressed what consumers are looking for in an experience:

> *Now, they want to have an interesting life, experience new aspects of life or new places, be entertained and learn in an enjoyable way. Customers are now looking for more than the mere product or service. Experiences fulfill this need.*

It is the experience itself that is the ultimate goal of consumption; thus the product, good, or service becomes an artifact around which the individualized and personal experience is created. When it comes to experiences, these may relate not only to classical commodities but also to activities in the context of culture, tourism, a website, digital technology, such as mobile phones or Internet services, and so on. This experience is based on the individual him/herself being involved and producing experiences as a creator—either on their own or with others—which results in the product or service being subordinate to the experience itself.

For this reason, the need for new innovations, new knowledge content, and new services are conditions for a dynamic market when it comes to creating symbolism and brand experiences in a global marketing environment. At the same time, this also illustrates the transition from mass production and mass marketing to individual, customized products and an increasingly individualized marketing. It means that the ideas that have been established and been around for a long time, regarding what characterizes marketing and consumption, need to be reviewed and questioned.

CHANGE PROCESSES IN SOCIETY

Three Social Waves

The transition that is taking place against an increasingly experience-based global consumer culture, primarily in Western and Eastern Europe, Japan, China, Korea, Australia, Brazil, India, and North America are rooted in the economic, cultural, social, and technological change processes that affect the development of society from one period to another. The effects that these processes of change have on marketing and consumption mean that new conditions often arise that affect both businesses and consumers.

Historically, various social stages were regarded as periods or waves, where the factors that have characterized the society have varied from one time to another (Table 2.1).

These characteristics have generally persisted for a long time and characterize the development that takes place in both the short- and long-term. One advantage with identifying this type of change is that you can explain what happens in a society at a given time, but also that one can predict what society might look like in the future.

The First Wave

Using a *wave-front analysis*, researchers, such as Toffler (1982, 1995), have examined the economic, political, social, and technological changes that have occurred during the last two centuries in the form of three waves of society.

The *first wave* refers to the development of the agricultural society, often referred to as the classic social stage, and it reached its end in the early and mid-1800s, when the Industrial Revolution began in England. The changes of economic, intellectual, political, social, and technical characteristics at that time were regarded as the foundation for the transformation of the old agricultural society.

Table 2.1 Characteristics of Different Stages of Societies (Jencks, 1987)

	Premodern	Modern	Postmodern
Production	Agriculture handiwork, farming	Industrial production, factory	Information production, office
Society	Feudal	Capitalism	Liberal capitalism
Orientation	Local	National	Global
Time perception	Cyclical	Linear	Parallel
Culture	Aristocratic	Bourgeois	Fragmented

That transition, which took place from the agricultural society to the industrial society, is called the great transformation or the modernist project called "the Enlightenment" (Polanyi, 1973). One of the most characteristic features of this transformation was the introduction of new forms of social life and socializing, as well as the emergence of the new social processes in comparison with the traditional way of life in the old agricultural society.

The Second Wave

The *second wave* refers to the industrial development of society, often called the modern social stage, and it is considered to have reached its peak in the mid to late 1970s. The transformation of the old agricultural society came to bring new effective methods and techniques for industrial manufacturing and food production, including the factory system, with division of labor and specialization, as a replacement for manual agriculture. Later, other forms of economic activities came to be the focus, compared to those earlier, which have become known as the breakthrough of capitalism.

This development led to the birth of the modern industrial society through what has come to be known as the Industrial Revolution. New business ideas, companies, and institutions arose, as well as new attitudes toward economic development. A development of new products and technologies began, as well as an increasing production of everyday items to create profitability and achieve gains.

New scientific methods were introduced relating to leadership and management of companies, in particular labor, which proved to be dynamic and logical as well as rational from an organizational, market-based, and technological point of view.

The Third Wave

The so-called *third wave* refers to the societal changes that took place during the past three decades in the late 1900s and early 2000s, often called the postmodern social stage. These changes in economic, political, social, and technological character have in many respects been contributing to the transformation of the modern industrial society. This is expressed through the often contradictory or paradoxical relationships in the private sector as well as the different spheres of social life.

Researchers, such as Inglehart (1997), argue that there is an ongoing cultural value shift, where the established ideas and understandings about the economy, family, religion, social relationships, business, and politics are questioned and reevaluated. Inglehart further argues that the modernization and the postmodernization of the society, as change processes, are to be considered as two basic cultural value systems related to economic growth and economic development. These two value systems are pivotal for how the socioeconomic conditions will be built and developed in a society at any given time.

CRITICISM OF THE MODERN INDUSTRIAL SOCIETY

Society's Postmodernization

In recent decades, sociological researchers have raised objections to classical sociological concepts and theories when it comes to studying the current development of society. The main argument has been that these concepts and theories are inadequate when it comes to interpreting and understanding the key issues and problems in the current society. The main reason for this is that there is a shift toward a new stage of society through postmodernity.

Postmodernity is usually associated with a temporal analysis of how social changes developed in the society from the 1970s onward. In contrast with postmodernity, modernity emphasizes the emergence of different kinds of social changes in a chronological order during the 1800s and 1900s, as a result of the Industrial Revolution.

In the transition from the old industrial society to the present society, through what is referred to as postmodernization, many sociologists argue that capitalism as an economic system is about to change in its basic character. Among other things, methods and structures by which companies make money are changing from an economic standpoint.

One of the biggest changes is the globalization of capitalism, which means that capitalism has become more global as well as more geographically separated and divided than before. Within many industries, production is outsourced to low-wage countries, and traditional manufacturing as well as manual labor are steadily declining in Western industrialized countries. At the same time, the service sector is expanding with a growing service industry and the recruitment of especially young people as a result.

> *In the early 1900s, the service sector constituted 3 percent of the employment in Sweden, whereas in 2000 it accounted for about 80 percent. Of all new businesses today, about four out of five service companies and three out of four Swedes engage in some form of service production. Overall, the service sector accounts for half of Sweden's GDP and about 45 percent of total employment.*

A number of sociologists have developed new concepts and approaches to create a different vocabulary, which have received a general expansion in recent decades. Some of the most well-known concepts and approaches have been *post-Fordism, disorganized capitalism,* and *flexible capital growth,* which analyzed and explained postmodernity as a different form of society.

The globalization of financial markets and the mobility of capital in recent years have emphasized the importance of postmodernity as a new form of society, especially when it comes to the relocation of job opportunities and investments within the automotive, electronics, and fashion industries to low-wage countries, primarily in Southeast Asia over the past decade, which today also include countries on the African continent. With this development, the classical industrial production has come to increasingly be replaced by knowledge and service production, placing new demands on economic adjustment, flexibility, and mobility.

A New Social Model

The so-called Fordism/post-Fordism model has aimed to illustrate some of the most prominent features of the earlier industrial society (Bilton et al. 2002) (Table 2.2). The model has been based on the idea of the assembly line, which was introduced by the American car manufacturer Ford during the 1920s. Furthermore, the model assumed that production has meant mass production of cars for a mass market in the form of the consumers of that time.

Fordism has been considered by many as an illustrative model of postwar economic development and growth boom from the early 1950s until the

Table 2.2 The Main Characteristics of Fordism and Post-Fordism (Bilton et al., 2002, p. 520)

Fordism	Regime of accumulation	Mode of regulation	Culture and worldview
Mass production standardized products	State manages the economy for growth and full employment	Class is the central social and political identity	Modernist culture belief in social and technical progress
Rigid bureaucracy Routinized work	Universal welfare provision	Work identity is more important than consumer identity	Emphasis on social justice as well as profitable production
High productivity and wage growth Strong, large trade unions Wages bargained collectively	Redistribution of incomes Strong interest groups influence policy and bargain with government	Collectivist class interest oppose groups with individualistic values in shaping politics	

(Continued)

Table 2.2 (Continued)

Fordism	Regime of accumulation	Mode of regulation	Culture and worldview
Post-Fordism Flexible specialization in production, using global manufacturing	Private welfare for core workers, basic state provision for the rest	Self-expression through consumption and lifestyle	Postmodern culture Commercial and artistic cultures overlap
Goods designed and produced for market niches	Resistance to planning or state coordination	Non-class issues and identities are the focus of political action	Mass-produced images more significant than individual art
Polarization of workers into core and secondary labor forces	Fragmentation of group interests Diverse social identities and interests	New social movements	Image and surface appearance more important than structure

middle of 1970. In the Western industrial countries, the public policy during this period of time focused on supporting full employment and welfare, as well as creating higher living standards.

From the late 1970s, new ideas of business and social life developed. This was a result of the first oil crisis and the increasingly tough competition in the world economy at that time.

With this, post-Fordism came to relate to the introduction of the new management methods and technologies in an increasingly global economy. Through concepts such as *flexible capital growth*, *flexible specialization*, and the *flexible company*, the development of Fordism to post-Fordism was analyzed and explained.

With flexible capital growth, it was no longer just the production and consumption of goods and services that were considered, but factors of production such as information and knowledge were also now seen as increasingly important. The main purpose of flexible capital growth was to improve the profitability of the company through lower production costs as well as higher turnover rates. The most common methods for achieving this were, for example, new production technology and new work processes, as well as new patterns of interaction between the producers and the consumers.

From Mass Production to Mass Individualization

In many industries, mass production as an idea, through market segmentation, is replaced by mass individualization (mass customization), which is derived from closer contact with the customers. Through the new digital information and communication technology, it is possible to divide a production volume of one or two products in more and cheaper variants. In this way, the introduction of automation and flexible manufacturing systems has resulted in mass customization, which the U.S. computer maker Dell can be considered an early example of. Dell offers its customers the opportunity to build a personal computer based on predetermined options, such as desktop or laptop, screen size, processor, and the software the computer will be equipped with.

Digital information and communications technologies, therefore, are a crucial driving force behind the globalization of ideas, brands, and products, as well as for the emergence of the new economy in the late 1990s. In a number of industries, companies' production has also been divided into complex or simple processes, with a national or global workforce, often spread across continents with large geographical distances. The products have also become more diverse and distinct from each other, at the same time as new services and service industries have arisen.

THE CULTURAL VALUE SHIFT

The Effects of Postmodernization

The ongoing transformation of the modern industrial society, through postmodernity, has substantially affected marketing and consumption. It has resulted in the establishment of new patterns of consumption, new family relationships, and new values, to highlight some of the major consequences.

The postmodernization of the society that has occurred in recent decades has meant that the importance of quality of life and well-being has come to have increasing significance, compared to the past (Inglehart, 1997). Since the 1990s, there has been a deliberate and obvious focus on the individual in terms of his/her needs, accomplishments, and experiences, which has not occurred to the same extent historically. A distinctive feature is that most people, as a result of the dynamic, diverse, social, and economic conditions in the workplace, politics, everyday life, or science, no longer have predetermined and permanent values.

> *"The new economic and social conditions have meant less collective, social responsibility, and the individual has received an even greater role."*

A similar basic value shift also occurred in the transition from the agricultural society to a modern industrial society. Then, it was believed that increased common obligations and social mobility were required as well as smaller collective responsibility to achieve economic growth and prosperity. In the modern perspective, absolute religiously based social norms were no longer prominent, but instead, individualism, innovation, and economic success appeared to be the crucial aspects for the development of society.

It was now possible for an individual to reach a social status through hard work and financial rewards, which previously was more related to "something you were born with." Instead, there was a worldview with new human values, which were totally opposite to the previous worldview, where common obligations, social traditions, and inherited status were based on religious norms and social nonmobility (ibid.).

Other main reasons for the economic growth of the modern industrial society were the organizational and technological developments. Further, it was also assumed that economic growth emanated from the bureaucratic society, the industrial company, the assembly line, and the trade union movement, which were pivotal for economic development. Then goals such as society's economic growth as well as corporate and individual capital growth became of great importance and are still a top priority today for most people in Western Europe and the United States.

Materialist and Postmaterialist Values

In the ongoing cultural value shift, many of the values that were previously associated with modern industrial society are questioned. The bureaucratic state is viewed as being less effective in the current society, where high technology and knowledge dominate; at the same time, there is less widespread acceptance of the bureaucratic state.

The industrial company and the assembly line—mass production's foremost symbols—characterized by workers with standardized procedures, considered as being "machines," are also questioned. This view originates from a dehumanization and a depersonification of the work that different individuals perform. Previously, many people in modern industrial society accepted the costs and the disadvantages that these tasks brought with them, which resulted in, for example, poor health and reduced quality of life to achieve economic benefits.

Inglehart (1990) also believes that the current cultural value shift is most clearly illustrated by both *materialistic* values, where economic and physical security are emphasized, and *postmaterialist values*, where quality of life and self-fulfillment are emphasized (Table 2.3).

In the book, *Culture Shift in Advanced Industrial Society* (1990), Inglehart analyzes the emergence of postmaterialist values and shows the value differences that have existed between the generations born in the 1950s

Table 2.3 Materialist/Postmaterialist Dimensions in Fifteen Countries (Inglehart, 1997, p. 112)

Materialist items	Strong Defense Forces, Fight Rising Prices, Fight Against Crime Maintain Order, Economic Growth, Maintain Stable Economy
Postmateralist items	Less Impersonal Society, More Say on Job, More Say in Government, Ideas Count More than Money, Freedom of Speech, More Beautiful Cities

Source: 1990–1991 World Values Survey data from France, Britain, West Germany, Italy, the Netherlands, Denmark, Belgium, Ireland, Norway, Sweden, Finland, Iceland, Canada, and the United States.

and the 1960s, in comparison with the generations born in the 1920s, 1930s, and 1940s. For the later generations, the basic physical and material needs, primarily in Western Europe and the United States, were satisfied through a vast majority of people obtaining a material standard of living and welfare.

As a result of the rising living standards, for the later generations, beginning in the 1950s and 1960s, there has been a value shift from materialism to quality of life. During the 1980s, the importance of higher quality of life, for many individuals, was expressed by the formation of political and social movements, such as Friends of the Earth, Greenpeace, and the environmental movement. It should be said that the latter two have an active political and social influence on marketing and consumption, even today.

> "To be able to create personal life strategies, material security and survival need to exist in a society."

In the analysis (Table 2.3), Inglehart concluded that previous generations born from 1886 to 1945 had shown a greater interest in economic issues than the later generations. This analysis has come to be supported by a British study, where it was shown that people between 18 and 34 years of age think of themselves as being more hedonistic than materialistic and have ensured that their own quality of life comes first. One of the conclusions of the study was that to "pamper oneself" has been accepted at the same time as postmodern values such as "to have, to be, and to break loose" have been accepted and have emerged (Wilkinson and Mulgan, 1995).

It should be said that economic efficiency has been less prioritized among people with postmaterialist values in comparison with the values related to quality of life and self-fulfillment. A conclusion has been that the individual and individual choice have completely different meanings in present society and that many individuals are not willing to bear the costs of bureaucracy, collective responsibility, and rigid social norms in the same way as before.

How Are Postmaterialist Values Explained?

As a researcher, I have asked myself the question: *How can the existence and development of the postmaterialist values be explained in current society?* One of the answers given by Inglehart refers to the individual's perception of whether his/her survival can be taken for granted or not in a society so that he or she can shape and influence his/her own life. In the case where survival can be regarded as self-evident, it is crucial to give the individual the opportunity to develop his/her personality and private life strategies.

Inglehart (1997) also asserts that the emergence of postmaterialist values have been dependent on material security and the survival within a society. In themselves, postmaterialist values do not manifest a negative value of either physical or economic security, but rather, they are valued as positive and considered to be important prerequisites for creating quality of life and achieving an individual's self-fulfillment in a given society.

Today, postmaterialist values are common in most European countries—especially the Scandinavian countries—and in North America, Australia, Japan, and China. One conclusion is that there is a systematic difference in terms of materialist and postmaterialist values between rich and poor countries. For that reason, marketing and consumption differ between these countries.

Inglehart claims that materialistic values have lost ground in favor of postmaterialist values just as the younger generations have come to replace the older generations. This has mainly been due to the age-related differences that exist between the different generations, which in itself has meant that the younger generations have not been regarded as being able to have materialistic values in certain areas, which I will discuss later in the chapter.

In a British study, Howard and Mason (2001) analyzed the ongoing cultural value shift. They chose to define what they named "Me-society" and "I-society," where the former is based on self-promoting, whereas the latter is based on independence and self-fulfillment. Their working hypothesis was based on the assumption that the Me-society was about to be replaced by an I-society, which is expressed as follows (p. 95, op. cit.):

> *Rather than focusing on work, money, and material acquisition for satisfaction . . . we are looking for new forms of fulfilment and sources of identity in a range of activities and values beyond these. People who are able to achieve a basic level of affluence are now more concerned with expressing their individuality and being independent—both mentally and materially.*

The study shows that low I-values are about materialistic values, safer work, and traditional gender roles, whereas high I-values are about work and financial independence. The high values are also about a more individualistic approach, where access to information via the Internet and other forms of communication success is emerging. One conclusion of the study is that high I-values will be prominent in a society in the future and that these values will be dependent on continued economic growth.

This leads to the conclusion that postmaterialist values, with an emphasis on quality of life and well-being, linked to economic growth, are given higher priority in a social culture where a secure survival exists to allow for higher quality of life and welfare. This allows for a greater degree of individualization, which becomes a crucial prerequisite for marketing and consumption in contemporary societal culture.

In its global youth study titled *Global Youth 2013*, the Swedish consulting firm Kairos Future reports on the dreams and values of 6,500 young people in 11 countries, including Sweden, the United Kingdom, Russia, India, China, and Australia. Out of these young people, almost two out of three believe that society has become too individualized and that the future is dim. Furthermore, many believe that their generation will have worse conditions than their parents. It should also be noted that faith in politicians is low and that concerns about not getting a job are great. Finally, it should be said that many young people share the dreams of a family, a good home, and a job, despite concerns over a dim future.

The ongoing cultural value shift, therefore, reflects the presence of both materialistic (or modern) and postmaterialistic (or postmodern) values. In my opinion, this points to the importance of the two different value systems, where there are different beliefs and understandings on issues related to economics and family relations, as well as corporate, individual, political, religious, or social norms.

SOCIETAL CULTURE AND VALUE SYSTEMS

Some Typical Features

Marketing and consumption are affected directly and indirectly by societal culture and the value system that prevails in current society. Some of the most prominent changes in the cultural value shift have touched precisely culture, knowledge, and everyday life.

When it comes to today's social culture, one of the typical features is what is called the time disorder, which allows for new experiences, perspectives, and identities for many individuals. This means that the consumption of goods, services, and experiences can happen anytime and anyplace, with the help of digital technology. Another typical trait is that design and style, as expressions of products and brands, are more important than content and substance, which reflects current societal culture.

Furthermore, another typical feature is the mixture of humor, reality, and visual surprises that often take place. Different postmodern themes recur constantly in advertising and television commercials. The distinction that previously existed between "reality" and its "representatives" in the real world becomes increasingly unclear and blurred.

Another defining feature of contemporary societal culture is that it covers both everyday experiences and popular arts, such as literature and art. The distinction that existed between art ("high culture") and popular culture has disappeared as a result of the ongoing cultural value shift.

Moreover, the differences between people, that is, diversity, is accepted and supported in everyday life, which can be said to represent the quality of life and well-being at the individual level. Also, different beliefs and ideas appear as to how current society shall develop, and there is skepticism toward any form of all-encompassing explanations that are based on a religion, a doctrine, or a social norm. The traditional understandings of everyday life, people, economy, business, and social life that have emerged in the modern industrial society are changing and are challenged when new values arise.

> During weeks 15–16 in 2010, ICA launched its Good Life collection, which was promoted in one of the company's commercials. In the film, Stig (main character) was asked by management to participate in one of the company's advertising launches, something that burdened him. Sebastian tries to encourage Stig but has difficulty finding the words when Stig shows the clothes that the company wants him to wear during the launch. Stig emerges wearing a pair of bright pink shorts that are a little too tight and a mint green, tight tank top that leaves little to the imagination. Added to this, he also has a white ICA sweatband and a pair of light-pink leg warmers.

Modern and Postmodern Value Systems

The contemporary social culture consists of and is characterized by two different value systems—the modern and the postmodern—which form the basis of the ongoing cultural value shift. The characteristic feature that has emerged and developed in the marketing environment can be linked to factors such as people and everyday life, facts and knowledge, culture and values, behavior and demography, economy and globalization, as well as markets and technology (Hultén et al. 2009) (Table 2.4).

In a societal culture, influenced by the cultural value shift, marketing and consumption are affected by both modern and postmodern values, resulting in increased complexity and diversity. This points to the importance of knowledge as a key factor for production and for assets for businesses, which can include everything from data, facts, culture, and symbols

Table 2.4 Culture of Society and Value System in a Global Marketing Environment (Hultén et al., 2009, pp. 27–28)

Factors and attributes	Modern value system	Postmodern value system
Human beings and everyday life	Custom and tradition Production as main task Work most important Social local context	Paradoxical and unsafe Consumption as main task Leisure most important Formal institutional context
Facts and knowledge	Positivism and science Objective generalizations A "real" world One possible truth	Subjectivity and knowledge Biased realities A "symbolic" world Diversity of knowledge
Culture and values	Human as object Collective meanings Materialist values Universal outlook	Human as subject Individual narratives Nonmaterialist values Personal outlook
Behavior and demography	Nuclear family Rising birth rate Limited time Unskilled consumption	Pluralism in living Declining birth rate Unlimited time Skilled consumption
Economy and globalization	Domestic competition Goods manufacturing Manual labor Industrial economy	Global competition Service production Knowledge manpower Learning economy
Markets and technology	Mass markets Manufacturing and distribution Consumers as consumers Uniformity and homogeneity	Fragmented niche markets Experiences and personalization Consumers as co-opters Diversity and freedom of choice

to values. Furthermore, intangible assets, such as know-how, patents, or brands are also considered as being more essential for the success of a business in comparison with classical production factors, such as workforce, capital, land, and raw materials. It must be said that the economic value of knowledge is not generally accepted, which is why it is difficult to measure and evaluate from a strictly business economics point of view.

One of the explanations for the importance of knowledge is precisely the complexity and the diversity that permeate the marketing environment in the current societal culture. It has become increasingly difficult for companies to reach out to their customers and target groups, because consumption is affected by an increasing number of factors in the transition from a homogeneous to a heterogeneous marketing environment. For that reason, science should search for the diversity of truths that exist based on individual, subjective feelings and intellectual thinking.

> "In each individual, the 'real world' is formed based on one's own experiences and social structures by using the 'symbolic world.'"

This is due to the fact that it is not considered possible for any person to experience and see the world by ignoring the structures that exist in every human being. In this perspective, the "real world" is a social construction, which is constantly changing and evolving, represented by our "symbolic world." This world is constructed and legitimized mainly through the language, values, and concepts that in turn represent the social reality.

In this way, knowledge of the social reality is individual, personal, and real. From a poststructuralism starting point, it means that all knowledge is relative and related to the place and time where it exists. Therefore, it is not possible for any individual to distance him/herself from the different economic, cultural, political, or social influences that have shaped him/her. All knowledge, all ideas, and all concepts, therefore, are based on a particular social context at a particular time in human history, which is why knowledge, ideas, and concepts cannot be regarded as objectively true.

The "Real" and the "Symbolic" Worlds

Contemporary societal culture becomes more and more fragmented from a greater diversity of knowledge based on both the "real world" and "the symbolic world." In recent decades, there have been various social movements, which in numerous ways have tried to defend their views and protest to voice their rights. But the most distinctive feature of these groups is that they do not define themselves, for example, by social class, professional status, or opposition to capitalism, as was the case in modern industrial society.

Instead, agendas and issues are driven in present society based on similarities regarding the perception of animal attitudes, peace, gender, food consumption, environment, senior citizens, religion, sexual preference, or weapons technology. These various groupings—or smaller units—have come to be called a *multiversum* in the society (Grenz, 1996). As a result, new attitudes and values have emerged regarding family formation, close relationships, and individuality. In varying degrees, more individualistic views have emerged and have become key elements in the design of the current social culture, which affects marketing and consumption in the short- and long-term.

In particular, diversity and differences are the main characteristics of everyday life in contemporary society. If it was previously necessary to identify what was good or bad with the economy, politics, or social life on a personal level, now it is the opposite. Instead, each individual has the opportunity to live as he/she wishes and to choose his/her own lifestyle. The so-called objective truth from the "real world" is not forced upon the individual, which is why the present society is a society full of contrasts and paradoxes, as well as different identities and understandings.

Because of this, the question of an individual's identity has become of importance and has come to be the focus in a new way. The fragmentation and diversity that characterize contemporary social culture have led to other consequences for the role that the individual plays, than before. As a rule, individuals are regarded as unknown "objects" in the modern production and consumption processes that have taken place in accordance with scientific, rational thinking in the modern industrial society.

But in the contemporary societal culture, most individuals no longer have a coherent, determined, and persistent identity, which can be explained by the constantly changing conditions of everyday life, work, economy, politics, or science. This means that a postmodern individual sees him/her as a "subject" consisting of fragmented, contradictory, and multiple identities at the same time.

Fragmentation and Identity Formation

Market fragmentation, target group adjustment, and customized solutions have become increasingly common in marketing in order to meet the individual needs of identity and lifestyle associated with consumption. This focus has come to replace keywords such as mass production and mass marketing in the modern industrial society. The Belgian Crock'In chain represents an example of the transition from the consumer as an "object"—built on industrialization and mass production—to the consumer as a "subject"—built on fragmentation and identity formation—in contemporary social culture.

Crock'In is a young Belgian brand that is fully committed to high food quality. Their stores are located in strategically selected locations in Brussels. The secret behind their success is: "Our special way of cooking. We do not buy our cakes, sandwiches, salads, or our soup in large quantities from industrial caterers. We cook everything ourselves in our kitchen with 24 hour preservability to ensure maximum freshness and quality, as if the food was cooked at home."

This example illustrates how Crock'In, as a brand, has become the symbol of—or link to—"the symbolic world." The brand stands for high food quality, traditional cooking, and preservability around the clock based on natural raw materials and caters to those individuals who want to build their consumption on these values when it comes to food culture.

The Ikea effect, coined by the American behavioral economists Norton, Mochon, and Ariely (2012), has as its starting point that the product or item that an individual has produced and created him/herself is valued greater than that which others have produced. Through a number of experiments, the researchers found that individuals value their self-produced furniture higher, like the furniture that is bought at Ikea, and become more satisfied.

More and more companies are trying different ways to build an Ikea effect in their brands to give individuals control over how a product is created and contribute to the individual's identity creation and personal experience. It is about customizing various goods and services or websites where mainly the design can be selectable. In this way, the individual's involvement is increased, and the time that is spent contributes to the Ikea effect occurring, which also increases the individual's freedom of choice.

In the current societal culture, therefore, the product—good or service, or a combination of both—no longer has just a functional meaning but also a symbolic meaning, which often has been called a social innovation. These social innovations are created and developed by aesthetic, institutional, human, and organizational solutions, which are linked to the product's basic functions.

Firat and Venkatesh (1995) discuss the conditions for consumption in contemporary social culture from a postmodern approach. They argue that consumption is increasingly changing and "With a growing awareness that consumption is more and more concerned with the consumption of self-images, the whole society becomes more and more a social spectacle" (ibid., p. 250).

Therefore, the present society can be seen as a spectacular society, where the consumption of goods, services, and products are based on a symbolic significance and meaning, which can result in both fictional and real experiences for different individuals.

Generations as a Force for Change

The most important role of marketing and consumption in today's global consumer culture is to contribute to the individual's identity creation and self-fulfillment, where the symbolic meaning is in focus. In this context, factors such as aesthetics, culture, symbols, and language are the most essential elements in the creation of identity, along with everyday life events and developments. Consumers are often regarded as rational, self-fulfilling, and sovereign, and in accordance with that, they strive "to maximize the value of their existence for themselves through personalized choice in a world of goods and services" (Du Gay et al., 1997).

> *"The new Barbie store in Shanghai, with an imaginative design, is built around a circular staircase surrounded by translucent, wrapped glass shelves with 800 Barbie dolls in natural sizes to create a creative environment."*

When consumption assumes that consumers are seen as producers of identities, images, and self-images in any consumption occasion, it means that many individuals are looking for products, goods, and services that can fulfill their dreams, hopes, and visions for them to become who they want. There is a freedom for many individuals to test and try out several different identities and roles, which can lead to a definite identity, and self-image can quickly be fragmented into a number of new identities and self-images.

With the help of products, goods, and services, the present society provides the opportunity for individuals to constantly create new, individual, and personal identities and experiences. This can be illustrated by the so-called lifestyle stories, which an increased fragmentation gives rise to, which are created by both real-world experiences and consumption of media, such as books, movies, or games. For many individuals, this leads to the identity creation that is based on a world of fantasy and imagination, which goes on to what is called *hyperreality* (Kellner, 1995). This hyperreality gives individuals the opportunity to experience both the real in everyday life and the unreal related to both today's society and the previous society.

Consumption then helps to create meaning and content on a personal level for many individuals through the social and cultural features that are found in physical goods, materials, products, or services. In various exchange and value creation processes, both marketing and consumption are of significant importance for how the individual's identity creation and self-fulfillment occur and how an individual's identity can be developed.

As a researcher, I have therefore asked myself the question: *What characterizes the younger generation's attitudes and values to achieve identity creation and self-fulfillment?* The generations born in the 1960s, 1970s, 1980s, and 1990s can consist of attitudes and values that can be attributed to a postmodern value system in the ongoing cultural valuation shift. The impact that these generations have on marketing and consumption represents, in my opinion, one of the most important driving forces in today's consumer culture (Table 2.5).

When it comes to mobility, in terms of physical mobility and social mobility, the X, Y, and Z generations are characterized by a desire to leave their homes to travel or work elsewhere. There is also a desire to want to see and discover the world beyond the traditional boundaries, which emphasizes the influence of globalization on these generations. This mobility has also contributed to the current society having a different international and multicultural character than before, which is reflected in the consumption of

Table 2.5 Values among Generations X, Y, and Z

	Generation X	Generation Y	Generation Z
	1965–1976	1977–1997	1998
Technology awareness	*Beginners* Little experience	*Pro's* In everyday life	*Freaks* Before school starts
Mobility	*Emancipators* Personal movement and life outside place of residence	*Globetrotters* International and multicultural	*Integrators* Cultural variation and diversity
Working life	*Independent* Free choice of career and free occupations	*Flexibel* Although professions for personal development	?

food, clothing, and services of various kinds, such as travel, education, and entertainment to name a few.

Furthermore, the X, Y, and Z generations are also characteristic in that they have different experiences of and familiarity with digital technology as a tool for information and communication exchange. Digital technology, including computers, Internet, mobile phones, and smartphones, is commonplace in one's everyday life and work life. The youngest generations, to some extent, have already received their computer skills at home, before they start school, which emphasizes the importance of digital technology as a force for change.

Generation X

Individuals born between 1965 and 1976 are usually defined as Generation X. This generation can also be called the 1970s generation, which as a group is often characterized by having two working parents, something that had not been as common in the past. The individuals belonging to the Generation X have had a childhood marked by personal mobility, which can partly be explained by a growing Swedish average income. This has allowed for increased consumption of travel, which has been of importance for identity creation and self-fulfillment.

> "Individuals in Generation X are regarded as liberators in both work and private life and belong to the most educated groups in society."

The fact that both physical and social mobility have become important characteristics has also made it possible for many individuals to live and work in a place other than their place of origin. They can therefore be regarded as *liberators* from the traditional notions of how work and private life should be shaped in the more traditional sense. A higher degree of personal mobility has also meant a different view on issues regarding family relationships, relationships, and sexuality than the view of previous generations.

Another distinguishing feature of this generation, in comparison with previous generations, is that many individuals have grown up with digital technology. They can be considered as *novices*, in many cases, with limited or little experience from the beginning. However, it has often led to a behavior later in life, which has meant that many individuals have become skilled communicators and extremely focused on media. There is talk that X Generation is often regarded as more or less aggressive communicators, because many of them like to express their opinions or make suggestions for new ideas, as they think of themselves as individuals who stand up for what they believe in.

In the 1970s generation, education was viewed as something positive; therefore, many have chosen to invest in a college or university education, in order to later in life be able to work based on personal development and increased independence. This may be viewed as consistent with how this generation sees themselves, as liberators from the traditional notions of how work and daily life should be formed. From a historical perspective, Generation X is also one of the most educated groups in contemporary society, compared with the previous generations.

When it comes to career choice, many of the 1970s generation prioritize tasks based on physical and social mobility, which also contribute to personal development and a higher degree of independence. They can therefore be regarded as *the independent*, because they question traditional notions of work and career choices. This is often done at the expense of achieving a higher status, compared to traditional occupations and opportunities to make money. Furthermore, many Generation X individuals prefer hierarchical work environments.

For Generation X, employment is viewed as a contract, meaning that loyalty to the work is of less importance. It should also be added that many individuals are prepared to take another job and leave their current employment to have the opportunity to change employers and for personal development in order to make a career. Therefore, Generation X can be seen as a generation that critically questions and expresses their opinions and wishes.

Generation Y

The 1980s generation is a common term for this generation, which includes people born in 1980 or later in the 1980s. There is some disagreement among scholars as to who should belong to the Generation Y group, and some authors argue that Generation Y should include people born between 1977 and 1997. Tapscott (2009) suggests that this generation shall be known as the *Net Generation*, because they are heavily influenced by digital technology when it comes to information and communication exchange.

This generation can be regarded as *professionals* when it comes to the use and exploitation of digital technology in comparison with Generation X. It also means, for example, that the Internet and mobile phones are more infiltrated in everyday life and seen as natural tools for information and communication exchange.

Another generation term for people born in the 1980s is the *MeWe Generation*, who alone can influence and shape their lives, which has not been the case previously. Many individuals consider themselves, therefore, to have a personal freedom without limits, which enables them to control and shape their future and their lives in an individual and independent manner.

> "Individuals in Generation Y are considered to have a personal freedom without limits and often question society's various standards."

Generation Y, or the 1980s generation, is often described as being ambitious, energetic, and progressive, although some disrespect may exist for authority, bureaucracies, and hierarchies. This is often expressed through a questioning of behavioral norms and codes of conduct (Parment, 2008). Parment believes that this can be explained by the fact that this generation has become accustomed to exposing and branding themselves on their own, without the help of the adult world, and that many individuals want to stand out from the group and be meaningful.

Furthermore, Generation Y is characterized as being more international and multicultural as well as more communication focused than previous generations, which lays the foundation for new consumption and lifestyle patterns (Parment, 2008). In the 1980s, Sweden developed, as a nation, toward greater ethnic and cultural diversity, which therefore came to characterize the 1980s generation as a generation.

Increasing globalization has also influenced this generation, which is expressed through a greater openness to the world. Furthermore, every third young person in Sweden has visited other countries around the world, outside the Nordic countries; thus the '80s generation can be seen as *globetrotters* when it comes to showing high mobility in the form of physical and social mobility. There are also writers who choose to call this generation *backpackers*, which refers to the fact that many people exhibit high mobility and often find themselves on the move.

There is in this generation a shift of values regarding attitudes toward work, which assumes that a person should be able to earn money from a job but at the same time have fun and develop on a personal level. The 1980s generation can be considered as the *flexible generation*, which can be seen as natural, given the increasing importance of identity creation and self-fulfillment in these individuals. It is common for them to believe that higher education is required in the workplace, because it has become increasingly difficult to get a job just based on high school grades. Two key concepts are highlighted for this generation's careers in professional life, and they relate to the importance of teamwork and creativity.

Generation Z

This generation refers to individuals born from 1998 to the present day and is also called *Generation Next*. This generation includes both older children (11–13 years), and younger children (6–10 years), and young children (1–5 years). It is not possible to analyze and understand more deeply the values that this generation have, or will have, because many are still children and have not yet reached the teenage stage. For this reason, it is only possible to try to discuss and speculate about the values that will arise and emerge in Generation Z.

Researchers such as Dillon (2007) maintain that Generation Z is characterized by all the information about the world being a click away. It is therefore assumed that many of this generation will follow in Generation Y's footsteps, where the use of digital technologies for information and communication exchange is in focus. In this context, it is also argued that there will be a greater emphasis on the ability to understand, analyze, and evaluate information rather than in the actual collection of information itself (ibid.).

The younger and older children in this generation can also be said to belong to the most influential generation in history. There is an endless supply of goods, services, and products that are designed for their use, which has made them very sophisticated consumers. They spend more time watching television and being on the Internet than being in school. For that reason, they become well-informed and engage early in having an influence over parental choice of brands regarding cars, computers, mobile phones, televisions, and other products and services.

This means that Generation Z, for the most part, will consist of individuals who early on become accustomed to computers, mobile phones, and other technical means in their daily lives. In that way, they will be *fanatics* and use digital technology more or less 24 hours a day. A distinctive feature of many individuals could be that this habit occurs early in life, before they take the plunge into preschool and the school world. Consequently, digital technology will make demands on the individual's adaptation to the technical tools at the same time as it offers different kinds of opportunities for information and communication exchange, such as greater influence on parents, as the following example shows:

> *Children exert an increasing influence over their parents' purchases, and the greatest influence they have over the family's purchases is over food. They also introduce new products and trends to their parents, while at the same time they themselves like to spend their money on clothes, shoes, cell phones, computer games, and sports equipment.*

When it comes to mobility, that is, physical and social mobility, the 1990s generation can be said to be *integrators* when it comes to multicultural variation and diversity. Therefore, Generation Z will from a very young age be accustomed to and receptive to the goods, services, or products developed to meet their needs and desires.

This means, in turn, that this generation early on has great demands and expectations of what the market can offer for individualization and self-fulfillment. Most likely this will also lead to the emergence of major differences between individuals and an increased variety, even between individuals in the same family with different backgrounds and experiences.

DIGITAL TECHNOLOGY AS A FORCE FOR CHANGE

Digital technology, as a force for change for marketing and consumption, is one of the most important personal tools for individualization and self-fulfillment. The use of the Internet and access to blogs, websites, and social media is an important part of the individual's consumption in the contemporary social culture. As soon as the technology is used for personal use in connection with information and communication exchange, it is regarded as consumption.

Most people today are looking for websites and social media that are devoted to their individual, personal interests regarding goods, services, or products. In this context, concepts such as individual choice, entertainment, and interaction are prominent; this is based on a fundamental curiosity about life. The emotional maturation process that especially young people go through influences the marketing of a brand in a whole new way in contemporary societal culture. This means that an emotional connection is required between a brand and the individual so that a young person is able to recognize it.

For that reason, a brand shall focus on special interest groups in different generations and not generic age groups, as was the case with traditional segmentation for a long time. This means that a brand is positioned in a group environment, where the group sees themselves as equal in terms of attitudes, interests, and values.

The younger individuals in Generations Y and Z represent the early followers of digital technology. Despite the parents' influence on the choice of technology in their homes, the children have a strong influence on what will be purchased and used. In this context, it can be said that the younger children, in particular, are driving consumption and are developing an entirely new behavior, compared to the older generations.

> "Individuals in Generation Y are considered to have a personal freedom without limits and often question society's various standards."

Digital technology is the most important tool in both daily life and professional life, in work, communication, entertainment, education, or health care. The main reason that technology has influenced everyday life and work is partly explained by what Atkinson (2005) emphasizes, namely, the so-called *imagined identity* from the 1960s and 1970s. Through various film and TV characters, a connection was created between the symbolic world and the real world, which film personalities such as James Bond could illustrate. It gave an opportunity, for example, for men to identify with their own masculinity and thus find their place in the current society's culture.

Over the past few decades, digital technology has grown rapidly, and Swedish households have had Internet access since 1994. Researchers such as Atkinson (2005) argue that it is difficult to determine what type of technology was first introduced and by whom and further proposes that technology may take different forms and expressions, and at the same time, it is complex to manage.

Information and communication exchanges between individuals and between companies and individuals have fundamentally changed thanks to digital technology, and the Internet has existed for the vast majority of individuals for almost 20 years. In this context, it shall be noted that access to broadband has been one of the most important prerequisites for this expansion.

One conclusion is that the Internet is a useful and simple tool—as opposed to what it had previously been considered as, somewhat prophetic or visionary—that provides information on various products and services in abundance. In Sweden, e-commerce in 2014 set new sales records, and growth increased by 16 percent in the first quarter, according to E-barometer. When it comes to product groups, construction/home improvement, consumer electronics, children's items/toys, as well as sporting and leisure have increased by between 20 and 40 percent. Seven out of ten consumers have made online purchases, and one in ten did so using their mobile phones.

When it comes to making purchases in a physical store or a virtual store online, it relates to the global phenomenon called *showrooming* and how consumers behave when searching for information about a brand and where the purchase takes place. This phenomenon means that consumers research a product in a physical store, but do not buy it on location; instead, they buy it at a later date either through their PC, mobile phone, or tablet. According to analysts, this purchasing behavior is most common in countries such as Brazil and China, where about nine out of ten consumers follow this behavior.

The phenomenon is less widespread for Swedish conditions, and it is not more than every other Swede who exhibits this new purchasing behavior, according to a study in 2013 by the consulting firm Accenture. In this manner, the product and price comparisons take place in a virtual store; thereafter, the product is tried and tested in a selected physical store and then purchased via the computer or the mobile phone. The phenomenon showrooming means that businesses in the future must integrate physical retail sale with digital channels for e-commerce and mobile commerce.

> "The cell phone or smartphone will be one of tomorrow's most important marketing channels for both individuals and businesses."

More than nine out of ten Swedes have a cell phone and mobile technology continues in expansive growth. Mobile technology offers marketers an additional opportunity to reach out to individuals through what has come to be known as mobile marketing. This technology, however, should not be compared with the Internet, which has a wider global distribution regarding both time and space.

In this context, the development of mobile applications (known as apps) and mobile-adapted websites that give consumers the opportunity to connect with a brand or a store through the mobile phone should also be mentioned. Furthermore, through the Wi-Fi network, there is an opportunity for consumers to search for information about products and services in the physical stores that are visited, which happens free of charge for more and more brands.

When it comes to Swedish conditions, the majority of companies in 2013, almost nine out of ten, offered some form of mobile marketing. The cell phone is considered a highly personal communication channel, because people usually always carry their phones with them, and at the same time two-way communication is possible. Because many Swedes are experienced mobile users, it is considered that they are open to allowing the cell phone to have some space in the relationship between businesses and consumers. Furthermore, it is believed that there is substantial growth within mobile marketing in Sweden, as the following example illustrates:

> Today, it is possible to offer consumers digital coupons via location-based marketing directly in the phone, which is triggered when a consumer is 100 meters or less from the actual stores. Furthermore, it is possible to offer consumers a purchase in a virtual store by using QR codes for different types of goods, such as ketchup, pasta, or milk.

A new lifestyle has also been established, where the creation of human networks are built on an individual's interest in communicating with others, regardless of time and space, which has also come to lead to new social structures. These networks have a greater power than what individuals previously could create on their own (Kozinets et al., 2008). It is manifested by the fact that many individuals are no longer passive but active, because they want to influence marketing and consumption in various ways, through personal engagement.

It has resulted in what has become known as *permission marketing*, emphasizing the individual's consent to a dialogue and participation expressed as an interactive relationship, where both the consumers and the businesses participate (Godin, 1999). This occurs both in traditional advertising and advertising through digital communications.

Network and Interaction

In today's global consumer culture, digital technology, particularly through the Internet, offers unimagined opportunities for interaction and networking for consumers and businesses. This can occur both between individuals and between businesses and individuals, which are especially characteristic of the Internet in comparison with other media, such as daily newspapers, direct advertising, or traditional advertising.

Without a doubt, digital technology gives individuals the opportunity to communicate and express themselves in a completely different way than in the modern industrial society. The new types of interaction that have been established in the form of blogs, *communities*, or social networking can involve many more individuals and allow for an increased information and communication exchange in connection with marketing and consumption.

> "Blogs have become consumers' truth in the market, whereas the companies' websites have become the official truth about brands."

When it comes to social networking sites, these are based on the assumption that individuals between themselves are engaged in an information and communication exchange on the same site based on both a public profile and a partially public profile. It is mainly the ability to visualize the users and an individual's social network that contributes to these sites having had a major expansion.

These social networks make it possible for many individuals to experience both emotional and rational benefits through interaction on the Internet. The most distinctive feature of this type of interaction is that it is based on two-way communication as opposed to one-way communication, which was common in the modern industrial society.

Even companies use social networks for internal information and communication exchange when it comes to giving employees the latest information on their own blog or their own website. Similarly, blogs are used by politicians, such as former Foreign Minister Carl Bildt, to create dialogue and interaction with the public on current political issues and positions. This points to the possibility that the Internet can establish and develop cultural as well as professional social networks, where people with similar interests can pursue a mutual information and communication exchange.

Social Media and Virtual Worlds

The social networking sites, launched back in 1997, have since expanded and become more and more prevalent. In some cases, sites have been shut down and in other cases, they have been expanded and developed further. One of the most famous examples of a social networking site in Sweden is Lunarstorm, which was established in the early 2000s but which was closed down in 2010. The well-visited youth website plummeted from a peak of 1.6 million visitors per week to around 78,000 when it was closed.

For the last ten years now, there has been a marked expansion of social networking sites around the world for information and communication exchange, both between individuals and between companies and individuals. Among the most famous are: YouTube, Facebook, Instagram, Myspace, and Twitter, all of which are considered among the leading sites on the net. When it comes to visiting the most well-known sites, YouTube is the most popular option among children between 9 and 12 years old, whereas Facebook is more popular for older youth.

When it comes to differences between girls and boys, it turns out that girls use social media to a greater extent than boys. This usage seems to peak at age 17, when four out of ten girls—compared to between one and two out of ten boys—spend more than three hours a day on the social sites. One problem with Instagram is the existence of so-called hate accounts, where crimes are committed against and by children, which refer to, among others things, defamation and bullying by peers and friends.

An alternative to social networks is to use blogs for mutual information and communication exchange, which is common in the younger subjects, aged 15 to 25 years. This forum allows for users to keep their families and friends informed about what is happening in their lives, and especially daily life, through words, texts, or images. A blog can also be used as a tool in order to influence others, and it also provides the opportunity for an individual to use a pseudonym.

It also occurs that an individual purports to be a different person than who he/she really is, and one in five Swedes write something in their blog that is not consistent with reality. The popularity that bloggers enjoy can be illustrated with the homeless in Stockholm who have free access to the Internet in exchange for them being active users of blogs.

For those who want to leave the real world, the virtual world provides unimagined possibilities for image creation and self-fulfillment in marketing and consumption. It allows many individuals to play other roles, live out their dreams and fantasies to become what they have always strived to be.

This may involve, for example, being a successful rock star, which has been a dream, or live a life like celebrities. This makes virtual worlds popular among many, as they reflect and reproduce a different behavior and life that fulfills the dreams and visions in a fictitious manner. When it comes to gaming, boys prefer games to a greater extent than girls, and boys play at least three hours per day in the 14- to 15-year-old range.

There is also the possibility, through the so-called network game, where individuals play against each other, of becoming the sports star that has always been a role model. In these networks, one does not just play against a computer but against other people. It allows for interaction and a communication exchange that many participants feel they are willing to pay for, which shows the value they actually get out of such participation.

New Behaviors and Structures

Digital technology, with its rapid development in the last five to ten years, has led to a rapid change in the individual's lifestyle. More and more younger people come into contact with technology, such as computers, tablets, and smartphones, already as a child. Today, nearly three out of four children aged 0–8 years old use the Internet, as consumption, several times a week, compared with three in ten children in 2010.

Furthermore, it should be said that the children's average age at onset of Internet use in 2013 was 3 years old, compared to nine years old in 2005. When it comes to the use of the Internet, it can be stated that today almost nine out of ten 15-year-olds use a smartphone for this purpose. Today's 8-year-olds surf the Internet in the same way as the 15-year-olds did three years ago, which shows how usage increases further down the ages.

Between 2010 and 2013, the daily use of the Internet increased for 9- to 12-year-olds from 32 to 55 percent, and from 62 to 93 percent for 13- to

16-year-olds. When it comes to consuming daily news online, it is the smartphone, instead of the television, that is most commonly used by today's 17- to 18-year-olds. Their use of newspapers has decreased substantially when compared to 2010.

An important observation is that slowly there is emerging a global Internet generation, where access to digital technology is an important prerequisite for both marketing and consumption. In the long-term, this results in a shift of power from the producers to the consumers, in terms of who is primarily influencing and controlling the information and communication exchange.

It is no longer possible for producers to influence consumer behavior only through one-way and one-sided influence; instead, consumers have the ability to independently determine how an information and communication exchange will take place. This means that individuals themselves can choose and decide the brands and products that consumption will build on in order to build an image and self-fulfillment.

One consequence of digital technology's increasing importance is the threat against traditional media, such as morning newspapers, radio, and television. This has resulted in advertising and promotion in traditional media increasingly moving toward Internet advertising for many companies in recent years. It can be mentioned that during the third quarter of 2007, the Internet passed as an advertising medium, in terms of turnover, television advertising, according to the Institute for Advertising and Media Statistics (IRM). When it comes to attitudes toward television advertising, a large majority of young people today believe that it is annoying and/or boring.

One of the advantages of digital technology is that companies can target their messages and their communication directly toward those individuals and groups who use social networking sites in their consumption. At the same time, companies can obtain information on individuals' behavior and consumption patterns in a completely different way than before, creating new opportunities in marketing.

The use of digital technology has also given rise to ethical issues. One of the most important issues relates to privacy and what user data will remain private and what will be public on such social networking sites. When it comes to Facebook, this site gives the opportunity for companies to gain access to information about users to reach out to different audiences in a more efficient and faster way. This is regarded as an invasion of privacy and criticized by many users.

Other questions relate to creating a safe and secure online environment to enable customers to shop and consume goods and services without the risk of intrusion from other users. Finally, it should be said that the issue of Internet addiction is always present, and many individuals think that they actually spend too much time on the computer for personal consumption.

REFERENCES

Atkinson, P. (2005), "Man in a briefcase: the social construction of the laptop computer and the emergence of a type form," *Journal of Design History*, 18, 2:191–205.
Bilton, T., Bonnett, K., Jones, P., Lawson, T., Skinner, D., Stanworth, M., Stephens, P. and Webster, A. (2002), *Introductory sociology*, Basingstoke: Palgrave Macmillan.
Dillon, N. (2007), "Educating generation Z," *American School Board Journal*, 194, 9:34–37.
Du Gay, P., Hall, S., Janes, L., Mackay, H. and Negus, K. (1997), *Doing cultural studies: the story of the Sony Walkman*, London: Sage Publications.
Elliott, R. (1997), "Existential consumption and irrational desire," *European Journal of Marketing*, 34, 3:285–296.
Firat, A.F. and Venkatesh, A. (1995), "Liberatory postmodernism and the reenchantment of consumption," *Journal of Consumer Research*, 22, December:239–267.
Fiske, J. (1989), *Understanding popular culture*, London: Unwin Hyman.
Fromm, E. (1976), *To have or to be*, London: Routledge & Kegan Paul.
Godin, S. (1999), *Permission marketing: turning strangers into friends and friends into customers*, New York: Simon and Schuster.
Grenz, S. (1996), *A primer on postmodernism*, Cambridge: Eerdemans Publishing Co.
Howard, M. and Mason, J. (2001), "21st-century consumer society," *Journal of Consumer Behavior*, 1, 1:94–101.
Hultén, B., Broweus, N. and van Dijk, M. (2009), *Sinnesmarknadsföring [Sensory Marketing]*, Malmö: Liber.
Inglehart, R. (1990), *Culture shift in advanced industrial society*, Princeton, NJ: Princeton University Press.
Inglehart, R. (1997), *Modernization and postmodernization—cultural, economic, and political change in 43 societies*, Princeton, NJ: Princeton University Press, p. 28–32.
Jencks, C. (1987), *What is postmodernism?* New York: Academy Editions.
Jensen, R. (1999), *The dream society*, New York: McGraw-Hill.
Kellner, D. (1995), *Media culture: cultural studies, identity and politics between the modern and the postmodern*, London and New York: Routledge.
Kozinets, R., Hemetsberger, A. and Jensen Schau, H. (2008), "The wisdom of consumer crowds: collective innovation in the age of networked marketing," *Journal of Macromarketing*, 28, 4:339–354.
Norton, M.I., Mochon, D. and Ariely, D. (2012), "The IKEA effect: when labour leads to love," Boston: Harvard University.
Parment, A. (2008), *Generation Y—framtidens konsumenter and medarbetare gör entré*, Malmö: Liber.
Polanyi, K. (1973), *The great transformation*, New York: Octagon.
Tapscott, D. (2009), *Grown up digital—how the net generation is changing your world*, New York: McGraw-Hill.
Toffler, A. (1982), *The third wave*, Stockholm: Esselte Info.
Toffler, H. (1995), *Creating a new civilization: the politics of the third wave*. Stockholm: Svenska Förlaget.
Wilkinson, H. and Mulgan, G. (1995), *Freedom's children*, London: Demos.

3 Sensory Marketing

This chapter presents sensory marketing (SM) as an emerging paradigm and an approach in consumer marketing. Initially, a number of theoretical issues with a postmodern view are discussed; this is the basis for a better understanding of sensory marketing, especially the individual's role and the importance this has for how sensory marketing should be designed in contemporary societal culture is analyzed.

Furthermore, the concepts that form the basis of sensory marketing are presented with respect to both businesses and consumers. Thereafter, a comparison is made between transaction marketing (TM) and relationship marketing (RM) on the one hand and sensory marketing (SM) on the other. In particular, the importance of service processes, sensory experiences, and sensory strategies are discussed with respect to consumer value, consumer experiences, and brand as image. Finally, the significance of sensory marketing as a model and a multi-sensory brand-experience is presented.

A POSTMODERN VIEW TO CONSUMER MARKETING

Emotions, Senses, and Experiences

In recent years, sensory marketing, as a new research field, has increasingly grown in importance for marketers, both from a theoretical point of view (Achrol and Kotler, 2012; Hultén, 2011, 2012; Hultén et al., 2009; Krishna, 2011, 2013; Krishna and Schwarz, 2014; Spence et al., 2014), as well as from a practical point of view (Lindstrom, 2005). The first scientific conference in sensory marketing was held in the summer of 2008 at the Ross Business School, University of Michigan, sponsored by the Marketing Science Institute (MSI) in the United States.

> *"The five senses help to create individual and personal experiences of a brand."*

As a researcher, I have asked myself the question: *What has caused this increased interest in the human senses and how can it be explained?* One of the primary reasons for the increased interest is that modern marketing, from either a theoretical or a practical point of view, does not sufficiently emphasize the importance of the emotions, senses, and experiences associated with different buying and consumption processes. On the contrary, a one-sided focus on the product attributes and the product benefits, such as function, quality, or price, has led to increasingly impersonal marketing, which has been questioned by more and more researchers and practitioners.

Researchers such as Pine and Gilmore (1999) assert that we are currently undergoing a transition from a service economy to an experience economy, where experiences are considered to be the most important value-creating factors in the future. One reason for this is the increasingly tough competition between brands, on both the national and global levels, for goods manufacturers and services industries. This has placed increasing demands on their ability to differentiate and position themselves in the market by creating and developing experiences. These are believed to contribute to increasing customer satisfaction at a deeper level, leading to an increased need for satisfaction, loyalty, and profitability.

In sensory marketing, one of the fundamental theoretical starting points is that firms, through their brands, offer customers sensory experiences in a more intimate and more personal way than transaction marketing and relationship marketing has succeeded with. By involving the five senses—sight, sound, smell, touch, and taste—an individual and personal experience of a brand is created on a deeper, emotional level, where the individual's lifestyle, personal characteristics, and social context are key drivers (Hultén et al., 2011).

Forces of change such as the cultural value shift and digital technology place new demands on sensory marketing, where such a deeper satisfaction of individual needs will increasingly become the focus. It is no longer enough for marketers to satisfy only the basic material and physical needs, but also emotional, intellectual, and experience-based needs have come to be recognized, which requires different concepts, models, and approaches. It is in this context that sensory marketing shall be understood, and it should be considered as an evolutionary development of modern marketing.

The Significance of a Postmodern View

Researchers such as Morgan (1992, p. 137) believe that marketing can be expressed as "a number of methods and languages, which help to establish and develop social relationships in modern Western societies." However, because a postmodern value system is emerging and becoming dominant in today's global consumer culture, these modern Western societies can no longer be considered modern in the old sense. Instead, new concepts, languages, and methods are needed to construct the image of sensory marketing where the markets, consumers, businesses, and society are united on the basis of postmodern views.

In my opinion, a postmodern view can help us to better understand the application and design of sensory marketing in a global consumer culture, as opposed to from a modern perspective. Among many critical marketing researchers, there is an interest in being able to contribute to the development of the marketing discipline using new perspectives and approaches in terms of both theory and practice (Brownlie et al., 1999). This shows how marketing, as a discipline and a practice, depends on context and processes where production and consumption can be united through new concepts, languages, and methodologies, which grow in a dialectical interplay between the different social environments and time horizons.

> "A postmodern view can give marketers a better understanding of today's consumer culture."

Brown (1993) is one of the researchers who early on recommended a postmodern view so that we can understand and interpret marketing from a theoretical and practical point of view. The author believes that the established concepts and models in the modern marketing discipline are separated from the *reality*, and many practitioners are not familiar with the concepts and model world that modern marketing revolves around, but instead they should more and more be based on a postmodern view.

A postmodern view as a methodological basis could contribute to the development of sensory marketing, because it is based on scientific pluralism and academic affiliation. Furthermore, Brown claims that such a view should not only be considered as an umbrella for "nontraditional" beliefs and attitudes. When it comes to theoretical scientific questions about objectivism versus subjectivism or hermeneutics versus positivism, many representatives of a postmodern view believe that it is a matter of *both* rather than a question of *either or*.

In this way, sensory marketing (SM), as a concept and model, is considered a development of the established theoretical concepts and models, which are mainly represented by transaction marketing (TM) and relationship marketing (RM). With this, I would like to clarify that there does not need to be any contradiction between these concepts and models, that is, on the one hand, TM and RM and, on the other hand, SM, as long as the application and design of sensory marketing is primarily based on the diversity and uniqueness that characterizes different marketing situations. I will return to a discussion of the key differences between the approaches to clarify this from a consumer marketing context (B2C), where the brand perspective will play the most prominent role for one to understand the meaning of sensory marketing.

Two Philosophical Bases

Brown also believes that a postmodern view makes it possible to better understand the main characteristics of today's marketing. Through a postmodern view, this is expressed as "the individual's preference," "different tastes for different people," and "do what you want," which is what a postmodern view advocates (1993, p. 26).

> *"Consumers should be seen as individuals and not as a homogenous mass with the average needs."*

In the most common marketing management literature concerning transaction marketing, consumers are considered as a mass or a segment of the mass with homogeneous and similar average needs based on objective generalizations. Both transaction marketing and relationship marketing are based on the idea that the consumer, as an individual, should be emphasized. But the individual as a customer and the importance of individual pluralism, diversity, or uniqueness are not emphasized; however, they are through a postmodern view, which distinguishes this from a modern view.

The second key feature is based on the fact that a company seeks to retain current customers, services, or brands, which relationship marketing emphasizes, as opposed to constantly attracting and recruiting new customers, as advocated by transaction marketing (ibid.). This means that a postmodern view makes it possible to establish and maintain relationships with consumers, as individuals, as a precondition for sensory marketing.

In the book, *TOTAL Relationship Marketing: Rethinking Marketing Management: From 4Ps to 30Rs*, Gummesson (1999) discusses how a renewal and development of established concepts and models can be made with the help of a postmodern view. One of the main arguments for this is that in marketing there are different kinds of phenomena, multiple perspectives, and ambiguity regarding explanations and interpretations. Furthermore, the writer presents that it is possible to use a postmodern approach in marketing, which is illustrated as follows: (ibid., p. 256–257):

> *We have seen that the organization, the supplier, the customer, and the competitor are ambiguous phenomena. Companies can be suppliers, customers, and competitors and they can own one another. The supplier and the customer are recognized as co-producers of services, and increasingly as co-producers also of goods and eventually of experiences*

and value ... Personal and organizational relationships, which contain both technical rationality and emotions, are central to marketing ... The imaginary organization is postmodern; it flows and changes ... To a large extent, successful marketing has always been postmodern and value-creating.

For me, a postmodern view is a philosophical basis of vital importance when it comes to understanding sensory marketing (SM) as a development of transaction marketing (TM) and relationship marketing (RM), especially when it comes to consumer marketing as a discipline and practice.

Individualization as a Lifestyle

In today's global consumer culture, the individual is viewed in a completely different way than previously, which, among other things, means that the brands play a critical role in satisfying emotional, intellectual, and experience-based needs on a deeper personal level.

It is generally accepted in consumer culture theory (CCT) that individuals' consumption of a brand leads to the creation of new self-images and identities. For many people, consumption is linked to the question of life's meaning and significance or the role that one has as an individual in his/her circle of friends or work. This points to the important role of consumption as a carrier of personal values in order to satisfy one's own ego and self-fulfillment in life as an expression of personal joy and happiness.

With a postmodern view to consumer marketing, unlike a modern approach, concepts such as consumer value, consumer experiences, and the brand as an image become prominent, from a brand perspective. The ongoing value shift from modern to postmodern values leads to an increasingly individualistic view of everyday life, which emphasizes the importance of quality of life and self-fulfillment.

In this context, individualization as a lifestyle can be said to be the most ultimate expression of today's global consumer culture, where consumption and shopping for many individuals play a crucial role in creating new identities and self-images on a personal level. Thus individualization is characterized as a lifestyle with three personal driving forces, which are self-fulfillment, identity formation, and sensory experience (see Figure 3.1).

Self-Fulfillment as a Driving Force

The individual's quest for *self-fulfillment*, which is expressed through new consumption patterns regarding both goods and services, is the first personal driving force behind individualization as a lifestyle. This need is particularly evident in areas with strong ties to the individual's physical and mental health, such as health coaching, medical care, recreation, cultural services, or education. In recent decades, there has been a clear shift toward

Sensory Marketing 93

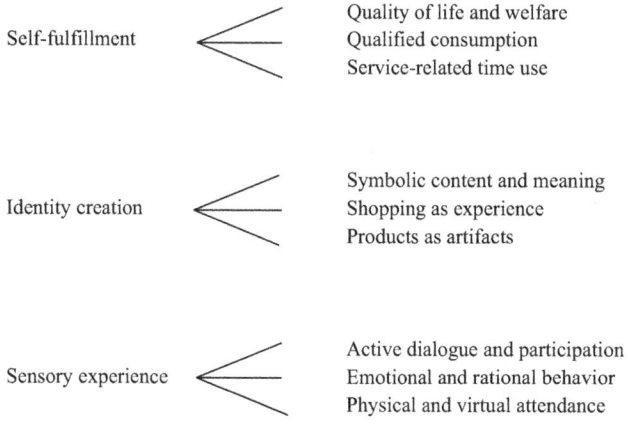

Figure 3.1   Individualization as Lifestyle (Hultén et al., 2009, p. 29)

a more qualified consumption that can be attributed to this need and has to do with, for example, personal well-being. In the media, for example, the Internet, newspapers, and television, articles or programs appear every week emphasizing individual self-fulfillment, such as through diet, exercise, or cooking.

> "Self-realization is about satisfying one's personal needs at a deeper, emotional level."

This can be exemplified by the consumption of services, where more and more individuals are engaged in *high value activities* as opposed to *low value activities*, where high and low is related to the individual's experience and the personal value of the services in question. This can be said to be the highest need in Maslow's hierarchy of needs, which is consistent with a postmodern view of the individual. There is also a clear shift in the consumption of food products to more health and environmental foods and services, which shows the importance of postmodern values when it comes to personal satisfaction needs and quality of life on a deeper, emotional level.

An increased focus on the self and self-fulfillment as a personal driving force is also expressed clearly by what is called service-related use of time. The fact that many individuals prefer to work less and get access to more free time means that there is room for many to realize their dreams and ideas through increased service-related consumption. This can be illustrated by more time being spent on leisure activities, such as visiting a good friend, going to a restaurant, or shopping. To buy and to go shopping can be an experience in itself and not just the later experience of the actually purchased goods or services. Furthermore, more time is devoted to personal self-care, for example, exercising, relaxing, or reading a book, but also for personal development by surfing the net, watching TV, or traveling.

Identity Creation as a Driving Force

If shopping and consumption are to be seen as carriers of personal values, then for many people it means that various goods and services are a critical part of their *identity creation*, which otherwise would not have been possible. In this way, identity creation, as a personal motivation, helps an individual to create his/her own unique identity and image with the help of the thousands of brands that are currently available both in stores and online. Therefore, today many individuals consider consumption and shopping to be a necessity for the production of their self-images and identities, which points to the importance of the symbolic content of many brands.

It also means that with a changed symbolic content, brands can change rapidly and disappear when they are not in agreement with the identity creation that many individuals strive for. This requires that companies recognize and adapt to today's global consumer culture and understand the currents and trends that affect individuals' need for satisfaction and identity creation. Thus consumption offers diversity and multiple choices, which contribute to the identity creation that gives

> *"Identity creation is about forming one's own identity and image by using different brands."*

the individual a high degree of personal satisfaction when it comes to creating a new role or a unique identity.

A common notion is that for many individuals, identity creation occurs on a personal level and is about being something, compared with what one believes one is. By buying a certain brand of pants, a person with a weak self-image can suddenly appear to be successful and give him/herself and others a different image of who he/she is. Often, this is about personal encounters with other people where you express who you are and define the role you have in relation to others, such as friends or colleagues. To create an identity and a certain image is therefore a matter of drawing a line between the outside world and the self, so that "the others" out there appear to be different from the individual in one way or another regarding, for example, hairstyle, clothing, or appearance.

Accordingly, the shopping and consumption of a brand plays a central role in the individual's identity creation and enables an individual to create his/her own identity and image. Some brands also create an identity in relation to others and enable each individual to be unique, yet at the same time belong to a collective, which many young people strive for in different sub-cultures. Identity creation, itself, becomes a way of life, which ultimately is about which identity and image an individual wants to build and create around him/herself.

It is evident that factors such as aesthetics, language, symbols, and sub-culture in this context are some of the most prominent features, along with events and happenings in everyday life, which point to the significance of emotions, senses, and experience's in sensory marketing.

Sensory Experience as a Driving Force

The third personal driving force is connected to individualization as a lifestyle and consists of the individual's pursuit of *sensory experience*. It occurs through the five senses and is controlled by both rational as well as emotional factors in a conscious or unconscious way in every individual. Sensory experience is affected by the individual's need for self-fulfillment and his/her quest for identity creation, which means that the individual is involved, active, and creative. In this context, therefore, different brands are used on the individual and personal level as symbols, and goods and services are no longer thought of from just a physical or functional point of view.

> *"A sensory experience is about taking part in a brand as a symbol of what one strives for."*

Thus the sensory experience is related to brands as symbols, which lays the foundation for the sensory experience that individuals strive for. Accordingly, it is no longer the product itself that is the ultimate goal of consumption, but it is the sensory experience that is the focus for the individual by contributing to the identity creation and ultimately to self-fulfillment, among other things. In this context, a product is "an artifact around which customers have experiences." Just the very emphasis on sensory experiences can be exemplified by products such as food and groceries, where these are increasingly developed from being used to *cook* to instead becoming "sensory experiences and contributing to the individual identity regarding aromas and flavors." In the same way, *technical equipment*, such as cell phones and laptops have instead become *mobile lifestyle entertainment*.

With a postmodern view, individualization as a lifestyle is a symbolic act, which for many individuals is linked to the self in the form of self-fulfillment and identity creation on the personal level. In this context, sensory marketing focuses on concepts such as consumer value, consumer experiences, and the brand as an image based on the five senses, which modern marketing has ignored for a long time.

THEORETICAL STARTING POINTS

Consumer Value

To understand the meaning of sensory marketing, my first theoretical basis is considering individuals as consumers, both as participants and coproducers in service processes and brand building, as well as helping to create value for themselves by using and consuming products and brands (Normann, 2001). It is also assumed that all types of resources are used as a service, which can include both goods and services, in the sense that they create consumer value and support individuals' value-generating and identity creation processes that are interactive.

Within what has come to be known as a service-dominant logic (SDL), it has been argued that a paradigm shift is taking place, from a goods dominant logic to a new service logic. It is argued that there is a transition from the exchange of visible goods to invisible goods, such as skills, knowledge, and processes (Vargo and Lusch, 2004). In this emerging approach, consumers are regarded as cocreators of value, which is expressed as the "brand becomes the experience" (Prahalad and Ramaswamy, 2004).

In a service logic, it is proposed that a company should take its starting point from consumers' value formation processes and especially support those processes where there is a potential for this, based on a company's skills and knowledge. It is believed that the values that consumers create emerge when they use the products, goods, and services in their consumption processes.

A customer or consumer perspective is considered to be of central importance in a service logic, where value and value creation are emphasized, unlike a goods logic, where only the exchange of goods for money has been dominant. The proposed service logic, therefore, has come to emphasize the consumer's or the customer's value creation as opposed to the goods logic, where this customer value creation was not emphasized for a long time.

In terms of value creation, it is thought that consumers create value in their daily buying and consumption processes when the products and brands are used and exploited for their own use. In this context, it is argued that consumers are value creators themselves and that companies should be seen as value promoters when it comes to developing various products and services for consumers. In this way, consumers are viewed as the *sole creators* of value, and a company offers various resources for this purpose in order to enable consumers to create value on their own in connection with the purchase and consumption (Grönroos, 2008).

> "Consumers create value for themselves by having the brand become the experience itself, because it is used and exploited for their own use."

This means that companies should promote the creation of customer value and offer different kinds of resources in their interactions with consumers to influence the identity creation processes in themselves. Different types of interactions affect the values that consumers understand and notice, either as interactive, relativistic, experience-based, or self-oriented values (Holbrook, 1999). This means that a company should knowingly support consumers in their daily activities and identity creation processes by providing goods, services, hidden services, information, and so on, as long as these elements generate consumer value.

In sensory marketing, consumers create value by collaborating with companies, as suppliers of products or brands, in their identity creation processes in the context of a number of different aspects. These can include everything from the design of a product to the final consumption of the product or the actual brand. Hence, consumers are considered as active, participatory, and coproducers, which means that consumer value is created and occurs in the identity creation processes that form the basis of the actual consumer experience.

Consumer Experiences

My second theoretical basis for understanding the meaning of sensory marketing is that a consumer experience is created and occurs through a firm's service processes, regardless of whether the company wants it to or not. In this regard, it is not a question of a strategic or tactical choice for a business, but all service processes lead to some kind of experiences of a product, a store, or a brand. On the other hand, a company can consciously create an experience to engage their customers, in which case, the importance of the individual as a consumer is absolutely essential when it comes to understanding what a consumer experience is really all about (Pine and Gilmore, 1999).

Early on, Holbrook and Hirschman (1982) focused on consumer experiences, from an experience-based perspective, in order to understand how consumers regard their purchase and consumption of products and services. The concept of experience was introduced by Schulze (1992) to analyze cultural behavior in society. Thereafter, Pine and Gilmore (1999) proposed that experiences, in themselves, should replace goods and services to become the primary source of value creation for businesses in the future.

In order to define the concept of experience, I have chosen to use Holbrook (1999, p. 8–9), who expressed the following:

> Finally, by **experience**, I mean that consumer value resides **not** in the product purchased, **not** in the brand chosen, **not** in the object possessed, but rather in the **consumption experience(s)**, derived therefrom (Holbrook and Hirschman, 1982; Woodruff and Gardial, 1996, p. 55)... In essence, the argument in this direction boils down to the proposition that all **products** provide **services** in their capacity to create need- or want-satisfying **experiences** (Morris 1941, p. 136). In this sense, all marketing is "services marketing." This places the role of experience at a central position in the creation of consumer value.

In experience-based consumer research, emotions, symbolism, and non-functional aspects of consumption play the greatest role when it comes to understanding the experiences that consumers have of their consumption. This means that consumer value of consumption does not relate only to the object itself, which may be a car or a mobile phone, but to the experience of those products during consumption. Therefore, the experience perspective broadened the view of consumer spending, which has come to include the flow of dreams, fantasies, joy, and emotions that an individual is looking for.

With this perspective, experiences of products and services are analyzed in connection with leisure, Internet, culture, tourism, and so on. It is also believed that an experience in relation to products and services can be considered as a supplement, that is, something that complements a product or a service in one or more respects. When it comes to a pair of shoes, the experience for one individual can be how fashionable they are and how they show to others who they are in relation to others. This means that the functional value of the shoes is supplemented with values relating to design, prestige, and symbolism for the individual during consumption.

Furthermore, an experience is thought to be completely individual, which is why the same experience would not automatically be the same for the individual with another pair of shoes. It is also possible that the shoes build on a story that the individual buys and consumes rather than the product itself (Jensen, 1999). Thus a story or a theme (i.e., story telling) is used to sell a product, regardless of whether it is a visible item or an invisible service, which may be the case with food, movies, music, shoes, a visit to a restaurant, or holidays, to lay the foundation for an experience.

> "A consumer experience of a brand is about both business and pleasure for most individuals."

One of the reasons that companies shall offer experiences is that consumers, as individuals, are looking for new aspects of life, and they want to learn new things in an entertaining and pleasant way. This is achieved not only through the product or service itself but requires experiences to fulfill these needs. It is through personal interaction with an experience that an individual becomes involved with a brand, which can be done in different ways with respect to background, emotions, associations, and interpretations. In this way, an experience challenges the human senses when it comes to creating awareness and commitment on the personal level (Darmer and Sundbo, 2008).

Schmitt (1999) suggests that marketers should use five types of customer experiences as a basis for experience-based marketing. In this context, consumers are viewed as both emotional and rational individuals who are looking for positive experiences. The author, therefore, suggests sensory experiences (*sense*), emotional experiences (*feel*), cognitive experiences (*think*), physical experiences through behavior and lifestyles (*act*), as well as social experiences related to culture and reference groups (*relate*). It is further assumed that the goal of experiences for an individual is to lay the foundation for a complete experience in the form of a "gestalt." In Gestalt psychology, it is argued that a person strives to understand different things as part of a holistic or complete picture, and in this context, the Gestalt illustrates the complete picture.

Each of these experiences can lay the foundation for marketing campaigns, which are based on offering consumers experiences. Furthermore, Schmitt discusses three strategic objectives of the senses as forms of experience, namely, the senses as a differentiator, stimulator, and value creator. These three provide the opportunity for companies to strategically differentiate themselves from their competitors and to build identities and images relating to their brands, which are based on experiences and not just on goods or services.

Schmitt also indicates that traditional brand building ignores the main task of a brand, namely, to create sensory, emotional, or cognitive associations, which lead to positive brand experiences. This can also be due to the notion that it is no longer said to be sufficient for a product to only offer functional attributes and characteristics, such as quality and price, but requires additional attributes, such as communication and entertainment, to provide and enhance customers' brand experiences.

It is also believed that a customer experience should be considered from both a cognitive process perspective as well as an emotional experience perspective, where the former is based on information search, evaluation of alternatives, and decision about the purchase (Frow and Payne, 2007). This process perspective was discussed in the previous chapter and is important when it comes to explaining consumer behavior.

The concept of customer satisfaction is discussed in connection with customer experiences, and it is believed that this can be seen as the culmination of one or more experiences (Meyer and Schwager, 2007). These may arise from the points of contact that a consumer has with a company in the form of direct and indirect contacts. Regarding the direct contacts, these often take place in connection with the purchase, service, or use/consumption based on consumers' initiative. This is in contrast to the indirect contacts, which occur when consumers encounter the products, services, or brands through advertising, media, recommendations, or similarly.

In addition, it is also possible to distinguish between the different kinds of experiences, such as product experiences, shopping experiences, and service experiences, as well as consumption experiences, which directly or indirectly influence the consumers.

The Brand as Image

My third theoretical basis for understanding the meaning of sensory marketing is that the brand as an image is created by the identity creating processes that consumers experience in their interactions with a company. The brand's image is based entirely on how consumers understand and experience the products and services in reality and the consumer value that is obtained, which is why consumers in this way participate in building the brand. The mental pictures that consumers have about a product or a service, as a brand, are the basis for the brand as image.

These feelings and thoughts that consumers have about a brand can be based on both the physical product and the service elements as well as other components, and also sensory dimensions, which help to form an image in the consumer's consciousness that is synonymous with the brand (Grönroos, 2008). This starting point is in line with what experience-based marketing is based on, namely, the importance of aesthetics, feelings, and symbolic aspects of the actual consumer experience of a product or a brand.

Among researchers, there is a consensus that the brand as an image has received remarkably little attention in the context of a service logic (Payne et al., 2009). Therefore, an experience-based, coproducer perspective has been proposed to emphasize the importance of the brand as an image and branding, where consumers are seen as coproducers of their personal experiences. This emphasizes the importance that both consumer value and consumer experiences are thought to contribute to the brand's image, and the mental picture that consumers have of a brand shows how it works in reality.

Regarding the relevance of the brand as an image from a consumer psychology perspective, as opposed to an information process perspective, Schmitt (2012) discusses how consumers may have different levels of psychological involvement. These levels are divided into what is called *object-centered*, where consumers seek information and beneficial aspects of the brand, *self-centered*, where the brand is seen as personally appealing, and *social*, where consumers consider the brand in a social context, which gives a sense of belonging.

Also discussed are the five brand-related processes, all of which are associated with the image that consumers have of a brand. The process involves *identifying* a brand and its category as well as creating associations and comparing it with the other brands. Another process is about *experiencing* a brand through affective, participatory, and sensory dimensions. Also, there is a process to *integrate* a brand by combining its brand information with a global brand concept, where both personality and relationship with the brand emerge.

When it comes to the process of making a brand significant for an individual, it means to use the brand as an information stimulus, an identity signal, or a cultural symbol. Finally, the process refers to *connecting* to a brand and how an individual creates an attitude and becomes personally attached to the brand and associates with it in different brand contexts.

Researchers like Schmitt also believe that these processes need not occur in any particular order, but can occur in different ways. The advantage of Schmitt's model is that it presents an integrative frame of reference for how consumers' brand-related processes occur, which in turn can be considered as contributing to the brand as an image.

Finally, it should be said that in the literature on brands, the importance of both customer value as well as customer experiences have received insufficient attention to understand how a brand is created as an image among consumers (Payne et al., 2009).

This means that the focus is shifting from the company's branding processes to the individual's identity creation processes so that one can understand the brand as an image among consumers. It is also stated that both consumer experiences as well as brand relationships are important to develop an understanding of how the brand contributes to the identity creation and self-fulfillment among the consumers. This is tied to experience-based consumption, which is why the brand as an image is of central importance in sensory marketing.

A Comparison of TM, RM, and SM

As previously stated, sensory marketing (SM) is based on theoretical concepts such as consumer value, consumer experiences, and brand as an image, which points to the importance of the five senses. In today's global consumer culture, individualization as a lifestyle requires new concepts and models to understand consumers' affections, cognitions, and actual behaviors. This has led me to pose the following question: *How is it possible for a company to meet the consumer in a more personal way when it comes to differentiating and expressing a brand?*

The deficiencies that have existed, both theoretical and practical, in both transaction marketing (TM) and relationship marketing (RM) have been the inability to meet and satisfy consumers on a deeper, individual level regarding their feelings, fantasies, and thoughts. Table 3.1 shows a comparison between TM, RM, and SM with respect to the management approach as well as strategic and tactical marketing.

Table 3.1 TM, RM and SM—A Comparison (Developed from Hulten, 2011)

	Transaction marketing (TM)	Relationship marketing (RM)	Sensory marketing (SM)
Marketing	Goods logic Exchange perspective Utility creation	Service logic Relationship perspective Value creation	Experience logic Brand perspective Identity creation
Strategic marketing	Product focus Customer acquisition Transactional strategies	Customer focus Customer retention Relational strategies	Individual focus Sensory experience Sensorial strategies
Tactical marketing	Price, place, and promotion One-way communication Production technology	Interaction and interplay Two-way communication Information technology	Dialogue and interactivity Multidimensional communication Digital technology

It should be said that since modern marketing's emergence in the 1950s, various concepts and models have focused on the marketing process with respect to businesses, consumers, nonprofit organizations, products, or services. TM, as a model, is based on microeconomic theory as expressed by the well-known marketing mix in the 4 Ps. This is done from a pure exchange perspective, where goods are exchanged for money through financial transactions, and no other parameters appear in the model.

Furthermore, TM assumes a physical goods logic, where producers and intermediaries are in focus and where mass marketing is the starting point. This is based on advertising and promotion in which the characteristics of the product and price are the most prominent features. TM is primarily aimed at recruiting new customers to a company and also assumes that there is an active seller and a passive buyer, which consists of consumers. In this context, consumers are viewed as a mass with an average need, without regard to the individual and personal preferences of sight, sound, smell, touch, or taste.

The development that has taken place with the RM model is based on the interaction and network theories, as well as the social exchange theories, when it comes to explaining the interaction of the various marketing processes between the buyers and the sellers. This interaction takes place both between companies and between companies and consumers on various goods and service markets through interactions, networks, and relationships between an active seller and an active buyer. This is in stark contrast to the TM model and shows the deficiencies regarding the interactions that are present with this model, which are considered by many as being too simple in design.

Furthermore, RM is based on regarding the consumer as an individual and a customer from a relationship perspective, where the issue of being able to retain a company's customers is the most prominent feature. This has previously been discussed in the context of consumer brand relationships, which is common in many goods and service contexts. RM mainly deals with a company's ability to retain and nurture its customers and suggests that this can be done with the help of long-term relationships, personal interactions, and two-way communication, where a company's customer relationship management is the focus of strategic and tactical marketing (El-Ansary, 2005).

When it comes to the relationships between companies and consumers, it is believed that the methods and techniques such as CRM (*customer relationship management*) and CSM (*customer-specific marketing*) within RM could help to transform anonymous relationships with consumers, such as individuals, more personally. This is seen as a way to build the long-term customer relationships, especially in leading retail chains, using customer cards and data-based marketing. The criticism of this has been that these methods have been more technologically advanced and not built on a more personal approach to consumers as individuals.

The developments taking place regarding sensory marketing means that the goods and service logic based on TM and RM are supplemented with an experience logic from a brand perspective. It should be pointed out that this is based on the individual as a participant and a cocreator of the service processes, which lay the foundation for the brand image that consumers have of a product or a service. It stresses the individual experience of a brand through identity creating processes and the consumer values it conveys through the five senses regarding both body and soul.

This does not mean that the product features of the goods and services lack significance, but rather poses the question as to how other elements in addition to these characteristics may contribute to different sensory experiences for an individual. In this context, both the TM and RM, through advertising and price offers as well as relationship-building activities, can help to reinforce the identity of and the image of a brand. There is, therefore, no contradiction between TM and RM on the one hand and SM on the other—either in theory or in practice.

SM can help to create emotional, aesthetic, and sensory elements of a brand, which an individual can understand and gain experience from in his/her use and consumption processes, something that TM and RM do not emphasize. In this way, SM can contribute to generating consumer value, consumer experiences, and laying the foundation for a positive brand image.

In strategic and tactical marketing, therefore, the focus shifts from the goods logic, through advertising and price messages (TM), as well as the service logic, through interaction and collaboration (RM), to experience logic, through the senses and identity creation (SM), as the basis for the individual's sensory experiences. Furthermore, the sensory experience in SM is considered to determine whether it is possible to recruit or retain an individual customer, which includes both TM and RM.

All this means that SM emphasizes the importance of sensory experiences and sensory strategies, also known as sensorial strategies, to attract consumers and make them aware of a particular product or a particular brand. On the other hand, transactional and relationship strategies are also required for advertising and price offers and relationship-building activities, which means that one strategy does not necessarily exclude the other in a strategic marketing context of a business. Rather, it is *both*, with a postmodern view, when it comes to understanding the meaning of sensory marketing and its possibilities in practice.

In conclusion, it can be noted that it can be profitable for companies to offer consumers sensory experiences and not just get them to buy certain benefits of a product, to create competitive advantages, segmentation, and positioning in accordance with TM. A sensory experience is deemed to lead to better competitive advantages through the company focusing on not only the product and its positioning but also on the experience of ownership and consumption.

In the campaign, Magic Ride, Coca-Cola used consumers' senses as the basis for experience-based marketing. In the campaign, consumers got to see a three-dimensional movie, listen to the digitized sound of a newly opened Cola, smell the aroma of the drink, and, finally, taste the carbonated beverage and get an experience.

It is important that a brand engages consumers' senses, which means that sensory stimuli and sensory perception are prominent processes for consumers' affections, cognitions, and purchasing behavior, as previously mentioned. The literature suggests that consumption, as an experience, that is, a form of consumption that appeals to consumers' senses, shall be matched to what is called experience-based marketing. I will now discuss the implications of sensory marketing as a development of transaction marketing and relationship marketing.

WHAT IS SENSORY MARKETING?

Two Research Directions

In the emerging marketing paradigm, sensory marketing shall be seen as a new theoretical and empirical contribution in terms of understanding the importance of products and services as sensory experiences (Achrol and Kotler, 2012). One way to try to define what is meant by sensory marketing is to first define what is meant by the mind and the senses, which are often thought to be more difficult concepts to define in the literature.

> "Concepts such as business sense, acumen, self-will, frivolity, presence of mind, or amentia can often describe a person's characteristics and condition."

In everyday speech, most agree that the mind is often synonymous with consciousness or a person's thoughts, but that it may also relate to reason or "common sense." Nonetheless, within the various sciences and religions, it can be described in different ways, making it more complicated.

Regarding the senses of sight, sound, smell, touch, and taste, individuals use them to retrieve information from their surroundings. However, the senses can also use stored information and develop the feelings that are linked to the specific memories, which are connected to the five senses. In this way, it is possible to describe the relationship between a person's mind and the five senses to clarify that sensory marketing is intended to assist or affect a person's mind both on a conscious and unconscious level through the five senses.

Krishna (2011) defines sensory marketing as "marketing that engages consumers' minds and affects their perception, judgment, and behavior" when it comes to understanding the importance of sensations and perceptions. From a behavioral science and consumer psychology perspective, this takes place in connection with concepts such as consumers' perceptions, cognitions, emotions, learning, preferences, selections, or evaluations, when it comes to explaining consumers' behaviors (Figure 3.2).

Krishna (2013) further believes that sensory marketing is about understanding the importance of perception and sensations based on the five senses, in terms of consumer attitudes, learning, and behavior. This means that research on sensory marketing presents many interesting questions, which concern both researchers and practitioners, on how successful sensory marketing can be designed.

> "Since 2012, the grocery chain ICA in Sweden has established a specialist function within 'sensory marketing' to develop this area of its business."

In contrast to Krishna, I consider sensory marketing with a consumer marketing and branding perspective, linked to issues of consumer value, consumer experiences, and brand as an image. Concretely, this means that sensory marketing might help to increase the understanding and knowledge related to how a company with the help of the mind, the five senses, and sensory strategies and stimuli can affect consumers' affections, cognitions, and actual behaviors in the buying and consumption processes.

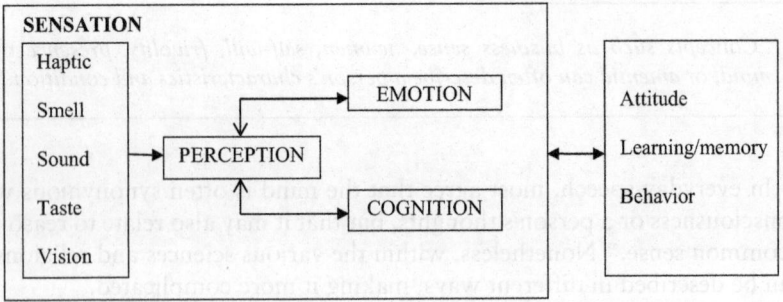

Figure 3.2 A Conceptual Model of Sensory Marketing (Krishna, 2011)

I define sensory marketing as "a service process that focuses on sensory strategies and stimuli with the goal of creating a multi-sensory brand-experience, in supporting the individual's identity creation through the mind and the five senses to generate consumer value, consumer experiences, and the brand as an image." For me, this means that the SM approach has its roots in the human mind and the human senses, where the mental flows and the psychological and neurophysiological reactions take place, resulting in a multi-sensory brand-experience. I will return to a deeper discussion of this concept at the end of the chapter.

Sensory marketing is based on how a business, by focusing on sensory strategies and stimuli in a service process, can contribute to consumer value, consumer experiences, and brand as image, which are related to the individual's personality and identity (Figure 3.3). Then sensory marketing has a natural and obvious link to individualization as a lifestyle, where self-fulfillment, identity creation, and sensory experiences are the key drivers for consumers' purchase and consumption processes.

Service Processes

One of the main reasons that sensory marketing is becoming increasingly important within B2C is that there are growing demands for an increased consumer orientation through various service processes. Above all, it requires a deepening and a refinement of the product and service offerings, which in a better way cater to consumers at a deeper level for marketing to continue to be successful going forward.

In the global competition, it also appears to be increasingly difficult to differentiate and distinguish one brand, because the price and quality are often considered to be equivalent for many products and services. For this reason, researchers such as Schmitt (1999) and Lindström (2005) have previously stated that it is necessary to focus on experiences in relation to the human senses, which enables companies to strengthen their brands to gain a stronger position in the marketplace.

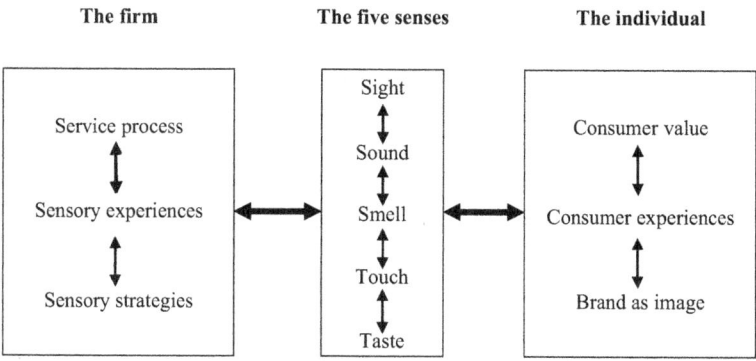

Figure 3.3 The Five Senses, the Firm and the Individual

Regardless of whether it is about a consumer product or a professional service, it is necessary that companies take into increased consideration how consumer value, consumer experiences, and brand as an image can be created in various service processes. In this context, branding is exclusively about how a brand is shaped in the customer's mind-set through the image that arises from the different experiences and perceptions of a product or a service.

Some researchers also argue that it is no longer possible for a company to simply satisfy consumers' functional needs by focusing on product features and advantages. Instead, it is important that consumers are activated and involved with a brand in different ways to achieve self-fulfillment and personal life goals. This can be done by creating memorable sensory experiences through sensory strategies and sensory stimuli that can contribute to consumer value, consumer experiences, and brand as an image through successful service processes.

Sensory Experiences

In sensory marketing, emotional, aesthetic, and sensory elements, in addition to product features and advantages, constitute the foundation of consumer value, consumer experiences, and brand as an image. In this context, consumer experiences are regarded as the sensory experiences that consumers get from a product or a service.

The German philosopher Alexander Baumgarten introduced the term aesthetics, which had its origins in the Greek word *aisthetikos*, already in use in the 1700s. It means to perceive something and refers to how a human being can experience a phenomenon or an object, particularly through emotions. At the time, rational thinking or logic, with truth as its primary objective, was dominant as a philosophical orientation. Then the term aesthetics was presented to allow a different interpretation of human actions and to show that aesthetics should be able to contribute to the emergence of knowledge about the senses of a person.

Within what has come to be known as marketing aesthetics, Schmitt and Simonson (1997) have defined marketing aesthetics as "the marketing of sensory experiences for a business or a brand, which contributes to the organization's or the brand's identity." Among philosophers, this is a supported reasoning, which is based on an individual achieving aesthetic satisfaction through symbols that in one way or another are perceived as pleasant and appealing, as the following example illustrates:

> *From the time we wake up to the end of a working day, we are dazzled by what we see, hear, taste, smell, and feel. Our personal tastes guide us in our decisions when it comes to choosing our neighbors, decorating our homes, choosing our clothes, or buying our cars.*

In Gestalt psychology, it is considered that the whole—or the Gestalt—is the most central to a person's perception, based on the holistic nature of perception. This means that the individual's perception can be influenced by, for example, shapes and colors as expressions of the aesthetic elements of a product or a service. This can be done without a conscious process and thus takes place in an unconscious way in a person's mind.

For this reason, aesthetic and sensory elements contribute in different ways to generate customer value, create sensory experiences, and reinforce the brand as an image. They are also able to contribute to greater loyalty and higher prices, to withstand competitors' marketing ploys, as well as create long-term thinking in brand relationships.

Aesthetic elements, therefore, can be considered as an emotional part of the sensory experience, which means that emotions will affect consumers' final choice of a product or a service. It is thought to be increasingly important to engage consumers on the emotional and mental levels in terms of emotional branding to create a positive sensory experience.

A sensory experience is deemed to affect the whole person and is a result of various events or activities occurring in the environment. It can be done, for example, by the influence of various stimuli associated with purchase and consumption. This often occurs through active participation and/or observation by an individual, which means that the sensory experience appears with the help of the marketing elements that exist.

In this way, different marketing elements contribute as stimuli to create a positive, neutral, or negative sensory experience for an individual. The individual experience that occurs is often related to the verb admire, attract, or hate, which then can be attributed to how the different stimuli are perceived and interpreted by the individual. Furthermore, the emotional, aesthetic, and sensory elements that exist, together with the functional elements, are viewed from a holistic perspective, which unconsciously lays the foundations for an individual's total sensory experience.

> *"The Swedish retailer Ikea has long succeeded in conveying an overall experience of the kitchen or bathroom in their stores, where both the aesthetic and functional elements are present."*

Within the framework of sensory perception of a brand, all the existing elements, such as name, logo, symbol, store layout, price, product, advertising, or staff, are the basis of the perceived consumer value. It also means that for the individual, the brand is related to his/her personal characteristics, lifestyle, and social context, which strengthen the established mental image of the brand or makes the brand appear for the individual.

I define a sensory experience as "an individual's perception and/or experience of the products or services or other elements through the five senses, which help to create customer value and brand as an image." The five senses lay the foundation for the actual sensory experiences through sight, sound, smell, touch, and taste (Figure 3.4).

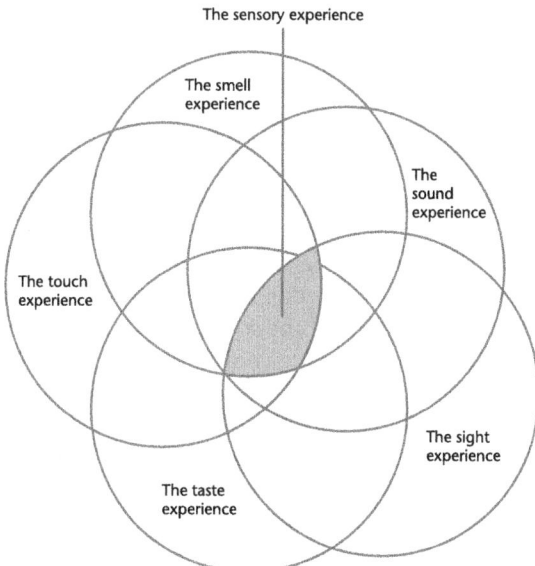

Figure 3.4 The Five Senses and the Sensory Experience. (Hultén et al., 2009)

Various stimuli contribute so that the senses react on a subconscious level, based on the emotional, aesthetic, and sensory—as well as the functional—elements that an individual encounters in an identity creating process. It is believed that a *change* in the environment regarding, for example, store layout or product design immediately attracts attention of the five senses, more than anything else. This has been expressed as follows by Howard Hughes Medical Institute in the United States (1995, p. 9):

> *Our senses are finely attuned to change. Stationary or unchanging objects become part of the scenery and are mostly unseen. Customary sounds become background noise, mostly unheard ... If something in the environment changes, we need to take notice because it might mean danger—or opportunity.*

The five senses have a vital role for every person, and without them, no sensory impressions would be created and experienced by an individual. Through the senses, either each one separately or in combination, we get sensory information about human life and the environment through sight, sound, smell, touch, and taste. It may be added that it is also generally accepted that humans have more senses than just the five, for example, a sense of balance, pain, or temperature.

> "The five senses receive stimuli that are converted into sensory information, which in turn become electrical signals in the brain."

For a long time, people have wondered how thoughts arise and where they come from, which has increased the interest in the significance of the five senses for affections, cognitions, and behaviors. Sense organs such as eyes, ears, nose, and mouth, which can be found on a person's head, convey direct impulses to the brain when a sensory impression is recorded. For the other senses, such as touch, impulses are transmitted through the nerves in the spinal cord to the brain. The sensory information that the sensory organs convey is sent through the sensory cells or receptors, which convert the information into electrical signals with regard to, for example, muscle tension and position of body, or emotions and feelings. It is, thus a person's sensory cells that transmit the electrical signals that a person reacts to, and they are based on the sensory information and the sensory impression that is received through the five senses.

Neuroscientists have long been trying to answer the question of how electrical signals arise and how these can cause different reactions in a human's behaviors and actions. In an experiment performed by the Nobel Prize Laureates David Hubel and Torsten Wiesel, they discovered that when a cat's eyes were exposed in a line in a particular position and at a particular angle, the neurons in the back of the brain, the visible neocortex, were activated. This result, which was not expected, has led to a focus in brain research on the identification of individual neurons' ability to manage and interpret sensory information, particularly with regard to the sense of sight.

In a human brain, there is also the cerebrum and the limbic system, where the latter deals with emotions that affect human actions and reactions. The cerebrum, on the other hand, controls thinking and memory ability, whereas the neocortex is responsible for a person's logic. It is widely believed that the cerebrum is dependent on the limbic system, because instincts and emotions largely govern human actions and behavior. Furthermore, it is thought that a conscious sensory impression occurs in the brain when a human becomes aware of a color, a sound, a smell, or a taste through sensory information and sensations through the nerve impulses. I will return with a more detailed discussion about the brain and the five senses in the next chapter.

Finally, it should be said that sensory marketing is about reaching an individual's feelings and thoughts on a deeper level by using the five senses, sensory stimuli, and sensory information to create consumer value, sensory experiences, and a brand image.

Sensory Strategies

In sensory marketing, companies create different sensory experiences through service processes that build on sensory (or sensorial) strategies, which are based on the five senses of sight, sound, smell, touch, and taste. It is believed that consumers have become what are called sensory producers and that they become emotionally and cognitively affected by both positive and negative sensory experiences in connection with purchase and consumption. Furthermore, consumers do not just put importance on functional elements of a brand, but also search for aesthetic, hedonic, or sensory elements in their identity creation.

I define sensory strategy as "a deliberate marketing strategy of a company's service process to create a sensory experience using sensory stimuli, which addresses and attracts a special sense or multiple senses simultaneously in an individual."

The importance that the five senses have for a company is illustrated by the following formulation by a store manager of a leading supermarket chain in the United Kingdom (Hultén, 2011):

Yes, we definitely believe in the senses . . . We tried a business with selling online, but that really destroyed everything we were trying to do—you can't touch it, or smell it, or see it. You are just relying on pictures. It didn't really work for us, so we are not going down that road again.

112 *Sensory Marketing*

Furthermore, a sensory approach can include goods, services, and products, which is why it can also contribute to both recruiting customers and retaining current customers. A sensory approach, therefore, is based on how various transactions and relationships shall be handled within the framework of sensory marketing (SM). For this reason, there is no contradiction between the transactional and relational strategies, on the one hand, and sensory strategies on the other hand. Provided that a sensory strategy can contribute to increasing the customer value, positive consumer experiences, and a better brand image, there is a natural consequence that consumer brand relationships also become more long-term and profitable for a company.

Table 3.2 presents the five senses, examples of sensory stimuli, and the kind of sensations that form the basis of consumer value, consumer experiences, and the brand as an image in consumers' identity creation processes.

Sensory Strategy for the Sense of Sight

The primary task of the sense of sight and an individual's visual system is to help him/her through the eyes to discover all the changes and differences in the surroundings. In the context of a visual marketing strategy, it can refer to, for example, a new store layout, a new design, or a different form of a packaging, where the differences are increased, especially regarding matters such as color and shape. That image, which is visually conveyed to the retina, is compared with past memories and experiences, which is why a new image has a link to the individual's past experiences.

Table 3.2 Senses, Sensory Stimuli and Sensations (Developed from Hultén, 2011)

Sense	Sensory stimuli	Sensations
Sight	Design, packaging, and logo Color, light, and theme Graphic, exterior, and interior	Visual
Sound	Jingle, voice, and music Atmosphere, attentiveness, and theme Signature sound and sound brand	Auditory
Smell	Product congruence, intensity, and sex Atmosphere, advertency, and theme Scent brand and signature scent	Atmospheric
Touch	Material and surface Temperature and weight Form and steadiness	Tactile
Taste	Name, presentation, and environment Knowledge, lifestyle, and delight Interplay, symbiosis, and synergies	Aesthetic/gastronomic

Using a visual strategy, a company's or a brand's identity is expressed visually and becomes a distinguishing feature in sensory marketing. This is a common occurrence and is often expressed through advertising, design, and style or by visual and verbal identity in the advertising context, at the same time as it can occur through electronic media, websites, or people. In connection with fast moving consumer goods, where the package provides a visualized identity, this is of importance for consumers when it comes to paying attention to a particular type of product.

> *"Because the human eye recognizes environmental changes, a visual strategy builds so that something will look different than before."*

Visual stimuli, either in isolation or in combination with other sensory stimuli, can contribute to highlighting and clarifying the visual experience that a brand wants to convey, with regard to a service environment, products, and services, as the following example shows:

> *Apple, with its iPhone, has chosen to design their mobile phone based on soft values to appeal to the five senses. Through the use of rounded edges and touchscreen as well as different colors on the phone, they have succeeded. The main argument has been to get away from the harsh values that technology and phones have represented.*

When it comes to visual stimuli, such as *design, packaging*, or *logo*, these are often more prominent in certain product contexts. In contrast, stimuli such as color, light, and theme in the context of both products and services exist, which also apply to stimuli such as *graphics, exterior*, and *interior*. I will return to a discussion of the importance of sensory stimuli, sensory perception, and sensory symbolism of the visual system in relation to societal culture, service environment, and brands in the next chapter.

Strategy for the Sense of Sound

Through the stereocilia in the ears and the auditory nerve, a person's sense of sound conveys the sounds that the brain then can interpret and give meaning to the environment and the surroundings. For several millennia, people have used sound to shape their identity and find meaning in life in different societal cultures. In this context, music and voices have been an important element in creating a better understanding and perception of reality in humans from birth.

With the help of sound strategy, a company or a brand identity can be expressed auditorily and become a distinguishing feature of sensory marketing. It is a common occurrence to create attention and arouse consumers' feelings for various products and services.

Generally, consumers give meaning to all kinds of sounds, whether they are perceived as pleasant or unpleasant, which means that there is a deeper interpretation of their meaning on a personal level.

> *"Most individuals respond emotionally to music or voices, which stimulates the human mind."*

Auditory stimuli, either in isolation or in combination with other sensory stimuli, can contribute to highlighting and clarifying the auditory experience that a brand wants to convey with regard to a service environment, products, and services, as the following example shows:

> *The fashion chain Abercrombie & Fitch expresses its brand through known songs, which are mixed to create the right atmosphere in the service environment. Often, music is played loudly to give the impression of a nightclub, and the songs build expectations that more things will happen. It so happens that both the customers and the employees begin to dance to the music, which creates the feeling of a live party.*

In this context, *music, voices,* or *jingles* become important stimuli to create a sensory experience of a product or a service. Likewise, sound can be used to help create an *atmosphere* in a shop or a mall and can simultaneously be present as a *theme*. This means that a company or a brand creates a listening experience that consists of a *signature sound*, or a *sound brand*, as an expression of its identity. A sound strategy need not just be about adding a sound to a service process, but it can also be about eliminating sound that is perceived as unpleasant or disturbing to the consumers.

I will return to a discussion of the importance of sensory stimuli, sensory perception, and sensory symbolism for the sense of sound in relation to societal culture, service environment, and brands in one of the following chapters.

Strategy for the Sense of Smell

The sense of smell and the olfactory system enables each of us to experience scents, which are closely linked to people's emotions. Thanks to the olfactory receptors in the nostrils, scent that is inhaled can be forwarded to the olfactory center in the brain. It is then that we perceive a scent as pleasant or unpleasant, which can affect an individual on an emotional level.

A human has around ten million receptors in the nose, in comparison with a dog's nose, which has about two hundred million. It also turns out that scents can create lasting memories in humans, which is why a scent from childhood can be drawn out in adulthood.

> *"In a service environment, a smell draws attention to a brand at the same time as creating a pleasant atmosphere."*

With the help of a scent strategy, a company or a brand identity can be expressed atmospherically, where scent's role is to create *awareness* and the fragrance component shall be considered as part of the identity. In daily life, consumer's give meaning to different types of scents, whether they are perceived as pleasant or unpleasant, which means that there is an emotional response.

Atmospheric stimuli, either in isolation or in combination with other sensory stimuli, can contribute to highlighting and clarifying the scent experience that a brand wants to convey with regard to a service environment, products, and services, as the following example shows:

> *The brand Citroën C4 gives its customers the opportunity to choose from nine different scents for the car's interior, which helps to create a positive new car smell and create a good atmosphere in the car. Furthermore, it is believed that scents such as lemon, lavender, lotus flower, or vanilla can contribute to safer driving. These have been developed in collaboration with fragrance experts to comply with the brand's identity.*

In this context, a scent's natural connection to a product—*product similarity*—and the scent's *intensity* are of importance for the sensory experience. It is thought that product-like scents can contribute to a positive sensory experience, whereas subtle scents have less importance. When it comes to a service environment, it is believed that scents could help to create a good *atmosphere* and increase *attention* as well as contribute to customers' increased satisfaction in shops and stores.

Furthermore, it is believed that scents contribute to the *recall* and *recognition* of a brand, which companies can achieve with the help of *signature scents* or legally protected fragrance brands. A scent strategy need not just be about adding a particular scent in a service process, but it can also be about eliminating scents that are perceived as unpleasant or disturbing to consumers.

I will return to a discussion about the importance of sensory stimuli, sensory perception, and sensory symbolism for the sense of smell in relation to societal culture, service environment, and brand in one of the following chapters.

Strategy for the Sense of Touch

The sense of touch (or the tactile sense) and the kinesthetic system make it possible for a person to experience physical contact with objects and people in their surroundings. The receptors that are found throughout the human body allow us through touch to feel the mechanical pressure on the skin. Furthermore, it makes it possible to examine three-dimensional objects and to obtain information as to whether an object is hard, oval, or sharp. It is widely believed that the sense of touch has the greatest impact on a person's health, and many of us can remember and relive how something feels just by seeing it or thinking about it.

With the help of a tactile approach, a company or a brand identity can be expressed in a tactile manner, where the role of touch is to create lasting sensory experiences. In daily life, consumers give meaning to different types of tactile experiences, whether they are perceived as pleasant or unpleasant, which means that there is an emotional response.

> "To touch a brand can lead to an emotional response, which would not otherwise have occurred."

Tactile stimuli, either in isolation or in combination with other sensory stimuli, can contribute to highlighting and clarifying the tactile experience that a brand wants to convey with regard to a service environment, products, and services, as the following example shows:

> Ikea chose to let their customers spend the night in one of their Norwegian stores so that they could try their beds during the night. The aim was to create a sensory experience at the same time as making it possible for them to gain experience about the beds' features and benefits. Sleeping over was free, and customers could choose between sleeping in a normal bedroom, a family room, or a honeymoon suite.

In this context, the tactile sensation is often expressed through stimuli as *materials* and *surfaces*, or *temperature* and *weight*, both in a service environment and for products and services. Other tactile stimuli, such as *firmness* and *shape*, contribute to a sensory experience in which the emotional feeling for the product is induced by the contact that occurs.

To create a sensory experience, it is necessary that products are physically available, which can enable the interaction that is required in a service environment. Then there is the opportunity to squeeze, feel, and turn and twist a product to evaluate it in a service process. It is considered that this type of touch results in consumers paying attention to the products that they otherwise would not have been bothered with, which at the same time can lead to impulsive and unplanned purchases.

When it comes to services, it is thought that a tactile experience is of importance in the moment of consumption in a service process. The emotional feeling that arises for a brand, for example, through hard or soft chairs in a cafe or a restaurant is found to have an influence on the experience that an individual has, which in turn is the basis for the brand image that arises.

I will return to a discussion of the importance of sensory stimuli, sensory perception, and sensory symbolism for the sense of touch in relation to societal culture, service environment, and brand in one of the following chapters.

Strategy for the Sense of Taste

The sense of taste and the chemical receptor system allows a person to use the taste organs in the oral cavity to experience the gastronomic tastes, the so-called inner taste. Thanks to the taste buds, which amounts to between five thousand and ten thousand of them scattered on the tongue, palate, and throat, a taste experience can be achieved. In each taste bud there are several kinds of taste cells, which means that an individual taste bud is sensitive to several different flavors.

> "Many people call it taste, but it's about everything: how it looks, smells, feels, and sounds."

There are five basic tastes, namely, sweet, salty, sour, bitter, and umami (savory), which form the basis of the taste cells. Furthermore, it is believed that the saliva helps so that the flavor can be absorbed by the taste cell receptors at the same time as the saliva protects the taste cells. It is also thought that the sense of taste interacts with both the sense of smell and the sense of touch in humans to create the overall taste experience, but it can be difficult to distinguish between the respective sensory contributions.

The opposite of gastronomic taste is aesthetic taste, so-called outer taste, which deals with the connection between the physical sense of taste and aesthetics. The old saying that you cannot argue about taste did not originate from the fact that taste was regarded as an individual, private matter. It was assumed that what felt or tasted good was both good and beautiful for every human being. This means that both internal and external taste have prominent roles in people's consumption when it comes to satisfying the self and achieving quality of life.

With the help of a taste strategy, a company or a brand identity can be expressed gastronomically/aesthetically, where the role of taste is to create lasting sensory experiences. In daily life, consumers give meaning to different types of taste sensations, whether they are perceived as pleasant or unpleasant, which means that there is an emotional response.

Gastronomic/aesthetic stimuli, either in isolation or in combination with other sensory stimuli, can contribute to highlighting and clarifying the taste experience that a brand wants to convey with regard to a service environment, products, and services, as the following example shows:

> *Heston Blumenthal, the founder of the restaurant The Fat Duck in England, has the following philosophy*: "Of course I want to create food that is delicious, but this depends on so much more than simply what's going on in the mouth—context, history, nostalgia, emotion, memory and the interplay of sight, smell, sound and taste all play an important part in our appreciation and enjoyment of food. ***Eating is a Multi-Sensory Experience.***"

In this context, the taste experience is often expressed through stimuli such as *presentation*, *environment*, and *knowledge* to contribute to a taste experience both in a service environment as well as for products and services. Even interactions with other senses regarding stimuli such as *design*, *scent*, *sound*, *texture*, and *weight* contribute to a culinary experience, which is based on *synergy*. Then a taste experience is often an expression of the individual's total sensory experience, as previously discussed see Figure 3.4.

The sense of taste is considered to be one of man's most distinctive emotional senses, which can be illustrated with concepts such as *sour*, *sweet*, and *matter of taste*. To create an emotional taste experience, therefore, a company's customers must "taste" the service environment or products and services in a service process through various interactions. Often this is done with the help of food and beverage elements to create taste experiences that can contribute to consumer experiences and the brand image. But it can also be done with the help of aesthetic and sensory elements such as color, sound, or texture, in order to emphasize the overall experience.

I will return to a discussion about the importance of sensory stimuli, sensory perception, and sensory symbolism of the sense of taste in relation to societal culture, service environment, and brand in one of the following chapters.

Multi-Sensory Brand-Experience

In sensory marketing, the goal is for companies to offer consumers a multi-sensory brand-experience through sensory strategies and stimuli in service processes. With the human mind and the five senses as the starting point, the mental flows and processes that occur in individuals lay the foundation for consumer value, consumer experiences, and the brand as an image.

My definition of a multi-sensory brand-experience is as follows: "*A multi-sensory brand-experience contributes to individual value creation and is related to how individuals react when a company collaborates with and supports their identity creating processes by engaging the five senses to generate customer value, consumer experiences, and the brand as an image.*"

The personal perception and subjective interpretation that takes place in a multi-sensory brand-experience is linked to the Gestalt figure and the holistic being that is strived for at the individual level. For that reason, every experience adds to shaping behavioral, emotional, cognitive, sensory, or symbolic values of an individual, which create what I call experience logic. This logic is completely personal and subjective and varies from one individual to another, demonstrating how SM differs from TM and RM, as previously discussed. Furthermore, the experience logic differs from the goods logic and the service logic in that it starts from individual, personal experience with products and services.

> "The experience logic is completely individual and subjective, which is why two people can have completely different experiences with the same brand."

Sensory marketing as an approach, therefore, differs in a crucial way from the TM and RM approaches by focusing on a multi-sensory brand-experience as the goal of a firm's marketing. In this way, SM emphasizes how a firm can differentiate and distinguish itself through sensory experiences and sensory strategies, which are based on emotional, cognitive, and value-based elements in relation to the human mind and the five senses.

This relates to how a product or a brand can be positioned according to the marketing theory, which was expressed by Ries and Trout (1982) as "Positioning is what you do to the mind of a prospect." In sensory marketing, this means that the sensory impression that a company has on an individual to differentiate themselves from their competitors is related to a deeper, emotional level of the individual.

Against this background, it means that the model of sensory marketing should have the goal to create a multi-sensory brand-experience when it comes to companies designing sensory experiences and sensory strategies based on the mind and the five senses (Figure 3.5). The figure shows the three levels that have been identified, and the model provides many options for action in the marketing process of products and services.

When it comes to the number of explanatory levels, these have been limited to three to make a classification that facilitates the model's construction

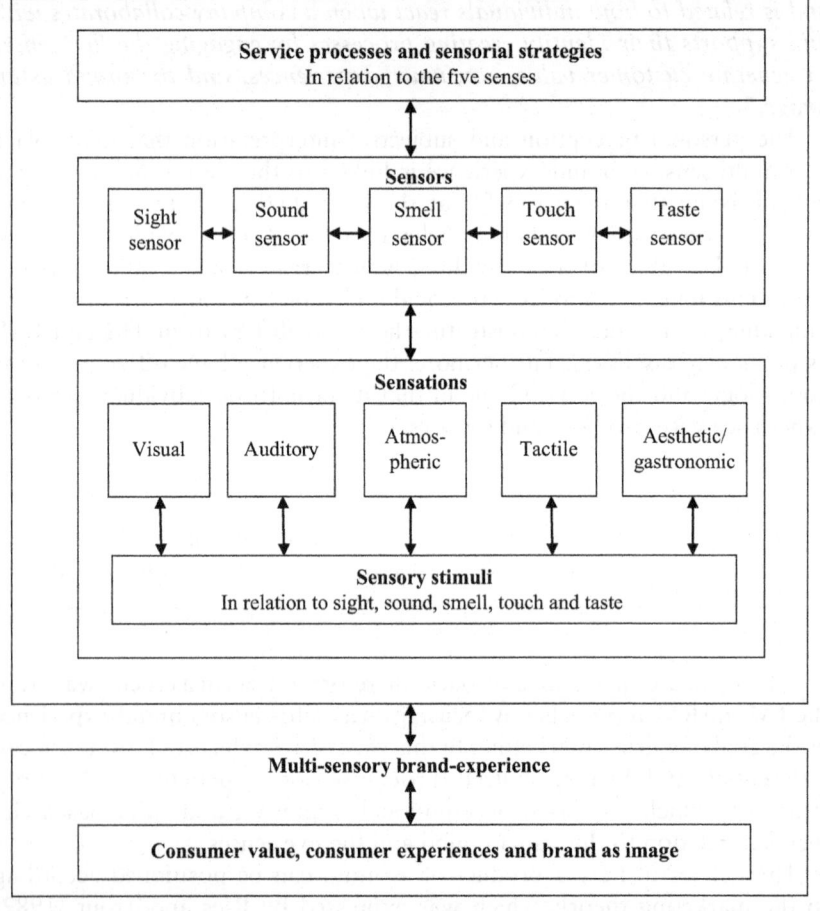

Figure 3.5 Sensory Marketing as Explanatory Model (Developed from Hultén, 2011)

and not make it too complicated and extensive. Furthermore, each level has a number of policy options in order for one to be able to develop successful sensory strategies in a service process with the purpose of creating a multi-sensory brand-experience, leading to increased consumer value, positive consumer experiences, and a stronger brand image.

The primary purpose of the SM model is to simplify the marketing process by grouping the possible options together on three main levels when it comes to marketing resources. Further, another goal of the model is to develop a more exhaustive classification than what has hitherto been possible to find in marketing literature. My assumption is that the three levels, paradoxically enough, are independent of each other and at the same time related to each other. This means that each level can occur together or independently of the other.

It should also be pointed out that at each level, different factors or elements arise in a service process that opens up for differentiation and variation with regard to how sensory experiences and sensory strategies can be shaped and developed. Finally, it should also be noted that there is an interdependence between the different marketing resources, which itself involves the creation of some kind of regularity in one or more respects in terms of how sensory marketing is expressed in a marketing process.

As previously discussed, sensory strategies and stimuli aim to differentiate and distinguish a company or a brand's identity with respect to the mind and the five senses. This must be emphasized in connection with a product or a service when the emotional and sensual elements are highlighted, compared with just price and quality.

In this context, sensory dimensions contribute to a brand in a more personal way to attract consumers when it comes to clarifying its brand identity and value. This means that a sensory marketing approach will facilitate a multi-sensory brand-experience by building on the use of resources such as sensors, sensations, and sensory stimuli, as shown in Figure 3.5.

In the model, the sensors aim to communicate sensations and sensory stimuli whose primary task is to convey a multi-sensory brand-experience to consumers. A sensor is defined as "a communicative tool, which sends sensations and sensory stimuli, or receives information through digital tools, technical equipment, or employees in relation to consumers."

Sensors are the basis of a multi-sensory communication platform with various types of influence, which include both traditional advertising and advertising websites in order to distinguish and express a brand's identity. In both service environments as well as virtual environments, such a communication platform strengthens the creation of sensory experiences and sensory strategies.

In the model, sensations, as mentioned earlier, aim to clarify and express a brand's identity as something distinct and distinctive in relation to the mind and the five senses. A sensation is defined as "an affection or feeling, which knowingly arises in the mind or the senses of an individual, coupled with a sensory strategy and stimuli."

When it comes to a brand's identity, the creation of the sensations is crucial for consumers to observe and pay attention to the brand. The mind and the five senses have the ability, on an unconscious level, to notice every little change in the environment, whether it comes from the service environments, products, or services. Moreover, various kinds of sensations can enable a multi-sensory brand-experience and contribute to consumer value, consumer experiences, and brand image.

Finally, in the model, sensory stimuli aim to express a brand's identity and uniqueness in relation to the mind and the five senses. Sensory stimuli are defined as "stimuli that clarifies a brand's identity and values with the goal of leaving an impression in a person's mind." The main reason for a company to make use of sensory stimuli is to reach consumers on a deeper, individual, and emotional level, as the following example from the American supermarket chain Whole Foods illustrates (Hulten, 2011, p. 268):

> *In a sensorial sight strategy, visual sensations and their sensory expressions belong to the interior with light colors like olive-green and yellow on the walls. The lighting is comfortable, with spotlights as sights sensors aimed at special products and style through colors and lighting expresses proximity to nature. Handwritten information as sensors, give the graphic feeling of a more personal sight experience.*
>
> *In a sensorial sound strategy, auditory sensations and their sensory expressions appear as pop music with soft voices, through such sound sensors as stereos and loudspeakers and the choice of music, which make it possible to say that the company has a signature sound.*
>
> *In a sensorial smell strategy, the atmospheric sensations and their sensory expressions welcome customers to the servicescapes with a soft intensity and at the entrance, there is a bakery with an oven spreading product-congruence scents of newly-baked bread as smell sensors. No artificial scents are used and the natural scents from fruit and cheese offer smell experiences as sensors.*
>
> *In a sensorial taste strategy, gastronomic sensations and their sensory expressions reinforce the taste experience through the interplay of other senses that allow synergies through staff who wear aprons as taste sensors, which emphasize a homely feeling and superb food. The company offers the presentation of real samples of tastes that are related to season and theme. This creates a setting where "food thinking" is part of the interior and invites customers to gain more knowledge, delight in and experience new tastes.*
>
> *Finally, in a sensorial touch strategy, tactile sensations and their sensory expressions invite customers to touch the products, because they are accessible in dishes or straw baskets that emphasize personal contact as touch sensors. No plastic material is used, and cold and hot foods are chosen by the customers themselves. There is a cheese room as a touch sensor with stable doors to keep the temperature at the right level for the taste experience."*

Societal Culture, Service Environment, and the Brand

A sensory marketing approach is about how a company uses the five senses to position a brand to an individual with the use of sensory (or sensorial) strategies and sensory stimuli. Accordingly, the question arises as to what environments, that is, in which different contexts can this be expressed both theoretically and practically and in what may be considered as characteristic for the respective senses.

I propose a model of the five senses in which societal culture (S), service environment (E), and brand (B) are included as contextual variables (Figure 3.6). The leading notion is that each of the five senses can be related to these three contexts, which then allow for the analysis and explanation of how sensory stimuli, sensory perception, and sensory symbolism might affect consumers' affective and cognitive reactions, as well as their actual purchasing behavior in different purchase and consumption processes.

In the model, it is assumed that the five senses lead to affective and cognitive reactions, which in turn result in an actual behavior in connection with the purchase and consumption processes, such as shopping and experiences (Spence et al., 2014). When it comes to purchase and consumption processes, these relate to both goods and services, because the latter is purchased and consumed simultaneously.

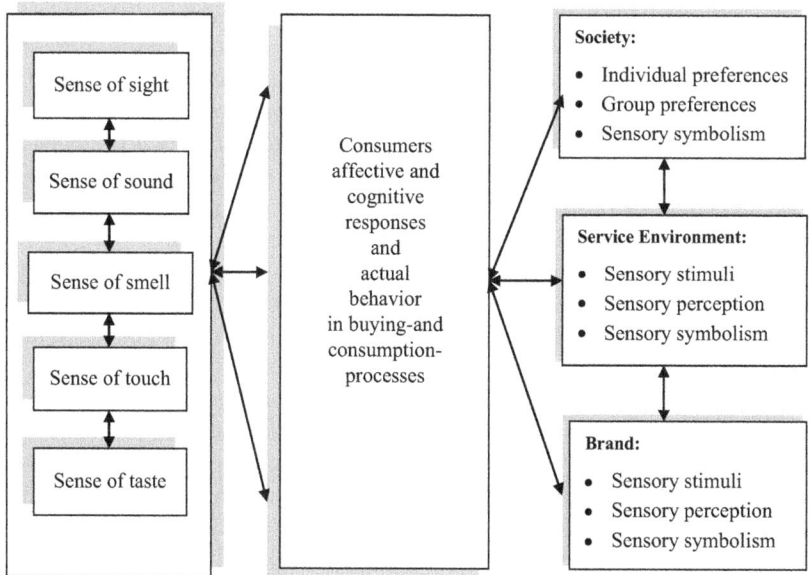

Figure 3.6 The S-E-B-model

SOCIETAL CULTURE

As previously shown, through the emergence of individualization as a lifestyle, *societal culture* plays a crucial role for us to understand how a sensory marketing approach can be used and applied. In every societal culture, different cultural codes convey the meaning or the meaning found in every person's subconscious about an image, an object, or a phenomenon. These codes explain the features found in different societal cultures in terms of the understanding and experience of what is in the environment.

In each specific societal culture, different experiences and feelings make unconscious impressions in each individual during his/her upbringing. These impressions lay the foundation for the feelings and thoughts that unconsciously affect a person's behavior. In this way, the brain delivers various cultural codes that on a subconscious level tell an individual how he/she will perceive a certain event or situation and behave in a particular cultural context. This lays the foundation for the specific features that can be identified in the different social cultures.

In terms of societal culture and its specific features, as contextual variables, I have chosen to highlight factors such as individual preferences, group references, and sensory symbolism to show how these may affect consumers' affective and cognitive reactions and their actual purchasing behavior.

SERVICE ENVIRONMENT

In the *service environment* that stores, malls, websites, or places represent, their designs have an especially significant role in a sensory marketing approach with regard to how individuals pay attention to and perceive (or interpret) their surroundings. It has long been obvious that human behavior is influenced by the natural or physical environment in which the behavior takes place; based on this finding, Bitner (1992) coined the term *servicescape*. Throughout this book, I have chosen to use the term *service environment* with the same meaning as the term *servicescape*.

Since the 1950s, research has focused on the physical attributes that characterize retail outlets and their personality through the concept of *retail atmospherics*. Already in the early 1970s, Kotler (1973) brought to attention the significance that the service environment would come to have and considered it to be the most important competitive advantage in the future. He also introduced the term atmosphere as a way to describe the surroundings and the physical factors involved in this and came to distinguish between the visual, tactile, olfactory, and aural dimensions in a store or a department store. The human senses came to play a prominent role in this definition early on, because the store atmosphere was described in sensory terms.

Research suggests that five main elements in the store atmosphere, namely, exterior, interior, layout, point of purchase, and people, laid the foundation for consumers' perceptions and experiences. Further research indicates that ambient stimuli, such as backgrounds, appeal to the five senses and thereby affect consumers' understanding and experience of various service environments. Sensory stimuli in the physical environment are also considered to help create positive feelings among consumers and increase store sales. But it is also evident that atmospheric elements are of significance in contributing to a hedonic shopping experience.

When it comes to service environment and its design, namely, contextual variables, I have chosen to highlight factors such as sensory stimuli, sensory perception, and sensory symbolism to show how these may affect consumers' affective and cognitive reactions and their actual purchasing behaviors.

BRAND

The *brand*, such as a good, a service, or a product, with its identity plays a prominent role in a sensory marketing approach with regard to how individuals pay attention to and perceive (or understand) a brand. A brand is defined by the American Marketing Association (AMA) as a name, a sign, a symbol, or another characteristic that distinguishes a seller's goods or services from other sellers.

Research shows that the brand is the identity that is created by a company for a product or a service, and it is an important part of an individual's brand image. Brand identity refers to the image of the brand that marketers want to create in consumers' minds. In the literature, brand is discussed as a relation to personality, which refers to how a product or a service can provide a symbolic content or symbolic meaning to consumers. It can be about characteristics of a brand, for example, straightforwardness, enthusiasm, competence, sophistication, and powerfulness, which can help to build a strong identity.

The desired identity results in an image of the product or service that later arises in consumers' thoughts. But it is always the consumer who decides whether the proposed brand evolves or not. In doing so, the brand as a concept is always the image that exists among consumers when they are involved and creating the brand. The claim that a company builds a brand is true only to a certain extent, because the brand as an image is always created in the customer's mind and imagination and nowhere else.

The brand is created after a number of contacts—interactions—between consumers and businesses in a relationship between both the parties. It takes place in the buying and consumption processes that develop a brand in the minds of consumers and where the human senses play a central role in the perception and experience of the actual brand.

When it comes to the brand, namely, contextual variables, I have chosen to highlight factors such as sensory stimuli, sensory perception, and sensory symbolism to show how these may affect consumers' affective and cognitive reactions and their actual purchasing behaviors.

In the next chapters, I will address each of the five senses and show the importance of societal culture, service environment, and brand based on what is known in research and literature.

REFERENCES

Achrol, R.S. and Kotler, P. (2012), "Frontiers of the marketing paradigm in the third millennium." *Journal of the Academy of Marketing Science,* 40, 35–52, 2012.

Bitner, M.J. (1992), "Servicescapes: the impact of physical surroundings on customers and employees," *Journal of Marketing,* 56, 2:57–71.

Brown, S. (1993), "Postmodern marketing?" *European Journal of Marketing,* 27, 4:19.

Brownlie, D., Saren, M., Whittington, R. and Wensley, R. (ed.) (1999), *Rethinking marketing—toward critical marketing accountings,* London: SAGE Publications.

Darmer, P. and Sundbo, J. (2008), "Introduction to experience creation." I: Sundbo, J. and Darmer, P. (ed.) *Creating experience in the experience economy,* Cheltenham: Edward Elgar Publishing, p. 1–12.

El-Ansary, A. (2005), "Relationship marketing management: a school in the history of marketing thought," *Journal of Relationship Marketing,* 4, 1 & 2:43–56.

Frow, P. and Payne, A. (2007), "Towards the 'perfect' customer experience," *Journal of Brand Management,* 15, 2:89–101.

Grönroos, C. (2008), "Service logic revisited: who creates value? And who co-creates?" *European Business Review,* 20, 4:298–314.

Gummesson, E. (1999), *Total relationship marketing, rethinking marketing management: From 4Ps to 30Rs,* Oxford: Butterworth-Heinemann.

Holbrook, M.B. (1999), *Consumer value,* London: Routledge.

Holbrook, M.B. and Hirschman, E.C. (1982), "The experiential aspects of consumption: consumer fantasies, feelings, and fun," *Journal of Consumer Research,* 9, September:132–140.

Howard Hughes Medical Institute. (1995), *Seeing, hearing and smelling the world—new findings help scientists make sense of our senses,* Chevy Chase, Maryland.

Hultén, B. (2011), "Sensory marketing: the multi-sensory brand experience concept." *European Business Review,* 23, 3:256–273.

Hultén, B. (2012), "Sensory cues and shopper's touching behaviour: the case of IKEA," *International Journal of Retail & Distribution Management,* 40, 4:273–289.

Hultén, B., Broweus, N. and van Dijk, M. (2009), *Sensory marketing,* Basingstoke: Palgrave Macmillan.

Hultén, B., Broweus, N. and van Dijk, M. (2011), *Sinnesmarknadsföring* (Sensory Marketing), 2nd ed., Malmö: Liber.

Jensen, R. (1999), *The dream society,* New York: McGraw-Hill.

Kotler, P. (1973), "Atmospherics as a marketing tool," *Journal of Retailing,* 49, 4:48–64.

Krishna, A. (2011), "An integrative review of sensory marketing: engaging the senses to affect perception, judgment and behaviour," *Journal of Consumer Psychology,* 22, 3:332–351.

Krishna, A. (2013), *Customer sense,* Basingstoke: Palgrave Macmillan.

Krishna, A. and Schwarz, N. (2014), "Sensory marketing: embodiment, and grounded cognition: a review and introduction," *Journal of Consumer Psychology,* 24, 2:159–168.

Lindström, M. (2005), *Brand sense*, New York: Free Press.
Meyer, C. and Schwager, A. (2007), "Understanding customer experience," *Harvard Business Review*, February:117–126.
Morgan, G. (1992), "Marketing discourse and practice: towards a critical analysis." I: Alvesson, M. and Willmott, H. (ed.) *Critical management studies*, London: SAGE Publications, p. 136–158.
Morris, R.T. (1941), *The theory of consumer's demand*, New Haven, CT: Yale University Press.
Normann, R. (2001), *Reframing business—when the map changes the landscape*, Chichester: Wiley & Son.
Payne, A., Storbacka, K., Frow, P. and Knox, S. (2009), "Co-creating brands: diagnosing and designing the relationship experience," *Journal of Business Research*, 62:379–389.
Pine, B.J. and Gilmore J.H. (1999), *The experience economy: work is theatre and every business a stage*, Boston: Harvard Business School Press.
Prahalad, C.K. and Ramaswamy, V. (2004), *The future of competition*, Boston: Harvard Business School Press.
Ries, A. and Trout, J. (1982), *Positioning: the battle for your mind*, New York: Warner Books, Inc.
Schmitt, B. (1999), "Experiential marketing," *Journal of Marketing Management*, 15:53–67.
Schmitt, B. (2012), "The consumer psychology of brands," *Journal of Consumer Psychology*, 22:7–17.
Schmitt, B. and Simonson, A. (1997), *Marketing aesthetics—the strategic management of brands, identity, and image*, New York: The Free Press.
Schulze, G. (1992), *Die Erlebnisgesellschaft: Kultursoziologie der Gegenwart [The Experience Society: Present Times of Culturesociology]*, Frankfurt am Main: Campus Verlag.
Spence, C., Puccinelli, N.M., Grewal, D. and Roggeveen, A.L. (2014), "Store atmospherics: a multisensory perspective," *Psychology and Marketing*, 31, 7:472–488.
Vargo, S. and Lusch, R. (2004), "Evolving to a new dominant logic in marketing," *Journal of Marketing*, 68, 1:1–17.
Woodruff, R.B., and Gardial, S. (1996), *Know your customers—new approaches to understanding customer value and satisfaction*. Oxford: Blackwell.

4 The Brain and the Five Senses

This chapter analyzes and discusses the human brain as the center for the five senses. The notions that have emerged about the organization and structure of the brain, as well as the role of the senses in the brain are covered in depth, based on the research and literature.

Furthermore, different memory systems and their significance for individual's learning, perception, and attention are presented. In this context, concepts such as emotions, rationales, habits, and impulsiveness are discussed. In addition, the differences between a male and a female brain are addressed in terms of organizational, emotional, and sensory differences. The emergence of neuromarketing as a research area is discussed, and its relevance to marketers is highlighted.

EXPERIENCE-BASED CONSUMPTION

Consumer Experiences and Consumer Value

In everyday conversations, consumption as a concept refers to an individual's consumption of goods and services, but in a marketing context, consumption has gained a wider and deeper meaning. Various activities are required in connection with the consumption of goods, services, or products for an individual to be happy and satisfied with his/her choice of brand. Here, a product is defined as a product that consists of either a good or a service or a combination of both in the same customer offering.

The product's use, function, and manageability are the basis of consumer experiences and consumer values that an individual obtains through his/her consumption. These experiences form the basis of what has come to be called the consumer experience or experience-based marketing, where companies develop and offer experiences of the brand to the consumers. This puts the brand experience into focus, which Brakus et al. (2009, pp. 52–68, op. cit.) defined as follows:

subjective, internal consumer responses (sensations, feelings and cognitions) and behavioral responses evoked by brand-related stimuli that are part of a brand's design, identity, packaging, communications and environment.

In sensory marketing, therefore, the focus with regard to experience-based consumption is the importance of creating memorable and positive consumer experiences of products and services. For many companies, it is no longer enough to simply develop marketing strategies, taking into account factors such as price and quality; rather, they need to consider how these are linked to the entire brand experience that will be perceived by consumers. Nowadays, it is generally accepted that the vast majority of individuals, particularly those in the X, Y, and Z generations, increasingly look for sensory experiences as discussed earlier.

Experience-based consumption can be defined as "An individual's consumption of goods, services, or products, where the experiences of these lay the foundation for the brand experience, which in turn is based on dreams, fantasies, feelings, and becoming physically and psychologically stimulated on a personal level." Then consumption is strongly related to individualization as a lifestyle (Hultén, 2011), where factors such as identity creation, self-fulfillment, and sensory experiences play a crucial role in how the brand is perceived, as the following example illustrates:

> *A Swedish teenager expressed that personal decision-making in itself was an experience in connection with shopping: "I feel good by doing shopping, mostly clothes, bags, and shoes. I get an incredible kick from deciding myself that 'I'll get this brand' and go to the checkout to pay. I often buy things I don't need, which I might just use once."*

In this context, five different types of experiences have been suggested in marketing, namely, sensory experiences, emotional experiences, creative thinking experiences, physical experiences, and experiences of social identity, which aim to create enjoyable and memorable experiences of consumption. These experiences can lead to an individual changing his/her behavior on a deeper level. An example of this is spiritual tourism, where a spiritual experience can lead to changes in an individual's behavior and lifestyle in his/her daily life. The actual change in behavior and lifestyle is the real experience for the individual.

Accordingly, the experience for the individual is about experiencing something fun and enjoying it, which is the basis for experience-based consumption. Providing consumers with sensory experiences can also lead to the creation of consumer values, which lead to engagement and long-term relations to the brand. In addition to these, consumption-based experiences are also things that are not directly linked to consumption in the form of either product experience—which may relate to the physical interaction in the buying process to investigate a brand—or the shopping experience in a retail store—which may relate to the physical or mental interaction with the service environment and its personnel.

The Holistic Nature of Perception

What distinguishes experience-based consumption from the traditional satisfaction of needs is the importance of the individual's perceptions and experiences with respect to his/her feelings, thoughts, and behaviors. This points to the need for physical and mental stimulation, which is something that both TM and RM have traditionally disregarded. The very fact that perceptions and experiences are related to both aesthetic factors, such as experiencing something with the help of emotions, and rational factors, such as experiencing something with the help of thoughts, has placed increasing demands on marketers when it comes to responding to consumers in the most personal way as possible.

The image of a brand that is created in an individual is based on the mental image or concept that the individual experiences during the purchase and consumption of the goods, services, or products. In this context, the brand is thought to be an image from a consumer perspective, as opposed to just being seen as a name on a product, such as a brand from a manufacturer's perspective. The individual's feelings and thoughts about the good, service, or product help to create the mental image or concept in the brain (or mind), which is the same as the brand image.

The ability of an individual to interpret and understand a brand is influenced by the individual's perception ability. The interpretation takes place through a perception process, where the individual is susceptible to various stimuli, which are interpreted and translated into a response. The holistic nature of perception is central to Gestalt psychology, where an important starting point is that the whole—or Gestalt—is greater than the sum of its parts.

> *"Ikea is often used as a model when it comes to creating an overall experience of the dwelling, where lighting, design, colors, and textures together create a kitchen or a bedroom."*

It has been argued that an individual's actions and experiences can be said to be characterized by organized Gestalt figures or holistic objects, where the parts cannot be seen in isolation from each other. Rather, it is assumed that the relations between the parts together create the figure, which is of greater importance than each of the parts individually. It is further assumed that these objects (Gestalt figures) are based on balance, simplicity, and good design and are divided into the background and the object, which indicates that relations between the elements rather than the elements themselves are relevant to form the Gestalt.

The holistic perspective—through the figure—is therefore crucial in order to be able to understand the meaning of experience-based consumption for an individual. Different aesthetic and rational elements together form the overall experience that an individual strives after, and the human's five senses contribute to this. In this way, perception, through the senses of sight, hearing, smell, taste, and touch, contributes so that the Gestalt figure plays a crucial role in the individual's perceptions and experiences.

In this context, the human brain (or mind) and what is colloquially called the black box has been of interest to marketers when it comes to how an individual, such as a man or woman, perceives and experiences the different buying and consumption processes. The technological developments have led to better opportunities to understand what happens in a human brain when it is exposed to different stimuli, which will be discussed at the end of the chapter through the concept of neuromarketing.

THE ORGANIZATION AND STRUCTURE OF THE BRAIN

Conscious and Unconscious Processes

One of the fundamental starting points in order to be able to understand how an individual handles stimuli, as input, in connection with marketing and consumption is to start with the human's five senses. It is through the five senses that the human brain processes the sensory information that is obtained by the various stimuli, either unconsciously or consciously. The feedback created in the brain can be seen as an individual's response to the stimuli that is created within our so-called black box.

The most important observation among brain scientists is that the brain works with both unconscious and conscious processes. One of the most common explanations for the unconscious processes is that "we cannot think of how we think, because we are not aware of the thoughts that we think of" (Pradeep, 2010, p. 4). This is because most of the work that a human brain does takes place in the unconscious processes beyond our human consciousness.

A person's five senses are thought to receive 11 million bits of information every second, most of which come in through the eyes. But even the other senses, such as smell, sound, taste, and touch, as well as spatial sensations, contribute significant information. The conscious processes, which deal with the part of the thinking where we are aware of what we are thinking, can only deal with about 40 pieces of information every second. The rest of the information is processed by the unconscious processes, which then correspond to more than 99.99 percent of all the information.

For marketers, this means that most of the information that is sent out does not actually get received by the human brain in a conscious way. Rather, they become unconscious processes that are crucial to how a product or brand is perceived and experienced by an individual. This points to the importance of understanding the brain's organization and structure and thus how human's five senses are important for a brand experience.

Some researchers assert that conscious processes shall be defined as immediate experiences of feelings and sensations (Gazzaniga et al., 2009). A person's experience is based on an experiencing self, which is a characteristic of conscious experiences, and it is considered to exist in an intimate relationship between awareness, on the one hand, and consciousness on the other. It is a common notion that when a person notices something, such as an advertisement or a brand, he/she is also aware of the advertisement or brand consciously, which makes it possible for some of the special traits or characteristics to be distinguished.

For a human being, the ability to be aware of something is critical for survival and provides the ability to understand what is happening in the environment. It also increases the understanding of a person's internal processes and can create awareness of how things are perceived as well as what feelings are present.

> "Every morning when we get dressed and wonder what we will eat during the day, a journey starts in the brain, where every action, word, or symbol has a code that the brain unconsciously helps so that the trip can be carried out."

But most of the processes that occur in the human brain are actually unconscious and can be localized to the right hemisphere of the brain. These processes are characterized in a way that an individual is not aware of or notices what is going on. This is the case when the pupils dilate to let in the light or when the light is converted to nerve signals and travels to the visual center of the brain via the eye lens and the optical nerve. Similarly, reflexes also occur that a person is not aware of or notices.

The unconscious processes can be viewed as difficult for an individual, because they affect and control a person's behavior and actions in different ways. But for most individuals, it is not possible to understand or explain these processes without deeper contact with the subconscious taking place. It is a very powerful process that affects human behavior in different ways and at the same time helps to shape and develop the domain of consciousness.

Researchers such as Rapaille (2006) believe that every culture with its rituals, customs, and traditions creates a mind-set that unconsciously teaches a person who she/he is. This is known as cultural unawareness, which can be considered to be related to cultural differences and is expressed, for example, by an American, an English, or a Swedish cultural unawareness. It results in that every culture gets its own patterns of behavior and thought, which at a deeper level molds a person to the specific culture that he/she has as a reference and starting point for "normal" behavior and thought. In this way, the unconscious processes are considered to be the basis for the development of personality traits and creativity.

The Triune Brain

A human brain is the basis of all consumer behavior, and the functions that must be performed each day are taken care of by the individual's brain in a completely unconscious way. The whole brain represents only 2 percent of the body mass, but it burns 20 percent of all the energy consumed. Furthermore, only about 20 percent of the energy is consumed in a conscious way in connection with the daily functions that must be performed in a human brain. The remaining 80 percent of the energy goes to keeping the brain in its resting state, a relationship that still mystifies brain researchers.

In the brain, there are a large number of complex neural networks, which are connected in an incredibly complicated and sophisticated way. It is precisely the many interconnections between the different parts or neural networks in the brain that allow us to go shopping, decide on a brand, or chew gum. The human brain can be more easily understood if it is considered as a system, where different regions or structures cooperate to work together so that a desired behavior occurs in an individual (Figure 4.1).

The human brain has become known as the *triune brain*, which is divided into three different types of brains. The three brains are the *cerebrum* (*primate* or *cerebral cortex*), the *limbic system* (*mammal*), and the *reptilian brain* (*reptile*), which together create the foundation of the brain's organization

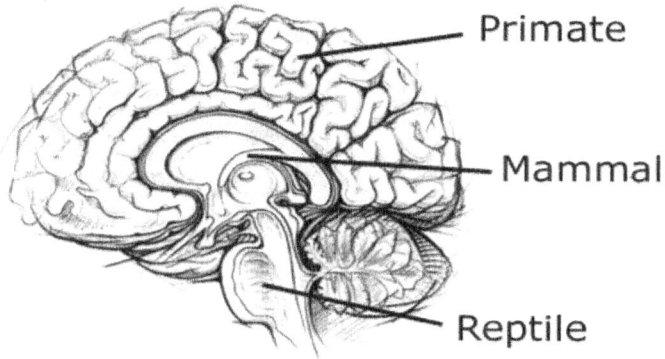

Figure 4.1 Brain Areas and Structures

and structure. We will now discuss and describe how experience-based consumption and brand experiences can be related to the brain as a center of experience in terms of its organization and structure.

The Cerebrum

The biggest part of the human brain is the cerebrum, which is evident from the name. Another name is the *cerebral cortex*, which consists of two different hemispheres or halves of the brain. These are often referred to in every day speech as the right and left hemisphere, which are united by the corpus callosum. It should also be mentioned that each hemisphere is divided into four different lobes called the parietal lobe, occipital lobe, frontal lobe, and the temporal lobe.

The outermost layer of the cerebrum, called the cerebral cortex, is considered to be the dominant part of the brain. It is only a few millimeters thick and covered by nerve fibers in several different layers. The surface of the cerebral cortex is folded so that there is room to fit as much cerebral cortex as possible. If the surface were smooth instead, then it would require a larger human head, because the folded surface allows for one-third more surface area. It is believed that another advantage with a folded surface is that it allows for communication processes in the brain to occur more quickly, because the nerve cells are located closer to each other.

Ingvar (2007) believes that a person's consciousness is in the cerebral cortex, and he expresses it as "knowledge and beliefs about ourselves and the world." Other scholars claim that the consciousness in the brain can be seen as a *global workspace*, consisting of a fast memory capacity, with the content distributed and dispersed to various specialized networks or unconscious processes.

In the cerebrum, there are several relatively independent areas and structures, which communicate both among themselves and with each other. Furthermore, the cerebrum is responsible for the intellectual functions that primarily distinguish humans from animals in the form of learning, memory, language, thinking, and perception. Communication takes place using different association pathways, where each area is, in principle, directly linked to a corresponding area in the other half of the brain. In this way, the right and left brain communicate with each other even though they are believed to contain different functions.

The Left and Right Brain Hemispheres

Visually, the two hemispheres are the same size and look symmetrical, but despite that there are significant functional differences. Most of all, the hemispheres are focused on doing different things, and the left brain is often regarded as dry and boring, whereas the right hemisphere is regarded as artistic and creative. Some of the key features of the left and right brain are shown in Figure 4.2.

A common understanding is that the left hemisphere is the dominant of the two. It has a linguistic focus and is often called the verbal hemisphere, but it is also responsible for logic and mathematical calculations. In this context, it should be mentioned that a linguistic specialization is regarded as having to do with whether an individual is right- or left-handed, where left-handers are generally associated with a lower specialization than the right-handers.

Unlike the left hemisphere, the right hemisphere focuses on managing emotions and is regarded as being superior when it comes to recognizing faces and interpreting various facial expressions. Research also shows that the right hemisphere is more sensitive and does not like to take risks, at the same time as being dominated by spatial perception and visual impressions.

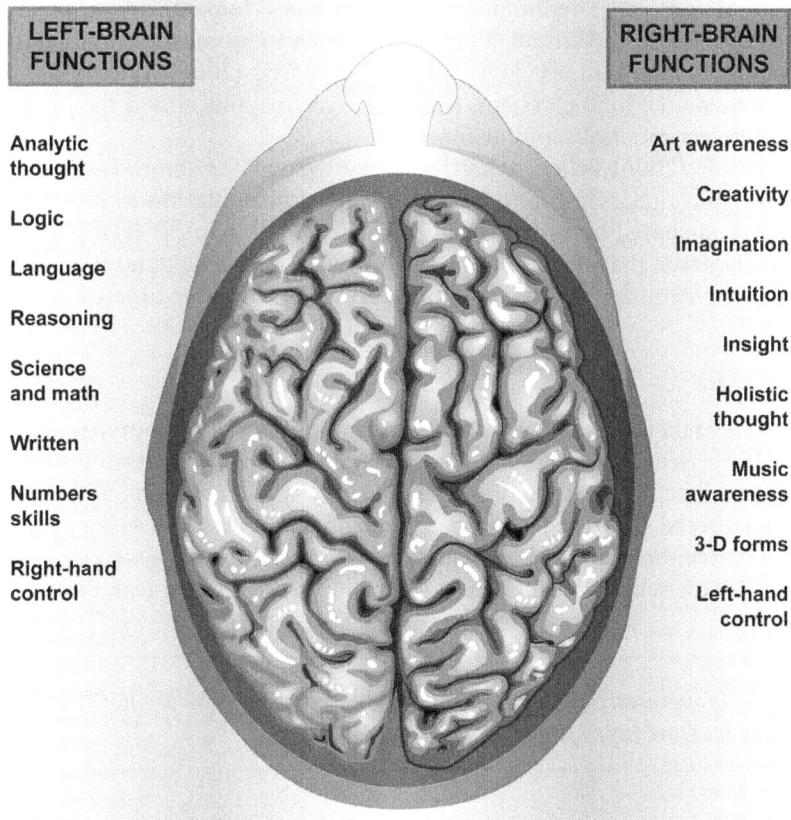

Figure 4.2 Left and Right Cerebral Hemispheres
Source: Shutterstock

Furthermore, it should be said that it is the corpus callosum that connects the two hemispheres via a large number of nerve fibers and provides opportunities for communication and collaboration between the two hemispheres. It is widely accepted that there exists functional differences, while at the same time the two hemispheres complement each other. In complex and compound tasks, both hemispheres of the brain are active and contribute with their respective specialties.

The Limbic System

This system serves as the prime location for a person's emotions, which is thought to be localized to the parts that are called the *hippocampus, amygdala,* and *hypothalamus.* Furthermore, the system is viewed as an internal border to the cerebral cortex and is also considered to be the interface for a person's reptilian brain, which I will return to.

The limbic system also has an important role for our learning, motivation, and memory. The limbic system determines, for example, which sensory expressions and stimuli a person will react to by constantly comparing new impressions with previous experiences. Martin (2008) states that if one understands the limbic system, then it is easier to understand the relationship between emotions and memory.

Rapaille (2006) believes that the limbic system's structure is influenced by the child's relationship to the mother from birth and up to four or five years of age based on the love and the warmth found in the relationship. It is also believed that the limbic system plays a critical role in how a person's emotions, learning, memory, and motivation develop over time.

Amygdala

The amygdala is a key region in the human brain for different types of emotional experiences and is found in the anterior and middle parts of the brain's temporal lobe. Its name comes from the Greek and means almond kernel. It should also be said that it is in the amygdala that a person's sensory expressions derive their emotional nuances and tone. Different nerve cell groups provide experiences that build on, for example, aggression, fear, or anxiety.

> "The brain researcher Antonio Damaso has expressed: 'We are not thinking machines that feel, we are feeling machines that think.'"

Furthermore, this region is connected to other regions or structures in the brain, such as the hippocampus. This specific connection means that an individual is thought to have the ability to save and remember different events and experiences on the emotional level. It is also easier for an individual to remember emotional events in comparison with neutral events, regardless of whether it is a positive or negative emotion.

It should also be said that there are very strong links with the other regions of the brain, such as the hypothalamus and the brain stem, in order for this structure to be able to express drives as well as emotions and affect behavioral responses.

Hippocampus

The hippocampus as a subsystem and a structure plays a crucial role in the individual's learning and memory. It is also called the seahorse, primarily because of its shape, and is found in the temporal lobe in one of the fluid-filled cavities of the brain.

For many years, the hippocampus has been linked with a person's memory, and brain imaging studies have shown that it contributes to both the recall of memory images and the encoding of information. This is achieved through interactions in the brain's association areas, that is, the place in the cerebral cortex where the memories are stored more permanently.

Hypothalamus

The hypothalamus is believed to be the area and structure that has as its primary fundamental task the control and management a person's vital functions, such as breathing, blood pressure, heartbeat, hunger, body temperature, sexual behavior, and thirst. This area is localized in the individual's middle brain where hormones are also formed by the nerve cells, which affect the organs in the body or are secreted directly into the blood.

It is also thought that this structure is involved in various emotional processes. Furthermore, there are different mechanisms in this structure that can influence and control a person's behavior regarding attack or escape.

The Reptile Brain

The reptile brain is a collective term for the cerebellum and the brain stem. The name derives from the fact that this part of the human brain has similarities with a reptilian brain. The most important functions of the *cerebellum* are to be responsible for a person's survival and reproduction. Because these two functions are essential for a human to continue to live, it is deemed that this part of the reptilian brain has the greatest influence on behavior and development.

Furthermore, the reptilian brain is thought to be the result of millions of years of evolutionary development and has as its main focus the task of processing visual stimuli to be able to handle threats in one's surroundings. The reptile brain prefers pictures before words and experiences before explanations, which makes it extremely selfish and egotistical in its nature.

Rapaille (2006) also believes that the reptilian brain expresses a person's instincts. In a battle between emotion, logic, and instinct, it is the reptilian brain that wins in the human brain. Especially in the case of an individual's relationships, well-being, and decisions concerning consumption. This is explained by the culture's influence on a person, which is considered to be part of the reptilian brain, where the culture can be seen as a glue for survival, which people inherit from one generation to another (ibid.)

The Cerebellum

The cerebellum is believed to be the region and structure for a person's movement coordination, where a network of information from the motion of the body's organs, such as joints and muscles, ensures that the muscles are used as the cerebrum wishes. The cerebellum, therefore, is an important part of a person's motor system and receives information from the skin, inner organs, or different motor organs, to name a few common examples.

This part of the reptilian brain is also called the *cerebellum*, which means the small brain. It is characterized by a substantial structure of nerves located above the brain stem. Furthermore, it should be said that the cerebellum is composed of cells and is estimated to have billions of nerves, which correspond to what the rest of a person's nervous system has all together. The cerebellum structure and appearance is often compared to a piece of cauliflower or broccoli, which is explained by the surface layer being thin and folded together into a packed mass.

Generally, the cerebellum is thought to be crucial to a person's posture when you go and perform movements, which require coordination. It is further believed that the cerebellum collaborates with the body's balance organs, which affect the entire interaction between a person's movements.

The Brain Stem

The brain stem is regarded as the extension upward of a human spine and is seen as a stalk, where both the cerebrum's right and left hemispheres as well as the cerebellum grow. This regulates and governs some of the individual's most vital reflexes, for example, that we stay conscious as well as the regulation of our body temperature. Even the control and regulation of the blood pressure and heart rate are some of the brain stem's prominent functions.

THE SENSES IN THE BRAIN

Perception and Sensory Impressions

The five senses—sight, hearing, smell, touch, and taste—as sensory inputs are the sources for a person's experiences, affections, cognitions, and behaviors.

In addition to the five senses, it is also believed that a person has a sense of pain, a sense of hot and cold, a sense of acceleration and weight, to name a few common examples. Furthermore, each of the five senses is composed of clearly separated components when it comes to treating various sensory impressions, for example, the sense of sight can distinguish shape, color, and motion as contrasts to brightness and structures.

> *"In comparison with animals, humans have weak senses. A person can hear sounds up to 20 kHz, less than a bat, which can hear sounds with ultrasonic frequencies."*

The brain analyzes various sensory inputs, which are then converted into perceptions that form the basis of a person's decision about how to act in a certain situation. It is thought that a human being can perceive the same sensory input in several different ways; however, at the same time, a sensory impression is only part of what a person becomes aware of or perceives. This means that a human can perceive something in particular, but without actually getting any sensory input.

The sensory input that a person gets is not always linked to the perception that a person has. Rather, a perception can be the same as the brain's educated guess about what one or more of the senses are trying to communicate via the different sensory inputs. It is also believed that the senses interact with each other in regard to their different sensory capabilities.

It is, therefore, important to distinguish between perception and sensory input, because perceptions can occur in more than one way, as several senses often interact together. The sensory organs that transmit sensory input give the brain the opportunity to perceive the same sensory input in more ways than one. It must be added that the brain is very selective when it comes to weeding out those sensory inputs that a person perceives.

In addition to sensory inputs, a person uses sensations inside the body, which generally one is not aware of. Different sensations tell the brain what the situation is with blood pressure, hunger, temperature, or thirst but also describe the location of the arms and legs, etc.

Most people are only aware of a very small portion of all the daily sensations that in different ways regulate their movements in their daily lives.

The Process of Perception

Within the framework of the psychological processes that an individual uses to interpret the different sensory inputs, cognition and perception are the most active in the brain. These two areas are not completely separated but overlap each other in some respect. In the area of cognition, the various brain functions relating to learning, consciousness, memory, language, thinking, and alertness as well as decision-making and problem solving are studied.

Cognition is a psychological term that includes the mental processes, often voluntary, which deal with information, knowledge, and thinking. In classical psychology, cognition, emotion, and volition, which are equivalent to thinking, feeling, and will, are deemed to be the three concepts that govern a person's mind or psyche.

It is believed that the mind's perception and interpretation are based on the experience and knowledge an individual has acquired, which then is a part of cognition, whereas others are contained within perception, which have to do with the sensory inputs, to be discussed in more detail now.

A person is affected by the various stimuli through the five senses; thereby, sensory information from the environment can form the basis in the final selection of a product. These stimuli are regarded as sensory input and are stored in the human brain. But it is only a small portion of all the stimuli in the environment that an individual notices and is aware of.

This means that each individual interprets and experiences different stimuli based on his/her own needs and experiences in a completely subjective manner, which is what the perception process is all about. Perception is the process by which different stimuli are received, organized, and interpreted through the five senses, which generate different types of responses in an individual (Solomon et al. 2010) (Figure 4.3). The information that an individual receives, using the five senses, determines the type of response that occurs for a particular product or service.

An individual's interpretations of various sensory stimuli are based on the attitudes and feelings that are on the individual level, where the expectations as well as the experiences play a major role in the choice of the final product in the form of a response.

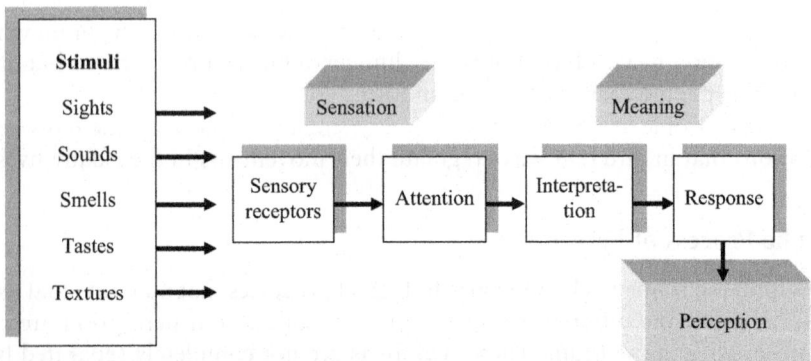

Figure 4.3 The Perceptual Process (Solomon et al., 2010)

The Spatial Location

When it comes to the location of the senses in the brain, it is thought that the cerebrum consists of three main parts, which are interconnected and hierarchically arranged so that the forebrain controls the midbrain, which in turn affects the hindbrain. When it comes to sensory inputs, vision and hearing address these first in the midbrain and then send them on to the other parts of the cerebrum, which can be said to function as a kind of leadership center for the entire human body. In the cerebrum, all the sensory information from the senses are handled, which together with the previous experiences lay the foundation for the cerebrum's assessment and decision. Figure 4.4 presents the spatial location of the senses in the human brain.

The cerebellum, which is the most distinctive part of the hindbrain, receives and handles a variety of sensory signals, especially the motor ones. This means that the cerebellum ensures that a person keeps his/her balance, stores memories of executed movements (e.g., bicycling), and coordinates the various muscle groups to achieve optimal movement patterns. In this manner, the practiced motion programs can be performed and also corrected as necessary.

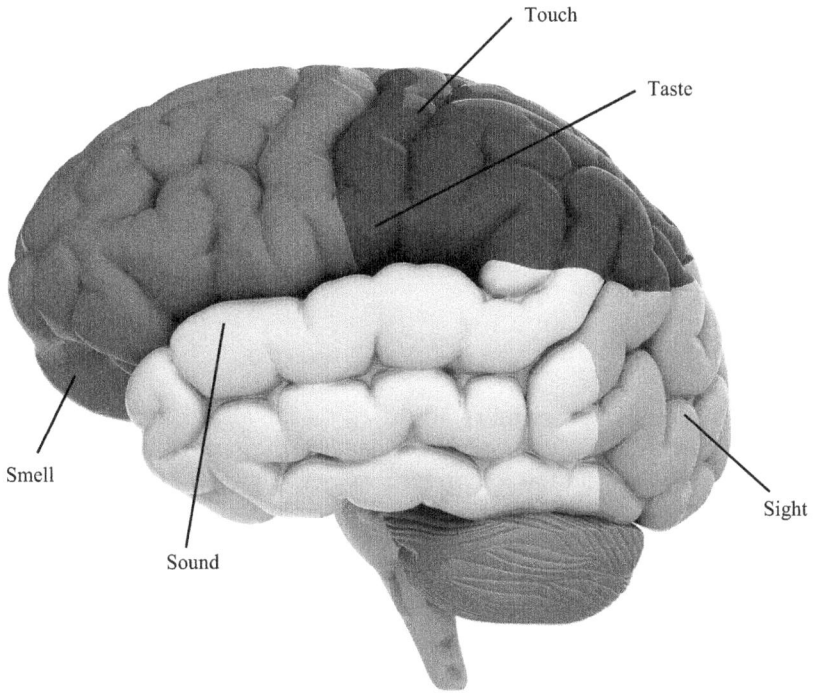

Figure 4.4 The Location of the Senses in the Human Brain
Source: Shutterstock

In the cerebral cortex, which is the cerebrum's outermost layer, important transformation of sensory information and sensory inputs take place in each person. There, the sensory information from the five senses is screened and becomes conscious perceptions, which then lead to conscious behavior and actions.

It should be noted that in terms of sensory signals, in relation to the right and left brain hemispheres, signals are processed from the left side of the right brain and vice versa. It is generally considered that both the hemispheres are aware of the outside world, but the right hemisphere does not put into words the perceptions, but rather, it is done with the help of the left hemisphere.

Regarding the cortex, it is divided into different areas by function, and the most fundamental difference exists between the motor and sensory areas. In terms of the latter, it is more common to start from the specific type of sensory information the areas receive from a particular sensory organ or a certain type of tissue. The visual inputs are transmitted through the eyes to the primary visual cortex, which is found at the back of the occipital lobe. The so-called somatosensory information, which comes from the body and the skin, is transmitted to an area called the sensory cortex, located in the parietal lobe.

These sensory areas of the cerebral cortex synthesize a form of pictures, maps, or spatial counterparts based on the sensations that are sent through the various sensory organs. For example, a map of the sensory inputs from the outside world is based on how the optic nerve, through an image on the retina, sends a "map" to the primary visual cortex.

This map is "redrawn" several times in the cerebral cortex using various subdivisions, each of which interpret and perceive a particular aspect of the visual impression. When it comes to the maps, these are not to scale; however, they are based on how big a certain sensory organ or a particular muscle group is, which affects the size of the actual spatial area in the cerebral cortex.

THE HUMAN MEMORY

Most theories on human memory are based on the idea that our memory consists of three different components, namely, the *sensory memory*, the *short-term memory*, and the *long-term memory* (Figure 4.5). Among psychologists, there is no consensus that memory consists of these three components, but this notion has come to be regarded as one of the most important models of the human memory. It has also become common to use this model when it comes to describing and explaining how an individual receives and processes information.

It is generally accepted that these three types of memory systems are necessary for us when it comes to processing, storing, and accessing information, taking into account the motivations, goals, and desires an individual has in connection with the various buying and consumption processes.

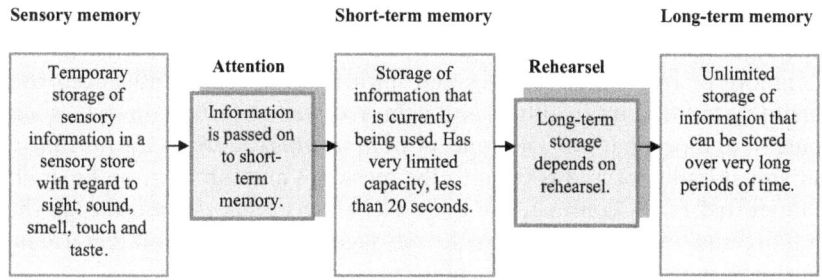

Figure 4.5 The Brain's Memory System (Jansson-Boyd, 2010)

The Sensory Memory

As the name suggests, the sensory memory stores information from the five senses, namely, sight, sound, smell, touch and taste, but for a very short time. While the senses are stimulated, the information remains present, and an individual saves this for further analysis of the most important parts. It must be said that human vision or hearing is not nearly as sharp as other animal species, which limits the ability to assimilate sensory information.

As an example, it can be mentioned that the visual information is lost within half a second, whereas the audio information lasts for two seconds. If this information is viewed as being interesting and important for the individual to process further, it is sent on to the short-term memory.

The senses also have some limitations when it comes to receiving all the sensory information that an individual encounters on a daily basis. A factor such as the *absolute sensory threshold* means that if a message is below our sensory threshold, then it is possible that it is not perceived consciously but only unconsciously. Furthermore, there is sensory discrimination, as a variant of sensory thresholds, which is about whether it is possible for an individual to detect differences between similar sensory information.

It has been shown that in taste tests, respondents found it difficult to identify a particular brand of chocolate in a blind test, although they described the taste before the test. Most of them believed that the chocolate they tasted was the same kind as the one they stated in advance. But that was not the case, which points to the importance of advertisements, packaging design, or the brand image and not just the taste for the sensory perception of a brand.

> "An individual who walks through a mall is exposed to a bombardment of various stimuli. But then there is a sound coming from a store, which captures the person's attention for a second or two. This leads to further processing."

There is a general perception that some individuals allow some messages and some information to get into the sensory memory, whereas others ignore or reject the messages and information. This is influenced by a person's attitudes, motivations, and values as well as his/her lifestyle, social context, and occupation. The concept of *perceptual alertness* means that an individual looks for and is open to the messages and information he or she is interested in. In contrast, the concept of *perceptual defense* means that an individual ignores or neglects the messages and information that are not consistent with his/her attitudes, lifestyle, and personality.

The sensory memory activates and processes the information that is presented to an individual through the five senses. In this context, it should be said that various events and experiences that are deemed to be emotionally engaging and stimulating are stored and processed in this memory. These memory images, in turn, affect how an individual reacts to new stimuli and the experiences they provide at a later date.

Short-Term or Working Memory

The information that is processed in the sensory memory and is relevant to an individual is then forwarded to the short-term memory. This is also called the working memory and stores, for example, data on someone whom we have just spoken to or a phone number that we have just gotten from someone. The function of the working memory can be said to be simple but very fundamental for a person's ability to solve various mental tasks.

This can involve everything from controlling one's attention to solving a logical, complex problem. When we play chess, we retain visual information in the working memory: "If I move the castle there, he will take the pawn with his horse." The working memory is needed for visual simulations and to remember the right moves.

One of the working memory's most important characteristics, in addition to remembering letters, instructions, or numbers, is to solve complex cognitive tasks, such as learning, logical thinking, and reading comprehension. In this way, the working memory is important for an individual's ability to solve problems by being able to retain and manipulate verbal or visual information and at the same time remember instructions, as well as control attention to a task.

The working memory, therefore, can store both verbal and visual information for longer periods of time, from seconds to minutes, and takes care of the information that is currently being processed by an individual. The capacity available for storage is completely individual and different from individual to individual. The working memory also has a limited storage capacity, however, not as limited as in the sensory memory. It is also this characteristic that differentiates the working memory from the long-term memory, which we will return to.

It is generally accepted in research that short-term memory is responsible for the temporary storage of information and stimuli. The memory is also regarded as an explicit memory, where an individual in a conscious way can produce data for a specific purpose, such as a name or phone number. It has been shown that the memory has the capacity to store more information if it is grouped into meaningful units, which are called chunks.

Another characteristic of short-term memory is that it can usually remember information that was presented at the beginning or end much better. This has come to be called serial position effect, and means that the first words of certain information are easier to remember because they have already entered into the long-term memory. One implication for marketers is that in the advertising context, the information that customers will remember should be presented either first or last in a message.

Long-Term Memory

This memory does not have a limited storage capacity—unlike the sensory memory and the working memory—but is seen as being infinite. As soon as our memories in the form of experiences have reached the long-term memory, they are permanently stored there.

> *"You use long-term memory when you park your car outside the mall to remember where it is parked when you come back. You use working memory to allow you to remember what to buy when you go inside."*

The memory also allows us to remember facts that cannot be linked to a specific learning opportunity, such as the meaning of a word or the name of the Moroccan capital. The term for the memory for activities or events is *episodic memory* and the memory for facts is termed *semantic long-term memory*. Among consumer researchers and practitioners, the difference between an episodic and semantic memory is thought to be of importance. This is emphasized frequently in advertisements and commercials that try to trigger or influence episodic memories by focusing on the experiences that many people share.

The main difference between the long-term memory and the working memory is that in the former, an individual memorizes something and then turns his/her attention to something else for a few minutes, one month, or one year and then recalls the information again. In working memory, however, that something is paid attention to all the time and is the focus of attention.

What determines how something is stored in long-term memory and moved from short-term memory has to do with its significance and meaning for the individual. This is partly about the information or stimulus itself and how these are related to the information that is already in the long-term memory. The more integrated the information in this memory, the easier it seems to be to remember it.

Another characteristic of long-term memory relates to how information is organized. It has been found that when multiple pieces of information are connected with each other, the information is more understandable and easier to remember. One conclusion has been that the pieces of information that are grouped together enhance an individual's memory capability.

Various kinds of stress can both positively and negatively affect a person's memory. During the in-coding phase, negative stress, such as rushing and time constraints, can result in it becoming harder to remember certain things. Furthermore, memory is affected by how stress is perceived, the nature of the stress, as well as how the stress creates an emotional response, which affects our memories and experiences.

It is possible to compare the long-term memory structure with a spider web, where every individually related piece of information in one way or another, directly or indirectly, is linked to the other information that is also stored in the memory. This allows an individual to create what has become known as a cognitive associated network, as the following example shows:

> *The first thing your brain thinks of when you hear the Volvo brand is perhaps "safe, childproof car brand." But if you continue to think of it, maybe you think of the country of Sweden and low consumption, and so on. This forms the basis of an associative mental network.*

It is considered that associations are formed either consciously or unconsciously between information and stimuli in the brain. By thinking of two concepts at the same time, we can form an association between these two, even if they were not related to each other from the beginning. A person's associative mental networks play an important role in what is called the key effect, which means that existing information guides and leads one's judgments about new information that a person comes across.

Attention, Perception, and Learning

In sensory marketing, it is important to create attention around a message or a brand so that an individual can be affected in a deeper, sensory dimension. Most people usually skim through various media, Internet, and television, to try to discover an interesting and exciting brand. There is, therefore, a deliberate search for relevant messages, through what is called the *initial attention*. If the individual encounters a message that is not sufficiently relevant, the search continues and the attention is preserved.

Most of us have *selective attention* in terms of marketing stimuli, and most things pass by us without us knowing. In order for us to notice an interesting and exciting brand, a focused attention to different messages is required. If marketing is to succeed in achieving this, it means that we as individuals will react and use our affective and cognitive resources in the brain to receive the message. Consequently, our minds are engaged, and both the emotional and rational elements of a message are valued and serve as the basis for a possible purchase decision. To create selective attention, various methods and techniques are used, such as color, humor, novelty, and movement.

> *"Most consumers are exposed to about 2,000 advertising messages a day, but in the best case, they will just notice 100 of these."*

It is increasingly important to create a sensory experience of a brand through selective attention, because the advertising noise that exists today makes it almost impossible to reach out with a message that most individuals notice. This means that the question of attention is increasingly important for many companies to enable them to deliver a sensory experience of a brand and compete in the market.

In this context, the human brain, like a black box, controls how a message or a brand is perceived and experienced by an individual. It is through the black box that it is possible to find explanations for consumers' experiences, affections, cognitions, and actual behaviors based on the information coming from the different sensory stimuli in the environment. It is through selective, or focused, attention, that the brain determines what information is to be processed and paid attention to or what information should be disregarded and neglected.

A person's brain, therefore, can be considered as an experience center, where the sensory information is received, processed, and perceived through the five senses. Furthermore, our experiences are stored in the brain as memories of the past experiences we have had of a message or a brand, and even our emotions have their place there and play a crucial role in the purchase and consumption decisions. It is important to know the most important concepts when it comes to understanding how an individual acts and thinks in the different buying and consumption processes if one wants to understand an individual's behavior at a deeper level.

Emotional Behavior

Our emotions and feelings are initiated in the right brain hemisphere and are widely regarded as a subjective experience. This is only feasible for the individual in question, who can experience the emotion that is the basis of the experience. It is widely believed that emotions awaken memories of previously experienced events and that there is an interaction between the currently experienced emotions and the previously experienced emotions. Furthermore, individuals have different emotional experiences with respect to experiences of the same stimuli. It should be added that emotions are also included in various social contexts, which also affect how different emotional stimuli can be perceived and received by an individual.

The right brain hemisphere plays a central role in our emotions and feelings when it comes to processing different types of information and stimuli. This applies to information from one's own body and information from other individuals and their tone of voice, as well as information from the environment. It is thought that dance, art, or music, as stimuli, attract an individual's emotions and feelings, which play a major role in our right brain. The emotional processing of the different types of information and stimuli occurs in the amygdala, where these stimuli are given an emotional meaning. It is believed that this occurs because it is our emotions that are stimulated by our senses on a deeper level, which then send out signals in the brain.

Emotions and feelings can also be thought of as aids when it comes to an individual navigating his/her way through daily life. It is believed that emotions help to evaluate the different situations emotionally, and the emotions tell an individual if the current situation should be perceived as negative or positive, which is what the term valence refers to. Most people, therefore, use emotions when various decisions and alternatives are to be evaluated. In this way, emotions and feelings have a pivotal role and have great influence in the different buying and consumption processes in relation to reason and rationality.

In research, it is generally considered that emotions and feelings can be divided into two dimensions, namely *arousal* and *valence*. It has also been shown that this two-dimensional classification can capture the differences in emotions between the different cultures. In heterogeneous cultures such as Estonia, Greece, Hong Kong, China, and Poland as well as in homogeneous cultures such as India, Japan, Croatia, Norway, Spain, and Vietnam, it has been shown that by examining both the facial expressions and the words, the differences in emotion can be explained thanks to dimensions such as arousal and valence.

> "A feeling of relaxation has the same effect on people's attitudes and assessments regardless of their cultural affiliation."

It turns out that emotions and feelings, in the form of either facial expressions or words, are classified in the same way in different cultures. In this context, both enthusiasm and relaxation contribute to positive valence across cultural boundaries. At the same time that enthusiasm is highly valued in terms of arousal, relaxation is valued lower.

Furthermore, emotions and feelings are thought to have an effect on how attitudes and evaluations are formed in the different contexts, which are based on a transfer of the positive or negative valence that can be associated with the emotions and feelings that arise. Therefore, it is assumed that similar emotions and feelings should have the same impact on the attitudes and evaluations regardless of the culture. It is believed that emotions and feelings play a crucial role for an individual when it comes to clarifying what is worth paying attention to in a message or a brand. For many businesses, therefore, it is about being able to understand and identify the emotional elements that mainly attract and influence the customers. Moreover, it is believed that there is a connection between emotions and learning in that the stronger the emotion is for something, the greater the probability that some form of learning takes place.

In marketing, messages are presented daily based on emotions and feelings, with the primary aim of attracting individuals and putting him/her in a positive state of mind. Among the most common manifestations of this include joy, humor, sex, beautiful people, or a surprise, and they are used to create an experience of a message or a brand (Söderlund, 2003). It has also been asserted that how an individual is affected by his/her emotions and feelings has to do with age, and it is assumed that the greater an individual's life experience and the older he or she is, the less likely that a message or a brand will influence him/her.

Emotions are very important in marketing and have proven to be able to explain an individual's behavior and the loyalty that many individuals show toward a certain brand. Furthermore, it has been shown that emotions and feelings can be connected to both positive and negative experiences. It has also been found that a person's mood affects emotions and feelings; similarly, the context in which a person finds him/herself can give rise to different emotional states.

> *"The more positive emotions that are created around a message or a brand, the more attention it gives rise to among consumers."*

Among researchers, there is a common belief that greater attention is created around a message or a brand by using positive emotions. Furthermore, it is believed that people who are in a good mood find it much easier to make a positive connection to the information and stimuli they encounter daily. There is the perception among researchers that thoughtful arguments, to a lesser extent, determine what an individual reacts to regarding the type of stimuli; however, it is about an emotional encoding.

It is believed that this occurs because it is the brain's emotional part, the right brain, which determines whether the emotions experienced are real or not. Especially considering that these emotions and feelings are based on past experiences and events, which are then perceived as either positive or negative.

In marketing, it is common that emotions and feelings can be created in an individual by means of a smiling store employee or a laughing celebrity in a TV commercial. Those feelings that others express can have a strong impact on an individual's feelings for a message or a brand. It is further assumed that more positive emotions are created with the help of a smiling face in comparison with a non-smiling face, which should be considered when you want to create an experience of a company and its brand.

As nonverbal communication, joy is seen as an important stimulus in the message and the brand. It takes no more than one hundredth of a second for a human to note if someone smiles, which may explain the existence of smiling faces in many advertising messages. Furthermore, the relationship between the emotions and memory can explain why an individual responds to superficial stimuli, because these can be related to previous memories, which in turn give rise to the emotions and feelings that are induced.

Finally, it should be mentioned that researchers such as Söderlund (2003) believe that emotionally charged marketing helps to create the effects that ultimately mean that an individual purchases the product, resulting in positive emotions and feelings. For this reason, emotionally charged messages have become a natural part in the advertising of different brands.

It is further assumed that the emotional elements play a crucial role in a multi-sensory brand-experience, where the emotional content can also be conveyed through a brand's identity and values in addition to more traditional elements. But such a brand experience is also about reason and being rational in order to satisfy an individual on a deeper level.

Rational Behavior

Rational thinking occurs in a person's left brain, as opposed to the emotions and feelings that arise in the right brain. Logic and rationality have long been considered as being characteristic of knowledge or, as it is has also been expressed, *cold cognition*, unlike the warm feelings. This information is processed by the individual who will make a purchasing decision regarding the uncertainties or risks that may exist.

> *"Cold cognition is commonly regarded as logical and rational related to the purchase, but it is the opposite of warm feelings."*

For centuries, people have analyzed and penetrated the question of how our thoughts are formed and tried to discover how logical reasoning arises. It is argued that structure completely gives rise to logical arguments and that it is about an individual creating a theory that is logical, whose arguments are based on a structure that supports the truth. In this context, it is also argued that logic is based on inductive reasoning, probabilities, or statistics, which then does not take into account the individual emotional states, such as self-interest or joy (Gazzaniga et al., 2009).

A common definition of rationality involves the ability to reason rationally and being able to draw well-thought-out conclusions. It is further intended that a rational decision made by an individual is often about choosing the best alternative over another alternative. However, it is pointed out that a number of variables influence rational decisions depending on the specific situation and the kind of situation the individual finds him/herself in.

In marketing, communications about a brand contain significant rational elements, which are considered to have a convincing influence on customers. It is further assumed that an individual makes a rational decision only after careful consideration of various alternatives, where new information can be added to the decision-making process. This rational behavior differs markedly from an emotional behavior, where the individual reacts more instinctively based on the emotions that arise in the decision-making process. These are generally also linked to the emotions and memories that are preserved from the previous positive or negative experiences.

Marketing has long been characterized as being rational, because the product's features and benefits, such as price and quality, have been at the center of attention. This is supported by various researchers who assert that many companies have chosen to focus on their core product and its benefits in their marketing planning, as shown in the following example:

> *In an ad campaign, the car brand Peugeot presented product benefits such as "Peugeot Diesel Premium 10,000 SEK, Webasto diesel heater with timer 0 SEK, particle filter 6,000 SEK in tax rebate, and comfort package only 4,900 SEK" to promote rational behavior.*

It is often argued that price is important for a buying decision, as long as consumers do not experience any major differences between the products or categories of products. This points to the importance of highlighting the emotional elements to differentiate and distinguish one brand in competition with others.

That marketing is rational means also that there may be an element of common sense, which is demonstrated by the company or personnel being able to evaluate the buying and selling situation that has arisen. It is about creating an understanding for the individual who just then finds him/herself in the situation of a purchase and consumption process, which can lead to a positive experience for the individual.

Furthermore, digital technology provides an opportunity for many companies to create websites through the Internet, where the question of how rational marketing can be expressed is raised. It may be that the brand will be available around the clock, that there should be access to data and information on current products, that it should be easy and quick to navigate, that it should be easy to contact someone, or that it should be possible to make purchases for those who desire it. This is confirmed by other researchers, who believe that the question of logic and rationality has a prominent role in e-commerce for this to be successful.

It is a common understanding that rationality and rational arguments should be included in an effective communication strategy through advertisements and commercials, because the intention is to influence consumers' product choices and decision-making. It is further argued that it is possible to convince individuals through the use of evidence-based and rational arguments on products and brands. It should also be noted that rational decisions are based on the individual's own analysis and reasoning, which usually take place under more or less controlled conditions in the store or at home (Biswas et al., 2009).

Finally, it should be said that researchers on brands believe that companies should build and develop a brand strategy that is based precisely on the individual's rational behavior. It means that this strategy should be simple and logical to understand and that an individual should be able to absorb the content of the message, which is almost exclusively based on facts, without any major difficulties. It can be about creating quality expectations in marketing, which is due to the product's actual quality through the use of logical and rational information that may affect the individual's understanding of quality and choice of product.

Habitual Behavior

In marketing theory, transaction marketing has advocated a unilateral focus for a long time when it comes to influencing and persuading consumers. Getting people to pay attention to a message about a product or a brand has mainly been through various advertisings and commercials in newspapers and television. The younger generations born in the 1980s and 1990s have generally chosen to forgo the morning newspaper at the kitchen table and instead have chosen to use the computer and cell phone for the latest news.

During the past decade, therefore, this marketing has increasingly been questioned, since new media has arisen at the same time as there has been an increasing awareness about the shortcomings of traditional advertising and promotional campaigns. The difficulties encountered in trying to influence and persuade consumers to buy a particular product or a particular brand can be explained by habitual behavior. It is agreed that habits, which are based on the behavior being repeated from one time to another, play a crucial role in the individual's purchasing behavior.

This means that an individual creates different habits, which implies that we can make the same decision regarding a brand or make the same purchase every time without thinking about it. In this way, we learn different habits through repetition, and these habits are then ingrained in our memory and our subconscious. It is believed that habits can be seen as automated responses to the sensory stimuli that are constantly in our surroundings and processed by our five senses.

On the other hand, it can be noted that the significance of habits or a habitual behavior regarding an individual's purchasing behavior has been tested empirically to a small degree. It is also not common that marketers discuss purchasing behavior from a habitual behavior perspective. But if this action is based on an individual's unconscious image of a product or brand, it is a challenge for marketers to take a seat in his or her subconscious. This process is called *behavioral marketing* and involves trying to get a consumer to choose a particular brand automatically (Martin, 2008).

It is generally accepted that an individual's habitual behavior can be explained by different sensory stimuli (or inputs). In this way, the five human senses—sight, sound, smell, touch, and taste—function as sensory channels for each individual, and the stimuli that is consciously presented are placed in the sensory memory. If these stimuli are strong enough, they are placed in the long-term memory and lay the foundation for habitual behavior through the subconscious processes that occur in the human brain. In this way, it is assumed that by linking the sensory stimuli together with a particular behavior, it creates habits in an individual, which then form the basis of a habitual behavior in the different purchasing and consumption processes.

But not all individuals react to the sensory stimuli that are available in a commercial environment, because it is also assumed that there is a learning effect related to them. For those stimuli that an individual is no longer affected by, he/she has become accustomed to and ignores, which means that they are irrelevant. There are many situations in daily life where an individual learns to disregard stimuli and eventually ignore them.

It has proved to be difficult for many individuals to change their behaviors and break their old habits. A habitual behavior is based on experience and learning, which many companies and organizations try to change through various advertising and information campaigns concerning, for example, health, food, and smoking. It is common for consumers to express preferences about a change in behavior, but it has been shown that habits are a powerful force for an individual's product selection and its impact on the different social processes. In this context, the individual's image, prestige, and self-image are of great importance and may partially explain the difficulty many when attempting to change habitual behavior.

On the other hand, habitual behavior means that we as individuals become more effective, psychologically speaking, by making use of a behavior that we have learned and that is automated and repeated. This means that it takes less energy, and behavior can be viewed as the result of how an individual has learned to respond to different stimuli in the environment. This can also be seen as a lack of conscious choice, because a habitual behavior occurs by itself, such as when an individual buys coffee without thinking about what other options are available other than the usual coffee brand. In such cases, it is important to have strong and clear signals from the store environment to influence a habitual behavior. Most of the choices an individual makes daily are based on well-established habits, which are often grounded in early childhood and adolescence.

This means that a brand that would form the basis of a habitual behavior must win the trust and confidence of customers in order to succeed. Some researchers believe that it is not until an individual has built this trust that a brand is chosen by habit. When it happens, the individual actively contributes to maintain a relationship with the brand and will choose to disregard the competitors. In this context, the promises made by a brand are of great importance, and the promises must be delivered on to win the individual's confidence and trust.

Starbucks is an example of a brand that has managed to create a habitual behavior, when it comes to choosing a coffee, which most Americans have learned to appreciate (Martin, 2008, p. 79, op. cit.):

> *Ask CEO Howard Schultz (Starbucks), why customers pay an average of more than 3 dollars for a cup of Starbucks coffee three times a week, and he will wax rhapsodic about the company's relationship with coffee growers, its emotional connection to customers, and its bond with partners (employees). But Starbucks' phenomenal success is arguably attributable to more mundane attributes.*
>
> *The first factor in the company's creation and domination of the chain coffee store market is the role convenience plays in creating habits ... Yet the ease with which customers can find and get to Starbucks largely explains the company's success. Starbucks is willing to open a store across the street from an existing Starbucks if traffic pattern analysis justifies it ... by the knowledge that you sell a lot more coffee if you don't make customers cross the street to get it.*

Martin (2008) also believes that it is important for a company and a brand to establish a habitual behavior in customers rather than just concentrating on customer satisfaction. In this context, the behavior that individuals display in relation to the brand is more important than the attitudes they may have, which do not always reflect the current behavior, in this case a habitual behavior.

Impulsive Behavior

If habitual behavior is based on the individual's habits, then impulsive behavior is the exact opposite. Then, most individuals act completely unplanned and make purchase decisions based on impulse, which they originally had not planned to. To create impulse behavior, companies should offer an interesting and exciting range of products and brands throughout the retail landscape, even in the more peripheral areas of the store.

People's daily behavior is often governed by impulses that add color to everyday life, which then leads to impulsive behavior. It may be about stopping for an acquaintance one meets on the street or making an unplanned purchase decision when shopping. Theoretically, impulsivity means that a person reacts hastily or without thinking it through, which is also a normal part of human behavior.

An impulsive behavior is usually divided into two types: dysfunctional and functional impulsivity. Dysfunctional behavior means that the behavior is characterized by a lesser degree of reflection, compared to most people, which then may lead the individual to problems and difficulties with regard to the impulses that are followed. Functional behavior, on the other hand, means that the behavior allows room for a higher degree of reflection, which can happen to an individual in unexpected or sudden situations. The individual can then with quick actions exploit the situation, which would otherwise have been lost.

In research, several studies have examined impulsivity as an important part of human personality, where it has also been defined as an inability to wait. Among some researchers, impulsivity is considered a personality trait, which includes behavioral as well as emotional and motor components that can vary in different individuals. It has also been shown in research that the cerebellum is of crucial importance for a person's impulsive behavior.

An impulsive behavior, or action, can be regarded as a sudden and spontaneous desire to purchase a product or a brand. Furthermore, impulsive action and behavior can be considered as being emotional and reactive in nature and without regard to the consequences of the behavior. The younger generation of consumers have often been regarded as reacting more emotionally than rationally in the purchase of products and brands. These generations have grown up with a different purchasing behavior than the previous generations, which had the result that many people chose to purchase products they originally had not planned to purchase.

> "When a customer comes into the store, Old Navy, in Manhattan, he or she is offered a black bag to put their goods into directly at the entrance, when he or she is shopping in the store. Then, at the checkout, the clerk asks if the customer wants to buy the bag, and the answer is often yes."

Underhill (2009) claims that both women and men exhibit impulsive behavior, especially in retail. Previous studies have revealed that about 60–70 percent of all daily purchases made by women and men can be considered as unplanned. Underhill believes that this shows that many companies can never form an understanding of or know what their customers are ready or willing to buy if the shopping experience cannot contribute to this.

Furthermore, Underhill believes that there are particular areas in a service environment that are better suited than others for impulsive behavior, and the checkout area is mentioned as an example. In this area, customers spend a lot of their time standing still, and the wait can therefore encourage impulse purchases. In addition, there are several factors that influence customers' impulsive behavior, particularly the placement of brands in the service environment.

Goods should be placed so that they are easily accessible to facilitate customer contact, and the goods, as a rule, should always be in sight. Even the placement of the shopping baskets can affect the behavior, and these should be available further into the service environment from the entrance. This is justified by the fact that many individuals are not susceptible to stimuli and do not start considering a purchase until they find themselves further into the service environment.

One of the main reasons for impulsive behavior is believed to be that people deviate from their habitual behavior. This is particularly evident in the service environments that are not known, making the daily routines disappear and often replaced with a more impulsive behavior. Airports and tax departments are often cited as examples of service environments that differ from everyday life and where an impending trip can help create a higher level of expectation and contribute to more impulsive behavior.

A FEMALE AND A MALE BRAIN

The Brain as a Gender

The image of the human brain that emerges stresses the importance of both emotional as well as rational behavior from an individual. The areas and structures that govern human behavior are intimately associated and interlinked with each other to be able to cope with the sensory information and those stimuli that an individual is exposed to in everyday life. I have, therefore, asked myself the question: *Do a man and a woman have the same type of brain or are there some fundamental differences between the sexes?*

A common view among researchers is that there are significant differences between a female brain and a male brain. This can be compared to the differences that exist between the physical appearance of women and men. Research suggests further that there are significant differences between women and men in terms of the performance of both simple and more complex tasks.

A person's genetic heritage and background is a contributing factor in the development of a female or male brain. It is believed that the mother's limbic system, which is responsible for human emotions, together with the hypothalamus, which is responsible for the man's vital functions, plays a crucial role in determining a brain's gender. It is explained by the fact that these areas and structures regulate and control the production of the hormones that lead to the gender a brain will obtain.

Even dopamine, which is a neurotransmitter in the nerve cells in the brain, may explain the differences between a female and a male brain relating to social behavior. These differences can be attributed to how much testosterone or estrogen an individual has been exposed to before birth.

It is, therefore, widely accepted that the differences between a female and a male brain are created even before birth. The gender is determined by the amount of hormones, testosterone for men and estrogen for women, which contribute to the differences that exist. I will now describe in more detail the organizational and emotional/sensory differences that are thought to exist in a female and a male brain.

Organizational Gender Differences

Two of the main differences between a female and a male brain relate to the brain's weight and size. Research suggests that a male brain is 9 to 12 percent larger than a female brain. This difference can easily be explained by the fact that a brain is proportionally scaled to the body size.

Another significant difference between a female and a male brain is its organization. It has been shown in studies of head and brain injuries, which occurred in the same place in men and women that the same kind of damage did not result. If the men lost their language ability, then the women retained that ability, even though it was a question of exactly the same type of injury. An interesting explanation for this is that the language center in men is found only in the left hemisphere, whereas in women it is distributed on both the left and the right brain.

It is also believed that there is a crucial difference between a male and a female brain when it comes to expressing oneself and finding the right words for the right situation. This is also explained by organizational differences, because girls generally have a larger vocabulary than boys. Already at an early age, girls are faster than boys when it comes to learning the first words and trying to build short sentences. Researchers argue therefore that women are often better than men in expressing themselves and have an edge when it comes to using the language. However, it should be said that there are areas within the language in which men are considered to be better than women.

When it comes to tasks relating to the so-called mental rotation, which means that a person should mentally imagine an object from a new angle, it has been argued that men often perform better than women. Furthermore, mental rotation is deemed to be important in being able to orient oneself in new environments or being able to navigate using a map, which mainly deals with spatial activities. Men are thought to cope better with this than women, which indicates that a male brain is superior to a female brain when it comes to overall spatial understandings.

On the other hand, women are viewed as having an ability to remember emotional memories better than men, and this is especially true when it comes to self-biographical, emotional experiences. This is mainly explained by the fact that women have a superiority when it comes to emotional language and social skills in comparison with men, which is thought to be due to more intertwined and developed communication regarding the left and right brain.

Emotional and Sensory Gender Differences

The organizational differences described between a female and a male brain also lead to women and men behaving differently. This refers to the emotional and sensory differences, which are expressed by men and women using different life strategies, evaluating things differently, and thinking differently.

It is generally accepted that a female brain is more empathetic than a male brain, which instead is more systematic. This is most clearly expressed by women who more often are thought to pursue altruistic and reciprocal relationships, unlike men, who instead value competition and power.

> *"Female brains strive after altruistic relationships and male brains strive after competition and power."*

When it comes to other emotional gender differences, it is more common for women to feel comfortable with seeking eye contact with others, compared with men. This is explained in that women, through a meeting that takes place face-to-face, have an opportunity to read facial expressions and body language. It is generally believed that women have a better understanding of body language and are better at reading facial expressions than men, which is explained by the fact that women generally use both of their brain hemispheres. Some researchers argue that this is an expression of women's emotional intelligence.

If women are assumed to perform better at direct eye contact, such a situation can often make men uncomfortable. Men prefer a more anonymous contact instead, for example, via e-mail or phone. It has also been pointed out that this is reflected in the retail sector, where men often prefer not to contact the store staff to ask questions about products, quality, and prices (Underhill, 2009).

Sensory gender differences exist between a female and a male brain, among other things, when it comes to the visual sense and then primarily visual appeal and including color selection. It is believed that women have better visual memory and night vision than men and that women have an easier time remembering visual details. When it comes to taste, it turns out that men can more easily distinguish different salty flavors than women, whereas women are more sensitive to bitter tastes than men.

In terms of sound and the impact of the sense of sound, it is thought that women notice and pay attention to sound more than men. This is explained by the fact that a female and a male brain are activated in different ways with the help of music, and it can bring both positive and negative emotions in an individual. Women process the positive and negative emotions that arise from the music only in the left brain hemisphere, however, in different parts of the hemisphere. In contrast, men process a positive musical experience in the left-brain hemisphere, whereas a negative experience is processed in the right brain hemisphere.

When it comes to perceiving smells, women have often proved themselves as being better able to detect, discriminate, and identify smells than men. It has also been shown in toddlers that the female sex has a better ability than the male sex when it comes to using the sense of smell.

Even when it comes to the sense of touch, there are differences between a female and a male brain; specifically, women are more sensitive and exposed to pain as well as reaction to pain, and their resistance to pain is different, compared with men. It is manifested by the fact that women often respond to pain in comparison with men, at the same time as women are more affected by it, mentally and physically.

Gender Differences in Purchasing and Consumption

Even though there are biological differences between a female and a male brain, every individual is affected by his/her environment and immediate surroundings. For many individuals, this means that one is expected to have a specific purchasing behavior or purchasing pattern based on his/her gender. This is thought to be particularly evident in the context of decision-making in the different purchasing and consumption processes, where the differences between the feminine and masculine behavior are often expressed in a more tangible way.

In the literature, it is generally assumed that women have a feminine, expressive tendency in their gender role, whereas men have a masculine, instrumental tendency. Furthermore, it is generally accepted that there are gender differences in many product and service contexts, where both women and men are involved, but these are not adequately documented and explored.

> "Women attach importance to the invisible factors, such as empathy and security, to a greater extent than men in the financial world."

Early researchers discussed the household decision-making in terms of femininity and masculinity. Various studies confirmed that women put more emphasis on love, affection, expressing warm feelings, and sharing feelings. It also emerged that women gave greater weight to both invisible factors, such as empathy and security, and visible factors, such as personnel, within the financial services industry, in comparison with men.

Several researchers have noted the lack of a specific gender perspective, in terms of relationships between buyers and sellers. Based on the relational concept, the strength of a relationship is defined and determined using a variety of behavioral variables. Among these variables are concepts such as trust, engagement, and satisfaction, which have been studied in a number of studies.

Bhagat and Williams (2008) believe that there are differences between men and women when it comes to the strength of a relationship. This refers to a qualitative difference in the motivation and commitment that exists, and the concept of commitment has been used as an important variable in a study of gender differences. They also suggest that previous research on gender differences has not paid enough attention to the concept of commitment.

In their study, they wanted to try to understand how men and women perceive the relationship with their doctors. The researchers concluded that women should be considered as being more relational than men. They put more emphasis on the personal and social aspects. Even the overall evaluation of the relationship is considered to be more important, compared with men.

When it comes to decision-making, it is widely believed that men and women make decisions differently. For men, the decisions are often linked to a specific purchasing situation, whereas women are interested in getting as much information as possible and making comparisons prior to making that decision. Men, however, are often considered as exhibiting more irrational decision-making and buying patterns associated with a purchase.

It is believed to be common that women use more analytical strategies than men, who instead look for a more holistic approach in connection with their purchasing decisions. This behavior is thought to be gender based, and it is supported by studies that have shown that if women are given more time to carry out a task, their performance improves. It has been shown that men often act more quickly than women when it comes to moving between the shelves of a store. This also suggests that women take more time than men in connection with purchasing decisions.

> "In connection with purchasing, men have a more holistic approach than women, who instead have more analytical strategies."

Underhill (2009) suggests that men may be regarded as more impressionable in comparison with women, which is explained by the fact that men usually want to get out of a store faster than women. Precisely for this reason, men are believed to be easier to convince when it comes to accepting a customer offer, which means that they can leave the store as quickly as possible.

At the same time, men make more and more purchases of food, something that previously was more related to women, which is why men are now involved in the purchasing decisions and purchasing work in a different way than before. This means that more and more companies need to adapt their offerings to both women and men, because the gender differences play an increasing role in the decision-making and purchasing patterns.

NEUROMARKETING

To Understand the Human Brain More in Depth

During the last decade, the scientific interest has increased greatly when it comes to learning more about how people make choices and purchase decisions based on the information and stimuli the brain receives. Within the framework of consumer behavior and consumer psychology, it has long been studied how consumers consciously process and perceive information on both the emotional and the cognitive level, as previously discussed. However, the research on how brands, as stimuli, are processed and perceived by the human brain in connection with selection and purchasing decisions has been relatively small so far.

There is now an opportunity to try to understand what happens in the human brain when there is a choice between two different brands. There has long been a desire among academics and practitioners to more deeply understand how the human brain is organized and structured to manage the selection and purchasing decisions consumers face in connection with purchase and consumption.

In neuroscience, as a research area, the aim is to try to get a deeper knowledge of the function and structure of the human brain in terms of how signals are encoded, how reactions to the environment occur, and how the brain regulates and controls the body. The Italian scientist Angelo Mosso is considered the originator of neuroscience; in his experiments in 1881, it was shown that the blood pressure monitor could record an increase in a person's heart rate and blood flow in the body when emotional or mental activities occurred.

Research in neuroscience is focused on trying to understand the basis for a human's decision-making, emotions, and memory in relation to stimulus and response. Various images of the brain's function and structure are used to analyze and identify how the human brain works and how it handles different kinds of information and input.

Some researchers argue that neuroscience as a scientific discipline is only at its beginning and is under further development. They also suggest that neuroscience should be seen as complementary to earlier consumer research with the intent to improve research and should not be considered as a challenger (Hubert and Kenning, 2008). Other researchers support this argument, claiming that it requires more knowledge about how people make economic decisions and that it is possible to obtain this knowledge using the latest technology.

In neuroeconomics, which combines scientific disciplines such as economics, psychology, and neuroscience, individuals are studied on how they make their choices and make purchase decisions. Various studies deal with the brain's role in terms of decision-making, risk taking, and rewards, as well as how these factors interact with each other.

What is Neuromarketing?

Neuromarketing as a research area has its base in both neuroscience and neuroeconomics, and its purpose is to analyze and identify an individual's unconscious feelings and reactions associated with the purchase and consumption processes. In particular, research has the task of obtaining new knowledge about how the human brain receives and processes the various stimuli and information from the environment and also to analyze and identify the driving forces that guide and influence individuals' choices and purchasing decisions relating to a brand.

As a research field, neuromarketing is relatively new and emerged in the early 2000s in the United States. The term neuromarketing is a combination of the two research fields, neuro—from neuroscience—and marketing and emerged organically without being connected to any particular individual as inventor. However, the company Bright House in Atlanta, Georgia, USA was the first to use the term neuromarketing in an article published in 2002. The new research field quickly gained ground among professional marketers, who felt that it could help to improve knowledge primarily about the effects of advertisements, which for a long time has been and even now is disputed.

There are still ongoing discussions about the scientific starting point for neuromarketing, and it is unclear whether the area is regarded as an established academic research field (Fischer et al. 2010). To achieve this status, concepts, theories, and models are required that can predict the types of stimuli or consumption-related problems research on the brain should be able to help solve.

In the literature, neuromarketing is defined in general as the application of various techniques to identify an individual's thoughts arising from the specific response in the brain in relation to products, services, advertising, or packaging. Through this definition, neuromarketing can be seen not only as a tool with commercial importance, but it has also raised the importance of research on a more general scientific level for the future.

> *"The purpose of neuromarketing is to capture brain activities using the latest technology in brain scans."*

The primary purpose of neuromarketing is to identify and explore what drives or triggers consumers to make specific choices and make specific purchasing decisions by looking at emotions and social interactions. In neuromarketing, the latest technologies in brain scanning and going beyond the use of focus groups and questionnaires are used to gain knowledge about the mental processes that underlie consumer choices and purchasing decisions. Rather, it is about being able to visualize how the brain evaluates its choices and makes its purchasing decisions, which is why brain activities should be captured using images taken of the brain.

Achrol and Kotler (2012) assert that neurophysiological studies of consumer behavior with respect to the sensory experiences belong to a new emerging marketing paradigm, as discussed previously. When it comes to studying individuals' perceptions and sensations, it is done today with a neurophysiological approach, which is based on cell biology. In this context, it is about identifying the different cell networks, which are localized in specific parts of the brain.

The authors also believe that tomorrow's research on consumer behavior and consumption experiences is inextricably linked to neurophysiological studies. This research is also naturally linked to yesterday's marketing through questions such as: What role does stimulus-response process have in consumer behavior? Is there a subliminal learning process after all?

With this, neuromarketing is considered to have a great potential to contribute to the development of new insights into consumers' choices and decision-making in purchase and consumption processes.

Neurophysiological Methods and Techniques

Neuromarketing enables researchers to further analyze and identify the effects arising from, for example, advertising and commercials or brand experience in terms of the brain's activity level. Some researchers claim that the more knowledge that can be developed about how individual behavior and decision-making are influenced by marketing, the greater understanding of how marketing itself can be achieved.

Among the neurophysiological methods that exist, techniques that measure the electrical activity (EEG) and magnetic fields (MEG) as well as functional magnetic resonance imaging (fMRI) are used, which are designed to measure different neural activities in the brain that can be linked to the degree of attention, emotions, and cognitions.

EEG, a proven technology in neurology, measures the brain activity through neurons that are a form of human cells, which constitute the biological basis. When the stimulus is presented to an individual, for example, as an advertisement, the neurons produce a weak, electrical current, which can increase. From these electrical currents, different pattern frequencies are developed, called brain waves, which can be attributed to the different stages of arousal in an individual. It appears that the EEG can measure brain activity up to ten thousand times per second, which indicates the speed at which an individual receives information through his/her senses and how quickly thoughts are formed.

Already in 1979, a model was proposed to link the electrical activities in the brain with emotions. It is believed that the incidence of brain waves in the left anterior brain area indicates that there are positive emotions, and in contrast, the negative emotions are thought to occur in the right anterior brain area in a human.

One of the drawbacks of the EEG is that the technology is not considered to have sufficiently good spatial resolution in different parts of the brain, which means that it is not possible to locate precisely where the different neurons respond to the stimuli. This means that it is difficult to argue that the emergence of brain waves in a certain part of the brain, as a result of a particular advertisement, is solely due to this stimulus. When EEG is used in conjunction with experiments, it is done without the consumers being asked about what kind of information or stimuli they are responding to—EEG records only those reactions that take place in the brain.

MEG, as a technique, is closely related to EEG and has received considerable attention over the past decade when it has been applied to being able to measure and take pictures of magnetic fields in the brain. MEG differs from EEG mainly with respect to the spatial resolution, which is higher, meaning that it is possible to trace the neural activity in the brain using various magnetic fields. Similar to EEG, it is limited to the brain's outer surface areas, and it is difficult to take pictures from the areas that relate to the prominent emotional or cognitive functions.

Regarding fMRI—functional magnetic resonance—this technology is used to analyze and identify an individual's emotional responses to different types of stimuli. This technique has become one of the most common when it comes to increasing the understanding of how the human brain and the individual's emotional and cognitive behavior work.

It is widely believed that the technique enables the mapping, with high precision, of those areas or structures of the brain that are activated when a person thinks of or experiences a brand. In studies of the human brain, fMRI is used in experiments when the brain does not do a specific task, to create a neutral picture of what is happening in the brain, and when the brain is activated by various stimuli or inputs, to analyze and identify the specific area or structure of the brain that is activated. Through fMRI, it is possible to obtain images with a ten times higher resolution than is the case with EEG and especially in deeper brain structures, which include emotional responses.

> "With the help of fMRI, it is possible to find out what happens in the brain when a person thinks of or experiences a certain brand."

During one such experiment, various stimuli or inputs led to the blood flow increasing in certain areas or structures of the brain, which revealed the activities that occurred in the brain. When an area or structure in the brain is activated or stimulated in this way, more blood is supplied, resulting in more oxygen and directly affecting the tissue's magnetic properties, which a magnetic camera then can easily identify.

With the help of a scanner, images are taken of the blood flow that is present, which are made evident when neurons are activated. This requires energy, which then in turn is transported through various blood flows and can be read through what is called BOLD (*blood oxygen level dependent*). When a particular stimulus, for example, an advertisement is paid attention to, it leads to a person's brain getting more oxygenated blood, compared with during the rest periods. This change in BOLD can then be read in the magnetic field and shows brain activity.

One reason that fMRI technology in recent years has received an increased application is primarily its ability to discern how different nervous systems can handle specific functions in the human brain. This is an enormous task, because a person's nervous system includes about one hundred billion individual neurons. The main advantage of the new technology is that it can produce high-resolution images in a fast way.

It should be noted that it takes up to a few seconds before an image is recorded by the new technology, whereas a reaction in the brain occurs within a few milliseconds, which is why an image always shows the aftermath of a person's reaction. Thus as the technology is refined and further developed, it will be possible to produce even better and more detailed images.

Other neurophysiological methods that are commonly used are: *eye-tracking*, designed to measure the degree of attention, and *skin conductance response*, or *galvanic skin response*, which evaluate the degree of arousal associated with selection and purchasing decisions. It should be said that both of these methods have their unique advantages and disadvantages when it comes to how they can measure and estimate the importance of different biological and psychological factors in individuals as well as the conclusions that can be drawn.

Pros and Cons of Neuromarketing

When neuromarketing has been applied, it has turned out that the usual questionnaire, which is often used in connection with surveys, does not give a sufficiently accurate picture of the brain's actual impression of a brand's attributes and characteristics. It is therefore believed that a questionnaire is of limited value, because it cannot reproduce or give precise answers as to which feelings and thoughts arise in an individual in his/her interaction with a brand. This points to the difficulty in trying to find out, retrospectively, by means of a questionnaire, how an individual perceives a brand experience and that such can give misleading information.

In this context, it is believed that the application of neuromarketing can provide a more realistic picture of what is really happening on a deeper level with respect to an individual's feelings and thoughts. This information could allow a brand to more clearly define new marketing strategies.

This also creates an interest in neuromarketing among companies, because it can provide information about how people react to different stimuli in the communication of a brand. An increased application of neuromarketing can also lead to a better understanding of the limitations of today's various marketing techniques, because there are often criticisms as to their superficiality and inability to reach customers on a deeper level.

The criticism directed toward neuromarketing is based on a fear that neuromarketing, through new knowledge about how the human brain reacts and responds to different stimuli, should be able to reveal a secret code to change our perceptions beyond a person's consciousness, which would not be regarded as ethically defensible. Furthermore, it is believed that this could lead to new marketing activities and promotional campaigns, which would lead to overconsumption in times when sustainability and increased environmental impacts are the focus of many companies.

> *"A disadvantage of neuromarketing is that new knowledge can lead to a person's perception being unconsciously influenced in the buying decision, which is considered unethical."*

But researchers such as Morin (2011, p. 132) believe that "ignoring neuromarketing as a way to understand consumer behavior would be as absurd as refusing to allow astronomers to use electronic telescopes." This has led to a continued discussion about questioning the ethics behind neuromarketing, which has also come to criticize the marketers who have used or are using neuromarketing in practice.

In 2011, a survey was conducted with the aim of identifying the academics' and the practitioners' ideas about neuromarketing and its applications

(Ezer et al., 2011). The quantitative study was based on data collected through the Internet from 111 marketing academics, 52 neuroscientists, and 56 professional marketers.

The results showed that the three most important factors in an assessment of neuromarketing are: 1) the interest and participation in the area, 2) knowledge and awareness about the area, and 3) ethics for all three respondent groups. Furthermore, it appears that neurologists and marketing professionals consider neuromarketing to be more advantageous, in comparison with marketing academics.

One conclusion of the study was that all the respondent groups agreed that the application of neuromarketing could not be considered as being a manipulative way to sell unnecessary goods and services.

Finally, it should be noted that there are critics of neuromarketing who argue for the need to have laws and regulations to prevent companies from infringing on consumers' privacy without their knowledge. This applies mostly to the use of stimuli and triggers, which in one way or another are built into their brands to manipulate consumers in connection with the brand selection and purchasing decision.

SCIENTIFIC STUDIES ON BRANDS

The Choice Between Different Brands

The first scientific study within neuromarketing is thought to have been carried out by a research team led by Read Montague at the Department of Neuroscience at Baylor College of Medicine in Houston, Texas (McClure et al., 2004). The main aim of the study was to identify how people's brains reacted when choosing between two different brands. The survey was conducted in the form of both a blind test and a passive experiment using an fMRI scan and included 67 respondents. They were asked to drink Coca-Cola or Pepsi anonymously in the blind test and drink Cola-Cola or Pepsi with knowledge of the brand while an fMRI machine scanned their brains.

The results showed that different parts of the brain reacted differently when individuals were unaware or aware of the brand that was consumed. In the blind test, half of the respondents preferred Pepsi and half preferred Coca-Cola, and it appeared that the choice of Pepsi elicited a stronger response in the brain, compared with Coca-Cola. When the respondents then were told that they drank Pepsi and not Coca-Cola, three out of four preferred Coca-Cola instead.

> *"A study has shown that the brain reacts differently when individuals are unaware or aware of the brand that is consumed."*

But when the Coca-Cola logo was displayed during the passive experiment, three out of four respondents preferred Coca-Cola instead of Pepsi at the same time as the brain activity was changed. The logo caused strong activity in the areas of the brain that are related to memories and self-images. This did not occur when the Pepsi logo was shown to the respondents.

It is clear that such a strong brand like Coca-Cola has power over the part of the area known as the frontal lobe and can be considered as owning the actual area. In this area of the brain, there is an execution function, which affects and controls our attention, our short-term memory, and our planning, that is, our thinking.

According to the study's results, this means that when individuals know that they are drinking Coca-Cola, they express that they prefer Coca-Cola over Pepsi, and their execution function in their brains lights up during the experiment. On the other hand, it turns out that if these individuals do not know which brand is consumed, then Pepsi is preferred just as often as Coca-Cola. In this case, the execution function does not light up, but older structures in the limbic system react to this. The study's findings are exciting and arouse curiosity about how the brain manages the choice of brands, but the results have not been able to show logically how brand selection actually works.

In another study concerning the choice between different brands, the relationship between price and quality was investigated in relations to how individuals perceive wines and was manifested by increased brain activity (Plassman et al., 2008). The investigation included 11 female students who expressed that they liked and occasionally drank red wine. Respondents were asked to try five different types of the French wine, Cabernet Sauvignon, which were marked with a price.

In reality, only three wines were tested, because two of the wines were used twice during the experiment. For that reason, the first wine was marked with its real price of $5 and some were labeled with a fictitious price of $45. The second wine was similarly marked with two prices of $90 and $10. Finally, the third wine was correctly marked with its real price of $35.

> *"A person's brain experiences more pleasure from drinking one rather expensive wine than a cheaper wine of the same variety."*

The results showed that after the experiment, respondents claimed to have tasted five different wines, even though there were only three in reality and that they thought that the more expensive wines tasted better than the cheaper ones. It was shown that an increase in the perceived price also led to increased brain activity, which was due to an associated increase in the taste experience.

One conclusion of the study was that if an individual learns that he/she is tasting two different wines, one with a high and one with a low price, although it is the same wine, then the part of the brain that experiences more joy is activated when the "more expensive" wine is drunk. This is due to the fact that the person tasting the wine believes that he/she is enjoying a more expensive wine. In this way, information about price can affect the individuals' perception of the real product quality, which in turn means that the price can change an individuals' perception of a brand.

This appears in a compilation by Kenning et al. (2007) through a number of studies that more closely studied the choices and purchasing decisions of brands. In most studies, fMRI has been applied as a technique to investigate how brands are perceived in the human brain.

Brand Experiences

A study by Esch et al. (2012) investigated how individuals' evaluation of brands, as a function of their awareness of these brands, could be related to neural activities in the brain. With the help of fMRI, it was revealed that the linguistic encoding was higher for unfamiliar and weak brands, especially in the regions of the brain where the encoding took place. Furthermore, a stronger activation of the brain's insula appeared for unfamiliar brands, in comparison with strong brands.

There also appeared neural activities in the brain that could be linked to information retrieval for familiar brands, which was not the case with unfamiliar brands. An additional result of the study was that eliciting positive emotions could clearly be attributed to the strong brands. Information regarding claims about the brand did not have the same meaning for the actual evaluation.

The conclusion that emerges from this study is that unfamiliar and weak brands lead to neural activities that start the temporary encoding and search processes. When it comes to evaluating strong and weak brands, it seems that the processing of positive information from previous brand experiences is important for the evaluation. In this context, therefore, it is argued that the existing models of brand equity and evaluation of brands emphasize the cognitive aspects too much, compared with the experience-based aspects.

In order to investigate the market potential for various types of cars, Ford and Daimler-Benz conducted neuromarketing studies. The results showed that those respondents who rated sports cars as attractive also showed more brain activity in areas of the brain that focus on rewards, in comparison with those respondents who preferred other types of cars than sports cars.

When it comes to brand relationships, as part of the brand experience, a study by Reimann et al. (2012) that was conducted with the help of consumers' *skin conductance responses*, showed the emergence of emotional arousal over the newly formed love relationship with a new brand. On the other hand, it turns out that for established close relationships with a famous brand, there is a lesser degree of emotional arousal.

Furthermore, the researchers examined the neural activities for established relationships using fMRI and found that the brain's insula is particularly involved in the close relationship that consumers have with a brand. One conclusion of these studies is that they offer a more nuanced picture of what characterizes consumers' close relationships with brands within the framework of the brand experience.

By scanning over 2,000 respondents' brains in a study, with researchers from Oxford University, Lindstrom (2008) concluded that branding has the possibility to optimize all the stimuli (or inputs) that a brand might include. The study examined how consumers reacted to health warnings, logos, product placement, or subliminal images in a variety of advertising and promotional campaigns.

One of the study's main conclusions was that an emotional attachment to a brand is the most important influencing factor, because many brand choices and purchasing decisions are based on emotional factors rather than rational ones. When it comes to different stimuli regarding a person's five senses, it is stated that what people hear and smell may be considered to be a more powerful stimulus than what they see. This statement is in contrast to previous research, which assumes that sight is the most powerful sense in people.

REFERENCES

Achrol, R.S. and Kotler, P. (2012), "Frontiers of the marketing paradigm in the third millennium." *Journal of the Academy of Marketing Science,* 40, 35–52, 2012.

Bhagat, P.S. and Williams, J.D. (2008), "Understanding gender differences in professional service relationships," *Journal of Consumer Marketing,* 25, 1:16–22.

Biswas, D., Biswas, A. and Chatterjee, S. (2009), "Making judgments in a two-sequence cue environment: the effects of differential cue strengths, order sequence, and distraction," *Journal of Consumer Psychology,* 19, 1:88–96.

Brakus, J., Schmitt, B. and Zarantonello, L. (2009), "Brand experience: what is it? How is it measured? Does it affect loyalty?" *Journal of Marketing,* 73, May:52–68.

Esch, F., Möll, T., Elger, C.E., Schmitt, B., Neuhaus, C. and Weber, B. (2012), "Brands on the brain: do consumers use declarative information or experienced emotions to evaluate brands?" *Journal of Consumer Psychology,* 22, 1:75–85.

Eser, Z., Bahar Isin, F. and Tolon, M. (2011), "Perceptions of marketing academics, neurologists, and marketing professionals about neuromarketing," *Journal of Marketing Management,* 27, 7/8:854–868.

Fischer, C.E., Chin, L. and Klitzman, R. (2010), "Defining neuromarketing: practices and professional changes," *Harvard Review of Psychiatry,* 18, 4:230–237.

Gazzaniga, M., Ivry, R. and Mangun, G. (2009), *Cognitive neuroscience. The biology of the mind*, New York: Norton & Company, Inc.
Hubert, M. and Kenning, P. (2008), "A current overview of consumer neuroscience," *Journal of Consumer Behaviour*, 7:272–292.
Hultén, B. (2011), "Sensory marketing: the multi-sensory brand experience concept." *European Business Review*, 23, 3:256–273.
Ingvar, M. (2007), "Hjärnbarkens funktion." (The Cerebral Cortex's Function), I: Österberg, K. (ed.) *Hjärnan* (The Brain), Stockholm: Karolinska Institute University Press, p. 29.
Jansson-Boyd, C.V. (2010), *Consumer psychology*, Maidenhead: Open University Press, p. 17.
Kenning, P., Plassman, H. and Ahlert, D. (2007), "Applications of functional magnetic resonance imaging for market research," *Qualitative Market Research*, 10, 2:135–152.
Lindstrom, M. (2008), *Buyology: truth and lies about why we buy*, New York: Doubleday.
Martin, N. (2008), *Habit—the 95% of behaviour that marketers ignore*, Upper Saddle River, NJ: Pearson Education.
McClure, S.M., Li, J., Tomlin, D., Cypert, K.S., Montague, L.M. and Montague, P.R. (2004), "Neural correlates of behavioral preference for culturally familiar drinks," *Neuron*, 44:379–387.
Morin, C. (2011), "Neuromarketing: the new science of consumer behavior," *Society*, 48:131–135.
Plassman, H., O'Doherty, J.P., Shiv, B. and Rangel, A. (2008), "Marketing actions can modulate neural representations of experienced pleasantness," *Proceedings of National Academy of Science*, 105, 3:1050–1054.
Pradeep, A.K. (2010), *The buying brain—secrets for selling to the subconscious mind*, Hoboken, NJ: John Wiley & Sons.
Rapaille, C. (2006), *The culture code—an ingenious way to understand why people around the world live and buy as they do*, New York: Broadway Books.
Reimann, M., Castâno, R., Zaichkowsky, J. and Bechara, A. (2012), "How we relate to brands: psychological and neuropsychological insights into close consumer-brand relationships," *Journal of Consumer Psychology*, 22, 1:128–142.
Söderlund. M. (2003), *Emotionsladdad marknadsföring [Emotional loaded marketing]*, Malmö: Liber.
Solomon, M.R., Bamossy, G., Askegaard, S. and Hogg, M.K. (2010), *Consumer behaviour—a European perspective*, 4th ed., Harlow: Prentice Hall, p. 119.
Underhill, P. (2009), *Why we buy—the science of shopping*, 3rd ed., New York: Simon & Schuster.

5 The Sense of Sight

This chapter analyzes and discusses the sense of sight, which is considered to be one of the strongest senses of a human being, with respect to sensory stimuli and sensory perception. The scientific notions about the fundamental role of the sense of sight are addressed initially with respect to both physiological characteristics and psychological aspects.

Thereafter, three categories of influential factors for the sense of sight, which relate to the importance of the societal culture, the service environment, and the brand, are presented. Considering this background, it is discussed how various factors affect individuals' affections, cognitions, as well as their actual behaviors in the different buying and consumption processes.

VISUAL CONSUMPTION

The sense of sight is widely believed to be the most prominent of the five senses for the perception and experience of a service environment or a brand, which is based on the existence of both affective and cognitive reactions. The sense of sight is thought to have a more crucial importance for the individual's sensory experience than the senses of hearing, touch, smell, and taste.

> "Throughout history and in every known culture, people have found joy in and meaning by using their eyes. They have deliberately tried to produce objects of beauty and have been fond of them."

For the vast majority of individuals, vision is the primary way to make a connection to the surroundings and the consumption experience, which emphasizes the importance of *visual consumption*. Visual consumption refers to the importance of vision when it comes to capturing the individual's attention to describe and clarify the company's and the brand's identity. In today's consumer culture, therefore, the question of vision and visualization is of vital importance for both businesses and consumers.

Visual consumption is based partly on how societal culture is shaped and how individuals interpret in various social and personal contexts. The growing importance of the sense of sight is increasingly reflected in the number of digital photos, movies, photographs, websites, television, and Internet advertising, which cater to generations X, Y, and Z, in particular. This is done at the same time as social media such as Facebook, Instagram, and Twitter are used for both commercial and social activities by more and more companies and consumers. When it comes to Instagram, it is a dedicated social photo service were participants share photos with each other and are offered a visual experience.

Some researchers believe that a company's competitive advantage is based on being able to visualize information regarding the brand and the meaning of this to connect with consumers in an efficient manner. In this context, this is done with the symbolism that different images convey, which is based on the cultural heritage that is present in the societal culture. This means that different images have their own inherent meanings, which is of paramount importance for marketers to understand when it comes to marketing communication and branding. In marketing and consumer behavior literature, discussions about vision, visualization, and its meanings have mostly focused on understanding the symbolism of advertisements or the meaning that consumers experience with their objects.

Several research studies demonstrate the importance of just the visual stimuli when it comes to influencing consumers' purchasing behavior in connection with sales, quantity of purchase, consumption, and product selection (Krishna, 2008). In other words, the visual experience can be decisive in determining whether consumers will be attracted to and aware of a product or a brand. This means that visualization provides companies endless possibilities to visualize and express a brand when it comes to conveying its identity, feelings, and values to consumers.

In this context, awareness is deemed to be one of the most important concepts that are related to the effects of visual stimuli. Advertising and commercials, as marketing stimuli, have long been focused on creating awareness around a product, which should be able to lead to an increased interest among consumers and a subsequent purchase of the actual product. In this way, the sense of sight has long been the focus of marketers and considered to be the most significant sense.

> "Four out of ten Swedish women remember that they have seen H & M ads when it comes to fashion advertising."

Visual stimuli such as design, shape, color, and packaging contribute in this way to build and establish strong producer and retailer brands and are considered to be a natural part of a branding strategy for a company. It is also clear from the research that design, as visual stimuli, positively affects consumers' perceptions of a brand. It has been shown that there is a high correlation between the design quality of the visual stimuli and financial performance.

In particular, product design connected to aesthetics has proved to be appealing to both cognitive and noncognitive, that is, affective, reactions. One observation made is that design draws attention to the attributes that make a product more or less attractive in the eyes of consumers. It also turns out that a pronounced preference for a product is more related to its design than to its functionality or brand. The shape of a product gives rise to an affective response based on an emotional evaluation, whereas the quality of a product is based on a cognitive evaluation.

Lighting can be used as another example of a visual stimulus that can be related to the importance of the sense of sight. Mehrabian and Russell (1974) identified the importance of lighting early on as an important component in a service environment, like a boutique or a department store. It is assumed that this component positively affects consumers' visual attraction to what is included in the service environment, including the range of products.

When it comes to the sense of sight and the importance of different visual stimuli, advertising and commercials are not the only marketing stimuli that affect a person's perception and experience of a brand. However, they have long been considered as the stimuli that have the greatest impact in mass marketing, even if many researchers have questioned the effects of advertising and commercials in the short- and long-term.

The importance that other visual stimuli, such as lighting, design, exterior, color, packaging, graphics, or interior, may have on consumers perceptions of a brand have long been overlooked in marketing research. To understand the importance of the sense of sight in sensory marketing, it is necessary to highlight visual stimuli other than just the traditional advertising and commercials in order to provide an understanding of the interaction between the visual stimuli on the one hand and the affective and cognitive reactions on the other hand which arise in consumers.

THE FUNDAMENTAL ROLE OF THE SENSE OF SIGHT

Physiological Properties

The sense of sight is the sense that is most used by us humans to get an understanding of the surrounding environment. Furthermore, the sense of sight is considered to be the most powerful and the most seductive of human's five senses, because the eyes are responsible for the collection of approximately 70 percent of all the sensory information the brain needs. The information an individual receives on a daily basis is mostly through the visual sense, and a person's ability to interpret external stimuli by means of visual impression is called *visual perception*. This ability is made possible by using a person's vision organ and the ability of each individual to interpret the impressions that the organ generates.

Through research in Gestalt psychology in the 1930s and 1940s, early interest arose in getting to know more about what affects the visual abilities of people. Through this branch of research, a number of principles are documented that show how a human brain could create an image based on visual impressions. The most prominent example is a person's ability to assemble the parts into a whole and the distance between the parts is very important for how this whole is achieved.

> *The German word Gestalt means the shape, form, or figure and represents an isolated, distinct, self-contained, and structured whole whose properties cannot be reduced to the properties of its parts. The motto of Gestalt psychologists was that the whole is more than the sum of its parts, in other words, a holistic approach.*

The principles of Gestalt psychology are of great value even today, especially the fact that a human brain makes a huge effort to interpret the information that sight conveys. Even if the visual information is for the most part incomplete or very incomplete, it is possible for a person to understand what an image represents and wants to say. However, Gestalt psychology failed to explain how visual perception takes place and works in practice.

Visual perception has to do with perceiving and interpreting various visual impressions and compiling them into a meaningful whole. For an individual, it means 1) seeing and 2) understanding what one saw. In this way, visual perception is an important part of the brain's cognitive process, which is the basis for decision and action.

This means that visual perception can be divided into two different components, namely, the *receiving* and the *cognitive*, where the first means that the eye receives the visual information and the latter means that the brain is able to interpret and understand the various visual stimuli. With regard to the cognitive component, it includes several visual areas, such as visual awareness, visual memory, and visual discrimination, which occur through a series of processes in the human brain.

It should be noted that all reading and writing for both children and adults are related to visual perception. People who have difficulties with visual perception have trouble perceiving, interpreting, combining, and remembering visual impressions. There are several different factors that can explain the perceptual difficulties, but a prerequisite is that the eyes and the optical system function properly, for example, one can see clearly, and the brain has the ability to interpret the visual impression correctly.

> *Computer games of the first-person shooters type greatly increase the players' visual perception. As little as 50 hours of training over nine weeks improved the participants' ability by an average of 43 percent and up to 58 percent, according to a study published in Nature Neuroscience. The results are very important, both for patients with visual impairment and for the training of police officers, pilots, and others where an increased perception ability reduces accidents.*

There is a general notion in the literature that the visual perception and the interpretation made of the impressions by sight need support from the other senses, such as hearing or touch, to make it possible to have a more accurate interpretation of the visual impression. The interpretation that takes place in an individual occurs through interaction with the sight organ and the central nervous system, where both color vision and depth perception play a big role.

Furthermore, it is believed that the collected impressions from more than one organ mean more than the impressions from the organs separately, i.e., the whole is greater than the parts. This suggests that sensory impression from multiple senses—not just one—is of great importance for the individual's sensory experience of a brand, which illustrates the importance of perceptual ability for a multi-sensory brand-experience. I will return to this aspect in Chapter 10.

It is widely believed in the literature that the eyes are a person's most important sensory organs, which is also evident by the fact that more than two-thirds of the body's sensory cells are in the eye. It is not possible for a person to perceive all the light that is around, however, it is only a small part that the human eye is able to absorb. For that reason, touch contributes so that infants learn different aspects of the surroundings early on, such as dimension, line, style, and structure. The eye receives the visual impressions upside down, and a newborn baby actually regards his/her environment upside and down, which is because it takes a while for the human brain to flip the image the right way.

But sight gives every person the opportunity to perceive the contrasts and differences that exist in the environment with regard to light and dark, large and small, or broad and narrow. The visual system gives everyone the opportunity to perceive the differences or changes that may attract the attention of the eyes, when it comes to, for example, a different design or a new packaging color (Figure 5.1).

Parts of the Human Eye

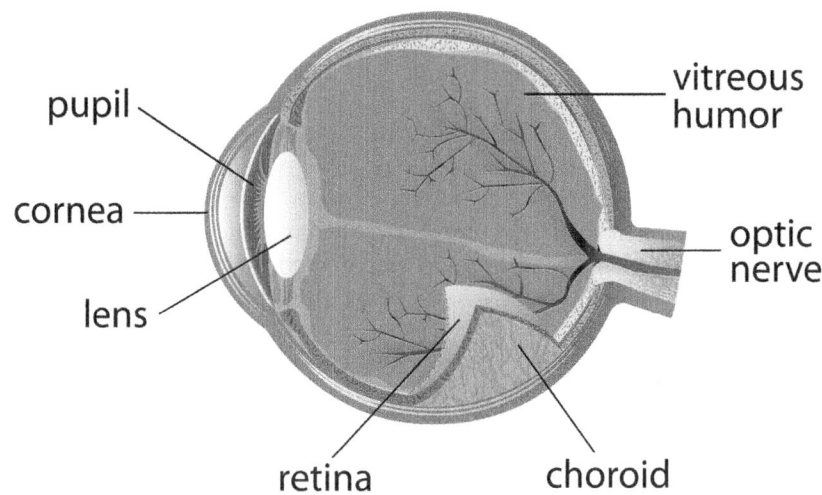

Figure 5.1 The Function and Structure of Vision
Source: iStock

When it comes to people's ability for visual perception, it has been shown in the research that an individual learns early on in his/her childhood to interpret the different visual impressions. This requires that the eyes be active and that the visual system be geared to capture the contrasts, movements, or differences that exist in the environment. The light absorbed by the eye is converted in the brain to the colors that form the basis of what a person actually sees. Thereby, the light is dissolved into a spectrum of six distinct colors, namely, red, orange, yellow, green, blue, and violet.

It is clear from the research that there are biological explanations as to why feelings can be coaxed by different shades of color, because color tones may be associated with specific physiological structures in humans. It is further suggested that the physiological process regarding color perception in a person shall be distributed on both a color shade that is warm/arousing, like red, and a color shade that is cool/relaxing, like blue. In light of the findings and conclusions that have emerged on the relationship between colors and emotions, a neurophysiological model of emotions has been suggested, which is based on color space.

From a physiological point of view, the eye's pupil filters the light that strikes the eye; moreover, the pupil has the capacity to expand and contract. The eye can be said to send images to the brain by light that is a form of electromagnetic radiation, which is refracted by the cornea and the lens. Thereafter, the light is led through the vitreous body and projected onto the retina, located at the back of the eye. When this occurs, the retinal sensors register the light radiation and these send signals on to the visual cortex at the back of the brain via the optic nerve.

From a visual point of view, an image appears on a person's retina, where the photoreceptors, in the form of rods and cones, transform the light into nerve impulses. This has led some to compare the eye to a camera, where the pupil corresponds to the aperture and its ability to regulate the light. Furthermore, the cornea and the lens are comparable to a camera's lens, which has the ability to refract the light rays so that an image is formed on the retina, which then corresponds to the film in the camera. The image that is created is always unique and compared with previous recollections, which means that each new image is always connected to the earlier visual experiences.

In the ongoing research on visual perception, it is proposed that the effects of visual stimuli can be explained through three interrelated conceptual structures (Raghubir, 2010). The first concept refers to the importance of attention and addresses the question of the extent to which the human eye observes or notices a certain aspect of visual information and the location of this focus.

The second concept refers to the importance of imagery and addresses the question of how the process of visualizing information occurs in the absence of visual stimulation.

Finally, the third concept refers to the significance of neural activation and addresses the question of the extent to which neurons in different parts of the brain light up in the presence of visual and other stimuli. It involves identifying the specific locations in the brain where these nerve activities may exist.

One of the most widely used scientific methods to detect different neuronal activities in the brain of an individual is the use of *eye-tracking*, where one of the starting points is that eye movements reflect how our information collection occurs with respect to both time and space. It is further assumed that the eye movements are closely linked to attention, that attention is of central importance in advertising and commercials, and that eye movements therefore reflect how advertising and commercials work.

PSYCHOLOGICAL ASPECTS

Cognitive Reactions

Given the importance that advertising and commercials, as marketing stimuli, have had for consumer behavior, two different research traditions have developed when it comes to studying the effects of visual versus verbal information for the sense of sight. One research tradition has studied the effects of memory, whereas the other research tradition has studied the effects on consumers' attitudes or overall judgment.

The first research tradition has generally assumed that visual information is superior to verbal information when it comes to remembering an advertisement for recognition. Already in the 1960s, studies revealed that people easily remember a print ad with a photo or an image, compared with an ad without an image or a photo. Later studies in the 1980s gave further support to visual information being superior to verbal information. Some researchers found additionally that the memory was reinforced when there was consistency between visual and verbal information.

> "Visual information in advertisements has shown to provide a more positive attitude toward a brand, compared with verbal information."

The second research tradition has assumed that visual and verbal stimuli have had an impact on people's attitudes. In one study, it was found that visually oriented advertisements were more effective, in comparison with verbally oriented advertisements, with regard to both creating a positive attitude toward the brand and communicating different product attributes. One of the conclusions was that visual information affected consumers' valuations of the products and thus created a more positive attitude and more purchasing intentions than verbal information.

When it comes to cognitive responses to visual stimuli, the perception of space has been studied for a long time. There is a well-documented effect regarding *clutter*, i.e., the amount of information in a visual stimulus, *extension*, i.e., the ratio between sides that have two- or three-dimensional spaces, *orientation*, i.e., vertical lines are perceived as shorter than the horizontal lines despite them being of the same length, as well as *categorization*, i.e., the dots between areas that are grouped together are perceived as less than the dots belonging to different groups (Raghubir, 2010).

In the research on perception, there are two studies that show the effects of visual stimuli as input and sensory experience. The first study, which dealt with contrast effects, showed that a volume was perceived as less than a weight. It appears that an object that is perceived as containing more volume is perceived as less, compared with an object that has the same weight. One of the explanations is that it is probably because the visual stimuli created an expectation that then was not matched by the actual sensory experience, which led to a reverse effect.

In the other study, it was shown that people perceive and believe that extended containers contain more volume than the actual experience shows, that is, the opposite relationship. This means that consumers believe that they have consumed less from a less extended container than from a more extended container, which has come to be called the *illusion of consumption experience*. It assumes that a long container is perceived to contain more volume and thus creates an association with a higher consumption. In the interaction between perceived volume and perceived consumption, there is a transformation effect of the extended container on the actual consumption (Raghubir and Krishna, 1999).

Researchers claim that the effects of visual stimuli on cognitive reactions such as intention, belief, and metacognition, are relatively unexplored. But in a study by Raghubir and Valenzuela (2006), the question of how the visual location of an object possibly affects individuals' assessments was presented. The results showed that individuals believe that the object that is centrally placed in a horizontal layout is more important than the other objects.

> *"People think that products that are centrally placed on a store shelf are more important than other products."*

One of the conclusions was that if people think that this is how information about the object's quality is shown, it could be used as an alternative stimulus to make a quality assessment with the fact that a centrally located property is important. It also means that if there are minimal cognitive resources, such as if there was a shortage of other information available at an assessment, then the centrally placed objects have a unique position in comparison with the other objects (Valenzuela and Raghubir, 2009).

In a later study in 2009, researchers concluded that consumers have a preexisting picture of how a store looks, in terms of its layout. This means that the most popular products are assumed to be positioned in the center of a shelf arrangement, whereas more expensive products are assumed to be located higher up in a shelf arrangement. It is further assumed that products that have pricing and promotional offers are placed in the horizontal part of a shelf arrangement, i.e., at the edges.

The conclusion that can be drawn is that products that are placed in the middle of a shelf arrangement (or a product distribution) are more popular than those appearing in the outskirts. This affects consumer's preferences and behaviors, regardless of whether the goal was to buy a popular product, a quality product, or a campaign product.

Affective Reactions
In recent decades, emotions and feelings have come to be increasingly important in understanding consumers' behaviors in purchasing and consumption processes. It has no longer been possible to explain these behaviors using only the cognitive, mental processes that take place in a person's brain. In several studies, feelings, as explanatory variables, have shown to influence individuals' behaviors and actions. Therefore, a number of models

have been proposed in the literature with different affective and emotional dimensions.

There is a general perception in the literature that people's emotional lives play a crucial role when it comes to perceiving and experiencing a product or a brand. For the sense of sight, this is clearly expressed, because different visual stimuli have the ability to create positive or negative feelings about, for example, an advertisement for a brand or a product's design, shape, or color. Several studies in advertising and commercials have shown that emotionally charged advertising and commercials are more effective than other types of advertising.

> *In a classic study in 1987, researchers Edell and Burke showed how consumers who viewed various television messages generated different emotions. It was also shown that these emotions affected the perception of the advertisement, which documented that the feelings that arise in the moment of exposure have an influence on the advertising process in the human brain.*

Research suggests that by making use of emotions in advertising and commercials, it is possible for a company to create a favorable attitude among consumers toward a particular brand. It is the feeling arising from the advertisement, which in turn passes to the brand and helps to create the favorable attitude in individuals. It has been shown that there is a strong positive relationship between the effects of advertisements and brand attitude in consumers; that is, emotionally charged advertising contributes in that a favorable attitude arises for the actual brand.

> *"A brown Starbucks bag has the text: 'Flavor my senses, set in motion my fantasies, and nourish my dreams.'"*

Emotional messages and advertisements are usually distinguished on the basis of the attitude that an individual has in response to them, which is expressed by positive or negative valence. It is further assumed that the feeling that the individual gets may also lead to a corresponding behavior. When a person's emotions are directed toward the message or advertisement, as visual stimulus, there is a positive valence, and when the feeling goes away, it produces a negative valence. Examples of emotions that can give rise to positive valence are joy, love, optimism, warmth, and friendship, whereas emotions that can give rise to negative valence are sadness, fear, shame, guilt, or remorse.

Various studies have also shown that an emotionally charged advertisement helps people to have a better state of mind, with a happier mood. In addition, it appears that such advertisements are easier to remember and that they are perceived in a more beneficial way, compared with ads that are based on a more neutral or worse state of mind. There are several different views on how this can be explained and what cognitive mechanisms influence the emotional process.

One view is that consumers with a positive frame of mind can be regarded as mindless, which means that they accept even the arguments of low quality in advertising. But another view is that those consumers who have a positive frame of mind would rather be considered as more flexible, creative, and effective in their thought processes, which creates greater association opportunities with regard to the product. There is also a view that asserts that a positive frame of mind is more efficient for an advertisement or a message because the positive mood, without being able to influence the information in the advertisement as a whole, can be transferred to the product in question in a more unconscious level in the individual (LaTour and Latour, 2009).

It is clear from research that visual stimuli, such as design and shape, create different psychological reactions in individuals. It refers to reactions having both cognitive and affective components, which can interact and occur simultaneously. Regarding cognitive reactions, the product's shape influences consumers' confidence in the product and the brand, and it depends on, for example, how easy the product is to use, its durability, if it is technically sophisticated or the value you get for the money. Furthermore, a product is categorized based on design and shape to a specific product category, which as a cognitive reaction means that one can distinguish between, for example, a standard car and a luxury car.

> *A study at the School of Design and Crafts, University of Gothenburg, on the rehabilitation of patients shows that if a patient's senses are stimulated with design, the opportunity for her or him to recover increases both physically and mentally. There is a developed concept where smart interior details, such as tables, chairs, cardigans, mittens, and rugs, are part of a good rehabilitation environment.*

There is also a discussion on whether a belief in the product comes from a holistic visual perception of the shape or from a linear processing of a design element at a time. As mentioned previously, the Gestalt psychology is based on a human perceiving the object as a whole rather than as atomistic, that is, each element separately. Researchers such as Bloch (1995) suggest that both perspectives occur almost simultaneously and that the product's shape is first perceived as a whole, and then the eyes of the beholder proceed to make certain features more prominent than others. If a consumer is going to buy an armchair, the armchair is first judged in its entirety, and then the colors, materials, or fabrics are studied.

In terms of affective reactions, it is believed that design and shape evoke aesthetic reactions, such as approval or disapproval. It is widely believed that this type of reactions can elicit some degree of attention as well as strong positive emotions to the actual product. It is further assumed that the design and sensory properties, rather than the product's functional features and performance, mainly trigger the aesthetic reactions.

Several studies show that colors can evoke emotions in humans in the same way as advertisements and commercial messages. It also turns out that variations in color shades, in a more systematic way, can affect the feeling of satisfaction with a product or a brand.

In recent studies, it was found that variations in color shades also lead to more systematic changes in the feelings for a product. One observation is that the short wavelengths of color shades like blue seem to elicit a stronger sense of relaxation, in comparison with the long wavelengths of color shades like red. Similarly, it seems the feeling of excitement is greater for long wavelengths of color shades, in comparison with the short.

INFLUENTIAL FACTORS FOR THE SENSE OF SIGHT

The sense of sight is without a doubt the human sense that has been studied the most within retail and marketing research and is the most prominent in the literature. Based on the previously presented SEB model, the factors that may be linked to the sense of sight's influence on an individual's affections, cognitions, and actual behaviors in the buying and consumption processes are presented (Figure 5.2).

First, the societal culture (S), as an influential factor, is addressed in relation to visual preferences on the individual and group levels, as well as the importance of visual symbolism. Second, the service environment (E), as an influential factor, is addressed in relation to the visual stimuli, visual perception, and visual symbolism. Third, the brand (B), as an influential factor, is addressed in relation to visual stimuli, visual perception, and visual symbolism.

SOCIETAL CULTURE

In research, the question as to whether there are cultural similarities or differences between individuals and groups when it comes to the importance of visual stimuli and visual preferences is discussed. This is deemed

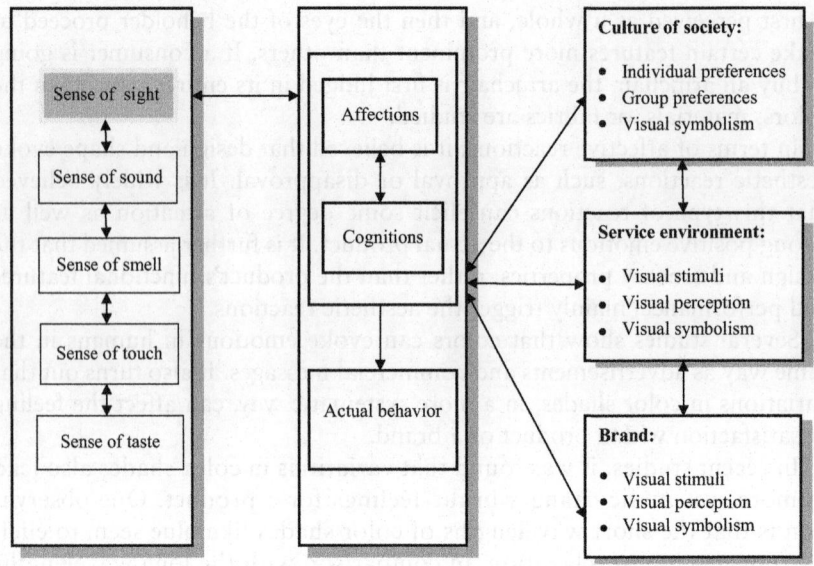

Figure 5.2 The Sense of Sight and the SEB-Model

to be very important in order to be able to understand and explain how humans through different visual stimuli, such as advertisements and commercials, design, colors, or characters, interpret and understand their environment.

As examples of culture's influence, it can be mentioned that colors have been linked to health for centuries; and in ancient Egypt, doctors washed their patients in brightly colored water to cure ailments among sick people. I will return to this issue concerning the meaning of visual symbolism later in this chapter

Individual Preferences

Every person has his/her own unique visual preferences, which is based on the fact that what an individual sees and receives through his/her vision is registered immediately and intensely in the brain. It means that what is seen receives faster attention and less energy is required to interpret that actual information.

> *Some people register one visual stimulus faster because they have visual sensory preferences that not all individuals possess.*

An important question in this context is: *What is the difference between the fact that an individual has visual sensory preferences and that she or he can visualize what is seen?* It is not a given that a person who can easily visualize things also has visual preferences. Having a visual sensory preference means for a particular individual that the brain quickly registers the visual stimuli in comparison with, for example, auditory stimuli or kinesthetic stimuli.

The term visualization means being able to create internal, mental images and differentiating oneself from having visual sensory preferences. It is possible for most people to train themselves to be able to visualize, which many athletes do before major competitions. Then you create a single, positive image of the contest to become less nervous and stressed. Similarly, most individuals can also train themselves to become more observant of things, regardless of the visual sensory preferences.

There are individual differences between individuals in terms of the ability to visualize, that is, create a visual picture language. Research suggests that this ability affects what a person has to rely on for existing visual stimuli in order to make an assessment (Raghubir, 2010). People with a better ability to visualize rely less on stimulus-based information than those who have less ability to visualize.

Individuals who have visual sensory preferences notice and quickly pay attention to differences or changes in the environment. Other people who can point out the details that differ can assist those individuals who do not have these preferences. This means that individuals have very different perceptions and expectations of how things should look, which completely depends on the properties and structure of the brain.

Research suggests that there is a large consensus when it comes to a viewer's visual preferences. These can either be influenced by visual attributes of images or by nonvisual associations, as these are common in many individuals.

In one study, the factors that influence the emergence of individual visual preferences in people were investigated, and to find out about these factors, the researchers developed a number of new abstract and visually disparate images (Vessel and Rubin, 2010). It appears that at the individual observation level, both the abstract and real images led to consistent and robust visual preferences. This occurred despite the fact that the abstract images, according to the researchers' opinions, led to fewer consistent preferences in comparison with the actual pictures. It was concluded that the abstract images might give rise to a higher degree of individual visual preferences.

The study's findings were that the visual preferences appeared to be influenced by the semantic content, that is, the linguistic meaning, in the actual stimulus. This seems to have led to similar semantic interpretations in people who in turn have similar preferences. But in further experiments, it was also found that the highest individual preferences could still be created for the real images in scenarios where the semantic associations were not emphasized. This indicates the importance of the semantic content for the creation of individual visual preferences.

> *"Individuals at a high emotional level react more favorably to a visual ad."*

The question about the extent to which the interaction between affective (emotions and feelings) and cognitive (thoughts and attention) affects an individual's ability to process verbal and visual information through images and words has been studied in the context of visual perception. In an exploratory study, four process groups, namely, high emotional stress/low cognition, low affective/high cognition, high emotional stress/high cognition, and low emotional stress/low cognition were tested as to how they responded to a verbal stimulus, a visual stimulus, and a combination of verbal and visual stimuli.

The results showed that individuals with a high affective level reacted more favorably toward a visual advertisement in comparison with other groups. Furthermore, it appeared that individuals with both a high affective and a high cognitive level reacted more positively to a combination of the verbal and visual advertisement.

The study's conclusion was that visual advertisements that contain emotional elements should be more effective for the affective group of individuals, in comparison with the cognitive group.

Female and Male

Research suggests that there are gender differences between men and women from a variety of aspects relating to visual perception and visual preferences.

One experiment examined whether gender differences between men and women were related to the women's greater verbal ability in comparison with men. A substudy was conducted with 246 university students in which recognition by memory afterward was studied for both named objects and abstract forms, as images on a computer screen. The results showed that women, to a significant extent, recognized more abstract forms and named objects, compared with men.

The experiment also included the study of women's greater compliance when it comes to following work instructions in comparison with men. A substudy was conducted on 105 university students in which a temporary learning task was intended to test the recognition of named objects. Even these results showed that women, more significantly, identified more items than men.

One of the conclusions of the experiment with regard to recognition afterward through memory was that the gender differences exist because women have a greater instinctive process of the surrounding stimuli than men are thought to have. This was discussed in view of the evolutionary development of humans and the importance that awareness of the environment has had so that we can take care of our offspring.

> *At Texas A & M University, a study was conducted with toddlers aged three to four months, using the eye-tracking technology, to investigate the choices made by 20 girls and 21 boys between a Barbie doll and balls. The children got to see animated images of balls, dolls, figures in a group and individual figures. It turned out that boys were drawn to balls, tools, and construction toys as well as playing in larger groups than girls. Furthermore, the study indicated that testosterone levels influenced the boys, whereas the girls were not at all affected by their hormone levels.*

Edens and McCormick (2002) conducted a study on how students were influenced affectively and cognitively by verbal and visual print ads. The study included 111 boys and 84 girls who were randomly selected for processing mainly visual print ads. Students were then asked questions that measured three dependent variables, namely, emotional response, conclusions, and memory of specific facts.

The results showed that the visual ads, for the most part, evoked the memory of more facts and conclusions as well as a more intense emotional response in comparison with verbal ads. It further appeared from the study's findings that girls drew more of their own conclusions, remembered more, and showed stronger emotional responses than boys. It should also be added that the girls noticed the advertisement's explicit statements more frequently than boys.

It was also shown by another study that there are gender differences when it comes to processing visual, emotional, stimuli. One study examined how 30 participants, including 15 women and 15 men, processed 75 pleasant and unpleasant pictures as well as neutral images in their brains.

The results of the study showed that women reacted more emotionally than men when it came to unpleasant pictures. It was suggested that gender differences exist in the processing of visual, emotional stimuli and that these differences should be taken into account in future studies.

In another study, the reactions of 28 women and men to both pleasant and unpleasant pictures were investigated using MRI. The starting point of the study was that visual stimuli of motivational character directly attracts attention and enhances visual perception. It was found that males exhibit greater activity than women for erotic pictures, which could be explained by the gender-specific visual mechanism regarding sexual selection.

When it comes to comparative advertising, a study showed that these types of ads encourage men, unlike women, to engage in the evaluation of the brand. Conversely, these kinds of advertisements encouraged women to draw conclusions about the manipulative content of the advertisements. These gender differences, in turn, led to the conclusion that men evaluated the advertisements in a more advantageous manner, which led to higher purchase intentions. For women, the result was the opposite, i.e., the advertisement was evaluated in a negative way and resulted in lower purchase intentions.

Group Preferences

Already through an experiment in the early 1960s, the renowned American psychologist Charles Osgood—inventor of the Semantic Differential scale—questioned whether the structure of a language affects a person's cognitive behavior (Osgood, 1960). The questions asked were of the type: "Do Navajo people, like us, see happiness as more up and sadness as more down? Do Japanese people, like us, imagine delight as colorful and calm as colorless? Are Navajo people different from others, when it comes to the connotative meaning of words like 'blue'?"(Ibid. p. 146–169).

The conclusions that Osgood presented were the first attempt to demonstrate that the visual/verbal relations that characterize a culture and its language are shared by people who experience different cultures and speak different languages. It was therefore suggested that there might be a common worldview that can be perceived as relatively stable, despite the differences that exist between the different languages and cultures.

Research suggests that there are cultural differences between population groups when it comes to the visual perception of places. Whereas people from Southeast Asia tend to pay attention to relationships between focal objects and the background elements, it appears that Westerners instead pay more attention to prominent objects.

> "Americans and Chinese people perceive visual objects in different ways, which depends on how the eyes are fixed on the object in question."

To investigate this relationship, a study was conducted where it was assumed that cultural differences arise as a result of culturally different patterns of movement in the eyes when a person is confronted with a natural place (Chua et al., 2005). The study measured the eye movements of Chinese and Americans who got to experience a number of photographs with a focal object against a complex background. The results showed that Americans fixed their eyes more on the focal object than the Chinese; moreover, the Americans tended to quickly fix their eyes on the focal object. On the other hand, the Chinese placed more importance on the background than the Americans.

Another study investigated cultural differences through two experiments by means of the so-called visual discovery paradigm. The results showed that people from Southeast Asia are better than Americans at detecting color changes when a number of colored blocks are expanded to include a wider area and, in contrast, are less able to detect these changes when the image is shrunk. On the other hand, Americans are quicker to detect color changes in the midpoint of an image or a screen.

Cultural differences also seem to exist in terms of visual perception and visual preferences related to the Internet and various websites. In a comparison between gender and cultural clusters in Asia, Europe, Latin and South America, as well as North America, it was presented that differences exist regarding the perception of and satisfaction with the design of various websites. People from Asia and Latin and South America have similar perceptions on the one hand, and people from Europe and North America have another. Furthermore, it appears that women in some cultures are considered to have a wider range of preferences regarding the attributes of a website, in comparison with men.

The question of whether color preferences are similar or not among different ethnic groups has fascinated researchers on color over the years. The literature is variable, and it is possible to find arguments for both similarities and differences.

Chattopadhyay et al. (2010) conducted a survey, based on three different studies, to identify whether there could be differences regarding color preferences between three Chinese ethnic populations. This study focused on color preferences and specific hue preferences. The results showed that there were differences regarding the perceived emotions evoked by blue and red hues. It turned out that blue color tones were perceived as more relaxing and were preferred over red hues in the two ethnic groups, namely, white-skinned and dark-skinned, which were studied.

It also appeared that the choice of a color shade was determined by the dominant cultural norms, but not always. There were cross-cultural differences in specific situations, which is the case when these standards are prominent in one culture but not in another culture. This was the case in one of the studies when it came to celebrating the New Year, where the choice of wrapping paper reflected the person's general color preferences. If there was not a specific cultural color associated with a specific event, such as Christmas or New Year, then people's choices of color seemed to be influenced by their general color preferences.

> *"There seems to exist a general similarity between population groups when it comes to color preferences."*

The conclusions of the study were that there is a general similarity in terms of color preferences among the three ethnic groups that were studied. Furthermore, there is a general preference for the blue color in all cultures and prominent color preferences probably attract stronger feelings; if these are developed, they affect an individual's color preferences.

It has also been suggested that there is a physiological basis for the relationship between color hues and emotions, regardless of people's cultural identity, where it is assumed that the effect of the color hues on emotions is proposed to be the same for everyone. This is because all humans have a similar physiology. It is also suggested that emotions should be interpreted in the same way across cultural boundaries and that feelings evoked by color hues most likely lead to the color shades being seen in the same way, regardless of the culture.

Visual Symbolism

There is a general perception in the literature that consumers choose the products they consume and the consumption experience they seek as symbols intended to create a person who brings success and status in the eyes of others.

In his classic article, Levy (1981) discusses the symbolic importance of the right products and their symbolic values. This may include, for example, the inherent symbolism of a shape, a color, a style, or a size, which can be interpreted in different ways by individuals. Levy asserts that a symbolic analysis is about interpreting people's fantasies about their personality, age, gender, or social status in relation to different products in order to identify the symbolic value of the products.

When it comes to the importance of visual stimuli, such as design, shape, and color, it is believed that their symbolic value lies in the meaning and the meaning they represent to consumers. In this way, the meaning is subjective, which also creates affective links between a product and an individual.

People have for a long time surrounded themselves with pictures, signs, or symbols in different cultures and sought to use their importance in communication where the sense of sight is the focus. In the interaction between a message and its readers, the meaning comes to be expressed, and the significance of the various symbols used is also included. For example, when an image gets an individual to react, one becomes aware of the effects this image creates based on the ideologies, connotations, or myths that are embedded in the actual image. Within the research field, visual semiotics, the significance of meaning and ideology, is studied by deconstructing various visual messages where the symbols are believed to play a prominent role.

A symbol is usually defined in the literature as something that represents something else, that is, a material item or object. It can be a letter, an emblem, a logo, a brand, or a sign, which is intended to denote or designate something. But it can also be an image, a phrase, a word, or something similar that can have a number of meanings, which in turn can be perceived as if it has intrinsic human values separate from what it should symbolize.

This means that the symbols found in a social culture perform its normal function, namely, to represent that which is to be symbolized. A sign as a symbol can be a word, a picture, or a sound and have the task of communicating the meaning that is intended. In the literature, it is generally believed that signs can mean different things to different people and especially nonverbal signs can contribute to both multiple meanings and complex symbols.

> *A study shows that marketers in Southeast Asia who are thinking of a brand's symbolic impact should be recommended to make use of folksy, taboo, supernatural, or religious meanings through colors, numbers, or other symbols. The supernatural element attracts most Asians—from card reading in China and healing techniques in the Philippines to ghosts in Japan. The same may be deemed applicable for making decisions on names, where "lucky name" and "lucky number" are important to create positive attitudes toward company and brand name.*

The research refers to the market as a *sign economy* where all kinds of characters are used to manifest a brand's meaning. In this way, characters work as symbols to differentiate and position a particular brand with respect to different audiences to communicate a particular meaning. When it comes to consumers' decision-making, it is generally accepted that characters, as symbols, are prominent and important as they help to create an image in the individual.

There are several examples of how cultural symbols are linked to celebrations, holidays, or religious contexts, such as the red color associated with Christmas celebrations in Sweden. The same goes for the black and orange colors that are linked to the Halloween celebration. But there is also an association between a context and a particular color, or shade of color, which is present in one culture but that does not exist in another culture. An example of this is the color red, which in China is associated with the Chinese New Year, whereas the Western New Year does not have a specific color hue associated with it.

> *"When Kalmar's new football stadium, The Goldbird in Sweden, was to be finalized, the coach, Nanne Bergstrand, saw to it that the opponents' dressing room was painted in soothing colors."*

When it comes to the issue of a corporate identity that is supposed to help to create an image among consumers, two questions are connected to visual symbolism. The first question concerns the choice of the company name, its products, and brands, and the second question concerns the selection of appropriate visual symbols, such as logos, labeling, or packaging. The question of visual symbolism is one of the key elements in a company's branding processes when it comes to identifying the most salient features of the brand from a visual standpoint.

Research suggests that letters and symbols contribute in that Chinese consumers consider a brand name based on the visual attractiveness. This is different from British consumers, who instead assess a brand name based on how it sounds auditorily. Furthermore, it is of importance that the writing style of a particular name be adapted to a feminine handwriting for a feminine product, and not vice versa.

Nonetheless, for Chinese consumers, it is not enough that a brand name looks good; they also require that it appeal to the Chinese way of thinking. This means that simple, memorable logos and names are preferred. Furthermore, it is important that names, logos, and other visual elements, for example, in advertising and campaign promotions constitute a coherent whole.

SERVICE ENVIRONMENT

In research, the cultural and social interaction between different places and consumers has gained increasing attention. Thus spatial capacity, when it comes to creating meaning, as the location for the interaction that occurs between societal culture and consumers, is considered in a continuously evolving relationship. This is an expression of a common cultural meaning, especially when a business exchange takes place. Among the contexts that create meaning for consumers, it should be mentioned that the mall is thought to contribute to the construction of personal meaning and experiences with personal values. Similarly, other places are thought to represent paradise or Utopia and nostalgia.

> Store space in retail can be considered to serve a more abstract, social purpose, and this space has been extended to include the broader shopping environment as expressed by the shopping street, galleria, or shopping center. These spaces have become places for play, pleasure, or consumption and thereby offer communication and interaction between people and the brand.

A general notion in the literature is that consumers feel the atmosphere in a service environment, such as location, through visual or other sensory stimuli, where both verbal and nonverbal stimuli are thought to contribute to creating an appealing atmosphere (Kotler, 1974). It is clear from several studies that nonverbal stimuli, which are the basis for the psychological sensations in individuals, lead to both cognitive and affective reactions to a service environment. This is thought, in turn, to influence the consumer's loyalty, either favorably or unfavorably.

In the literature, the term visual marketing refers to how companies strategically use commercial and noncommercial visual symbols and signs to communicate interesting and useful messages and experiences to consumers. In visual marketing, a prominent component is how the visual communication is designed, which includes the design, for example, of advertisements, packaging, and logos.

Theories of visual marketing are processed within disciplines such as cognitive psychology, social psychology, and visual science, where the latter is by nature, interdisciplinary. Central within visual science is that sight is responsible for the calculation of how the world is shaped around us, with the help of the eyes and the brain. For this reason, visual science can provide knowledge about what consumers really interpret as key or consciously in front of a shelf in a supermarket, what they interpret peripherally or subliminally, or which aspects of the various visual stimuli they are affected by.

Visual Stimuli

In the well-known stimulus-organism-response model (S-O-R) by Mehrabian and Russell (1974), it is believed that different stimuli in a service environment affect consumers' emotional states, which can lead to a response by either approach or avoidance behavior (Figure 5.3). The main idea of the model is that individuals evaluate a service environment based on the degree of emotional stimuli they receive, with the result that they either approach or avoid the actual service environment.

The model shows that the different emotional states are considered to be the mediating variables between the stimuli in the service environment and consumer behavior. It further appears from the compilation done by Turley and Milliman (2000) of over 60 scientific studies that there is a significant relationship between a manipulated service environment and shopping behavior. Numerous studies have confirmed that consumers really react to different types of stimuli (cues) in a service environment.

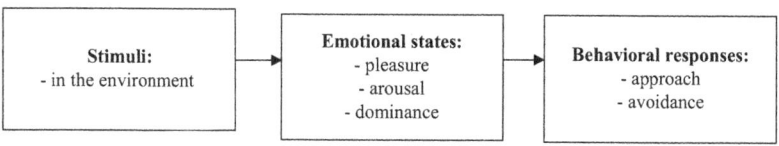

Figure 5.3   Mehrabian-Russell-Model (Mehrabian and Russell, 1974)

The literature reveals different classifications of stimuli that can be used in a service environment. One classification proposed by Booms and Bitner (1982) is based on signals such as architecture, lighting, paint, interior design, layout, and temperature. Later, Bitner (1992) proposed a classification of atmospheric conditions, spatial layout, and functionality along with signs, symbols, and artificial objects. It should also be added that a classification was proposed based on the use of the shop exterior, general interior, design, layout, decoration, and place of purchase.

There is a general perception in the literature that design affects customers' actual behaviors by creating attention, evoking emotional responses, and communicating different messages through those signals and stimuli that are in the service environment, which *retail design* refers to. Furthermore, a classification has been proposed of *ambient factors*, design factors, and *social factors*, where the latter two are of relevance to analyze and discuss the importance of visual stimuli, as shown in Table 5.1.

Both the design and the structural aspects of service environments and indoor shopping areas prove to affect the importance of the relevant information, thought processes, and responses in individuals. Researchers such as Meyers-Levy and Zhu (2008) have proposed three categories of structural factors that occur in consumption and shopping environments, namely, architectural elements (e.g., ceilings, windows), independent store elements (e.g., showcases, cabinets, mirrors), and broader contextual elements (e.g.,

Table 5.1 A Classification of Stimuli in a Service Environment (Adapted from Ezeh and Harris, 2007)

Ambient factors	Background stimuli exist below our awareness	Air quality: – temperature, humidity, ventilation Sound – level, pitch, genre Scent – intensity, cleanliness
Design factors (interior/exterior)	Stimuli exist at the forefront of our awareness	Aesthetic and functional: – architecture, layout – lighting, light – color, comfort – scale, signage, material – texture, pattern – shape, style, accessories
Social factors	People in the environment	Audience (other customers) Number, appearance, behavior Service personnel Number, appearance, behavior

Ezeh, C. and Harris, L.C. (2007), "Servicescape research: a review and a research agenda," *The Marketing Review*, 7:159–178.

nearby stores with the same or complementary product categories). But the knowledge of how structural aspects in indoor environments really affect consumers in terms of perception, judgment, and decision is limited.

> *"At an airport, it is important to ensure that passengers check in and pass the security check; at the same time, the service landscape must be attractive in a sensory way and appealing."*

There is a general consensus that visual stimuli, to a greater extent than other sensory stimuli, are the basis for the image that individuals create in a service landscape. In terms of ambient factors, these will be discussed in connection with the senses of sound, smell, touch, and taste, as stimuli in the following chapters.

Aesthetic and Functional Stimuli
As visual stimuli, design factors are proposed to be either *aesthetic* or *functional*. Factors such as comfort, layout, and signs are considered to be more functional than aesthetic. The difference between the aesthetic and the functional is proposed to lie in how individuals evaluate the artistic quality with respect to the physical features of a service environment. Architecture, lighting, decor, color, light, materials, scales, and style are viewed as aesthetic elements.

There is also a general perception in the literature that although the aesthetic and functional stimuli are closely related to each other, the aesthetic stimuli promote, to a large extent, sensory gladness in the experience itself, whereas the functional stimuli facilitates the customer's behavior. There are also several studies that have shown how design factors affect consumers' behaviors in a service environment.

It is generally considered that visual stimuli, such as visual information, are the stimuli that are most useful to get a person's attention regarding a retail environment or a specific product. In a comparison between the visual and tactile information, the latter requires labor, which is not the case with visual information. Regarding the significance of visual information, research in consumer behavior has traditionally focused on the visual, aesthetic experience, and how noninstrumental qualities give rise to emotions and feelings in different individuals.

In this context, the consumer's aesthetic reactions build on the product attributes, such as color, shape, congruence, size, symmetry, or proportion, which are thought to help to differentiate a product from competing products on the market. It is further assumed that these types of product attributes also have symbolic content, which leads to the development of relationships between consumers and the brand.

Some researchers claim that the aesthetic value of a product is more important to the individual than the functional benefit. It has also been shown that aesthetic stimuli directly affect consumers' satisfaction with fashion products, such as clothing and shoes. One study analyzed how the aesthetic dimensions of a product in connection with product evaluation and decision-making affected consumers. The results of the study showed that aesthetic stimuli, such as expressions of product aesthetics, have a significant effect on consumers' choice of products, such as microwave ovens, sunscreens, and radios. One conclusion was that the aesthetic value of a product is relevant to consumers' choice, which applies to different product categories.

In service environments, such as stores, malls, websites, offices, places, restaurants, or cities, the aesthetic stimuli, including architecture, lighting, color, interior, and signs, have an impact on consumers' visual experience. Research suggests that the effects of visual stimuli on the customer's reaction have been further investigated with regard to perception, sensation, influence, memory, cognition, and behavior.

Architecture
When it comes to the impact of architecture, it has been shown that high ceilings, which are considered to be ever present in a service environment, can improve both the way people process information and think and their response (Meyers-Levy and Zhu, 2008). The ceiling height is also intimately linked to individuals' sense of freedom, which is believed to contribute to the data integration and abstraction, or limitations, which are thought to contribute to more concrete, specific thinking. It has been shown that high ceilings are ranked among the three most important architectural features that contribute to consumers' psychological well-being.

As an architectural element, windows are viewed as being able to influence consumers' thought processes and responses to products in a shopping environment. It is also assumed that the lack of windows in a shopping environment could lead consumers to be more concrete, rather than to feel free and be creative. If there are windows, it can be assumed that this would help individuals to come up with more creative ways to use the products; however, if there are no windows, it could rather lead to the functional attributes being the focus of attention.

> *"Aircraft manufacturers enhance consumers' experience of a cabin by using higher ceilings, even if it is just an illusion."*

The appearance and contours of the walls are also thought to influence consumers' perceptions of store products, because this influences the context in which the actual product is found. It is clear from several studies that the appearance of the walls, such as color and material, are reflected in the perception of the product, which affects an individual's assessment and purchasing decisions. Regarding the contour, it is assumed that this is predominantly seen as straight or curved, which may relate to the male or female bodies. It is, therefore, assumed that the contour of the walls means that consumers can identify with their own sex, which can also mean that gender-related products can be associated with a particular wall contour.

When it comes to places and cities, such as Manhattan in New York or King's Park in Malmö, the architecture affects a person's well-being. The researcher Matilda Annerstedt at the Swedish University of Agricultural Sciences found in a study that experiencing nature in the form of beautiful greenery and the chirping of birds affects the parasympathetic nervous system in a favorable way for a person's rest and recovery. The blood pressure dropped and the pulse became slower, which illustrate the importance of landscape architecture as stimuli for a service environment outdoors.

Lighting

The effects of lighting on consumers' affections, cognitions, and their actual behaviors received attention in several studies early on. The underlying theory is related to the model proposed by Mehrabian-Russell, where an approach or avoidance response is affected by which emotional state is elicited in an individual through the actual lighting.

Several researchers have pointed to the importance of lighting as a prominent component in a retail environment, because it is believed that this positively affects an individual's visual attraction to the entire store environment, including the product range. It is also believed that the lighting not only conveys information about the place or space itself, but that it can also convey the content and meaning.

One study showed that the lighting in a store landscape had a significant impact on how shoppers investigated and handled the assortment of wine in a wine shop. However, it demonstrated no significant effects for the time spent in the store or the total purchases made.

Furthermore, another study showed that extra lighting in a store display had a positive impact on consumer behavior. A significant correlation was found between lighting and display, indicating that additional lighting in a store can be helpful to both attract and retain customers.

The cognitive processes of consumers are affected by whether the service environment is dimly lit and gives a dim impression or if it is brighter and more enlightened. With dimmer lighting, many individuals react more concretely to the stimuli that are presented through more individual and personal reactions. This has been shown through more creativity and less inhibitions in relation to the products, which indicates that a more dim service environment can increase interest in the products and put into motion consumers' dreams and fantasies.

Color

Initially, it should be said that light can be broken down into a spectrum of six distinct colors, namely, red, orange, yellow, green, blue, and violet. It is believed that red has the longest wavelength, whereas violet has the shortest. Regarding the classification of colors, red and yellow colors are viewed as warm, and blue and green colors are viewed as cold, but the difference is considered to be more or less relative. White, gray, and black colors are considered neutral.

Research suggests that a person's color experience varies from one individual to another, so it is not possible to know how another person experiences colors. Furthermore, the effects of color on a person's personality are not clear in the research on color theory; however, there is evidence that there is a physiological response as part of the human experience. In contrast, there is no evidence that you can connect specific colors to specific responses; such attempts have proved to be fruitless.

It is also clear from the literature that colors can exert a significant influence on the individual's cognitive interpretations and actions in the shopping environment. It appears that this effect occurs both on the consumer's emotionally related moods and on the consumer's activity-related arousal. One study showed that visitors of different retail environments actually preferred blue environments as opposed to red, because the color blue was perceived as being more relaxing and led to longer periods of searching for products as well as a greater propensity for purchases.

Numerous studies have confirmed that consumers are actually influenced by colors, and useful results have also been presented in terms of how consumers react to, for example, different combinations of colors and lighting.

Interiors and Signs

Within retail, window displays have existed for a long time to bring attention to the products that are marketed and sold in a service environment, such as shops and department stores. In recent decades, visual merchandising, i.e., various sales promoting measures, has increasingly been linked to a design coupled approach, where both the outer and the inner design of the store environment have come to be emphasized.

When it comes to signs of products on the tables, shelves, or benches, these are made of surfaces, which are made of materials of glass, metal, plastic, or wood. Some researchers believe that people associate glass with modern society, because it dominates in modern buildings, whereas wood is associated with nature and is a natural material. In this way, a surface on a table or shelf can give an individual an association with a particular context and affect the assessment that is made.

Social Stimuli

In the literature, it is believed that the service environment not only consists of tangible stimuli but also of social stimuli, which include the people who play a crucial role in influencing consumers' actual behaviors. It is believed that the people who are in a particular environment, such as a restaurant or a supermarket, determine the type of human environment they represent because it is not possible to separate individuals and the human environment from each other.

There is a consensus in research that social stimuli in the service environment include the human factor through the number of service personnel, conduct, and behavior, number of visitors (customers), conduct and behavior, which together constitute the human aspect of a service environment. Furthermore, it is believed that the behavior

> *"In a service environment, the personnel's style and behavior are of particular importance, as it affects the corporate and brand image."*

of the human factor, in terms of both service personnel and customers, either suppresses or enhances the sensory experience, which in turn is considered to lead to either an approach or avoidance behavior in relation to the service environment (Bitner, 1992).

Kotler (1974) pointed out early on the importance of personnel to the atmosphere in a service environment and believed, for example, that aircraft personnel were selected according to their ability to create confidence among customers. The service personnel's behavior and style, therefore, are considered to be particularly important factors, because these people contribute to shaping the corporate and brand image.

The importance that visitors or customers have to create a positive atmosphere in the service environment is highlighted in the research. A general idea is that customers can help to create content and meaning in different activities and thereby become cocreators of value for both the company and the customers, as a social stimulus.

Visual Perception

Visual perception in a service environment relates to how individuals recognize and interpret the visual stimuli that exist in the environment. The stimuli that are paid attention to are also perceived and interpreted by an individual selective process in different individuals.

Initially, it should be said that visual perception is based on the concept of ambient or environmental perception, where the perceptual process is the basis of human behavior in a particular environment. It is further assumed that the process itself is the source of all messages or signals in the surrounding environment, which in turn stimulate the human senses with more messages than what is possible to process effectively. Some researchers argue that it is not possible to isolate individuals from an environment in which they find themselves in during the perception process, because the process is based on interaction with the environment and this affects perception.

It is believed that the interaction between individuals and the environment is characterized by a number of different stages. First, the surroundings must stimulate individuals through the senses so that perception and cognition can occur and for an evaluation of the physical environment to take place. It is believed that this perception process involves both senses and perception, where the senses are regarded more as a physiological process, in comparison with perception, which is based on a psychological process and differs in structure and content.

It should also be mentioned that perception, in the sense of how an individual receives and interprets external stimuli, begins as a sensation process and can be said to constitute a selective process. It is generally accepted that if an individual does not notice a stimulus, it will not be perceived or interpreted. Most people spend the majority of their time on things that they have an interest in, and enjoyment of, which in turn creates satisfaction. Every individual's perception therefore is unique, and consumers respond to advertisements, packaging, products, and similar stimuli in light of their own motivations, their attitudes, and their social situations.

In terms of perception studies in research, psychologists seem to be more focused on studying the perception of objects, compared with the perception of the surroundings and its significance for individuals. Researchers such as Mehrabian and Russell (1974) claim that perception of the surroundings may be considered more meaningful, because it is linked to the concept of spatial perception. This is considered to encompass both visual spatial perception and auditory spatial perception and is seen as a psychological process in which individuals interpret the surrounding area, the surrounding objects, and the current situation through their senses. In this three-dimensional space, an individual weighs things in his/her mind and makes assessments based on distance, height, and direction in time and in every place. It is thanks to visual stimuli and the individual's past experiences that he/she is able to understand and evaluate the different situations.

In a study by Chandon et al. (2009), the effects of retail activities at the *point-of-purchase* at supermarkets were studied in terms of the individual's visual attention and evaluation. It has recently become more common to consider the point-of-purchase in a store as an advertising medium to create long-term brand awareness and a long-term image. The researchers chose 11 leading brands in each product category based on the market share and added a twelfth brand, which was not known in the United States. Specifically, 348 adult shoppers were recruited from different shopping centers in eight U.S. cities. Participants were offered $10 for their participation and were aged from 24 to 69 years. They had at least secondary education and a minimum annual income of $25,000.

Using the experimental and eye-tracking method, where the eye movements are measured, the effects of the number and the placement of the shelf facades using twelve different planograms were investigated. Planograms refer to a diagram that is used for a particular product category, where the location and the number of shelf facades are shown for each stocked product at a retailer. The attention was measured for each participant and product category, as the total time the image was studied and the eye's fixation with respect to both the position and duration in time for the actual brands.

In the experiment, three levels of shelf facade manipulation (4, 8, and 12 shelf facades) were used, which corresponded to a certain area on the image. Furthermore, four levels were used relating to the actual brand's vertical positioning on the shelf, namely, first, second, third, and bottom shelf, and four levels regarding the horizontal positioning, namely, the far left, left of center, right of center, and far right.

> "Products that are placed on the top and in the middle on a shelf get more attention than the products that are placed further down."

The results of the study showed that visual attention, and thus also brand evaluation, were strongly influenced by the number of shelf facades. For the occasional users of the brand with a low-market share, a doubling of the number of shelf facades meant that the eye fixation increased by 26 percent (from 63 percent to 80 percent) and brand choice by 67 percent (from 3 percent to 5 percent). For the average brand, a doubling of the number of shelf facades meant that the eye fixation increased by 28 percent and the brand choice by 10 percent.

Furthermore, a conclusion that was drawn was that the products placed at the top and in the middle of a shelf facade got more attention than products that were placed further down. It should also be noted that only those products that were at the top were selected for a brand evaluation and any subsequent brand selection.

In another study, the effect of lighting on visual perception was studied in connection with a sporting event, and 260 spectators aged 15–60 years of age participated as respondents. It is believed in theory that good lighting can reduce eyestrain, help to speed up the recognition of objects, prolong vision, and improve the quality of the visual experience. A well-designed lighting environment enables an individual to see the object sharper and can help to avoid eye fatigue due to overload. It is further assumed that different lighting conditions can cause varying visual perceptions, which can affect the atmosphere at sporting events.

With the help of the quantitative method, the relationship between lighting and visual perception was analyzed. The results showed that poor lighting quality degraded the quality of the audience's visual perception, which is why the recommendation is to improve and develop the lighting at sporting events. This could help to increase the potential enjoyment for spectators.

When it comes to websites on the Internet, a study has examined closely how the various verbal and visual presentations influenced the attitudes that consumers have relating to products and purchase intentions. The objective of the research was to determine the effects of verbal and visual information with respect to both consumers' attitudes toward products and purchase intentions and to evaluate the importance of verbal and visual information in product presentations.

The study was conducted as a web experiment in which a fake website was used. There was a fictitious brand name for a retailer to avoid the influence regarding effects and attitudes from well-known brand names. In two separate experiments in which 160 female American university students participated, fashion products for women, such as tops, blouses, pants, skirts, and dresses, were the focus. Participants were instructed that they had enough money to buy the product they wanted, in order to minimize the effect of monetary limitations on purchase intentions.

The experiment involved participants taking part in four different verbal and visual combinations, where the verbal content was high or low and the visual content small or large. Subsequently, two fashion products should be evaluated in each combination, with a total of eight fashion products. The order in which the eight products were presented was completely random. Furthermore, a questionnaire was used in which respondents were asked to answer questions about the perception of image size and the amount of information in the first experiment. This questionnaire was modified in the second experiment, because questions of perception were removed.

The results demonstrated that both verbal and visual information have a significant impact on cognitive and affective attitudes toward fashion products, whereas only verbal information has a significant impact on purchase intentions. In previous research, visual information has been considered superior to verbal information, but in this study, the results showed the opposite. It is possible that the effect of visual information was less in comparison with the verbal information, because both the verbal and the visual stimuli conveyed the same message about the products, particularly with respect to the information about the model and the construction details. One conclusion from the study was that more detailed verbal descriptions of products are of importance to positively influence the consumer's purchasing decisions.

Visual Symbolism

For centuries, people have surrounded themselves with symbols, images, and characters of different kinds for visual communication. The intention has been to help express meaning and content with symbols as a result of the interaction between the message and the receiver. Within the research field of visual semiotics, different messages with regard to signs and symbolic patterns have been closely analyzed.

> "Most car drivers recognize the red octagon as a symbol for 'STOP,' and stop."

In the literature, it is widely believed that a brand represents a complex symbol with different properties and values. For many individuals, the brand means different things and can be interpreted based on one's own perspective of the symbolic content with respect to both a service landscape and a product. I will return to the product as a brand in the next section. Symbolic meaning refers to something that represents a physical entity, an idea, or a process. The main aim of symbols is to communicate content and meaning to different people. Personal names are symbols for individuals, and numerals symbolize numbers.

> *The American fashion retailer Abercrombie & Fitch has a retail concept called Hollister, where dark environments, loud music, and English speaking staff are in focus. Inside, the stores use spot lighting for the colorful fashion garments that are placed on shelves made from dark wood. Furthermore, Hollister has a seagull as a logo, which is to be associated with the American dream of freedom.*

When it comes to places in nature, as a service environment, the forest has a special significance in terms of landscape symbolism. Some researchers have linked the symbolism of the forest to Mother Earth, which both creates food through the animal and plant kingdoms and contains threats in the form of snakes and other wildlife. Furthermore, early on in the human culture, the forest was thought of as a nesting place for demons, evil spirits, and diseases, which meant that the forest as a place came to be dedicated to the gods.

Trees have also long been one of man's most important traditional symbols and have been interpreted as standing for life's universe. It has long been regarded as sacred to plant a tree, because masculinity was considered to be expressed by a man building a house, planting a tree, and fathering a son. From a person's concrete consciousness, a tree functions as a way of connecting hell, earth, and heaven, which it does with the help of its roots, its trunk, and its foliage. Many trees have therefore come to stand as special symbols of human culture, for example, as the tree of knowledge, family tree, and the Nordic mythological cosmos tree, Yggdrasil, which represents the universe's center.

In this way, the tree is a symbol of fundamental meaning for people, because it is easy to identify yourself with a tree when it comes to defeating and overcoming storms and winds. The trees also remind us often about childhood, when you climbed a tree and hid there and it was also possible to get shade under the treetop. The significance of the tree as a symbol shows up when people become tree huggers and are willing to fight for the survival of the trees.

BRAND

When it comes to a brand, regardless of whether it is a product or a service, the visual impact is crucial for individual perception and sensory experience. This section describes and analyzes how different visual stimuli can lead to a memorable visual experience of a brand for consumers.

Let us first note that we as consumers are exposed daily to a hundred explicit advertising messages through newspapers, television advertising, SMS advertising, outdoor advertising, or the Internet. Add to this all the messages that reach us in a more implicit way, through various types of product packaging in the home and in the stores. When it comes to the place of purchase, there is everything from the store signs to the visual message on the personnel's clothing, which makes it impossible to escape the visual impact that is ever present in today's everyday life and prevailing social culture.

There is no doubt that for consumers who experience a brand on the web, the visual experience dominates, because the sense of sight is the only one of the five senses that can navigate in a completely computer-based environment. Visual images, therefore, mean more today than ever before for how products and brands are produced and marketed to consumers.

> "If 'to see is to believe' and 'to believe is about shopping,' it is true then that it is important what consumers actually see and notice."

From a marketing standpoint, it is important, on the one hand, to distinguish between a company's overall visual communication to convey its corporate identity and on the other hand, a brand's visual communication should convey its brand identity. In many cases, it is difficult for consumers to experience any difference between the two identities, because the corporate identity that is expressed by means of a special logo often occurs in association with the brand identity. Apple is an example of this, where the graphic logo in the shape of an apple is always presented with a product name such as iPhone or iPad.

Visualization, therefore, is about creating a graphic design for the visual stimuli that expresses the company or brand identity, which includes design issues relating to advertising, design, color, packaging, logos, names, and websites. It is generally considered that the visual context in which the brands and products are presented can influence consumers' affection, cognition, and behavior.

But it is important to stress that the importance of textually based information and other sensory categories (*modalities*) cannot be excluded under the so-called visual aspects of a brand. In the literature, it is believed first that a text as a visual format can affect the consumer's behavior and experience in exactly the same way as a color, a logo or word can. In this way, both pictures and texts are considered to be visual.

Second, a single word can evoke intense and vivid images, which lead consumers to react by being present or purchasing the product. This is in contrast to a single image, which may convey or transfer thousands of words to create awareness among the consumers. In this way, the visual effects of a text or word play a crucial role in the visualization of a brand.

It should also be said that the processing of the images and texts could either be in conflict with or cooperate with each other. The research has shown that the consumer's images have been affected by textual descriptions, which in turn have affected the memory of the images. As a result, the linguistic vocabulary associated with consumption has been changed and come to refine the consumption experience and the memory of it. This, in turn, has been shown to affect the consumer's future behavior.

Finally, it should be mentioned that research also shows that the sense of sight and other senses work together when it comes to completing a task, such as a purchase or a shopping experience. This has been found in the development of visual music linked to today's smart phones, where images are at the core of the visualization of the brand.

In the research, there is a growing realization that sound, smell, and other sensory stimuli, in addition to visual stimuli, have a strong influence on consumers' affections, cognitions, and actual behaviors in the buying and consumption processes. I will address the issue of multi-sensory interaction in a later chapter.

VISUAL STIMULI

Advertisements
In the literature, it is believed that advertising, as stimuli, helps to create visual attention and interest in a brand for consumers. Because advertisements are

geared toward mass populations, it is generally believed that product advertisements are regarded as legitimate by many consumers because of their public nature. This applies regardless of whether it is an ad in the newspaper or commercials on television or on the web. Furthermore, it is believed that ads are very expressive in that they present the products using visual images and printed words as well as colors and sounds.

A common perception is that advertisements can help to build and create a long-term image of a brand, while still being able to provide a rapid response in the short-term. On the other hand, it is believed that advertisements are impersonal and are based on one-way communication with consumers who feel that they do not need to either pay attention or respond to them.

Research suggests that two terms, namely, *recognition* and *recall*, are used to measure an advertisement's visual impression on consumers. When it comes to recognition, a number of respondents were asked whether they have seen the advertisement before or not. This is in contrast to the remember test, where consumers were asked to remember from memory previously obtained information on the brand. It turns out that both terms are important in connection with consumers' purchasing decisions.

It is generally accepted that advertisements create both cognitive and affective reactions and actually affect consumers' purchasing behavior. In terms of affective, i.e., emotional, advertisements create every possible emotion, from disgust to happiness, which has a direct impact on the attitudes that arise toward a brand. These reactions, in turn, affect the memory with respect to what the advertisements contain as a message.

When it comes to emotional dimensions, three such have been identified in the research, namely, joy, excitement, and fright. The types of emotions that can be evoked by an advertisement are divided into positive emotions, such as amused, delighted, or playful, and warm feelings, including affectionate, passionate, and hopeful.

In addition, negative emotions are evoked, such as critical, defiant, or angry.

In the literature, there is a common notion that advertisements should be entertaining, funny, or sexy. Despite this, and the importance of eliciting positive emotions, the effectiveness of advertisements have been questioned by researchers, and it has been asked whether consumers really feel the emotions that advertisements are meant to provoke. It must be added that advertising has also been considered as manipulating people's emotions and playing on them to create attention and interest in a brand.

Design

There is a general consensus in the literature that the color or shape of a product creates attention in consumers. The shape and appearance helps to communicate the relevant information about the brand and helps consumers to draw conclusions about the properties of the product. In this manner, the shape and appearance of the product, in general, are the first impressions in the same manner as the price can be.

> "A beautiful shape and appearance of a brand stimulates the five senses and can cause sensory delight."

Regarding the term "product," there is a consensus among marketing researchers that it shall be deemed to include visible goods, tangible goods, invisible goods and, nonspecific services. Then the shape of a product can refer to all the components that can be mixed and designed as a whole, with the aim of achieving a particular sensory effect. It is in this context that designers make different choices for a brand relating to, for example, shape, color, logo, material, ornamentation, tempo, or texture, and its mutual coherence.

Furthermore, it is believed that the shape and appearance can affect consumers' quality of life by enabling them to perceive and use the products with a good design and beautiful appearance. This, in turn, gives rise to sensory pleasure and stimulation of the human senses beyond the sense of sight, like sitting and enjoying in a comfortable chair and drinking a cup of tea. Similarly, an unattractive shape and appearance of a product may induce a dislike for that product. On the other hand, a product's design and appearance have lasting effects, mainly thanks to its aesthetic features. Some products may affect both users and nonusers for a long time and become part of the sensory environment, for good or bad.

Design is considered the most potent expression of a brand's sensory experience (Hoegg and Alba, 2008). It is generally considered that product design, as visual stimuli, appeals to both cognitive and affective reactions in people, particularly in relation to aesthetics. In this context, design is about what product attributes make a product more or less attractive.

> *In the case of Absolut Vodka, the bottle's shape and color are the distinctive features, whereas in the case of the BMW, the timeless style is expressed through the divided engine grille that provides a clear distinctive trait. When it comes to Apple, this trait is the apple as a logo and a stylish design, with the colors black and white, and together these components form a visual whole for the customers.*

When it comes to cognitive reactions, it is generally believed that the product's shape and appearance can affect the belief that consumers have about the product's attributes such as usability, durability, prestige, or technology status. For that reason, designers choose to design a brand with unique components to proactively encourage consumers to create the desired belief about the product in question.

There are different opinions about whether consumers' perceptions of products comes from a holistic, visual interpretation, or from an atomistic interpretation of the product's design and appearance. In Gestalt psychology, the idea that dominates is that consumers regard an object as a whole rather than as consisting of different parts. But there is also a notion that consumers pay attention to individual stimuli, which is the basis of atomistic interpretations. It is, therefore, suggested that one way to solve this problem is to assume that a product is first considered as a whole and then goes on to be considered from some prominent individual components, such as color, style, or texture.

In terms of behavioral reactions, it is thought that these are expressed as either an approach to or a rejection of the product's shape or appearance, which the earlier Mehrabian-Russell model showed. When a certain form or a certain look elicits a positive reaction, it is thought that consumers seem to engage themselves in approaching with activities such as taking a closer look, listening to, and feeling the product. There is a perception that this type of reaction should be seen as part of the aesthetic experience and in and of itself indicates an individual's desire to become exposed to the product's shape and appearance at a deeper level (Mehrabian and Russell, 1974).

In research, it is believed that visual aesthetics are intended to distinguish a brand from the competitors, primarily through superior design, and achieve recognition in a competitive market. Furthermore, it is thought that visual aesthetics, through its symbolic function, can contribute to how consumers understand and interpret a product. This can be expressed, for example, by an image of elegance, youthfulness, or an innovative look that marketers can use to develop the appearance of new products. It is also considered that the appearance of a product is the first element in the creation of consumer-product relationships, which can be attributed to the sensory experience itself.

In terms of affective reactions, it is believed that the form and appearance can elicit affective, that is, emotional, reactions in consumers. It manifests itself mainly through the product's form creating interpretations, as positive response, by one liking a brand, or arousing strong aesthetic reactions by one falling in love with the brand.

Aesthetic reactions are based on a stimulus intrinsic element, which leads to different degrees of attention and commitment among different individuals. Furthermore, it is deemed that aesthetic reactions may be related to product design and sensory properties rather than their functional properties or performance/execution. On the other hand, it is also common for aesthetic and functional values to occur simultaneously, and it is believed that the most successful brands offer both parts to consumers.

In this context, the hedonic element of a product reflects its aesthetic appeal and its ability to please or to speak to one or more of our senses. The importance of an enjoyable use and experience of the product should also be added to this, which means that designers should think about making products engaging and fun for their users and not just have a one-sided focus on appearance.

Furthermore, in the literature, it is believed that reactions to a product's shape and appearance does not occur in isolation but are linked to factors such as consumer tastes. It turns out that when the product's shape and appearance are consistent with the individual's tastes and preferences, the product is evaluated positively, whereas low agreement leads to negative reactions.

Finally, it should be said that the social context in which the product's shape and appearance appears influences the consumer's reactions. It is considered that the product's exterior also helps to create an image of the user, i.e., the consumer, and that reference persons can affect different individual's appreciation of the brand in a significant manner. A store employee who expresses a positive perception of a product's shape and appearance can lead to a consumer with a negative attitude at first, changing his/her perception.

Color

The literature reveals that color, as visual stimulus, helps to differentiate and identify a brand to consumers. Several studies have indicated that color is deemed to have an inherent meaning, with respect to the names, logos, and fonts, in the image of a brand that is conveyed. It has been shown that color is a valuable signal that can be retrieved from memory in both adults and children.

It should be added that color can communicate a brand's desired image and thereby evoke different associations for an individual. This means that color perception is thought to have a positive and significant effect on memory and purchase intentions.

The inherent meaning that colors have has been investigated in one study using temporary word collections, which described various personality traits, emotions, and salient features for marketers. In a study that surveyed American students, it was found that the black color was associated with power and wealth, the red color with love, the gray color with high quality, the yellow color with joy, the blue color with confidence and high quality, and the purple color with progress.

A common notion is that colors attract consumers' attention better than black and white, which I will return to in the next section. It is also thought that various colors are different when it comes to creating attention for an ad or a package. It is believed that red has the greatest attention value, and this is because it is a warm color.

Furthermore, warm colors are perceived to move in the direction of an individual and contribute to an object being perceived as larger than it actually is. Similarly, cool colors such as blue and white appear as if they are moving away from the direction of an individual and contribute to the actual message perhaps being less perceived than it actually is.

A British study, which was conducted using experiments, showed that functional colors like blue were better suited for functional products, whereas sensory/social colors like red were better suited for social products (McQurrie, 2008). This should convey the inherent and suitable value of a brand.

For consumer goods, particularly food, the red color is of particular importance in both packaging and price labels to capture the individual's attention. Because many consumers make their buying decisions in front of the shelf in a supermarket, it is important that the brand is visible and that it can reach the individual's consciousness among all the stimuli that are available.

> "It is considered that the product's exterior, like shape and appearance, also creates an image of its users in different social contexts.

Also, it is believed that consumers buy the products that appeal to them most regarding different colors. In this context, it is clear that color brightness can have a major impact on the consumer's behavior. Bright colors are associated generally with goodness and purity, whereas dark colors are associated with evil and sin. It is also believed that consumers prefer colors that are consistent with their own emotional state when the attitude toward a brand is positive. Correspondingly, colors that are not in agreement with one's emotional state are preferred when there is a negative attitude toward a brand.

When it comes to the web, a study shows that the prevalence of colors affects how quickly a website is download—colors that give rise to a sense of calm result in a person choosing to download a website. Furthermore, as evident from another study, background colors and images on a web page may affect the significance of different product attributes and product selection, in a superior manner. In particular, this applies to colors on pricing, because a green dollar sign was considered to characterize the best price, whereas the orange and red colors were deemed to characterize safety and not price.

Finally, it should be mentioned that in one study, different colors and shades were examined, which led to the realization that the basic colors that exist may reduce consumers' search times more than other colors. One conclusion was that the use of basic colors could help one to design and develop sales and promotional materials that provide both consumers and the brand advantages in the purchasing process.

Packaging

In the literature, packaging is viewed as having both a functional task and an aesthetic task, where the former refers mainly to transport and storage of the product, whereas the latter refers to the shape and design of the packaging itself. When it comes to the function of packaging, this is regarded as a hygiene factor, which means that it should just work as intended for the consumer.

When it comes to the aesthetic task, the packaging design has a decisive role in a purchase decision, as this enables consumers to identify the actual brand at the place of purchase.

Beyond that, the packaging design and design space provide information and text, often with logos and signs, describing the characteristics of the actual product, which can facilitate the visual perception.

In many contexts, product packaging is of great importance, because consumers have had some lasting and unique images of a brand in their memories. These images, thus, represent the associations with the brand and reinforce the importance of different visual stimuli, which then remind the individual what the product actually stands for.

Retail chains can then choose to use packaging design as a reminder of the well-known supplier brands in their attempt to be perceived in the same way. This is one of the reasons why the supplier brands strongly defend their logos and graphic designs by taking legal action when apparent plagiarism occurs.

Name

In the literature, the name of a brand is viewed as one of the key elements of visual communication. The main reason is that the name can cause individuals to have a positive and special association to a brand. Furthermore, it is believed that an established brand name can achieve rapid associations, which take less time, compared with personal sales and advertising.

Also, a name should be simple and easy to pronounce, which often may be deemed to apply to low-engagement products, such as chocolate (Japp), detergent (Yes), coffee (Zoégas), and yogurt (Yoggi). Then consumers can more easily remember and memorize the brand in connection with their purchasing decisions. When it comes to high-engagement products, such as cars, refrigerators, banking services, and brokerage services, the names are often more complex. This means that consumers find it more difficult to remember and memorize them; thus the brand name should not be too difficult.

Furthermore, a brand name should be based on consumer knowledge so that it is perceived as important and well-known. To accomplish this, there is the opportunity to make well-known associations and use animals, events, people, or places that are often already established in consumers' memories. In this way, a brand helps to evoke a mental, internal picture of a property or an image factor that proves to be of great importance for an individual. The more specific a brand name, the easier it is for a person to create a mental image and perception of the actual brand, which means that the Siamese is preferred over cat and Orrefors before Småland.

> "It has become increasingly common for television celebrities to create their own brand for a type of wine, as Per Morberg and Maria Montazami have done in Sweden."

A brand name can also be based on a known person's name or persons to create associations and feelings between the brand and the individual. When it comes to fashion products like clothing, there are examples of names like Bjorn Borg, Salming, and Victoria Beckham. It also happens that the name of the founder of a company is used to create associations and personalize a brand, as is the case with Amelia, Filippa K, and Ralph Lauren.

It is generally accepted in research that consumers consider a brand as consisting of a number of personal characteristics, which is where the concept of *brand personality* originates. This means that a brand name can be the name of a person, in a natural way, where associations arise linked to the individuals, either fictional or real, that personify the brand, for example, Harry Potter, Ronald McDonald, and Mother Anna's Gingerbread. Finally, it should be said that foreign names have proven to be perceived and interpreted as more hedonic, i.e., pleasurable, when they are pronounced in French, in comparison with English.

Logo

It is evident in the literature that logos more effectively communicate a brand compared with a brand name, because consumers perceive and interpret images in a faster way than words. For that reason, logos are expressed through words, pictures, and/or symbols, as the most common way to identify the sender of an advertisement or outdoor advertising.

Furthermore, a logo is thought to be part of a brand along with other visual stimuli to create attention and recognition. It is common for logos to include classy brand names, such as Apple, Coop, or Ikea, as abstract symbols, but some logos use symbols with closer connections to the brand name, such as KF's eternity symbol, Lantmännen's sprout, or the Mercedes star. But there are also logos where names and symbols are combined to create associations with the brand.

In the research, it is generally considered that an effective logo should create meaningful associations, evoke positive feelings in individuals about the brand, and be easy to recognize. One of the reasons that logos can evoke positive emotions is that most individuals are attracted by the aesthetic logos and stylish designs. Furthermore, the positive feelings are transferred from the logo of the brand to the company, which means that both the corporate image as well as the brand image are influenced by the visual communication.

It is believed that consumers' attitudes toward logos have to do with the extent to which they can contribute to sensory pleasures, that is, how the eyes are attracted to the logo with respect to visual perception. In connection with this, it is also believed that a logo's color has significance for both how enjoyable it is and positive emotions; for example, the red color is viewed as more social and emotional in comparison with the color blue, which emphasizes more functionality and rationality.

Visual Perception

The general consensus in the literature is that the individual's perception is associated with the image, i.e., the mental perceptions and thoughts that are established in an individual about a product or a brand. Positioning a brand in the consumer's mind-set, therefore, is about getting an individual to perceive and interpret a product in a way that positively agrees with the needs and attitudes of the individual, as well as his or her values about the product's importance and role in a social context. Thus visual perception is about visualizing a brand's characteristics with respect to how the eyes and the sense of sight can be made aware.

In order to catch the eyes attention, pictures have gained increasing importance in advertisements, at the same time as the proportion of written text has declined in recent decades. This has been a consistent trend throughout the 1900s until today, which means that the mass media, such as newspapers and magazines, contain advertisements with fewer words and more pictures, which occupy the entire advertising surface (McQurrie, 2008).

In research, there are two perspectives, namely, the *cognitive* and the *rhetorical*, when it comes to analyzing and explaining consumers' reactions to the content and the complexity of the advertisements. From the rhetorical perspective, one distinguishes between "what is said" and "how it is said," which assumes that any context whatsoever can be expressed in more ways than one. In marketing, the content of an advertisement can explicitly state that a brand contains a particular property, or to be more explicit, which requires that a conclusion be drawn, and this can be expressed either through pictures or verbally. In this case, it is about stylistic choices, which differ from the content itself.

Furthermore, it is generally considered that the visual elements of an advertisement are based on the visual arrangement of images, texts, and brand components. With pictures in this context, it is about that part of the advertisement that is not about text or brand identification, which, in itself, can be a mixture of visual and verbal elements.

In terms of stylistic choice for an advertisement, either a documentary layout or an illustrative layout is suggested. In a documentary layout, it is proposed that an advertisement be designed to be read, where the words are the focal point for the reader, who is expected to want to explore the advertisement. In an illustrative layout, it is suggested that readers are inspectors, who just look over an ad, and that requires the colorful images to create attention and interpretation.

Another aspect of the stylistic choices has to do with how pictures take form in an ad, either in the form of "see-through" pictures or "see-right-on" pictures. For the "see-through" pictures, it is proposed that one should get readers to think in a particular context or a certain situation, and in this case it is strictly a photorealism expression of the visual style. The opposite situation is proposed for the "see-right-on," pictures where readers instead get ideas directly conveyed by the visual structures and images that the advertisement contains. In this case, it is also suggested that genres and rhetorical figures can be present for the readers to be able to stay there and read through the advertisement (McQurrie, 2008).

Finally, it should be said that a general notion is that images in advertisements are noticed and interpreted, which is not the case with words. On the other hand, it is difficult to design an image from which specific conclusions can be drawn or that can easily be translated into words. Thereby, words are deemed to be superior to images, but at the same time, most readers of advertisements know what the message is, for example, "This is the cheapest brand to buy because . . ." and in such a context, an image can draw attention and lead to other interpretations of the brand.

In terms of physical exposure of products in grocery stores, in comparison with price advertising, Swahn (2011) shows in his doctoral thesis how sensory descriptions of tomatoes on the signs affected consumers' choices in the store. Usually, there are no sensory descriptions in the advertisements for perishables, making it difficult for consumers to make a sensory analysis of the product's characteristics. Using various experiments in the store environment, the influence of sensory information was studied, taking into account price and taste. By comparing pricing, sensory descriptions, and the tomatoes' visual appearance with each other, it was concluded that sensory descriptions influenced consumers' choice of tomato.

During the study, an important observation was revealed, namely, that when the tomatoes were presented by appearance, consumers were less interested in making their choices. In that case, the decision-making was rather quick, compared with when the sensory descriptions were included.

One of the conclusions was that the sensory information that consumers could read through the sensory descriptions on the signs made them choose the kind of tomato that was in best agreement with their taste preferences. An important question is whether the sensory information, which might affect consumers, should be presented on the sign or on the packaging. In the latter case, this allows an individual to reevaluate the product when it is consumed, as opposed to just reading about it on the sign at the shelf in the store.

To further investigate the interaction between vision and touch, a study by Lindahl and Stark (2013) analyzed the importance of visual stimuli for increased contact and time spent on the product evaluation. The intention was to more closely find out how visual stimuli in the form of two different signs with both a price message and a product message at the *point-of-sale* would affect shoppers' purchasing behavior.

The investigation was conducted in the form of a field experiment in a selected zone in the interior design department of a Swedish department store called Åhlens. The experiment included a control group (n = 100), an experimental group 1 (n = 100), and an experimental group 2 (n = 100), with a total of 300 observations of shoppers who visited the department store for three weeks, especially from Friday to Sunday. In addition, a manipulation control was conducted with the help of some 20 interviewees.

The specific zone had been selected in view of its location in the stores department, where most shoppers chose to pass through in order to more closely partake of the products and the range. The zone included three tables: the first table presented bathmats; the second pots, sheets, and stools; and the third table had shower curtains, towels, and soap dispensers. During the experiment, the same tables were used for both the control group as well as the two experimental groups in order to be able to find any differences in the shopping behavior.

The control group was studied in an unmodified product environment, which was in the zone where the experiment took place. On the three tables, there were the named products along with a small white square price tag that was attached to the product. In addition, there were no changes, and the product environment was identical to that which normally greets the store's customers.

In the first experiment, a visual stimulus was introduced in the form of a price label on all three tables to communicate a price message. On the sign, there was the actual name of the product on the three tables, and the sign was in the form of a white A4 paper and the price was written in black. The aim was to identify the impact of the price message on the number of shoppers who would conceivably be affected by the product as a result of this being introduced.

The second experiment had the same visual stimuli in the form of a sign, but the price message was replaced by a written product message such as: "Feel the quality," "Soft for your feet," and "Sleep well in soft duvet cover" for the products that were on the three tables. The actual text was framed in black on a white A4 paper. The aim was to

---

"A product message may be more important than a price message in order for shoppers to touch the products for a longer time."

identify the impact of the products' messages on the number of shoppers who could conceivably be influenced by the products as a result of them being introduced. It should be said that the messages that were investigated were developed together with the researchers and the personnel at Åhlens.

The results showed that of the two messages, the price message did not have any significant positive impact on the shopping behavior in terms of the shoppers touching the actual products. It also meant that the price message did not mean that shoppers bought more products when a price tag was placed on the product.

When it came to product messages, it was clear that this had a significant positive impact on shopping behavior in terms of the shoppers feeling the product before they studied the price.

It appeared that 51 shoppers touched the products in the control group while the corresponding figure was 65 shoppers in experimental group 2, which represented an increase of 28 percent, i.e., almost a third of the shoppers were influenced by the product message.

When it came to the impact of the product messages on how long shoppers touched the actual products, there was a significant positive impact. It appeared that shoppers in the control group touched the products for 9.84 seconds on average, whereas the figure was 16.77 seconds for experimental group 2. This corresponded to a percentage increase of 70 percent, as the time of contact was influenced by the product message. When it came to comparing the price message and the product message with respect to how long the shoppers touched the actual products, there was a significant positive impact for the product message. It was evident that the product message had a greater impact on shopping behavior than the price message.

The conclusion of the current study was that a product message, in comparison with a price message, has a significant impact on shopping behavior when it comes to touching a product and that it occurs over a longer period of time. The most interesting is that the product message may be a greater attention getter than the price message, probably because shoppers are more receptive to a message that says something about the properties and quality than just what the product costs.

Visual Symbolism

Visual symbolism means that individuals consume the brand from a symbolic perspective, where the notion of the brand fits the mental picture the individual wants to create for him/herself in a social, cultural context. Then, the images and perceptions of the brand have received a central role in the creation of interpretations and experiences for the individual.

The fact that people use consumption as a way to identify themselves in relation to others has resulted in symbols gaining an increasing importance in everyday life. The so-called *symbolic self-completion theory* assumes that those people who perceive

> "Mercedes-Benz uses the star on the front of the car to create associations with quality and German engineering."

themselves as having an incomplete definition of the self use different symbols to complete their own self-image. It is particularly important in personal and social contexts to symbolize appearances and show off. For young men, macho products such as cars and cigarettes help to reinforce their masculinity.

Furthermore, it is believed that many individuals choose products with the greatest symbolic value to match the self-image they seek. Therefore, there exists a correspondence between symbol usage and self-image. But the research also shows that there is a difference in symbol usage with regard to whether an individual seeks the ideal self or looks at the current self. In order to achieve the ideal self, expressive, social products such as clothing, perfume, and shoes are of importance, whereas everyday, functional products are of importance for the current self.

It is widely believed in the literature that a *symbol* has the ability to induce a broad spectrum of both associations and feelings in an individual, which is thought to contribute to creating a sensory experience at a deeper level. A symbol is usually regarded as a sign that is linked to one product to create associations with the product in question.

A brand can be expressed as a symbol by using form, figure, color, logo, character, or text, and many customers therefore can remember a certain brand by seeing only part of its characteristics (see Figure 5.4). It is possible to distinguish between *word brands*, such as Google; *image brands*, such as Starbucks; *emblems*, such as Linnaeus University; or *abstract/symbolic brands*, such as Volvo, which are presented here as pictures.

It is common for marketers to use symbols to communicate a message, which consists of three parts—the *object* itself, that is, the product or the brand; the *sign*, which is the actual sensory image of the object; and the *meaning*, which is how the recipient perceives and interprets the actual message. It is common to relate the message symbols directly to the product or the brand to create associations and evoke emotions. When it comes to how the symbol in a message is used to create associations, the cowboy used by the cigarette brand Marlboro is a classic example and should be interpreted as the image of the individualistic, American man, who smokes.

Among consumer researchers, it is a common notion that many products and brands contain symbolic aspects that are of more importance to consumers than the functional benefit. This means that among some individuals, the psychological and social meaning of the product is more prominent.

Symbolic innovations refer to how a product can convey an associative meaning, which for an individual may mean that he/she is part of a certain

Figure 5.4 Different Types of Brands

reference or social group. It is not a question of a new product in itself, but how an established product instead has come to get a new symbolic meaning, for example, through new packaging, logo, or color.

> "When it comes to jeans, it seems that the jeans image and "personality" symbolizes different personal values of an individual."

Research has shown how cultural symbolism with respect to the meaning and content of a product affects consumers' affections and cognitions. It is therefore considered that cultural symbols, such as color, shape, or character, have great influence over the individual's purchasing decisions and partly lead to a higher degree of self-realization. It is also common in many product contexts that symbols from prominent sub-cultures are modified to become regular features of the general social culture. This phenomenon can be illustrated by rap music, which initially was only associated with young African Americans, but which today has become widely accepted as musical entertainment.

When it comes to the Internet, it is regarded as society's symbolic pool, which allows for the presentation and selection of various changes and trends in social culture. Visual images with different symbols can result in quick impact and offer new symbolic innovations, especially in design and fashion, which can lay the foundations for new styles and expressions among consumers.

REFERENCES

Bitner, M.J. (1992), "Servicescapes: the impact of physical surroundings on customers and employees," *Journal of Marketing*, 56, 2:57–71.

Bloch, P.H. (1995), "Seeking the ideal form: product design and consumer response," *Journal of Marketing*, 59, July:16–29.

Bloch, P.H. (2011), "Product design and marketing: reflections after fifteen years," *Journal of Product Innovation Management*, 28:378–380.

Booms, B.H. and Bitner, M.J. (1982), "Marketing services by managing the environment," *Cornell Hotel & Restaurant Administration Quarterly*, 23, May:35–39.

Chandon, P., Hutchinson, J.W., Bradlow, E.T. and Young, S.H. (2009), "Does in-store marketing work? Effects of the number and position of shelf facings on brand attention and evaluation at the point of purchase," *Journal of Marketing*, 73, 6:1–17.

Chattopadhyay, A., Gorn, G.J. and Drake, P. (2010), "Differences and similarities in Hue Preferences between Chinese and Caucasians." I: Krishna, A. (ed.) *Sensory marketing: research on the sensuality of products*, New York: Taylor and Francis Group, p. 201–217.

Chua, H.F., Boland, J.E. and Nisbett, R.E. (2005), "Cultural variation in eye movements during scene perception," *Proceedings of the National Academy of Sciences of the United States of America*, www.pnas.org./content/102/35/12629.short

Edens, K.M. and McCormick, C.B. (2002), "How do adolescents process advertisements? The influence of ad characteristics, processing objectives, and gender," *Contemporary Educational Psychology*, 25, 4, October:450–463.

Ezeh, C. and L.C. Harris (2007), "Servicescape research: a review and a research agenda", *The Marketing Review*, 7:159–78.

Hoegg, J. and Alba, J.W. (2008), *A role for aesthetics in consumer psychology*, New York: Taylor & Francis Group, p. 733–754.

Kotler, P. (1974), "Atmospherics as a marketing tool," *Journal of Retailing*, 49, 4:48–60.

Krishna, A. (2008), "Spatial perception research: an integrative review of length, area, volume, and number perception." I: Wedel, M. and Pieters, R. (ed.) *Visual marketing: from attention to action*. New York: Erlbaum, p. 167–192.

LaTour, K.A. and LaTour, M.S. (2009), "Positive mood and susceptibility to false advertising," *Journal of Advertising*, 38, 3:127–142.

Levy, S.J. (1981), "Symbols, selves, and others." I: Mitchell, A. (ed.) *Advances in consumer research (Vol. 10)*, Ann Arbor, MI, p. 542–543.

Lindahl, C. and Stark, M. (2013), *The strength of the visual word on customers touch behavior*. Bachelor thesis, School of Business and Economics, Linneaus University, Kalmar Sweden.

McQurrie, E.F. (2008), "Differentiating the pictorial element in advertising." I: Wedel, M. and Pieters, R. (ed.) *Visual marketing—from attention to action*. New York, London: Psychology Press, p. 91–113.

Mehrabian, A. and Russell, J.A. (1974), *An approach to environmental psychology*, Cambridge, MA: MIT Press.

Meyers-Levy, J. and Zhu, R. (2008), "Perhaps the store made you purchase it." I: Wedel, M. and Pieters, R. (ed.) *Visual marketing: from attention to action*, New York: Psychology Press, p. 193–223.

Osgood, C.E. (1960), "The cross-cultural generality of visual-verbal synesthetic tendencies," *Behavioral Science*, 5, 2:146–169.

Raghubir, P. (2010), "Visual perception—an overview." I: Krishna. A (ed.) *Sensory marketing: research on the sensuality of products*, New York: Taylor and Francis Group, p. 201–217.

Raghubir, P. and Krishna, A. (1999), "Vital dimensions: antecedents and consequences of biases in volume perceptions," *Journal of Marketing Research*, 36, 3:313–326.

Raghubir, P. and Valenzuela, A. (2006), "Center of inattention: position biases in decision making," *Organizational Behavior and Human Decision Processes*, 99, 1:66–80.

Swahn, J. (2011), *If I can taste it, I want it… Sensory marketing in grocery retail stores*, Academic Thesis, Örebro University.

Turley, L.W. and Milliman, R.E. (2000), "Atmospheric effects on shopping behaviour: a review of the experimental evidence," *Journal of Business Research*, 49, 2:193–211.

Valenzuela, A. and Raghubir, P. (2009), "Position based schemas: the center-stage effect," *Journal of Consumer Psychology*, 19, 2:185–196.

Vessel, E.A. and Rubin, N. (2010), "Beauty and the beholder: highly individual taste for abstract, but not real-world images," *Journal of Vision*, 10, 2:1–14.

6 The Sense of Sound

This chapter analyzes and discusses the sense of sound, which is considered to be one of the most intimate senses of the human's five senses. The scientific notions about the fundamental role of the sense of sound are addressed initially with respect to both physiological characteristics and psychological aspects.

Thereafter, three categories of influential factors for the sense of sound that relate to the importance of the societal culture, the service environment, and the brand are presented. Considering this background, it is discussed how various factors affect individuals' affections, cognitions, as well as their actual behaviors in the different buying and consumption processes.

SOUND FOR EMOTIONS AND EXPERIENCES

A person is surrounded both *in utero* and after birth by sound, and the mother's heartbeat is the first sound that meets each one of us. The sense of sound plays a crucial role in an individual's perception and experience of his/her environment, because it is always on and contributes to shaping a person's identity, as shown in the following example:

> *Every morning many of us wake up to a jingle on the clock radio or to the harp on the mobile. At the breakfast table, the TV shows the first commercial, which is listened to. In the car on the way to work, advertising flows through the car radio. At the end of the day, you go to the grocery store and get to listen to music as well as voices from the in-store customer radio. At night, you turn on the TV again to see your favorite show, with breaks for commercials. There is no doubt that the sense of sound has been fully occupied most of the day.*

Each of us often expresses our identity by using sounds of various kinds, and we use the verbal ability to talk about who we are, what we stand for, and how we are to be perceived by raising our voice, crying, laughing, or screaming. In this way, sound can often provide a different understanding of a person's feelings and state of mind than a facial expression.

There is no doubt that the importance of sound for the sensory perception of a brand has long been overlooked by marketers when it comes to expressing a brand's personality.

Jackson (2003) believes that sound has several different qualities, which are possible for a company to use in marketing. One of the most remarkable aspects of sound is that it is actually a science.

When it comes to creating a sound experience of a brand, it is common to use both voices and music. The latter is considered to primarily help create positive emotions and solidarity with a brand, since many people see music as a natural part of everyday life. You can listen to music and voices at home, at the train station, at the nightclub, the concert, or on the plane or the train. This is often done with the help of digital technology in a smartphone or via Spotify, around the clock. Music and voices are also available in many public contexts, such as sporting events, New Year celebrations, as well as political and religious contexts.

Furthermore, music is used, mainly with famous artists and their songs, to give many individuals the opportunity to form associations and to be able to remember past events in life. A melody or a song from early childhood can bring up strong memories and feelings later in life. In this way, music is ever present, and it can be quite difficult for an individual to avoid hearing or listening to music in everyday life.

> *Brands such as Hästens and BMW started to use digital and personal voices to create an audio experience. One result was that sales increased and the brands had a stronger identity.*

For millennia, music has been around in political, religious, or social contexts to create emotions and a sense of solidarity between people. But it was not until the latter half of the 1800s that German researchers became interested in the importance of music, in various empirical studies (Stumpf, 1883).

For centuries, to remember a melody or a song, before the technology breakthroughs, people learned to memorize. This has allowed people to keep the music alive, and in this way, memorable melodies and songs have passed on from an earlier generation to a later one using the human brain.

When the cassette tape and CD-ROM were introduced, the ability to memorize music was of less importance to many people. In recent years, there has also developed a number of new online solutions to enable access to both new and old music, mainly through streamed music, which is different from downloaded music. This has meant new opportunities when it comes to both listening to music and accessing music around the clock. The streaming music services have increased in recent years, mainly thanks to the launch of the Swedish Spotify in 2008. These services are growing the fastest, in comparison with downloaded music, and for players like Apple's iTunes Store, Google, Rhapsody in the United States and Wimp in Sweden, it is estimated that the annual turnover for streamed music will soon reach eight billion.

Digital technology, which is expressed through computers and smartphones in today's societal culture, has meant that music has become both easy to handle and easily accessible to individuals and businesses. This means that music can be consumed and provided in a volatile manner at the same time in many different contexts and may not be perceived as qualitatively as before by many people. For companies, this development opens up new and unexpected possibilities when it comes to creating a sound experience of a brand.

THE FUNDAMENTAL ROLE OF THE SENSE OF SOUND

Physiological Aspects

In daily life, most people encounter various sounds, which, as a form of stimuli, tell us what is happening in the immediate surroundings. There are sounds that we do not notice, and which are filtered out, whereas both low and high sounds are easily noticed by us. It can relate to a continuous, low frequency noise, such as the sound of a computer, a refrigerator, or a fan. Most of us react with relief when the sound disappears or ceases.

> *Even silence is perceived in an individual's brain, which is immediately compared with the possibility that a sound can emerge to break the silence.*

The physical process of hearing consists of every human experiencing sound by the eardrums being set into vibration by sound waves that are in the air around us (Figure 6.1). The strength of the sound is considered to be due to the size of the pressure variation, and all sound is measured in decibels (dB). A person can perceive the lowest level of sound as zero decibels, whereas the pain threshold of what a human can tolerate is considered to be around 120 decibels.

It should be said that a normal conversation between two individuals is around 60 decibels; moreover, a rock concert is around 100 decibels, whereas a whisper is around 20 decibels. The sounds that evoke the most

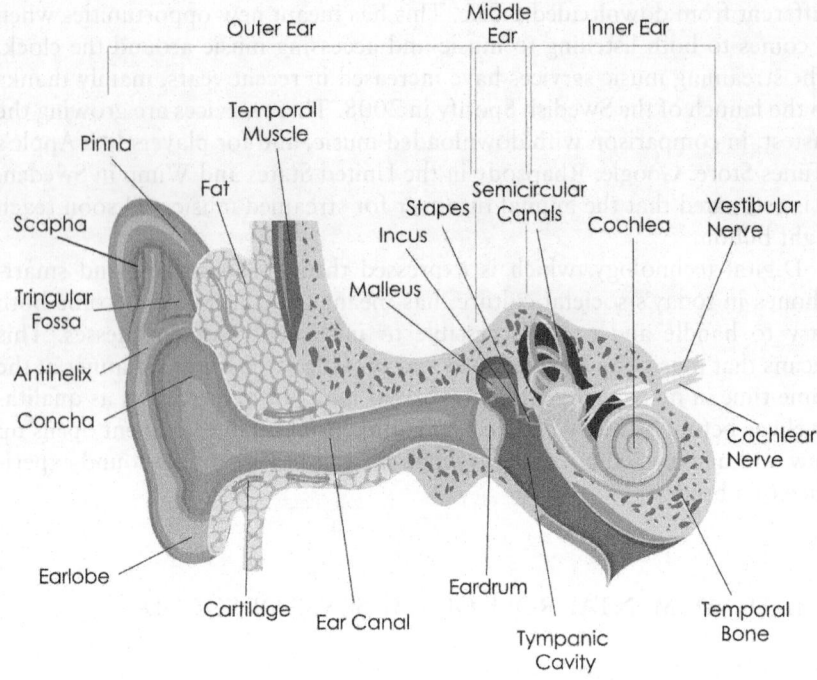

Figure 6.1 The Structure of the Ear
Source: Shutterstock

discomfort, such as a child crying or scraping noises, most of us react to even at low decibels.

This is equivalent to the sound of the highest octave on a piano and activates the brain's amygdala, which influences the onset of phobias and fears. A person's sensitivity to sound is innate but also environmental, which explains how unpleasant sounds can affect a sound experience in a negative way.

The Three Different Elements of the Sense of Sound

It is generally accepted in research that sound has three different elements, consisting of *ambient sounds*, *voices*, and *music*. An ambient sound is a sound that does not come from a human or from a musical instrument, and common examples of this are animal sounds, birds chirping, or different sound machines.

A voice is a sound that comes from a person, which can be classified as a voice. It can refer to a scream from a baby or a song by Pavarotti but also words spoken by someone. The left hemisphere of the brain contains the concepts and words that constitute the building blocks of human language from which all communication is based. It is becoming increasingly common in marketing to use recorded voices in everything from the bank's telephone customer service to the design of television advertising where the voices of the spokeswoman or the spokesman are crucial for how a message becomes the basis for a sound experience.

Jackson (2003) believes that there are sounds that consist of both words and music. In the right hemisphere, a song can be processed, and when the words are associated with a particular melody, the words are understood using sounds. This means that the words are not understood or interpreted in any rational sense by the left brain, but instead are processed and stored, for example, the text of a song is stored in the right hemisphere where it is remembered and memorable.

The left brain can simultaneously remember words and sentences of words as well as construct sentences; however, the word order in a song and how it goes, the right brain can produce verbatim. This is considered valid also for rhyming and rhythmic elements, which can only be processed and stored in the right hemisphere. In this way, it can be explained how various jingles, songs, or slogans as sound experiences get stuck in our heads and live on in our memories longer.

Music is the sound of a song, instruments, or a combination of these to create beauty, harmony, and emotional expressions. There is a general understanding that music as a sound has a special capacity to influence people's emotional state. In this context, psychological studies on the impact of music have particularly focused on cognitive and perceptual processes, where the experience of music has been in focus.

One reason for this approach has been that researchers have assumed that these types of processes have been considered to be universal, whereas cultural and social norms have determined the subjective emotional responses that music may give rise to in an individual. Despite this, it is assumed that there is a complex interaction between music, emotions, and intellect, and the link between music and emotions is still thought to be unclear, although a number of possible theories have emerged about how it can be explained.

Psychological Aspects

The Greek philosopher Heraclitus did justice to listening early on, and in early philosophy, the conversation between two people was in focus. Then, it was about listening, and it was believed that through listening a human could understand that "the universe is one." But at the same time, vision was thought to be the central sense, and so it has been in Western thought for thousands of years.

In modern philosophy until today, the starting point for knowledge is visual input. Some philosophers argue that sight limits and defines, because that which is observable is easier to find than the hidden. In this context, the ears and hearing, by listening, can lead a human to be able to understand what is said without observing it. Then the sense of sound can respond to processes and change, whereas the sense of sight tackles the stable and static objects.

> In classical conditioning, it is assumed that music evokes a mood that is directly transferable to a brand.

The sense of sound is different from the other senses, especially sight, because sound is experienced more intimately and inside our heads. The objects that are studied and experienced through sight are experienced entirely outside the head, which means they are separate from a person's true self. They are not an integral part of the sensory experience on a deeper, more intimate level but rather a part outside a person's true self. It is because of this that music or voices can be considered as the most powerful examples of sound's unique importance for a sensory experience.

There is a generally accepted understanding in research that sound contributes to a person's frame of mind and various psychological states. The sense of sound, therefore, is thought to help create peace and quiet in a person's soul, at the same time as the mind warns of dangers and surprises, which can cause unpleasant experiences. The fact that sound has a special ability to arouse intense emotions has often been observed and was highlighted already in the 1930s.

Emotions and Reason

Rational (cognitive) processes, as opposed to emotional processes, such as reasoning, planning, and remembering something, are deemed to occur in an individual in the context of what has come to be known as the information process paradigm. To have an understanding of human perception, thoughts, and actual behaviors, a computer may be used as a metaphor in this context.

A common understanding is that sensory information is treated by different mental processes in the brain, via the sense of sound, where the features that suit the individual are classified, transformed, brought forward, and interpreted. These processes are assumed to end with an individual, as output, experiencing different physical or mental conditions as negative or positive emotions (Thompson, 2009).

> In a study at Cornell University, students' ability to recognize music was investigated regarding music perception and cognition. Krumhansl (1997) studied how long students needed to listen before they recognized a song. It turned out that within four hundred milliseconds, students could name the artist and title of the song. Furthermore, it was possible to determine the decade, from the 1960s to today, the emotional content, and style.

The question posed by many researchers is whether emotions are a part of cognitive processes or if they can be regarded as something that falls outside the scope of cognition? One perspective is that cognitive processes lead to emotional responses, such as the feeling of joy or sorrow, which in itself is regarded as the result of a number of cognitive processes where the characteristics of the event in question are classified, interpreted, and finally evaluated. It is assumed that the interpretation of the event itself is a cognitive process, whereas the evaluation that takes place leads to the point where emotions arise.

Another perspective is that emotions are created independently of cognitive processes, which has received support in both psychological and neurophysiological research. Some researchers argue that there are two different brains in humans, the emotional and the rational, which is demonstrated in that a person who knows something about something, from a rational perspective, can react quite differently on the emotional level.

A third perspective is that emotions are intimately connected with reason. In this context, it is assumed that emotions arise to prepare an individual for important events, such as threatening conditions, feeding and mating opportunities, and so on, in daily life. With this functional starting point, it is thought that humans are the product of an evolutionary development and that it may be considered possible to understand emotions based on this perspective.

Damaiso (1994) proposed the concept of *bodily marker* in his theory of emotion and reason, where a physical marker may be associated with sensory image, i.e., mental images or ideas. These markers are considered to be emotional labels that mark each image with an emotional association, which can be illustrated by a dog lover associating joy with a picture of a dog, whereas other people associate fear with the same image.

Furthermore, Damaiso believes that physical markers increase the efficiency of decision-making by reducing the number of opportunities an individual faces in daily life. It is also argued that this can be considered as though emotions may have a possible adaptive function, from a cognitive perspective.

In the literature, there is a common perspective to distinguish between basic emotions and secondary emotions to define a person's emotional state. Basic emotions involve questions about the individual's physical and psychological survival, whereas secondary emotions depend on the cultural context and are regarded as social constructs. There is some disagreement among scholars as to what are considered to be basic emotions and secondary emotions, but it is suggested that anger, happiness, fear, and sadness should be considered as being basic emotions for most people.

Furthermore, it is assumed that emotions are essential if the task is to contribute to an individual's survival, if they have some particular emotional expression and whether they can be found in all human cultures.

Emotions and Music

There is no doubt that music plays a significant role in people's everyday lives, because it contributes in different ways to how life and the world are shaped and experienced. Already 20 years ago, the renowned management guru, Peter Drucker, stated, "music affects the nervous system as a key in a lock by activating the brain processes with the corresponding emotional responses" (1994, p. 10).

It is believed that film music, in particular, contributes to the creation of a universal interpretation and understanding of the language of music, because sounds and music together influence our experiences. In the context of a film experience, the combination of sound and music often amplifies dangerous or exciting situations.

In the literature, it is assumed that music communicates content and meaning in two main ways. It is both about transferring a clear meaning by imitating concrete sounds, such as birds singing or traffic noise, and transferring a special associative ability to convey images, emotions, or thoughts about a particular event or particular phenomenon to a listener.

Music is believed to be characterized based in three different aspects, namely, *sound, behavior*, and *concept*. When it comes to music as sound, it is defined as that group of auditory signals that are produced by musicians and perceived by an audience. Music as behavior has to do with activities, such as dance, ritual, or performance, which are usually of great importance for a musical experience. These activities have often been the subject of a thorough historical, psychological, or social analysis, where the actual piece of music has come to embody this behavior. Finally, as for music concept, this generally has to do with the interpretation that is made of a song or melody associated with a particular social group in society.

> *Music therapy is used to create physical, emotional, and mental well-being, which can lead to a positive attitude to life and good self-esteem.*

What is it that makes music act as a bodily marker and become an emotional label on a brand? Burner (1990) argues that people are influenced by music through both emotional content and experience-based, emotional reactions. An example given is that fast music can be regarded as happier than slow music. In research, it is common to describe and analyze music in light of three basic factors: the *tempo or time, pitch or tone,* and *structure in the form of the instruments and volume.*

Two categories have been suggested, namely, *contour* and *convention*, to describe the relationship between music and emotions. In this context, contour relates to the "natural" link between music and emotions, whereas convention does not appear to have any natural connection. As an example of contour, slow tempo is mentioned, which naturally conveys sadness or melancholy and can be expected to illustrate a sad person who walks in a slow, painstaking way.

It is assumed that different music styles, tempos, and melodies illustrate the feelings that characterize human behavior. When it comes to conventions, Kivy and some researchers speculate that these are developed from natural connections and are seen as the link between specific musical styles and special emotions based on a person's needs, fantasies, and experiences in daily life.

The term *valence*, which has a crucial role in Lewin's field theory and was designed in the 1930s and 1940s, is about the value that a piece of music or a song can have on an individual's emotions and feelings—in other words, how large of an attraction the actual music has (expressed through positive valence) or how repulsive it is (expressed through negative valence) for an individual. The term is used to characterize the emotions and feelings an individual experiences based on the actual music.

This means that there are phenomena in everyday life within the world of music that can arouse emotions and feelings with either low or high valence. Joy, for example, is an emotion that has high positive valence, unlike anger, sadness, or rage that has high negative valence. It is clear from the research that valence, whether it is a musical piece or a song that is perceived and experienced as attractive or repulsive, is of great importance for what an individual will or will not remember.

Cooke (1959) claims that there is a specific emotional quality in different melodies and in their patterns. Many composers use these patterns and deliberately try to capture the emotional nuances that melody or music can give rise to in the listener. In this way, melodies and music are created to become a kind of emotional language whose parts and structure serve to represent different emotions and emotional states (Thompson, 2009).

> *Per Thorgaard, chief physician at the Ålborg University Hospital in Denmark, believes that music can calm patients in ambulances.*

Furthermore, Cooke (1959) discusses the issue of whether the emotional associations that different melodies or styles of music convey are to be considered as universal. What then can explain the variety of musical styles that exist in different cultures? The answer given is that different social cultures choose to express their viability and vitality in various ways. In every culture, a special style of music has developed, which is supposed to reflect the attitudes, the characteristics, and the lifestyles that characterize and reflect the particular social culture.

When it comes to Western culture, Cooke claims that in different ways it has influenced the music style in other social cultures. The emphasis that has existed in Western culture in material happiness has come to oust established musical styles, often with an emphasis on more mournful music in other social cultures. One of Cooke's most important contributions to the study of emotions and music is the demonstration of how certain melodies and musical styles are used to convey and transmit similar emotional qualities during different time periods.

Reactions to Music

A general view is that music reminds many people of their everyday lives and the world they live in. Each of us has at some point experienced the vicissitudes of life, from the deepest seriousness to true happiness, and music is seen by many as a way to express our innermost emotions and feelings. In this way, music is thought to showcase the diverse emotions that are present at a higher general level in all of us rather than simply expressing individual emotions and feelings. If so, this means that music as a phenomenon has more to do with an abstract understanding of people's emotional lives.

When it comes to the impact of music, the cognitive approach claims that the emotional meaning of music creates reactions in listeners. It could mean that a listener can recognize sadness in a certain genre of music, but the music itself does not create sadness. In contrast, the emotional approach argues that music can evoke an emotional response in a listener. However, many scholars, including Kivy as previously mentioned, have argued against this view and assert that music expresses feelings but does not create them.

In research, the question about the relationship between music and emotions is not fully understood. It is possible that the influence of music can be explained by both of the aforementioned approaches. On the other hand, several studies have shown that there are physical reactions in people when they listen to music, which suggests the emotional approach. There are examples where individuals have experienced faster breathing, increased blood pressure, chills, tears, and higher heart rates as a consequence of the music they listened to.

In a study by Krumhansl (1997), the listeners' reactions to six pieces of music were closely reviewed. The survey was conducted using 38 music listeners, and 12 physiological measurements were taken of respiratory rate, respiratory volume, blood pressure, finger temperature, and heartbeat.

On average, the music increased respiratory rate and blood pressure, and there was a decrease in the respiratory volume, heartbeat, and finger temperature, which meant that the measurements showed a significant influence of the music. The conclusions showed that the established physical changes were the same regardless of the specific emotional association, such as happy, sad, or frightened, made with the music.

In the research project, "The Body's Musical Score" at the Sahlgrenska Academy in Gothenburg, Sweden, in 2012, researchers managed to create a physical and spiritual state, which has been detected in a number of involuntary biological reactions. During the study, 20 people had access to the blues, enthusiastic, or soothing music, and examples of horror music. When the music changed its character from the blues to soothing or from enthusiastic to frightening, it was possible to measure the body's neurophysiological responses and any differences.

Measurement points included breathing, fingertip temperature, perspiration, heart rate, and levels of stress hormones such as adrenaline and oxytocin. The results indicated that different stress values in the body continued to drop after the patients had been listening to soothing music and did not return, as expected, to normal values. It showed that the heart was clearly influenced by the music. The researchers' goal was to be able to use music in connection with surgery or pain management in clinical practice. This could then be seen as a complement to classical school medicine.

In a study using EEG, Travis, Harung, and Lagrosen (2010) investigated how professional classical musicians, in comparison with amateur musicians, react to different tests and stimuli. It appeared that the professional musicians reacted more strongly to stimuli than the amateur musicians, but both groups were characterized by high brain integration. This means that an individual is good at understanding the whole by putting together the parts that might be a part of the big picture, which can also lead to a better understanding of the more complex context.

One of the conclusions of the study was that an individual's effectiveness in a particular area of the brain is affected by brain development in terms of affections and cognitions as well as ethics and morality. The more highly developed the brain, the greater the brain efficiency seemed to be in a certain area. It was evident that professional musicians were better at reasoning about ethics and morality, compared with amateur musicians, despite the existence of high brain integration in both groups. One explanation for this was that it is possible to train the brain, and it can be done with the help of music.

INFLUENTIAL FACTORS FOR THE SENSE OF SOUND

In terms of the sense of sound, music is undoubtedly the stimulus that has been studied most in retail and marketing research. Based on the previously presented SEB model, the factors that may be linked to the sense of sound's influence on an individual's affections, cognitions, and actual behaviors in the buying and consumption processes are presented (Figure 6.2).

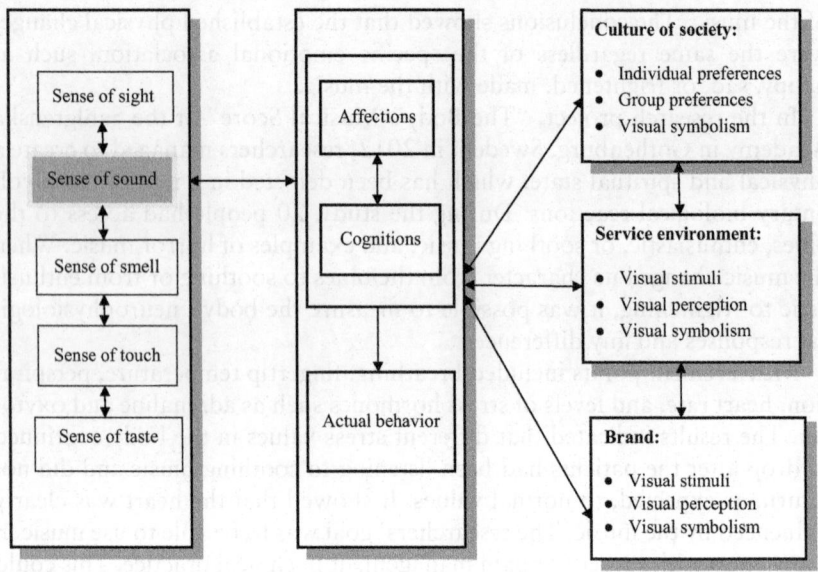

Figure 6.2 The Sense of Sound and the SEB-model

First, the societal culture, as an influential factor, is addressed in relation to the different preferences on the individual and group levels as well as the importance of sound symbolism. Second, the service environment, as an influential factor, is addressed in relation to sound stimuli, sound perception, and sound congruence. Third, the brand, as an influential factor, is addressed in relation to sound stimuli, sound perception, and sound symbolism.

SOCIETAL CULTURE

Auditory communication, as sensory information, plays a prominent role in a societal culture, primarily through the use of primary stimuli words, language, or sound (Meyers-Levy et al., 2010). These can be expressed in many different ways between people, mainly through music and voices, to contribute to the affections and cognitions elicited at the individual level.

Individual Preferences

In each societal culture, sound, such as music and voices, is of central importance to the individual's emotions and sensory experiences. It is clear from the research that individuals make use of music in everyday life to create a good and positive mood. There is a general notion that pure instrumental music can convey or transmit a specific meaning, which can be shared by listeners.

In an empirical study as early as 1935, Gundlach found that "music can elicit in many listeners a fairly uniform characteristic only through factors, which have its place in the musical structure." In another study, it was found that regardless of musical training or habit, three out of four listeners could correctly understand and interpret the intended meaning of unknown composed music. In the early 1980s, American research showed that among untrained and trained listeners, the aesthetic expressions of classical music were perceived in a surprisingly similar way.

> *Many individuals use music as personal expression to communicate their attitudes, self-image, and values.*

It is generally accepted in research that sound stimuli, such as music, words, or voices, touch an individual on a deeper level in comparison with visual or tactile stimuli. This assumption leads to a belief that sound stimuli have a more intense and rapid impact on the human brain than the corresponding visual stimuli. This can be illustrated with a picture of a woman laughing in a newspaper advertisement, which may make the reader smile, but it is not until the woman's laughter can be heard that the reader can begin to laugh too. An analogy is to see a picture of a war with dead people, which can be experienced as deeply offensive; but to simultaneously listen to bomb explosions and death screams, of course, is much more painful.

One study showed that children experienced and responded positively to the emotional message and content of new forms of music. This is regardless of whether they had listened to the music before or if the music was aggressive, happy, or sad. One of the conclusions from the study was that there is significant evidence of the existence of musical archetypes, which means that people react and feel the music in a special way regardless of mood, context, or past associations.

Personality and Musical Styles
In studies of music, it has emerged that an individual's personality is influenced by music preferences. This means that music helps to shape the personality in the same way as the physical and social environment. Many individuals, therefore, choose their own style of music to create an image of their self that they want others to perceive. If an individual chooses hard rock as a personal music style, it can lead to him/her being perceived as an individual who is "tough and hard," which may in fact not be the case.

Research has also shown that it is mostly younger men and teens with a strong circle of friends who harbor a particular fondness for music styles such as hip-hop, hard rock, and rap. It has also been shown that individuals who may be described as reckless, who like to take risks, and who can be said to be more aggressive and violent are also attracted to these musical styles. These musical styles, therefore, are also called "problem music" by some researchers.

In sociological research, it has been shown that there is a relationship between music preferences and social class. This is manifested by "intellectual" music genres, such as classical music, opera, or orchestral music being preferred by people from higher social classes with higher educational backgrounds. On the other hand, "nonintellectual" music genres, including country, gospel, and rap, seem to be preferred by people from the working class with low educational backgrounds.

Furthermore, it has been shown that people who have some knowledge about different musical genres can gain an understanding of other individuals and their group affiliation. It is also clear from the literature that individuals with more optimistic personalities prefer musical styles, such as jazz and fast-paced music, whereas the preference for classical music reflects sensitivity.

With regard to the individual's musical ear, Canadian researchers claim that people who play an instrument have better hearing than others. One of the conclusions that researchers drew was that it probably came from playing an instrument their whole life, because music practice can help to delay age-related changes in the brain's auditory system.

Female and Male

Research also shows that it is possible to distinguish between female and male music preferences. It has been shown that there is a link between masculinity and "hard" sounding music and, on the other hand, femininity and "soft" sounding music. The difference between hard and soft sounding music lies in how music is perceived by men and women, respectively. Specifically, the hard music is associated with male aggression, domination, and rebellion, whereas soft music for women is associated with emotions and relationships.

> Women generally prefer classical music, compared with men. Men prefer, however, more hard rock, compared with women.

In one study, the differences between men and women were examined with regard to their physiological reactions to music. The researchers were interested in finding out the individual's ability to react to two musical stimuli, which would help to develop some specific physiological and psychological reaction patterns. The results showed that women tended to show a hypersensitivity to negative (aversive) music stimuli, unlike males. One of the conclusions was that one should take into account gender differences in the use of music to create emotional reactions.

One of the main conclusions of a British study by sociologist Denora (2001) was that music must be considered as one of the most powerful tools to bring about emotions and feelings in people. The researcher conducted a groundbreaking study on how individuals with completely different backgrounds and sub-cultures made use of music in their daily lives. She found that British women primarily use music in everyday life to regulate, enhance, and modify their emotional states. These women considered music to be one of the most effective tools for managing the emotional labor required to maintain a positive emotional state, such as relaxation or enthusiasm, or to eliminate a negative emotional state, such as stress or fatigue.

Through laboratory experiments, it has been shown that music has a significant impact on the levels of the hormone testosterone in the body of women as well as men. The aim of the study was to identify whether there were any gender differences when it came to listening to music and the extent to which this affected the levels of testosterone.

The experiment was conducted using 70 university students, of whom 35 were women and 35 men, aged 19 to 25 years with a mean age of 21 years. Forty of them had taken music as the first choice for their college degree, whereas the other 30 had not. During the experiment, participants were given six choices, and they had 30 minutes in which to listen to their favorite choice. They could choose between (1) favorite music (n = 10; five women and five men each), (2) Gregorian chant (n = 10), (3) Mozart (n = 10), (4) jazz (n = 10), (5) popular music (n = 10), or (6) no music at all (n = 20).

Women and men were separated from each other during the experiment, which was carried out in a quiet laboratory between the hours of 2:00 and 5:00 p.m. To measure the levels of testosterone, saliva samples were taken both before and after each stimulus. The results showed that the testosterone levels decreased during silence, compared with when participants listened to music but not in a significant way. In contrast, it was found that music had a significant effect on both sexes, which meant that for women the testosterone levels increased, whereas for men it decreased.

One of the conclusions was that music has a biological and evolutionary function, which is linked to both love and the ability to reproduce one's own species. Furthermore, it was found that music could help to control aggressive and sexual behavior among both women and men. In this way, the lower testosterone levels in men contribute to avoiding confrontation, whereas the higher level of testosterone in women suppresses sexual behavior. By comparison, the researcher Hajime Fukui mentions that music, even animal sounds, works to increase the tension or effort between people, brings joy and happiness as well as strengthening social ties or cohesion between people (Fukui, 2001).

Group Preferences

In each society's culture, sound, such as music and voices, is central to group emotions and group experiences. It is clear from research how different groups in a societal culture use music to stimulate their emotions and moods.

The Tuamotus people on the French Polynesian island of Futuna see music as a way to express and stimulate feelings and experiences in the musicians and the singers as well as those who listen. The primary purpose of music is to express longing and passion through love songs, grief and anger through sad songs, or to create songs that express religious devotion.

> *In the Swedish societal culture, the midsummer celebration with its famous tunes and songs is an expression of the feelings that the bright summer gives rise to.*

When asked why they make melodies and songs, the Basongye people in the Congo say that they produce music of love and happiness to evoke joy. The construction of a melody or a song often includes emotions, and musicians should always express joy, because the musicians believe that the audience can relate to a number of individual emotions by seeing and listening to the performance. It is assumed, for example, that a funeral song playing even though there is no funeral can cause great sadness in those who listen.

The question we can ask ourselves is whether there is a natural, universal connection between music and emotions that can be considered valid regardless of the cultural background. In one study relating to the influence of Indian music on Western listeners, it was found that Westerners responded with the same emotions and feelings as the Indian listeners.

The survey was conducted by asking expert Indian musicians to implement a number of musical numbers with the intent to convey emotions such as happiness, sadness, anger, and tranquility. The Western listeners were then asked to evaluate each piece based on the four emotions. When it came to happiness, sadness, and tranquility, it was found that Westerners could relate to the basic structural characteristics of the Indian music on an emotional plane, such as tempo and complexity.

One of the study's conclusions was that there are strong arguments to suggest that at least some of the demonstrable links between music and emotions may be considered universal and thus exist regardless of cultural belonging.

Researchers such as Thompson and Balkwill (2010) have discussed the example with two different musicians from two different cultures, A and B. The two musicians have composed a piece of music that will bring joy to the audience. It was assumed that they probably would compose the piece in a scale that would bring joy to their respective cultures. This means that musician A might make use of complex harmonies, together with a simple rhythm for an instrument with a high pitch. This would perhaps get the audience in culture A to recognize the music as "the joyous flute." Musician B might instead use an unaccompanied melody with a complex rhythm for a string instrument. This might cause the audience in culture B to associate music that is in a fast pace with joy.

Thompson and Balkwill believed that although there would be superficial differences between the two pieces of music composed by the musicians, there would be elements that would strengthen the recognition process for those listeners who belong to the same culture. Among these elements, there should then be psychological stimuli such as music tempo or pitch, as well as culture-specific stimuli, such as harmonic progression, specific instruments, or tone to convey a culture-specific experience of the actual music piece.

Sound Symbolism

When it comes to the meaning of words, which are formed by sound, there is no established link between the sound of a word and its meaning. Despite this, the sound that is embedded in a word can contribute to a person's semantic understanding of the word. For that reason, there is extensive research that tries to shed light on the connection that exists between the sound of a word and its meaning for us humans, known as sound symbolism.

Researchers examined early on how nonwords such as "mil" and "mal" with the i-sound and an a-sound could be associated with either a large or a small table. A number of respondents were asked which of the two words might represent one of the tables. The study showed that more respondents associated the short i-sound in "mil" with a smaller table, in comparison with the a-sound. One conclusion was that the sound of a word, as stimulus through language, could evoke specific associations in many people.

In consumer research, several studies have investigated how the sound of a word can influence consumers' perception of products through sound symbolism. It has been clarified that an a-sound as in "father" and the o-sound as in "bought" have been associated with larger objects and that the symbolic associations, which arise from how a word sounds, cannot be considered to be language specific.

It has also been shown that sound symbolism means that many consumers may infer which product benefits a particular brand may have. In a study, it was revealed that consumers' perception of an imaginary glass brand called Frosh respective Frish was affected by how the brand could be perceived as a word sound. There were differences in opinion between an o-sound (Frosh) and a shorter i-sound (Frish), and respondents graded Frosh as creamier, softer, and richer in comparison with Frish. It was also revealed that respondents were more likely to choose the Frosh brand at the time of purchase.

> The sound of a word can influence consumers' perceptions of a brand and convey what product benefits the brand may have.

Finally, it should be said that the sound symbolism enables us to more deeply understand consumers' perceptions of different brands, which are produced daily in different marketing messages in a social culture. Each word itself can form the basis for pronunciation, and the meaning that the sound gets is the natural focus of how the sense of sound perceives the brand. In this way, words, language, and sound interact in a natural way in different social cultures and provide the opportunity to shape a unique sound experience.

It should also be added that the symbolism conveyed by musical lyrics are deemed to have a stimulating effect on visual imagery. It is also believed that music promotes a person's cognitive stimulation, provided that the listener in question tries to analyze and categorize the music and its technical aspects. Against this background, it cannot be considered surprising that music via the sense of sound often has an effect on consumers' decision-making, actions, and product selection.

SERVICE ENVIRONMENT

In a service environment, such as a store, mall, or a department store, sounds, music, and voices are used to influence the atmosphere for a shopping experience. Retail companies, in particular, have been using music to enhance the experience of the store environment's atmosphere and attractiveness. This can involve everything from the pulsating disco music from the nightclub in the fashion boutique to the classical flute sound in the old mall. There may even be an attempt to increase the pace of consumer shopping behavior by playing background music at a higher pace.

Television commercials use both voices and music to draw attention to a message and get the individual in a better mood so that she/he can easily remember the brand.

> *To align their personal message more directly to individual customers, two grocery stores in Sweden, Coop and Ica, started using directional sound. It involves using the so-called "sound showers," directing a sound to a place in the supermarket that attracts customers. The sound, which may consist of both music and voices, is created by speakers, which are placed in the ceiling and send out a sound beam to the part of the store where it is desirable.*

Sound Stimuli

Research has examined the role and significance of music, as sound stimulus, in a service environment by studying the effects of music styles such as classical or diverse, the music's tempo as slow or rapid, the music's volume as high or low, as well as the degree of recognition. Through several studies, there is clear scientific evidence that music has an overall positive impact on consumers' affections, cognitions, and actual behaviors in service environments.

> *Music can shape individuals' behaviors, and movement is the most important sensory response to music. Think of how a fast melody on your iPod can get you to increase the pace when you walk or run.*

Research has shown that mood music, as stimulus, has a positive impact on cognitive variables such as understanding and service quality, and emotional variables such as joy, humor, or arousal, as well as on behavioral variables such as customer frequency and time spent in the store, to name a few of the most common examples (Turley and Milliman, 2000; Garlin and Owen, 2006).

It was revealed in a study that fast background music, as mood music, in a medium-size store belonging to a well-known American chain had a positive impact on both consumers' pace of shopping and total sales volume. The study included 1) no music, 2) slow-paced music, and 3) fast-paced music. On the other hand, slow background music had the result of calmer customer traffic in the store, compared with faster music.

It has also been found in another study that slow tempo music has resulted in restaurant guests spending more time during their restaurant visits. Thus their average expenditure also increased, because they spent more money on drinking compared with before. In contrast, the music itself had no impact on the purchase of food, serving time, or when one left the establishment.

In a field study by Dubé and Morin (2001), the effects of background music on the degree of pleasure that different individuals experienced were studied. This measure was related to attitudes toward both the service environment and the sales staff. The survey included 85 women and 25 men, who visited a store in a shopping mall. The shop was part of a national retail chain specializing in selling trendy clothes in the middle price range for young men and women. The music selected was organized according to the beat and tempo and was adapted to the store's atmosphere and design.

The results showed that different degrees of happiness, which arose from the background music, had an impact on customers' attitudes toward both the service environment and the sales staff. One of the conclusions was that the background music had an impact on customers' perceptions of the store by positive emotions being created. These feelings then had the ability to change customers' attitudes toward the service environment as well as the store staff. Finally, the researchers believed that there was an atmospheric stimulus—in this case, the background music—that helped to enhance the store's attractiveness and image, rather than just personal service by the sales staff.

In a meta-analysis of the effects of background music on consumer behavior, researchers such as Garlin and Owen (2006) examined 32 studies conducted over the past few decades. They were interested in documenting ordinary, observed effects on consumers' behaviors and the circumstances under which these effects could differ in a retail context. Among other things, the authors concluded the following after their review of the literature:

1. The mere presence of music has a positive impact on consumers.
2. Familial/popular music has a positive impact on consumers.
3. Slower pace and lower volume means that consumers remain marginally longer in one place, compared with when both the tempo and volume are high or when the music is less familiar.
4. The music tempo is found to have the highest impact on consumer excitement.

Effect on Product Selection

An American study examined how music affected the time spent in a store, which was based on Milliman's previous studies. In a department store context, the music playing was manipulated, and the researchers compared the effects of the foreground music (top 40) and the background music (instrumental style) on an experimental group and a control group, where music was not present.

It was revealed that younger shoppers felt that they had spent more time shopping with instrumental background music, whereas older shoppers felt that they had spent more time when the foreground music (top 40) was played. One of the study's conclusions was that unfamiliar music could negatively affect consumers' perceptions of time, in terms of how much time is spent on shopping.

Research suggests that the specific type of mood music, often background music, not only has an impact on the perception of speed and time but that it can also affect the product selection through the associations that are created thanks to the music.

In a study by North et al. (1999), the extent to which the purchase of French and German wines is influenced by mood music was studied. During a two-week period, French and German background music was played on different days in a store that had signs for both French and German wines. The results of the experiment were that the French background music led to French wines being sold more than the German wines. Similarly, the German music led to the sale of more German than French wines. When respondents were questioned, it was revealed that they were unaware of the music's effects on their final product selection.

One conclusion was that music with strong national associations could have the effect that consumers bought wine from the respective countries because their relative knowledge of the countries was activated in the brain.

> *Pub guests buy more expensive wine in the restaurant's wine cellar when classical music is played.*

In a study by Areni and Kim (1993), it was revealed that when classical music was played in a wine cellar, wine purchasers bought more expensive wines than cheap wines. Through a field experiment in a centrally located restaurant with a wine cellar, the effect of classical music on customer behavior was investigated. The assumptions were that the music would increase the amount of products that are 1) investigated, 2) handled, and 3) purchased, as well as 4) increase the time customers spent in the wine shop, compared with when the top 40 music was played in the background. Those who visited the restaurant could go down to the cellar for a visit with a view to try or buy a wine.

The results of the study showed that there were no detectable effects of the background music regarding investigated shelves, the number of purchased goods, the number of handled products, or how many wines were tasted. Even the time that customers spent in the restaurant turned out to not be influenced by the background music. Nevertheless, the amount of money that customers spent on the wine was influenced by the music, and they bought more expensive wine when classical music was played as background music in comparison with the top 40 music.

The study shows that music must fit in context to enhance the credibility of the actual service environment, which will be discussed in more detail in the section "Music Congruence." The study's findings contribute to support the hypothesis that classical music can affect an individual's perception that a store's products have a higher price range. It is also generally accepted in the literature that music gives rise to mental associations, primarily in terms of social class, price, or status.

Effect of the Service Level
Research suggests that mood music can help so that queuing may be perceived as more pleasurable by invoking positive evaluations of the waiting times.

A study using a field experiment in the banking environment was conducted. The experiment had four different musical stimuli with ten levels of music valence (positive and negative). For the control group, there was no music at all. The intention was to test three different concepts, such as perceived waiting time, emotional evaluation of the service landscape, and the emotional response at having to wait in relation to both the background music and behavior toward the bank.

The results showed that music, regardless of valence, helps to improve the emotional evaluation of a service environment, which in turn has a positive effect on the customer's behavior toward the service provider. It was evident that the more positively valued music—as opposed to the negatively valued music—stimulated and created a clearer emotional response among customers regarding having to wait.

The findings showed that customers perceived a longer waiting period when the background music was played. It also turned out that even if the music seemed to increase the perceived waiting time, there was no negative emotional response, but rather a positive response from having to wait. In this context, it turned out that music has a distracting function, by creating positive emotions, which in itself seems to reduce the negative effects of having to wait. In this way, background music is considered to be an effective tool to get customers to be satisfied when they are waiting.

> *It was experienced as easier to wait in a queue when background music is played, and customers become more satisfied.*

In another study, Cameron et al. (2003) investigated customers' perceptions of the cost of having to stand in line and wait. The researchers were particularly interested in how the effects of music, the length of the waiting period, and customers' moods influenced the overall experience of standing in line at a supermarket. Low-cost waiting, i.e., having to wait at a low cost, differs from high-cost waiting, where there is also a social/emotional cost involved.

The results showed that music had both cognitive (no waiting time evaluation) and emotional sensory impact. It was apparent from the study that music's positive contributions mainly proved themselves by mood, not by waiting time evaluation. Mood was found to have a direct impact regarding the overall experience of having to stand in line.

One of the conclusions was that atmospheric stimuli, such as background music, could help to improve the mood of customers waiting in line. This reinforces the general perception that music in the general public—and classical music in particular—can contribute to an improved experience of a service environment. For supermarket checkouts, where customers often have to stand and wait at a low cost, this means that cost may be perceived as less or perhaps even eliminated.

Deterrent Effects

The type of music can also cause people to easily go away from a store or a restaurant, which an example from McDonald's in Camberwell, England, can illustrate. It turned out that when classical music was played through the speakers outside the restaurant, teenagers no longer gathered in crowds outside the restaurant.

A similar example of how music can have a deterrent effect can be shown from the underground in London. In January 2005, tests were conducted using classical music in selected metro stations to prevent thefts. It turned out that thefts decreased by 25 percent, vandalism of trains and stations fell by 37 percent, and assaults on the staff decreased by 25 percent.

Sound Perception

It is generally accepted in research that tempo and time indicate whether the actual music is perceived or experienced as fast or slow. If the tones are in major or minor and have falling or rising tones, the music's pitch will answer. Without a doubt, both the tempo and the pitch of music are the most important properties and contribute to how it is perceived and experienced in different service environments.

When it comes to the structure of music, which provides the desired aesthetics and color to music, it should be possible to distinguish different instruments from one another so that it gives the desired sound experience. Furthermore, it should be said that the structure is also about music orchestration, where the different instruments as individual audio elements are linked together to provide the overall sound experience of the actual music.

> The American clothing chain Abercrombie & Fitch is known to discourage adults from visiting their stores by playing loud music.

Three different types of responses to music as stimuli were identified in a study that was conducted. It appeared that joy, excitement, and amazement were related to three identified music features such as tempo, tonality (pitch), and structure (classical music or pop music). One of the study's conclusions was that it is necessary to have a better understanding of both the music as the stimulus and the listener's response when it comes to creating knowledge about the multidimensional nature of the music.

Various studies show that the tempo of music is generally linked to the rate at which shopping is conducted in a service landscape. Consumers who listen to music with slower tempos also do their shopping activities slowly. Above all, this is thought to be due to a slower rate, which means that a consumer spends more time in a shop or a restaurant with a longer service meeting. This, in itself, leads to the finding that slow music gives consumers greater purchasing opportunities and thereby influences the purchasing quantity.

It is also shown by other studies that many consumers cannot recall the characteristics of the music played in a service environment. Furthermore, in many cases it has been found that consumers have been unaware that music has been played at all in the actual service environment. Rather, it appears that consumers, most likely in an unconscious way, associate slow music with a slower pace, which in itself can cause a calming effect on the shopping experience.

In the same way that slowly paced music can get consumers to be calm, fast-paced tempo can cause many to react with excitement. One study examined how excitement evoked by music had a positive effect on consumer behavior at a bank. The faster the music that was played, the greater the excitement, thus there was an increase in consumers' positive attitudes toward the bank staff. Furthermore, it was found that consumers who had been subjected to fast music also stated that they were more likely to say hello, smile, or chat with bank employees.

When it comes to the effect of music on the consumer's shopping experience, from a hedonic or practical utilitarian perspective, this has been studied by Eroglu et al. (2005). The researchers were interested in finding out how the interaction of the music tempo and congestion would affect the consumer's assessment of the shopping experience in a service landscape. The survey was conducted in a shopping center and involved 47 respondents, of whom nearly two-thirds were women aged 23–54 years. Respondents were asked to answer a questionnaire with statements about their shopping experience.

The results showed that the shopping experience, from a hedonic perspective, was linked to slow music as well as high congestion, whereas from a practical utilitarian perspective, fast music and low congestion were emphasized. Furthermore, it appeared that many would avoid shopping in the actual shopping center in the future if the fast music were retained, which was shown to have a significant impact on shoppers' behaviors.

One of the study's conclusions was that by using music as an atmospheric element in a service environment, it might be possible to minimize the negative effects of congestion in a shopping mall. Depending on whether it is a high or low degree of congestion, the effects of slow or fast music can be tested. In a rather empty service landscape, therefore, perhaps fast music should be put to use to make the shopping experience more lively and inspiring, whereas slow music might be used to lower the tempo in an already crowded and too full service landscape. In this way, the music can contribute so that consumers' perceptions of crowding can be changed and lead to a positive shopping experience.

The importance of developing the right sound design in a service environment is illustrated by the following example:

> At the shopping center Emporia in Malmö, Sweden, the acoustic experience was already planned from the beginning with architects and sound designers. To remove noise from the escalators and waterfalls, other sounds are present to create a whole. They have chosen to have quiet walkways; however, a personal voice talks about the services and the offerings. The parking garage plays music from the 1950s with a connection to the car.

When it comes to the effect of music volume on consumers, a study has shown that consumers spent less time in a store with high volume, compared with low volume, music. Despite this, there proved to be no significant differences in terms of sales or customer satisfaction.

> The cognitive work when purchasing is facilitated by soft music, whereas high, arousing music makes it more difficult for an individual to think.

The effect of music on an individual's cognition, i.e., the cognitive functions that process and manage the information and knowledge, has been studied to a lesser extent. The research has assumed that the effect of music on emotions and feelings has been instrumental in consumer behavior and chose to ignore the cognitive functions. In older psychological theories, cognition has also been viewed as the opposite of emotion (emotional life) and volition (decisions in life).

In another study, the effect of music on cognitive processes such as information management and thinking was investigated. Of the conducted experiment, it was evident that soothing music, which was both pleasurable as well as low inflammatory, increased the cognitive activity in individuals when other cognitive stimulation was low or weak. The most common example of this is when sales arguments are not strong enough to convince the consumer of the actual product's good functional properties.

The results of the study showed that calm music was causing low excitement, which helped to increase the cognitive response when it came to customer service and sales figures. This means that the individual's cognitive activity becomes stimulated by calm music. Other studies have shown that music, which is highly exciting, hampers the cognitive activity, which suggests that calm music helps to facilitate the cognitive processes.

One conclusion of the study was that certain musical stimuli could probably enhance the cognitive activities and that these stimuli have an impact on the attitudes that consumers have about the shop and the products they encounter. This appeared to be particularly true when the level of engagement with the product was low or when the sales personnel's arguments were weak.

In an experimental study, Haegermark et al. (2011) surveyed parents and children's responses to sound stimuli when buying groceries in a grocery store. In conjunction with the introduction of a new sound system, which included 13 different stories for children with a human voice, the effects of the parents and the children's behaviors during the shopping visit were investigated. The study included 200 families in the control group and 131 families in the experimental group and was performed using field observations in the store. Every family that participated in the experiment received an MP3 player free of charge. Adjacent to each category, there was a rack where the children could listen to the stories.

Often, parents experience various forms of stress when younger children accompany them to the store, and by introducing the sound system, it would give children a positive listening experience and the parents a more pleasant shopping experience. The various stories had to do with adventurers who used the shop to store their treasures from past adventures. By following a number of stations, in categories such as milk, meat, or cheese, the children would take part in the stories. The aim was both to entertain the children and to educate them about the various products that were included in the categories.

The results showed that the children's voice levels were and that their movement patterns decreased when they listened to the stories. Furthermore, the stories resulted in both the children and the parents being able to determine in which direction they should go during the shopping trip, which previously was a problem, because children and parents often do not want to go in the same direction. It was also shown that parental stress decreased as a result of this and that the parents stayed longer in the store environment.

One conclusion of the study was that sound stimuli, in the form of sounds and voices, affect both children and their parents' behaviors in a positive way. This is especially true when buying groceries in a supermarket, which is in itself a source of stress with everything that is offered to children in the form of ice cream, candy, and toys, to name a few. When the kids got to experience a positive listening experience, they also became preoccupied with an interesting task, namely, to follow the stories, which offered both joy and excitement. The research showed that the introduction of sound stimuli, in this case sound and voice, were perceived positively and affected both children and their parents' shopping behavior.

Music Congruence

Based on what has emerged so far from the research, mood music and the music's tempo and the volume influence consumers' emotions, thoughts, and behaviors. There is no doubt that music as a phenomenon has a strong effect on an individual's listening experience in a service environment. But the question that remains to be answered is how consistent should the music be with the whole atmosphere of a certain type of service environment through what is called *music congruence*? By music congruence, it is meant music is in full agreement with the interior, the character, and design of a store, a mall, or a restaurant.

> *If the music matches the service environment, the customers will be satisfied.*

In a field experiment, Demoulin (2011) examined the effects of music congruence with the whole atmosphere in a service environment. As a starting point for the study, a holistic perspective was used, and the researcher was interested in studying the effect that music congruence could have on emotional and cognitive aspects, as well as on behavioral intentions.

The experiment was conducted in a French restaurant with the help of both congruent and noncongruent music, which was considered to be consistent with or inconsistent with the restaurant's atmosphere regarding the interior, character, and design. Before the experiment was conducted, interviews took place with the owner and the staff to clarify what might be considered to be the "right music" for the restaurant. Regarding the nonconforming music, a popular French radio station was chosen, which sent timeless popular music.

The results showed that music congruence led to a low degree of arousal, which resulted in high pleasure for the guests. The fact that high pleasure arose also led to an increase in their evaluations of the quality regarding service environment and service quality. In turn, this led to a positive impact on the visitors' intentions of returning to the restaurant again.

One of the study's conclusions was that consumers perceived and experienced music congruence regarding the service environment and the music that could be considered "right." The holistic experience resulted in many individuals getting more excited and feeling a greater pleasure on an emotional level, which also affected their attitudes toward the whole atmosphere and quality of service in a more positive way than without music congruence.

The reported study showed the importance of music congruence and its effect on individuals' emotions and feelings. But there are also studies that examined how music congruence affects individuals' information management and thoughts through cognitive activities.

> *Nordic Light Hotel in Stockholm, Sweden, has deliberately chosen to use music to clarify the meaning of the brand's identity. There are about eight hundred songs in the music collection, and the music can be "streamed" via the Internet. Throughout the day, music is played that is consistent with the hours of the day; and in the morning, a news channel is played when the guests eat breakfast. Even the volume varies depending on how many guests are on the premises.*

In the advertising context, it is believed that music can contribute to a message becoming attractive and can also create attention. It is also a known fact that slow music creates a low degree of attention, whereas fast music can lead to a higher degree of attention. In this manner, attention-creating music can lead to an advertisement and its message being noticed and thereby strengthening the receipt of the message. On the other hand, sometimes there is a paradox that many individuals just listen to the music and do not get the message.

One study investigated how listeners received the message in a radio advertisement. Authors, together with experts, created the advertisement and 40 pieces of music were tested, which were instrumental and nonfamilial. The survey included 110 respondents who were asked to rank the music pieces regarding attention value and how familiar they were considered to be. Furthermore, respondents were asked to write down their thoughts while they listened to the music.

The results showed that respondents got different images of the products, which amazingly seemed to be consistent with the group's understandings of the relevant product categories. The conclusion drawn was that an advertisement and its message is received and recognized more easily by an individual when the music, having an attention value, contributes by communicating a congruent message. In those cases where the music does not match the message, this would probably mean that many listeners do not get the message that the advertisement would like to convey but instead ignore it. In this way, music congruence is of relevance also for information management and the thoughts that arise in an individual when an advertising message is to be received and evaluated on a personal level.

BRAND

Both the music and the voices of famous artists and personalities can help create a memorable listening experience of a product or a service. This means that companies and organizations can make use of sound through music and voices to clarify its identity and values. For this reason, sound is used almost daily to communicate with and convince consumers, as well as to strengthen a brand's image in consumers' minds. It is even considered that sound is a crucial element of the brand experience itself, as is the case with the bang that is heard when a wine bottle is uncorked.

As previously shown, there is extensive research that clearly points to the link between music, on the one hand, and cognitions, on the other hand, in both the societal culture and the service environment. However, research has mainly dealt with music's effect on the atmosphere and mood in different service environments, such as stores or shopping mall, has been perceived and experienced by different individuals. However, music's effect on consumers' emotional and cognitive processes as well as behaviors in conjunction with the product evaluation of individual goods or services, such as a car brand or a dentist appointment, has been addressed to a lesser extent.

> On Loka's website, they offer customers the ability to listen to Veronica Maggio, who interprets "Must Continue" to strengthen the brand image.

Sound Stimuli

In advertising and promotional campaigns, music, as sound stimuli, has for a long time had a prominent role—especially when it comes to television and radio commercials, which most consumers are in daily contact with. In recent years, advertising on the Internet has also increased in scope and has come to contribute to an increased exposure to advertising messages and promotional offers.

Some researchers believe that music helps to trigger different emotions and moods, which in turn creates and allows attitudes toward advertising and brands. In this manner, the music functions, as the representative of a particular brand, as an outward, persuasive stimulus in advertising and campaign promotions. As previously stated, it is a common perception that the background music in the ad context has a positive effect on consumers' attitudes toward the brand in question.

The researchers found in a study that consumers' ability to address a brand's distinctive features could be hindered by music. In this case, music, as a distractor, seizes the individual's attention, or cognitive resources, and hinders the receipt and processing of the actual advertising message.

Researchers believe that this type of involvement or distraction is likely to occur in individuals with low engagement in connection with their product choice, because uninvolved individuals seem to be more aware of the peripheral, external stimuli rather than information from the message. For individuals with high engagement, however, there is a risk that the music may make it difficult for them to focus on and really process the actual message of the advertisement.

> The home ice cream truck jingle has been played in many neighborhoods when the ice cream truck comes to visit. This jingle can be considered one of the most famous audio brands in Sweden during the last decades.

Researchers such as MacInnis and Park (1991) suggested instead that music, through its involvement, could have a tendency to trigger powerful emotional memory experiences that are associated with music on a deeper, inner level. In one study, they found that for individuals with low engagement, music increased their ability to process the message of the advertisement. This occurred primarily because the music reminded these individuals to devote their attention to the actual message. But the music, which also had been correctly assumed, was a distractor for individuals with high engagement, because the music triggered their emotionally charged memory experiences so that it became impossible for these individuals to embrace the advertisement message.

It is also shown by research that the understanding of the meaning of an advertising message is facilitated when the music is congruent rather than incongruent with the message. Music congruence is considered to be easier for an individual to process the message, strengthen the brand, and remember the same.

Mood and Music

In marketing, music has long been used as a secondary sound tool, even though it has been shown to have a strong influence on consumers' behaviors. When it comes to advertising, music has been shown to contribute to a positive mood, develop a brand image, or influence the onset of favorable attitudes toward a brand and consumption of the brand in general.

It has also been shown that music can help create either a pleasant or an unpleasant mood among consumers in connection with advertising messages. One study examined whether arousing music could be used to manipulate an individual's state of mind. The results showed that an individual's state of mind was influenced by music, especially if the advertising message had a vague emotional tone. It also turned out that it was the fact that the music was highly arousing that influenced the evaluation of the advertising message more positively in comparison with the music that was low arousing.

In another experimental study, it was studied how attention to product information in the advertising message in a television commercial was influenced by music. In the experiment, classical conditioning was used as a method. It turned out that when individuals listened to popular or not popular music at the time of product exposure, their product preferences were influenced. The results of the study showed that the simple relationship between the product as a conditioned stimulus, on the one hand, and music as a unconditioned stimulus, on the other hand, had an impact on consumers' product preferences.

Researchers have early on discussed how studies of music in advertising contexts have regarded music as a nonsemantic, emotional stimulus independent of meaning or context. Some further argue that music is often separated from its syntax of visual and verbal stimuli, which is reflected in the methods used to investigate the effect of music on consumers' perceptions of the advertising message.

Instead, others convey that this ignores the individual's ability to assess and interpret music as part of the overall rhetorical intent of the advertising message. For that reason, an alternative theory is proposed, which assumes that music is both meaningful and linguistic, which requires both interpretive and empirical research to create more explanatory concepts of the role of music in advertising and campaign promotions.

Brand Embodiment
The fact that a structure of an advertisement message, like a certain mood, can be influenced by music also means that the advertising message can induce general, hedonic emotions in many individuals. Here, hedonic means emotions that lead to joy or happiness in one's own self in the first place. It is widely recognized in the literature that these feelings are related to the significance of the music's embodiment, because they are considered to be independent of its context.

> *A nursery song can bring up memories of childhood, and listening to an unknown fast melody can create thoughts on frivolity.*

These hedonic feelings arise as a result of the sound music embodies, such as its instruments, rhythm, tempo, and pitch or just the joy of something new. It is widely believed that music with a fast pace elicits more positive emotions than calm music, just like music in major, unlike the minor form or with a high pitch also encourages more favorable emotions.

Remarkably, regardless of listeners' musical experience and training, it turns out that there is a broad consensus on the interpretations that are made by the importance of music embodiment. This shows that the importance of music for one's self is context-dependent, learned, and arises from an interaction with the concepts in the surrounding world, which the music can trigger based on previous experiences.

In this way, music in advertising contexts has an effect on the individual's emotions and feelings as well as the cognitive processes that take place in order to perceive and interpret the actual message in the advertisement. Therefore, there is reason to pay attention to how the music that is presented embodies the brand—a product or a service—that the current advertisement message wants to convey, in a company's marketing communications.

Voices in Advertising
In research, the importance of voices, as opposed to music, in advertising and advertising messages has been analyzed and investigated in several studies. It turns out that the two most significant factors are pitch and rate of speech when it comes to listeners' response to verbal communication and

getting a personal understanding of the speaker, that is, the person behind the voice.

Impact of Pitch

Within psychology and linguistics (general linguistics), it is generally suggested that voices with a low pitch are evaluated more favorably in comparison with voices that are high pitched. In one study, it was shown that an increase in a speaker's pitch led to listeners perceiving the speaker as being less competent and less friendly.

Three experiments were conducted in a study that examined how the audience reacted to a speaker's normal pitch level, compared with a decrease, respectively, and an increase of 20 percent. In the survey, the listeners got to experience different tape recordings in which the pitch varied. The results showed that listeners preferred a speaker with a low pitch as opposed to a high pitch. This was because the speaker in the latter case was considered to be less empathetic, less credible, and more nervous.

> *If a brand is pronounced high and clear repeatedly, consumers' product evaluation and selection of the product is influenced in a significant way.*

In several experiments, Argo et al. (2010) analyzed the emotional reactions in response to sound and suggested that the brand name should contain a phonetic sound repetition. If the brand name is pronounced with a loud human voice, the brand is recognized and evaluated more favorably than in the case where the sound repetition does not take place or where the brand name is pronounced quietly. One of the conclusions of the study was that phonetic sound repetition positively affects the consumer's evaluation and selection of a product in terms of both multiple brand names and product categories.

Effect of the Rate of Speech

In research, attention has been directed to the importance of the rate of speech in different advertising messages on the radio and television. It turns out that there is extensive research that has demonstrated the relationship between a speaker's faster speech rate and enhanced powers of persuasion when it comes to an individual being influenced by the advertising message. Numerous studies show that listeners attribute a speaker's faster speech rate with greater competence and credibility.

Furthermore, it also appears that a speaker's faster speech rate has an impact on listeners in that they perceive the speaker as being more intelligent, knowledgeable, and impartial as well as more empathetic, serious, and compelling.

It is generally accepted in the research that speech rate is determined by two components, namely, the speed with which a syllable is pronounced and the pauses that exist between the various phrases. The syllable rate refers to the rate at which a syllable is articulated, which is assumed to be approximately five seconds in normal speech.

In the advertising context, the effect of speech rate on the listener's propensity to absorb the actual message has been analyzed in a number of studies. This has been done with respect to how changes as well as the speed at which syllables are articulated and the pauses between different phrases affect the listener's response.

In one study, a radio commercial context was used to both compress and expand the speaking rate, either by shorter or longer pauses between the phrases or by changing the speed of the syllables articulation. The results generally showed that listeners respond more effectively to a faster rate of speech and that they have a better attitude toward the spokesperson in question. In contrast, a slower rate of speech gave listeners the opportunity for a greater cognitive assessment of the actual advertising message. These results were consistent with previous results that have been found in the research, which is why there seems to be a clear link between the speech rate and the listener's reactions, on both an emotional as well as a cognitive level.

One study examined what happened to the listeners' reactions at a faster rate of speech. It turned out that the listeners were then more focused on the pitch stimulus. The results showed that a faster rate of speech in the TV and radiobroadcasting context seemed to interrupt listeners' processing of the advertising message rather than to reinforce the same. One of the study's conclusions was that it is the individual's motivation to process the advertising message that was important and not its ability, which seems to support that a faster rate of speech should be combined with a low pitch in order to be noticed.

Orator's Voice
When it comes to the importance of voice in the radio and television context, factors such as pitch and rate of speech were examined a number of decades ago. In recent years, research has paid very little attention to the importance of how female voices are perceived in marketing by listeners.

It has generally been the case that male voices have been used in psychology and linguistics when studies on the importance of the voice in marketing have been investigated—even though there is enough evidence that a female voice is different from a male voice in a systematic way. Some research has been conducted that has attempted to identify desirable voice qualities, but it has faded away theoretically or has been able to demonstrate the existence of gender differences.

> For ten years, BMW has used the famous British actor David Suchet's voice in its commercials.

Some studies have shown that there are no gender differences, but these studies seem to be the exception rather than the rule. There is evidence to suggest that a high-pitched voice is better suited for women than for men, and that a low-pitched voice fits better for men than for women.

Sound Perception

Marketing research has, only to a small extent, addressed sound and, foremost, music's effect on how consumers perceive and experience a brand in association with product evaluation, although this usually occurs within the framework of the service environment where the mood music has proved to be of great importance for both emotions and feelings as well as cognitive processes that influence consumers' actual behaviors.

But in connection with product evaluation, it is not just about mood music, which is used to make the service environment more pleasant and appealing, but also about how music can help to enhance the listening experience of an individual brand. In this context, music congruence also plays a big role, because there should be a natural connection with the music that relates to the individual brand.

One study found that in evaluating pens with one or two color combinations, consumers more frequently chose the pen that was clearly associated with the music they liked. This was done by letting consumers listen to both the music that they liked as well as music they disliked to find out how this would affect their product choice. It was found that consumers chose the alternative pen when the preferred pen was associated with the music that was disliked.

With the help of an experiment, the effect of music on consumers' mood was investigated in connection with the evaluation of new products. The experiment was carried out in such a way that the music would contribute to a good mood or a bad mood and respondents would not be aware of what was behind their good or bad mood. Respondents had the task of evaluating the performance and quality of new stereo speakers during the time they listened to music they liked or disliked. Thereafter, a number of questions were posed about the music's influence on respondents' mood.

The results showed that when respondents were not aware of what affected their mood, then the products were assessed more positively when the respondents were in a good mood than when they were in a bad mood. But it turned out that when respondents were aware of the music, there were no differences in the product evaluation between those who were in a good mood and those who were in a bad mood.

One of the conclusions was that generally music had an influence on the mood, which the music came to generate in the respondents. The researchers explained this by saying that consumers recognize their own feelings and decide on the basis of these; but if one is not aware of his/her mood, then they use their own feelings as information in the product evaluation context.

In a literature survey, researchers such as Spence and Shankar (2010) mapped out how sound affects people's experiences of food and beverages as well as their behavior in the context of taste experiences. It appeared that both music and other sound stimuli could have a dramatic effect on how food and beverage are perceived. There is a significant effect regarding preferences, taste evaluation, and consumption levels, which are explained by including other multi-sensory interaction, which I will return to later.

When it comes to sound in the product evaluation of different brands, it is considered that this plays a crucial role in consumers' acceptance and purchasing decisions. A product's sound gives the brand an identity and tells the consumers how the product works and functions. So without a sound, it is impossible for many products to be identified, which is why the sound of a product can be said to embody the brand, just like the music genre, tempo, or key signature can embody a brand.

It is also common for consumers to identify and think of a product in terms of its sound, which can be either more of a pleasant sort or directly unpleasant. In the automotive industry, most buyers want to purchase a car with a quiet engine, which car manufacturers in different ways also try to satisfy as much as possible. The sound of a car, therefore, can build up an image of a brand, such as a sports car, and the sound can be used in the advertising context to reinforce the identity of the brand. Then, the sound of a new, quiet car door in a TV commercial can reinforce the image of the brand that wants to convey exclusivity and quality.

Sound often has a supporting role when it comes to showing how the actual product works in different ways. In this way, these sounds have a substantial contribution to how a product's features and functions can be perceived and experienced by consumers. It is often considered that a car door that sounds hollow and rattles when it closes signals the car's quality, just as a car horn can say something about the personality and size.

> *The hotel chain Crowne Plaza offers snorers a special room with anti-snoring pillows and soundproofing so that they will not interfere with other hotel guests.*

But sound is not only pleasurable, there are also unpleasant sounds characterizing products such as vacuum cleaners, computers, household appliances, or washing machines. The sounds coming from different types of electrical motors are perceived by many consumers as disruptive noise. For a vacuum cleaner, the sound may be considered a paradox, because it illustrates both the power to suck up dust and dirt while creating dissatisfaction in the user in question. Despite a high functional quality when it comes to sucking up dust and dirt, it can create discontent and dissatisfaction in many consumers in the long run.

It should also be said that many consumers use sound to evaluate a product, since a sound, for one reason or another, does not sound like it should. This includes products with both motors and those without, and it provides the opportunity for a brand to focus on sound's role in order to create an identity and an image of the actual product.

Sound Symbolism

Spence (2012) believes that sound symbolism is about how an individual implicitly associates an experienced sound with a characteristic of a particular stimulus. In this way, the pronunciation of a name or emphasis of a particular letter can influence an individual's perception of a certain brand.

It is clear from the research that sound symbolism is considered to have a significant effect on consumers' product perceptions of product categories. Researchers such as Lowrey and Shrum (2007) have found that the product evaluation of a brand was positive when the product benefits were brought forward with the help of a language sound that was congruent, i.e., in line with the expectations of the evaluated product.

In one study, it was found that by manipulating certain properties, such as the sound level and the frequency of electric toothbrushes, they were perceived as hard or less pleasant. In the case of an ordinary lighter, it emerged that a luxury brand was associated with a saturated and low sound or a sound that was clicking, strong pitch, and soft.

The concept of *audio branding*, which translates to sound brand building, relates to how different types of sounds can be linked to a brand. The starting point in sound brand building is brand identity, which is based on a number of core values, such as dynamic, flexible, personal, or challenging. In the automotive industry, these core values are often used to build and establish a brand identity over time, as has been the case with brands such as Audi, BMW, Chrysler, Ford, Mercedes-Benz, Toyota, and Volvo.

To communicate brand identity, there are a number of different elements that are directed toward one or more senses, including sound. Primary brand elements have been proposed such as *product sound* and *brand sound* to establish the brand directly, whereas secondary branding elements such as music cooperation and ambient music can indirectly enrich the brand.

In terms of *product sound*, this includes all types of sounds that can be linked to the product itself, such as door sounds, engine noise, or other disturbing noises while driving. Often, this is about sounds that can be directly linked to the physical characteristics and that can affect the sound experience in a positive or negative way. When it comes to dealing with product sound, generally engineers, acousticians, and hearing experts are involved to create a sound environment that is as attractive as possible.

> Porsche's product sound, as well as the engine noise, conveys a sense of dynamics, power, and sportiness.

When it comes to *brand sound*, this includes all types of sounds that can also be connected to the product, but which are deliberately created, such as the jingle, music, song sound logo, soundscapes, voice, or brand theme. Often this sound is used to create personal and symbolic associations with a specific brand based on one or more types of sounds. When it comes to dealing with brand sound, generally, communications, audio, and brand experts are involved to create a sound that can be communicated through various contact points, such as the Internet, trade shows, radio, and television.

In the literature, it is not considered that product sounds and brand sounds are independent of each other but rather that they should be connected together to create an agreement within the framework for the whole brand. Just think of the sound that is heard when starting your PC or turning on your cell phone, which can be said to be equivalent to both product and brand sound.

Audio logo (or signature sound) means the acoustic identification of a brand, which is often combined with a visual logo, as illustrated by the example here.

> When Microsoft developed the Windows Vista operating system over 18 months, they looked for a signature sound for the brand that would sound simple and clean. At the same time, it needed to create attention and awaken the rhythm of "Windows Vista." To succeed with this, the signature sound came to consist of four chords during four seconds, where the number four also symbolizes the four different colors in the Windows Vista logo.

When it comes to *jingles*, which first came about as early as the 1920s, it is believed that it is a song traditionally played in the radio context. Originally, the jingle in people's ears became a synonym for a radio station, which conveyed the advertisement's message about different brands. The American company General Mills was the first company in 1926 to launch a jingle for their breakfast cereal Wheaties in the United States. Since then, jingles have commonly been used to symbolize known brands. In recent years, McDonald's jingle "I'm Lovin It" has been launched in global advertising campaigns in collaboration with the famous singer Justin Timberlake.

A *brand song* is regarded as a more commercial song with the aim of creating an association and a relationship to the actual brand. It is possible that a brand song can become a real acoustic brand, and it usually develops for special target groups or specific applications.

Brand voice means a voice that is capable of inciting associations and feelings for the brand through the voice itself. It is not just about a singing voice but a speaking voice. In this context, it is important that the person's actual voice, in terms of character and personality, really fits with the actual brand.

> *Ikea Germany uses a voice that speaks German, but with a typical Swedish accent, to communicate their advertising message.*

Sound icons, like sounds symbols, are considered to be short acoustic signals used to emphasize a particular aspect or benefit of the actual brand. It is evident also that sound icons are integrated into a sound logo or a brand song. For many years, Coca-Cola has used the clicking sound of a newly opened bottle to illustrate the product's freshness.

It should also be mentioned that there are *hymns* or *songs of praise (corporate anthems)* within the framework of sound (sonic) branding that cover the entire corporate and brand name. This can be applied to general meetings, internal representation, mobile phones with special ring tones, or e-mail boxes with special sound design on company computers. This can be seen as part of strengthening and developing staff participation and creating emotional connections to the corporate and brand name.

Research suggests that there is a significant effect regarding music and voice alignment with the brand in advertising with respect to various acoustic elements. The elements that fit with the brand receive significantly better results in terms of advertisement recognition, brand awareness, and purchase intent in comparison with the music that does not. It was also found that inappropriate music could even affect the brand negatively (North et al., 2004).

Finally, it should be said that the significance of sound on a brand experience—in comparison to sight, smell, touch, and taste—has been neglected in research for a long time. Therefore, there is reason to highlight the importance of sound in research to come.

REFERENCES

Areni, C.S. and Kim, D. (1993), "The influence of background music on shopping behaviour: classical versus top-forty music in a wine store." I: McAlister, L. and Rothschild, M. (ed.) *Advances in consumer research (Vol. 20)*, Ann Arbor, MI, p. 336–340.

Argo, J., Popa, M. and Smith, M.C. (2010), "The sound of brands," *Journal of Marketing*, 74, July:97–109.

Burner II, G.C. (1990), "Music, mood, and marketing," *Journal of Marketing*, 54, 4:94–104.
Cameron, M.A., Barker, J., Peterson, M. and Braunsberger, K. (2003), "The effects of music, wait-length evaluation, and mood on a low-cost wait experience," *Journal of Business Research*, 56, 6:421–430.
Cooke, D. (1959), *The language of music*, London: Oxford University Press.
Damaiso, A.R. (1994), *Descartes' error: emotion, reason, and the human brain*, New York: Avon Books.
Demoulin, N.T.M. (2011), "Music congruency in a service setting. The mediating role of emotional and cognitive responses," *Journal of Retailing and Consumer Services*, 18, 1:10–18.
DeNora, T. (2001), "Aesthetic agency and musical practice: new directions in the sociology of music and emotion." I: Juslin, P.N. and Sloboda, J.A. (ed.) *Music and emotion: theory and research*, Oxford: Oxford University Press, p. 161–180.
Drucker, P.F. (1994), *Post capitalist society*, Harper Business, p. 10.
Dubé, L. and Morin, S. (2001), "Background music pleasure and store evaluation intensity effects and psychological mechanisms," *Journal of Business Research*, 54, 2:107–113.
Eroglu, S.A., Machleit, K.A. and Chebat, J. (2005), "The interaction of retail density and music tempo: effects on shopper responses," *Psychology & Marketing*, 22, 7:577–589.
Fukui, H. (2001), "Music and testosterone: a new hypothesis for the origin and function of music," *Annals of the New York Academy of Sciences*, 930:448–451.
Garlin, F.V. and Owen, K. (2006), "Setting the tone with the tune: a meta-analytic review of the effects of background music in retail settings," *Journal of Business Research*, 59, 6:755–764.
Gundlach, R.H. (1935), "Factors determining the characterization of musical phrases," *The American Journal of Psychology*, 47, 4:642 ff.
Haegermark, H., Kvarnvik, M. and Persson, G. (2011), *Sound marketing*, Master Thesis, Linneaus University, Vaxjo, May.
Jackson, D.M. (2003), *Sonic branding*, Basingstoke: Palgrave Macmillan, p. 27.
Krumhansl, C.L. (1997), "An exploratory study of musical emotions and psychophysiology," *Canadian Journal of Experimental Psychology*, 51, 4:336–352.
Lowrey, T.M. and Shrum, L.J. (2007), "Phonetic symbolism and brand name preference," *Journal of Consumer Research*, 34, October:406–414.
MacInnis, D.J. and Park C.W. (1991), "The differential role of characteristics of music on high- and low-involvement consumers' processing ads," *Journal of Consumer Research*, 18, September:161–173.
Meyers-Levy, J., Bublitz, M.G. and Peracchio, L.A. (2010), "The sounds of the marketplace." I: Krishna, A. (ed.) *Sensory marketing: research on the sensuality of products*, New York: Routledge, p. 138.
North, A.C., Hargreaves, D.J. and McKendrick, J. (1999), "The influence of in-store music on wine selections," *Journal of Applied Psychology*, 84, February:271–276.
North, A.C., Hargreaves, D.J., Mac Kenzie, L. and Law, R. (2004), "The effects of musical and voice 'fit' on responses to adverts," *Journal of Applied Social Psychology*, 34:1675–1708.
Spence, C. (2012), "Managing sensory expectations concerning products and brands: capitalizing on the potential of sound and shape symbolism", *Journal of Consumer Psychology*, 22, 1:37–54.
Spence, C. and Shankar, M. (2010), "The influence of auditory cues on the perception of, and responses to, food and drink", *Journal of Sensory Studies*, 25, 3:406–430.
Stumpf, C. (1883), *Tonpsychologie (Vol. 1)*, Leipzig: Hirzel.
Thompson, W.F. (2009), *Music, thought, and feeling*, Oxford: Oxford University Press, p. 121 ff.

Thompson, W.F. and Balkwill, L.-L. (2010), "Cross-cultural similarities and differences." I: Juslin, P.N. and Sloboda, J.A. (ed.) *Handbook of music and emotion—theory, research, applications*, Oxford: Oxford University Press, p. 765.

Travis, F., Harung, S.H. and Lagrosen, Y. (2010), "Moral development, executive functioning, peak experiences and brain patterns in professional and amateur classical musicians: interpreted in light of a unified theory of performance," *Consciousness and Cognition*, doi:10.1016/j.concog.2011.03.020

Turley, L. and Milliman, R. (2000), "Atmospheric effects on shopping behavior: a review of the experimental evidence," *Journal of Business Research*, 49, 2:193–211.

7 The Sense of Smell

This chapter analyzes and discusses the sense of smell, which is considered to be strongly associated with both emotional and cognitive reactions in a person. The scientific notions about the fundamental role of the sense of smell are addressed initially with respect to physiological characteristics and psychological aspects, as well as the importance of the effects of scents.

Thereafter, the three categories of influential factors for the sense of smell, which relate to the importance of the societal culture, the service environment, and the brand, are presented. Considering this background, it is discussed how various factors affect individuals' affections, cognitions, as well as their actual behaviors in the different buying and consumption processes.

THE UNCONSCIOUS SENSE

Since ancient times, people have used scents in the form of perfumes and incenses as an important element in societal culture in order to clarify power, social status, and wealth. Already in ancient Egypt, both perfumes and incenses were perceived as royal gifts; and in the Roman Empire, scents were prominent in perfumed bath water. In this way, scents have been used for centuries for different purposes in both Western and Eastern cultures, and gradually, increasingly sophisticated methods have been developed to preserve and to develop scents. For a long time, the fact that an individual could smell good was believed to be something luxurious.

> *Since three hundred years ago, in the perfume capital of Grasse in France, recipes have been developed for the secret perfume scents for leading brands such as Armani, Chanel, Dior, Gucci, Kenzo, and Versace and marketed to a certain age group or clothes style. Becoming a perfume composer, that is, to be a nose, belongs to the male world, and the profession is often handed down from father to son. It has been explained that women's hormonal fluctuations are not fit for a nose's sensitivity. In total, there are two hundred noses in the world capable of developing new, secret fragrances. These noses should also be able to distinguish between 1,400 different scents to cope with the task!*

It is generally accepted in research on the sense of smell that scents in the environment, natural or artificial, affect people in different ways. The sense of smell is stimulated unconsciously by fragrances and affects a person's mood either in the positive or negative direction, indicating scents' ability to contribute to a sensory experience.

Furthermore, it is considered that the function of the sense of smell and scents' properties directly affect an individual's associations and memories, as a result of the reactions of the emotional life. Therefore, it is possible for an individual to remember scents and to relive a fragrance from childhood in a context later in life. The sense of smell, therefore, is considered to play an important role in people's everyday lives; although in comparison with the senses of sight and hearing, it is not as important for an individual's survival.

The sense of smell is the sense that develops the earliest in a person, even before birth; and after twelve weeks, the sense of smell is fully functional in an unborn child in the womb. This means that during the fetal stage an individual can learn different scents that arise when a mother eats, which contributes to the experience of aromatic chemicals. This early development of the sense of smell can be compared with the sense of sight, which develops more slowly after birth, and it can take years for a person to get fully developed vision.

When it comes to a person's physical or gastronomic taste, smell is absolutely crucial to an individual's taste perception. It turns out that taste perception, for the most part, is based on scents and that they generate 80 percent of the individual's perceived taste. With regard to brands such as Coca-Cola and Sprite, these would taste the same if scents did not play such a crucial role in the taste. People who lose their sense of smell by anosmia (the Greek negative an and osme, 'smell') experience their daily lives as more depressing and boring. These people have lost an emotional dimension in the experience of everyday life, which can also lead to feelings of depression.

> The most classic example of the sense of smell is the smell of freshly baked bread, which unconsciously captures a person's attention.

It has become increasingly common for companies to make use of scents in marketing, through what has become known as scent marketing, to create scent experiences. Scents can be used to create awareness around a product or a brand in the short-term in a store or advertising campaign, which is a common occurrence.

But scents can also be used to differentiate, position, and strengthen a brand's image in the long-term in a strategic marketing context. Research regarding scents, as sensory stimuli, also shows that the introduction of different scents with regard to both the brand and the service environments affect both sales and profitability.

Both retail chains as well as service providers make use of scents as part of their effort to create a positive scent experience in a particular purchase situation or retail environment. It is thanks to the so-called nebulization technology that it has become possible to spray liquid aerosols in different service environments, making the practical application of fragrances easier to implement.

Using the technology, it has become possible to convert liquid oil to dry steam, which can be present in different environments. Then, a fragrance can easily spread in a shop or a restaurant either with the help of a fan or via an air and ventilation system. As the technology to handle smells is refined and developed, scent marketing becomes increasingly common.

The consultancy company Scent Marketing Institute in the United States estimates that by 2016, roughly the equivalent of 3.5 billion SEK will be spent on scent marketing. Both manufacturers and retailers are developing new innovations for products and brands when it comes to adding fragrances to them. For service providers, the application of scents means that companies can make their services more visible and contribute to the creation of positive scent experiences of an earlier, perhaps unknown, brand.

THE FUNDAMENTAL ROLE OF THE SENSE OF SMELL

Physiological Properties

It has long been a mystery for man how the sense of smell has worked and reacted to different sensory stimuli. This happened despite the fact that people in daily life have been able to distinguish different scents and remember the smells that they come into contact with in their environment. But thanks to Richard Axel and Linda Buck, the 2004 Nobel Laureates in Physiology or Medicine, and their unique mapping of the structure and function of the olfactory system, the mystery has finally been solved (Axel, 1995; Buck, 2004). This discovery is considered by many to be a great scientific progress because of the significance of the sense of smell for human experiences, memories, and well-being.

Based on research from the 1920s, it was previously believed that a human could detect over ten thousand different scents, with over five million olfactory cells located in the nasal cavity. However, following new theoretical calculations, a new American study in the journal Science shows that the sense of smell can detect more than a trillion scents. This means that the sense of smell is superior to other human senses when it comes to sensory input.

From a physiological point of view, every human being experiences scents through about a thousand different types of olfactory cells in the nose, where each individual cell is specialized in individual scents. The olfactory cells work to send electrical signals to the olfactory bulb, which is the brain's basic odor area. It then passes the signals on to specific parts of the brain, and it is in the cerebral cortex that information is combined into a pattern that may be deemed to characterize a particular scent (Figure 7.1).

It is thanks to this ingenious design that it is possible for a human to consciously experience the smell of a newly bloomed rose in early summer but also to recall the fragrance experience through memory at a later time. A person can perceive an incredible number of different combinations of scents, and it is possible to perceive and remember them because each fragrance is composed of several different scent molecules. This is also why different combinations of receptors form different smells, just as different letters form words when one speaks or writes.

The sense of smell is considered to be the slowest of the five senses, and the time it takes to sniff a particular scent until it is recorded in the brain is estimated to average 400 milliseconds. This is equivalent to almost half a second and should be compared with the 45 milliseconds it takes for the brain to register a visual image that falls on the eye's retina. Then, add the time it takes for the brain to react positively or negatively to the actual scent, which in reality means that it takes twice as long to perceive an odor.

It should be added that the sense of smell is also considered to be a synthetic sense, which means that if two scents were perceived simultaneously, the whole would not be the same as the sum of the parts. If, for example, licorice and chocolate were to be mixed together, it would not smell "chocolate licorice" but smell like something new. It is difficult to predict what the "something new" will smell like; therefore, it is deemed to be impossible to predict the perceptual experience of a new scent, especially when the new scents are based on their specific chemical compositions, which is also considered to be a major obstacle to technological advances in the fragrance industry.

> *Different types of scents tell an individual whether he or she is in a pleasant or threatening environment.*

Furthermore, it is possible to distinguish two explanatory factors that affect a person's experience of different scents, namely, trigeminal stimulation and genetic differences (Herz, 2007). Trigeminal stimulation means that scents can have an emotion linked to a specific odor. This means that the temperature, touch, and pain fibers, which are found in the face and nose, allow for one to have a sense of a fragrance. As an example, a mint smell is often perceived as cold, and an ammonia odor is perceived as giving a burning feeling.

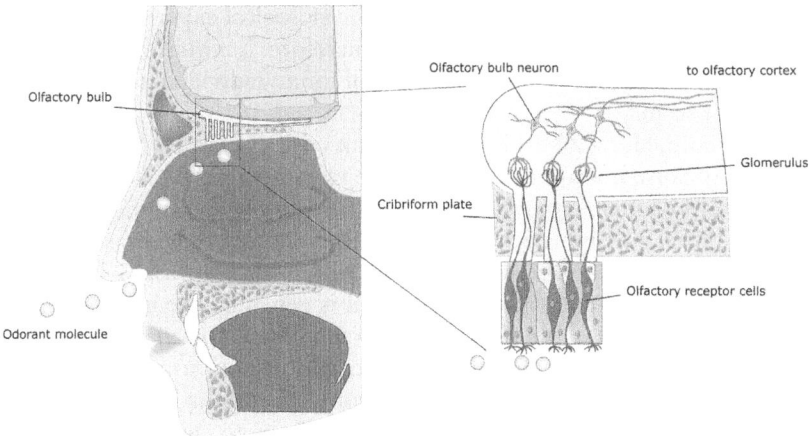

Figure 7.1 The Structure of the Smell Sense
Source: Shutterstock

The organ for the sense of smell is small and detailed, and its location is at the top of the nasal cavity, which is divided into three floors. In normal and quiet breathing, inhaled air usually passes the bottom two floors. It is not until you "sniff" a scent that the inhaled air passes on to the third floor. This moves the scent molecules closer to the olfactory receptors, which are located in the back of the nose, and the scent is smelled more clearly.

This means that different scents stimulate the trigeminal system in various high and low grades. A rose scent stimulates the trigeminal system to a lesser degree, compared with the smell from a skunk, which may be perceived to be so strong that it brings an individual to tears. This is also the reason why we get tears in our eyes when we, for example, chop onions or we sneeze when we get the smell of pepper.

Nevertheless, it is not just trigeminal stimuli that might explain how a person experiences different scents in the environment. There are also differences between people at the individual level, which can be explained by the genetic code that every human being possesses. It is believed that more specifically, these differences may be attributed to the fact that each individual, who, of course is unique, has different genetically constructed olfactory receptors that directly affect how an individual perceives and experiences the different scents (Herz, 2007).

Psychological Aspects

Research suggests that a person experiences different scents physically first and thereafter, emotionally and/or cognitively. It is only in the latter case that a scent experience can be defined as positive or negative. For an individual, it is not about being able to opt out of the physiological experience, because it always occurs automatically. Generally, therefore, it requires very little or almost no emotional or cognitive effort at all for an individual to experience the different scents.

Furthermore, Herz (2010) believes that an odor can be likened to binary opposites, because it is about an immediate response, such as to like or dislike, or to approach or avoid the actual scent. Feelings work in the same way in that an individual approaches what is perceived as good, charming, and joyful and avoids what is perceived as bad, sad, or dangerous.

With this background, the sense of smell is generally the most direct of the human's five senses, which also makes it difficult for an individual to distort a scent experience. Thus there is no opportunity to correct a scent experience retrospectively with regard to thoughts or translation. When an individual remembers a scent, this results usually in an emotional memory association, because scents are mainly linked to our memories.

It is believed that smells, in comparison with other sensory stimuli, elicit more emotional memory experiences in an individual. Furthermore, it is thought that scents that can be associated with such memory experiences can stimulate special feelings, with a direct impact on the mood and behavior, which I will return to later.

The human's sense of smell is the sense that is most closely linked to the part of the brain where memory functions are found. In comparison with other sensory stimuli, such as design, color, or texture, scents have a special ability to trigger our emotions and can fill a person with either joy or rage. It may even go so far that an individual can be so affected that tears come flowing out or the heart aches. Scents, therefore, can arouse strong memories from an individual's past experiences, because each person can associate scents to happy or unhappy life events.

> *Have you ever suffered from a sense of fear without knowing why and then noticed a specific scent?*

The most characteristic for the sense of smell is the direct response that arises from scents. Upon the experience of a scent, every individual makes an immediate assessment of whether it is liked or disliked. This assessment is based on the emotional experience, and it is possible to argue that the functional experience and the emotional experience are the same thing when they occur almost simultaneously. The immediate reaction by an individual to a scent can be said to be of a binary type, because a positive and a negative experience are in contrast to each other (Herz, 2010).

It has been shown that a person either likes or dislikes a scent, which also determines whether that person will approach the scent or try to avoid it.

Often, emotions work in the same way, because a person usually approaches something that feels good, pleasing, and loving.

Similarly, generally, most people avoid something that feels bad, dangerous, or scary, which can cause a person to be sad. Researchers such as Herz (2007) even claim that the human emotional system can be a highly developed cognitive version of the basic behavioral motives that are initiated by the sense of smell in animals.

A comparison between how scents and sounds are perceived by a human shows that this occurs equally intimately and inside our heads in both cases. The crucial difference lies in how scents can be associated with previously experienced events and thus result in an individual experiencing the same emotional state again at a later time. If there was not a previous relationship with a scent in the memory, then an individual would instead make a direct assessment of whether he or she likes the scent or not.

> *Memories that are invoked by scents, as sensory stimuli, are considered to be more alive and bring the individual back to the original time and place in comparison with the memories that are awoken by the other sensory stimuli.*

But at the same time, the individual would also associate the scent with the actual event or situation that he or she was in at the time of the scent experience. It is clear from the research that scent stimuli tend to evoke memories that are more emotional in nature than the memories that are evoked by verbal, visual, auditory, or tactile stimuli.

Affection
A common notion in the literature is that scent preferences are innate and embedded in people's genes, as shown by the studies conducted in the case of infants and their scent experiences. However, researchers such as Engen (1988) and Herz et al. (2004) have shown through their studies that the perception of a particular scent—and what one thinks about it—is something that is learned rather than innate.

Their result implies that an individual's scent preferences are not built into the genes and thus can be considered as natural. It is also why children are indifferent to scents for a long period of their childhood when they have not learned to understand what smells good or bad.

Associative learning assumes that a person learns which scents can be linked to his or her previous experiences in the context of hedonic scent perception. This can take place because an odor can: 1) induce an emotional state that is associated with a previous exposure to a scent and impact an individual's mood and 2) be experienced in itself and filled with hedonic content that the emotional response generates (Herz, 2010).

Research suggests that there is strong evidence that associative learning, with emotions as the mediating variable, controls an individual's scent hedonic perception. One study showed that mothers of young children who consumed alcohol or garlic or smoked cigarettes during pregnancy affected their children's preferences for the actual odors, compared with infants whose mothers had not done that.

> *Mothers who drink coffee, eat garlic, and smoke during pregnancy affect their children's smell preferences early on.*

The sense of smell may be deemed to be closely linked to a person's memory functions, and in literary contexts there are many examples of how the scent experiences can be revived with the help of memories. Similarly, the scent experiences trigger a person's memories, and it is worth noting that such an experience is considered to be more emotionally significant to an individual than the memories that arise through other sensory stimuli. At the same time, scents, unlike many other sensory stimuli, are invisible, and a person usually has difficulty precisely locating the scent in a natural environment. It could be a possible explanation for why people often look for an external context to find meaning behind the smell.

Cognition

Beside the fact that scents are the basis of a hedonic scent perception and affect a person's mood, they also affect a person's cognitive behavior. Studies have shown that humor and mood can affect an individual's creativity, and it is thought that people who are in a good mood exhibit a higher degree of creativity. This is especially true in comparison with persons who are in a bad mood.

Research suggests similar cognitive effects when scents are present in different service environments. In one study, it was found that the introduction of a pleasant ambient scent, in comparison with a disagreeable scent, improved the problem-solving ability. It has also been shown that employees who work in an appealing service environment with pleasant scents have reported that they are more effective, set higher goals, and make use of more efficient work strategies in comparison with colleagues, working in a non-scented service environment.

It is clear from the literature that humor and mood, such as affection, generally affect human cognitive behavior, for example, through increased productivity and a willingness to assist others.

Effects of Scents

It is generally considered in the literature that the sense of smell is a direct sense, but reacts slowly to scents that are present in the surroundings. This means that it takes a relatively long time for a person to perceive the presence of different scents, which also leads to a person's scent processing being considered to be a slow process. The scents' duration, i.e., how long they are in the environment, depends on the ambient airflow and temperature, which in itself means that the duration can vary from place to place.

But scents also stick to the walls, which means that many times the only way to get rid of odors from a room is by repainting. In a store, it is good to know that smells that spread out can stick on the walls, the furniture, and the goods that are to be sold.

Scents can also create a synthetic feel, which is often the case when two different scents are combined. But the mixture of chocolate and licorice, as stated before, do not become a scent that can be called "chocolate licorice," but this blend will smell like something completely different, which in turn is unpredictable. In this case, it is possible to say that the whole will not be the same as the sum of all the parts.

Research suggests that people have an ability to adapt to a fragrant environment. This means that after a while in a particular environment, our awareness of scents in the environment disappears. But by going out of the store, for example, an individual can neutralize the scent experience. In stores where perfumes are sold, small cups with coffee beans can help the customer to neutralize the scent experience through the nose, and thus enable him/her to remain there.

Scents have an ability to create a personalized meaning for the individual and also have a tendency to be associated with events, environments, experiences, objects, items, and other people (Kirk-Smith and Booth, 1987). Pleasant scents are associated with what is elicited by positive emotions, such as being happy or in love, whereas unpleasant scents elicit negative emotions, such as being sad or feeling lonely. It is this power of association that is the basis for why a smell can attract or warn us of a person or the environment.

> *It is difficult for an individual to put words on a smell, but an individual can remember a smell better than a visual image.*

Furthermore, research shows that people often find it very difficult to put a word or a symbolic value on scents, which may also be the reason why people add weight to finding the meanings behind scents. From a psychological perspective, a person's reaction to scents is simple and mostly about a response that is based on the individual's approval or disapproval. An interesting observation in this research is that a person remembers smells better than visual images, indicating scents' effect, which may be considered more far-reaching, even if the response can be considered to be uncomplicated.

Among many theorists, it is argued that the very fundamental "liking" can be seen as an expression of a person's complex emotional system. In addition, the experience of smells and feelings are entirely internal, primal, and cannot be verbalized. This means that a person has the same difficulty describing his/her emotional experiences, such as love, to someone, and expressing his/her scent experiences, such as saying what vinegar really smells like using words.

INFLUENTIAL FACTORS FOR THE SENSE OF SMELL

When it comes to the sense of smell, it should be said that scents are one of the sensory stimuli that have received attention early on in retailing and marketing research. Based on the previously presented SEB model, the factors that may be linked to scent's influence on an individual's affections, cognitions, and actual behaviors in the buying and consumption processes are presented (Figure 7.2).

First, the societal culture, as an influential factor, is addressed in relation to the different scent preferences on the individual and group level, as well as the importance of scent symbolism. Second, the service environment (or the surroundings), as an influential factor, is addressed in relation to the scent stimuli, scent perception, and scent symbolism. Third, the brand, as an influential factor, is addressed in relation to the scent stimuli, scent perception, and scent symbolism.

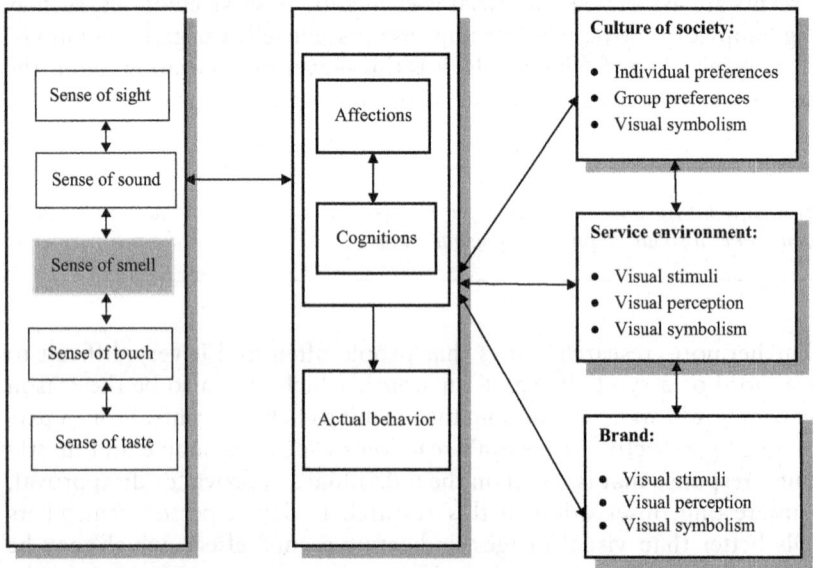

Figure 7.2 The Sense of Smell and the SEB-Model

SOCIETAL CULTURE

In every societal culture and its environment, scents exist in everyday life, which everyone can experience. It is common for many people to engage in some form of ritual on a daily basis such as a bath, shower, or brushing in the morning, where bad smells, that is, odors are eliminated. Because these types of odors often cannot be hidden from other people, they are unpleasant, regardless of whether it is about old food, old garbage, or body sweat, because people in one's surroundings will be aware of them and not like them.

It may be considered as belonging to the social norms of a societal culture that an individual represents him/herself with some kind of respectable scent. In this way, it is also possible to define what can be considered a "good" or "bad" smell in relation to other people. At the same time, by using these standards, an individual in a specific societal culture can determine how respectable people should smell. Then an individual can get a compliment like: "You smell so good," which means that there is an acceptance among others in the surroundings for how that person chooses to present him/herself to others with the help of scents.

Individual Preferences

Each person's scent perception is individual and unique, and it is thought to be due to this ability that each person has, which is innate. This ability is completely personal and consists of an affective or emotional assessment of the impact a scent has on the individual in the moment it is perceived. The scent experience that occurs in an individual is valued only on the basis of approval or disapproval, meaning it is not analytical but hedonic in nature.

In research, it is believed that the hedonic perception helps people to evaluate that which one mostly likes, which is also the most basic and immediate reaction an individual has for a scent. The assessment that is made of the scent takes place almost entirely automatically, without an individual wondering whether the scent can be considered pleasant or not. Therefore, the sense of smell does not react analytically when it comes to scents, like answering the question: "What is that smell?"

> *Each individual has his/her own unique scent identity or so-called fragrance fingerprints.*

It is believed that there are three basic factors, namely, the scent's pleasantness, familiarity, and intensity, which affect the individual's perception of a scent. Research suggests that it is the degree of pleasantness and familiarity that a scent has, which is positively correlated with the individual's scent preference for the smell. This is explained by the fact that pleasant scents are perceived as pleasant, and familiar scents, in other words, known scents, tend to be more liked than unfamiliar scents.

When it comes to the intensity of a scent, it turns out that this affects both the scent preferences as well as the scent experience itself. But it turns out that the intensity of a scent is complicated in relation to whether an individual likes the scent or not. For example, the scent of lilac is perceived as more positive with a high intensity, until this scent reaches such a high level of intensity that the scent suddenly becomes too strong. This can then result in the individual perceiving the lilac scent as unpleasant.

Even unpleasant smells can be accepted in certain environments; for example, the fish smell in a store's fish department. But when the intensity of the smell/odor increases, then the hedonic value for the individual becomes too negative.

Even other factors that have to do with the individual's genetic differences influence the perception of scents. It has been shown that the number and type of olfactory receptors affects an individual's sensitivity to a particular scent and his/her perception of it.

One study showed that some scents seemed generally perceived as unpleasant by most people, and those scents came from decayed plants, old milk, and that emitted by the skunk. By contrast, floral scents are generally perceived as agreeable to most people. In another study, it was found that newborn babies can react to pleasant food smells only a few hours after birth, as has been observed by using their facial expressions.

> In the author Patrick Süskind's book, *Perfume—The Story of a Murder*, there is a description of how scents can affect individuals. The book is based on the main character totally lacking body odor, making others around him uneasy without knowing why. However, he is born with a special sense of smell; he never forgets a scent. With the help of his unique skill as a perfume developer, he can manipulate the emotions and behaviors of people around him by giving himself different scents. The main point of the book is that scents create an effect, but those who react to the scents are largely unaware of it, which also emphasizes scent's mysterious nature.

There is an ongoing debate in the literature about whether human scent preferences and hedonic responses to scents are innate, natural, or if these should be regarded as learned. One view is that innate scent preferences mean that an individual has a predisposition to either like or dislike different types of scents. It would mean, for example, that the reaction to the scent of roses as a good scent, on the one hand, and the scent (odor) of a skunk as a bad scent, on the other hand, would be innate.

However, it is not generally believed that innate scent preferences are empirically validated to a sufficiently high degree due to scent being closely associated with taste experiences and the sense of taste. I will return to this discussion in Chapter 9, where the relationship between scents and flavors is addressed. It has been shown that a drop of quinine on a newborn baby's tongue will evoke a grimace on the baby's face, and a drop of raw sugar will evoke a smile. This shows the importance of taste for a taste experience.

From a learning perspective, it has been argued instead that every person is born with a hedonic tendency to like or dislike scents. This means that if an individual prefers a particular scent or not depends on his or her acquired emotional association to the scent. Scent preferences then become associative learning, and it is considered to be the basis of a person's scent perception, which can be regarded as a function of his/her past experiences of scents in relation to items, objects, or people.

Generally, it is believed that the associative learning theory regarding hedonic scent perception may be regarded as meaningless stimuli. Instead, emotions are regarded as the stimulus itself, which can be associated with the presence of scents. For this reason, a scent can: 1) elicit an emotional state associated with an earlier exposure to a scent with a general effect on mood and 2) lay the foundation for a scent experience that gives a hedonic meaning, thanks to the emotional response that is elicited by the scent.

> *Imagine that there is a stimulus called A. When you meet A, your reaction is A+ and not just A. Imagine a different stimulus called B. When you meet B, you have no reaction to B. Then A and B are joined together and the following happens: When you are introduced to A again, you still react with A+. However, when you are reintroduced to B, your reaction now is also A+. This happens because B, which was previously meaningless, has now associated itself with A and taken on A's properties. Associative learning is considered to be the basis of human cognition and behavior, as well as for classical conditioning.*

This, in turn, determines the hedonic perception (the understanding) of the actual scent, which shows that associative learning takes place largely with the help of emotions as the basic explanatory variable.

Some researchers have shown that scent preferences influence food and taste preferences later in childhood, whereas other researchers have shown that this also continues into adulthood. However, research is still required to show the importance of previous hedonic reactions to scents.

A common understanding in the literature, therefore, is that scents should be considered to be a strong stimulus because the memory of scents last longer than, for example, visual memories. This notion is based on both anecdotes as well as empirical studies, which show that the effect of a scent associated with a particular event or experience will be remembered and remembered much later by an individual.

Gender and Age

Research suggests that there are differences in scent preferences when it comes to gender and age. In the tests that have been performed on a person's olfactory ability, which means being able to detect, discriminate between, and identify scents, women have often gotten better results than men. In other studies, it has been shown that this difference could be identified in infants, where the female children tended to perceive scents better than their male counterparts.

> Women in general have a stronger sense of smell than men.

But there are also conflicting results, which indicate that gender differences in themselves are not entirely reliable, although some scents can be perceived better by women than by men. One possible explanation, which has often been ignored in many studies, is women's menstrual cycles. It turns out that women can be up to ten thousand times more sensitive than men during the ovulation period, in comparison with the menstrual period. It is, therefore, possible to argue that the female sensitivity to scents could be higher during these periods, compared with males.

It is also believed that women are significantly more likely than men to suffer from oversensitivity to scents. For those individuals who suffer from this, it can lead to nausea or illness, taking into account the scents that are present in the surroundings, such as perfumes.

Furthermore, it appears that people's ability to feel and perceive scents is due to their mental and physical health. Individual differences such as impulsivity and age have been shown to have an effect on scent preferences (Morrin and Chebat, 2005). It is also believed that a very healthy 80-year-old has the same sense of smell as a young adult. On the other hand, it turns out that people's sensitivity to smells begins to deteriorate as early as their twenties. There are also studies that claim that this process starts already at the age of fifteen.

In a study by Chebat et al. (2009), it was found that the ability of a mood fragrance to affect customers' willingness to make purchases in a shopping mall was significantly decreased among older shoppers. In another study, results indicated that scent preferences of three-year-olds regarding whether they like or do not like a scent are substantially the same as that of an adult.

In an American study, subjects aged between 20 and 30 years old sniffed at three smell samples from different age groups, and it was found that older people's smell was not as intense as those who were younger and was more appealing. When it came to approaching one of the two smells, either coming from an older person or a younger person, it was found that the older men were considered to smell better in comparison with the younger and middle-aged men. The older men were also thought to smell better than the older women. One explanation for the older men smelling better than others was believed to be the declining levels of the sex hormone testosterone.

A British study found significant results for both men and women when drivers were subjected to both pleasant and unpleasant odors. The subjects were tested in a car simulator; and with a pleasant scent, such as lemon, the ability to handle the car on the road was affected in a positive way. It appeared that the men did a little better than the women. Regarding the ability to brake quickly, it was found that both men and women improved equally. One of the conclusions was that environments with pleasant scents could make a person more alert in some everyday situations, compared with unscented environments.

Group Preferences

Scents have been a part of human civilization since ancient times and they still are today. As stated earlier, people have developed both a social status through the use of scents and an ability to preserve the memory of a scent. Then it is legitimate to question whether scents can evoke the same emotions in people of different cultures or if it differs between cultures.

> The American military has tried to create a stink bomb, but it was impossible to find an odor that was unanimously considered unpleasant across different ethnic groups.

Research suggests that there is evidence that the scent preferences of people belonging to different cultures differ. There is a significant difference in how people like or dislike scents. As an example, the smell of cheese is very popular among individuals living in Western Europe, but the same scent is regarded as a rotten odor among many in Southeast Asia.

Therefore, it is important to understand how people in different sub-cultures or groups build up a perception of smells and how a culture can help to create this perception through scents. It has been shown that young children learn early on to perceive scents but are indifferent to different scents until they are about eight-years-old. As an example, babies like the smell of feces and are indifferent to what adults consider as being a pleasant or an unpleasant scent.

With the help of associative learning theory, which assumes that a person's perception of a scent occurs when he or she first comes into contact with the scent, it is possible to explain how individuals in different cultures perceive scents in their surroundings. In other words, it is a cultural phenomenon that gives rise to both the individual scent perception and a memorable scent experience, as demonstrated by some different examples.

> *The Ethiopian people, Dassanetch, experience the smell of cattle as attractive, because the smell is an expression of social status and fertility. For this reason, they wash their hands in cattle urine and smear it on their bodies. Among Chinese people, the burnt smell is an expression of heat in the same way as the bitter taste, the color red, and so on. The Suyá Indians of Brazil and the Serer people of Senegal have developed their own scent classifications, which makes it possible to distinguish between different scents and give meaning to them.*

Researchers such as Lwin and Wijaya (2010) have attempted to explain in a study how individuals in different cultures associate scents with emotions and meaning. The purpose of the study was to examine the significance of different attributes of scent associations between and within different cultures in order to find answers to how the multitude of olfactory preferences are expressed in different cultural contexts. In this way, they wanted to try to answer the question about the significance of emotions in explaining the emergence of cultural associations with scents.

The study was conducted by the formation of eight focus groups of eight to ten respondents in each group, representing eight different cultural backgrounds. These were then divided into four subgroups called Indian, Chinese, European, and American. Respondents were evenly divided regarding gender, men, and women, and age groups from 20 years up to 43 years.

The focus groups were instructed to discuss the cultural contexts that might contain two types of olfactory experiences: one with a low emotional context and one with a high emotional context. In each context, two questions were asked of the respondents, which were considered suitable when it came to finding out what characterized a low emotional experience and a high emotional experience. It should be mentioned that a low emotional experience of a context was whether a place was clean or unclean, whereas a high emotional experience of a context was about excited, happy, and sad emotions that could be linked to a specific scent (Table 7.1).

The study showed that scents have characteristics that elicit a variety of previous experiences, no matter what culture a person comes from. It was shown that there was also a great engagement to describe positive or happy contexts using scents and less so to describe negative contexts.

Table 7.1 Cultural Associations of Smells in Low and High Emotional Contexts (Lawin and Wijaya, 2010)

Context	Germans/U.K./French	U.S.	Pakistanis and Indians	Chinese Singaporeans, Chinese, Chinese Malaysians
Low emotive: Clean Place	lemon, mint, VIM, freshly washed clean sheets, mountain smell, Alps, ventilated, freshly cooked food, GLADE.	pine, chlorides, detergents like TIDE and CHEER, fresh air, lemon, strawberry, orange, grape fruit, mountain breeze, ocean breeze.	Citrus, airy, meadows and mountains, lemon and lime; orange; sunny smell, VIM, TIDE detergent, paint, flowers.	lemon, lime, lavender, floral, DETTOL, TIDE, sunned, citrus; mint, lime, woody, running water, Alpine mountains, air freshener, fresh paint, detergent, KIWI, GOOD, MAID, air fresheners.
Low emotive: Not clean place	garbage, old food, musty, stale air, dirty clothes.	garbage, spoiled food, sewage, stuffy, stale.	garbage, stale, spoilt food.	garbage, salted fish, smoke, sour, burnt, still, dust, rotten food, stuffy.
High emotive: Happy/Celebratory	Christmas smell, forest, candles, beer, wine, cookies, Christmas food, warm, homely, fireplace, sausages.	pie, ham, Christmas tree, pine, cake, candles, turkey, chocolate, eggnog, snow, champagne.	curry, spices, sweet smell, cake, herbs, oil lamps, incense, whisky.	fresh notes, Chinese cookies, barbecue pork, coconut oil, cake, fried chicken, oranges, money smell, liquor, carbonated drinks, fireworks, herbs.
High emotive: Sad/Funeral	church smell, flowers, stones.	flowers, candle, earth.	burning, Bhopal leaves, incense.	joss stick, floral, ash, incense, burnt paper, porridge.

Furthermore, the study indicated that in a lower emotional context, the scent association tends to be fairly universal. This could be illustrated with the scent of a clean room, which was associated with citrus, air spray, and mountainous and natural fragrances. It is interesting to note that mountain and natural scents exist in this context, because many people in the actual cultures have never been near a mountain.

One possible explanation for why these scents are mentioned among the responses is probably attributable to the advertising and promotional campaigns that take place with the help of marketers, where clean rooms are associated with mountain and natural scents. In this way, marketers have been successful and helped to create unnatural associations, which are not directly attributable to the cultural context in which the individuals find themselves.

One of the study's main conclusions was that highly culture-specific scent associations are developed in a high emotional context, which emphasizes the importance of the influence of one's own culture when it comes to understanding scents. This was emphasized in a clear way through the different types of cultural celebrations, such as Christmas and Chinese New Year, with their connection to specific scents. Therefore, each social culture itself has a big effect on how people perceive and experience different scents, especially in connection with a high emotional context, where emotions play a prominent role. However, when it came to a low emotional context, it seemed that this could be considered more universal, where the scent experience was not only related to the specific event, but also to the influence of the mass media on what may be considered to characterize a good or bad scent.

Scent Symbolism

Research suggests that people often have trouble putting a word or a symbolic label on scents, something that is also called the tip-of-the-nose effect. But it is still possible for an individual to distinguish the many different scents previously experienced in different contexts.

It is also possible to set different emotional values on how scents influence an individual, mostly by reading anecdotes and literary works. The personal memories that are evoked by scents can be read about in Marcel Proust's opus on memory, where forgotten experiences from the past suddenly appear when a particular scent is perceived. In the book's case, some recollections arose when the person in question dipped a biscuit in Indian tea, which evoked memories of the past through the scent that arose.

> It is difficult to be against the smell of bread, which may be due to the smell of bread, for many individuals, being linked to positive memories.

This phenomenon has become known as the Proust phenomenon, i.e., memories that are characteristically filled with vivid emotions are suddenly evoked by a scent. At the same time, the memories that are evoked through scents are always significantly more emotional than the memories that are evoked by other sensory stimuli. This is mainly because people experience a feeling of having been transferred to the memory's correct time and place. Because scents can evoke emotional memories stronger than other sensory stimuli, by associations with emotional scent experiences, they can also highlight specific emotions, which have a direct effect on the individual's mood and behavior.

Within the area of eroticism, scents, as symbols, have been used for decades by performers and artists to evoke emotional, psychological, and cultural connections. One reason for this has been that the sense of smell has directly come to include the entire physical body, which has led to immediate internal reactions in an individual who has not been able to just relate to that which is possible to detect with the help of the eyes, that is, the sense of sight. Accordingly, perfumes and other scent signals have come to surpass the visual images, which symbolize the power and strength of the sense of smell in human relations.

Even in ancient times, it was believed that different scent signals, such as perfumes and incenses, had the ability to break down an individual's resistance to various erotic and sexual temptations; smell was nicknamed "the secret seducer." One of the reasons for this is deemed to be that scents in general seem to work on a more subtle level, which is considered to be below the conscious perception. In this way, a scent, as a symbol, helps change a visual experience of a phenomenon to instead become a holistic experience.

A general notion in the literature is that the typical scents, as symbols, are related to different social groups or races with distinctive features. It is believed that body odors from different cultures may differ largely due to genetic factors and which foods are consumed. Furthermore, it is thought that most people give off scents but that one usually does not notice odors from other individuals because one is so used to his/her own personal odors and those derived from the group one belongs to. In the early 1900s, odors were a common way to highlight the social identity and social differences in a societal culture, prompting researchers to assume that scent connectedness was considered to be an important means of preserving a group of like-minded people.

It is worth noting that the use of perfumes by men in Western Europe declined during the Industrial Revolution and the introduction of machines. In the new world, men refrained from using fragrant scents, which was considered to be in contrast to the sterile, insensitive machine. Some scientists believe that this dichotomy between scents and machines—because machines do not smell—may explain why the Western media completely avoids scents. This is not only because the machines do not smell, but also because its sterile expression symbolizes something nonfragrant.

Finally, it should be said that every societal culture has its own hierarchy in terms of the five senses and that the ranking varies from one time to another and from one social culture to another. In this way, scents play a different role, and the symbolism that scents want to convey often have meant more in an earlier period of societal culture than it might today. At the same time, scents, unlike many other sensory stimuli, are invisible and therefore cannot exactly be pinpointed in the physical environment. Consequently, individuals are more likely to find meaning behind scents through external contexts.

SERVICE ENVIRONMENT

As indicated in the previous chapter, scents are related to the nonverbal stimuli, which can help to create an attractive and pleasing atmosphere in a service environment. It is also considered that this type of stimuli creates various psychological sensations in individuals, which lead to both affective and cognitive reactions to the experiences in a retail or restaurant environment. Using scents in shops, restaurants, or shopping centers, therefore, are common occurrences to influence the atmosphere and create a positive shopping experience.

> *The introduction of pleasant mood scents in a casino increased the games on slot machines significantly.*

In recent years, marketing research has increasingly started to pay attention to the effect and influence of scents on consumers, where individuals' mood, evaluation, memories, and purchasing behaviors have been the focus.

Scent Stimuli

It is generally believed in biological research that scent signals of various kinds are used to convey messages between animals, on the one hand, and between plants and animals, on the other hand. It occurs in the form of airborne chemical substances produced by an individual of one species and used as information by another individual of a different species.

In the same way, companies can make use of scent signals, or scent stimuli, to transmit messages and information to different individuals in a service environment or in connection with a brand. Therefore, I choose to define scent stimuli as a signal, which aims to transfer the message using natural or synthetic chemical substances with the aim of creating atmospheric sensations.

As discussed earlier in the chapter on the sense of sight, researchers claim that there are four different environmental factors in a service environment, including scents, in addition to hearing, sight, and touch, which can affect a person's senses. Other researchers have pointed to the importance of various ambient factors, beyond design and social factors, such as air quality, noise, smells, and cleanliness. I choose, therefore, to continue to treat scent stimuli as a mood factor.

Research has produced a number of empirical studies, which highlight the influence that scents have on consumers' affections, cognitions, and actual behaviors in buying and consumption processes. The vast majority of studies have their theoretical basis in the well-known stimulus-organism-response model (SOR) by Mehrabian and Russell (1974).

This model assumes that different stimuli in a shop environment affect consumers' emotional states, which can lead to a response by either an approach or an avoidance behavior. This is thought to be based on an emotional response, which can be explained by means of either a positive or a negative mood. In this context, a scent, as stimuli, should be able to explain avoidance by a scent being perceived as smelling bad, or an approach by a scent being experienced as pleasurable. I will return to the question of mood in the next section.

Especially in shops, supermarkets, hotels, and restaurants, scents appear in different service environments to create sensory experiences, which are considered to contribute to a memorable shopping experience. Scents, therefore, can occur in different types of environments in order to get customers to stick around and spend more money on purchases. Concerning the presence of scents, this seems to apply to both goods and services, and in the latter case, a scent can make a service more tangible and concrete. The uniqueness of scents is that they can only be experienced by customers in a physical store or a restaurant environment; it is only there that one can create a scent experience.

Mood Scents
Scent marketing refers to the application of ambient scents, i.e., how companies can choose to use one or more fragrances to create an attractive and appealing atmosphere and mood in a service environment. This can apply to a store, a hotel, a casino, a shopping mall, a restaurant, a hospital, a department store, or a university, all of which are characterized by a physical environment.

Research suggests that scientific studies that have examined the effects and influences of scents on consumers have generally chosen to apply mood fragrances. This type of scent, unlike a product-specific scent, has the ability to influence consumers' perceptions and experiences of a service environment. A mood scent can be considered a scent that is not specifically related to a particular object as a product or a brand but is prevalent in a particular environment.

It is clear from existing studies that the introduction of mood scents in a shopping center, such as the aroma of fresh coffee or freshly baked bread, helps more people become motivated to help strangers with finding the right store or right way. Furthermore, it appears that staff working in the presence of a pleasant mood scent believe that they are more effective, set higher goals, and are more likely to use effective strategies in their daily work.

> Scents have the ability to create comfort in the customers, a feeling that also remains.

With regard to the effect and impact of ambient scents on consumers' behaviors, researchers such as Gulas and Bloch (1995) claim that there are two important aspects. The first aspect is about scents that can be directly associated with an object, which can be illustrated with the scent of a particular product or staff. The second aspect is about scents that can indirectly be associated with and considered as part of the wider environment in a service environment. In this way, a mood scent is transferred to all products that are represented in the environment, because it is a question of creating an attractive and appealing atmosphere from an overall perspective for the store or restaurant (ibid.). But then it could prove that mood scents have an effect and influence on consumers' reactions and behaviors in relation to any products or services that exist in a particular environment. As such, this also means that this includes the products and services that may be considered indecent or inappropriate to apply any scent, which could be detrimental to the company in question.

Furthermore, ambient scents are regarded as environmental stimuli with an aim to achieve an affective response from customers, either an approach or avoidance. In terms of approach in a service environment, it is generally considered that such behavior can lead to longer time spent in the environment, generate a more positive evaluation of products and services, and also lead to future intentions regarding time spent and increased return visits.

It is clear from the research that various empirical studies have chosen to analyze the importance of scents in the service environment based on 1) olfactory congruence/consistency with the environment, 2) scent presence, and 3) scent's pleasantness. When it comes to scent's congruence/consistency, this dimension is about how well natural scents fit with the products that are marketed and sold in a service environment. An example of this is that a flower store smells of flowers and a restaurant smells of freshly cooked food and so on.

> It is about the scent fitting into the context in which it occurs.

The second dimension is about how only closeness to a scent can have an impact on consumers' affections and actual behaviors. In one study, it was shown that the negative effects of queuing and waiting time have been countered with the help of an ambient scent.

The third dimension deals with how comfortable or pleasant scents can be perceived, which shows that this type of scent has a positive emotional or behavioral effect on consumers. It also means that unpleasant and disagreeable scents, often what is called odorants, have a negative impact and lead to a negative response from customers. But it should also be said that the use and development of comfortable/pleasant scents can be problematic when there are differences between individuals in terms of scent preferences, as previously mentioned.

Scents as Associations
In the literature, a scent's product resemblance is generally how well a scent can be considered to have a natural connection to a product, which can be the basis for a positive scent experience. This means concretely that an orange should smell like an orange and nothing else. Furthermore, it is believed that product-like scents improve the consumer's perceptions of a product and contribute to a more flexible and variety-seeking behavior, because the consumer is looking for a suitable product (Bone and Ellen, 1999). It is deemed important that product-like scents are present even in a service environment; however, it may be difficult in many cases to determine what can be considered a special product-like scent in such a context.

In a study by Parson (2009), the application of associated scents was examined for the first time in more detail in retail stores, where smells do not normally appear. The experiments, which took place both in a laboratory in the form of a field study and in an existing store, were designed so that it would be possible to determine if an associated scent, as opposed to a nonassociated scent, could affect customers' perceptions and shopping behaviors.

Several empirical studies have previously only studied scent's pleasantness for customers, but scent's associations with the retail environment have generally been neglected. In his study, Parson raises the question of whether there is an appropriate scent that fits into a store environment, which is otherwise naturally odorless. Electronics stores and fashion boutiques are mentioned as examples of this, whereas in other types of stores, such as a florist, skincare shops, or perfumeries, there are natural scents in the environment.

In the study, there were three ordinary stores where it was considered unlikely that there could be a product-specific scent with a connection to the environment. I will return to a discussion of the importance of product-specific scents linked to a brand later in the chapter. The three stores were a bookstore, a lingerie store, and a kitchen appliance store, and they came to be characterized by three distinct scent scenarios, namely, an associated scent, a nonassociated scent, and no scent at all (Table 7.2).

Table 7.2 Associated Scent Experiment (Parson, 2009)

Type of scent	Bookstore	Lingerie	Appliance
Associated	Coffee	Perfume	Soap
No scent	–	–	–
Nonassociated	Soap	Coffee	Perfume

A pilot study was conducted, where the aim was to produce the correct association scents by asking a number of customers about which scents they would consider to be associated with the products in the stores. It was found from the results that a coffee aroma could characterize the bookstore, a perfume scent could characterize the lingerie shop, and a soap fragrance could characterize the kitchen appliance store. Figure 7.2 shows the selected associated scents, nonassociated scents, and no scent at all when it comes to the application of scents for the three retail scenarios.

In a laboratory experiment, 180 customers were included who were randomly selected to participate in the three retail scenarios, and they were divided into three groups of 60 people in each group. During the experiment, when the selected scent was introduced, the customers got to see a video of the store for 90 to 120 seconds. Subsequently, each participant got to fill out a survey, which aimed to measure the influence of the actual scent on customers' perceptions and behavioral intentions. A field study was also conducted at a bookstore to confirm the results obtained from the laboratory experiment.

The study's findings showed that for stores that were normally odorless, an associated scent could mean a positive response from customers. It was also highlighted that a comfortable and pleasant scent that was not related to the stores' products and services could lead to negative affections or behaviors. The study, therefore, goes a step beyond the previous empirical studies when it comes to the importance of a pleasant smell by highlighting the importance of consumers' scent associations. It is therefore not enough, as previous research assumed, to just introduce a pleasant scent in an odorless store, but it should tie in with the store concepts, products, and services.

In practical terms, the results of the study mean that the introduction of scents could be an easy and cost effective way for many odorless shops to create a new shopping experience for customers by using relatively small means. For the stores that already smell, such as bakeries and florists, there is a natural connection to products and services, which is why it would be difficult to change a scent that customers expect to face when they come into the store. But the question still remains as to what associations do different products and services provide, because the vast majority of shops, supermarkets, and department stores may be considered as being odorless.

Scents as Markers

In research, there are studies that have examined more closely the role of ambient scents and their deeper impact on the consumer's affections and actual behaviors. It is thought that retailers have an opportunity to apply scents to achieve an effect on the consumer's memories in two respects. First, the positive associations can be evoked by means of, for example, the aroma of freshly brewed coffee or freshly baked bread and, secondly, memories can be evoked that are linked to a certain specific scent in connection with a shopping experience in a retail store or a department store.

In the latter respect, a specific scent helps to create positive affective experiences, which in itself may contribute to these experiences being attributed to the scent itself. The first category refers to experiences outside the store, which are naturally linked to the individual's experiences with his/her family, close friends, colleagues, or other situations. The second category refers to retail and shopping experiences where companies can independently develop and apply unique scent experiences for customers.

Sensory marketers can use scents in two ways: 1) by associating a specific scent to the product attributes and 2) by linking a specific scent to the atmosphere/environment in the actual service environment to influence the customer's behavior.

When it comes to getting customers to connect a certain specific scent to a store or a mall, the concept of place markers is presented. This means the ability of different scents to evoke a special feeling for a place, which can be explained in that a city, a square, or a street can have a unique scent. In this manner, the scent works as a place marker.

> *Ikea follows the Allergy Association's recommendations not to introduce scents in their odor-free stores.*

Furthermore, it is believed that retail businesses should not primarily use scent as a place marker. Rather, they should use scents to help create a store's image, which can then be linked to a specific location, such as, for example, an urban center or a square. Thus these two factors can overlap each other, because a specific scent can be used to create a sense of place, a specific store atmosphere/image, or vice versa.

This reasoning can be illustrated by the fact that the scent of roses can help to create a feminine and romantic atmosphere/image of a store for customers. But the scent of roses, in itself, does not necessarily mean that it contributes as some kind of place marker, which is directly linked to the store in the customer's consciousness. When customers encounter the scent of roses outside a store, it does not mean a direct association to the store, but the smell of roses can help stimulate customers' feelings and memories.

> *Fragrances of different locations can also be used to recreate memories by having vacationed at a location. Something that Miami has done is it has a unique signature scent that will make any visitor associate the scent with the city. This fragrance is a combination of citrus and baby powder, something that captures the feeling of excitement, sun, sea, and Miami's essence.*

The general understanding in the literature is that if you create a feeling for a place through scents, it builds on both the past and present experiences of an individual. It is further considered that the feeling of a location is based on the interaction between the individual and the environment in question where the scents can be regarded as place markers linked to the overall impression of the service environment.

Scents Effect on Time Spent and the Propensity to Buy

The literature reveals that the primary purpose of using scents in a service environment is to create a pleasant and attractive atmosphere for customers. This is considered to result in customers being stimulated, which is expressed through both increased visiting time and increased propensity to buy.

It has been shown that when a mood scent was introduced in a store, it contributed to customers staying longer, which was also thought to increase customers' propensity to buy. Other empirical studies have shown that consumers spend more time collecting and processing information about products when there is a match between the actual scent and the environment in question. In a field study, it was shown that the scent of lavender (but not lemon) increased the time spent in a pizzeria by 15 percent, compared with a control group in a non-scented environment.

Spangenberg et al. (1996) found that pleasantly scented environments help in that one perceives the time spent in a simulated retail environment as longer than the actual time spent there. In research, there are contradictory results regarding the effects of ambient scents on the actual and perceived time spent in a store environment. Therefore, there is a need for further research to clarify the effects of ambient scents in this respect (Morrin, 2010).

In a study by Spangenberg et al. (2006), it was presented that shoppers spent more time in a clothing store when a mood scent was used in some departments, which was consistent with the kind of clothes that were showcased. It involved the application of a feminine fragrance in the female departments and a masculine scent in the male departments. This points to the importance of having an agreement between the scent, gender, and product, which is relatively unexplored in the context of a service landscape.

> An ambient scent that matches the product in question leads to customers staying longer in the store.

When it comes to increased propensity to buy in a store environment, studies show that under certain specific circumstances, consumers spend more money on purchases when a pleasant scent is introduced in the service landscape.

Scent Perception

With scent perception in a service environment, it refers to how individuals recognize and interpret the scent stimuli that exist in the environment. The stimuli that are noticed will also be perceived and interpreted by an individual, selective process in different individuals.

As previously discussed, there is research showing that a person's scent preferences are innate or inherent in consciousness from birth. With time, these scent preferences become conscious and learned through the experiences an individual has with different scents. In many cases, the connection between the experiences, for example, to have fun, and the scent constitutes the prerequisite for a scent preference to occur and be learned.

For marketers, this means that a scent should not be introduced without a correlation with the experience that the actual service environment will give to customers. Table 7.3 shows how the different scents are believed to stimulate people's moods and actual behaviors.

Research suggests that on average it takes quite some time before a person perceives and interprets existing scents in the service environment. It should be said that as a comparison, it takes ten times as long to perceive a scent, approximately 450 milliseconds, and for a visual image, about 45 milliseconds. In one study, it has been shown that the sense of smell is considered to be a slow sense, because a person's autobiographical memory, which is stimulated by a scent, takes twice as long time to develop the memory of the smell in comparison with the visual or verbal stimuli.

Furthermore, it is thought that scents are slow as stimuli, however, more enduring and challenging, which means that they are hard to resist and

Table 7.3 Examples of Impact of Scents

Citrus	The scent can improve mood and cognitive performance.
Mint	The scent reduces stress and increases mental concentration.
Vanilla	The scent is one of the most attractive scents for increasing comfort and reducing stress.
Lavender	The scent has a relaxing effect and eases anxiety and insomnia.

avoid in a service environment. Therefore, it appears that many individuals can recognize and recall scents that have previously been smelled, even long after the scent coding and the scent perception have taken place.

A general notion in the literature is that scents have the ability to influence an individual's mood through scent perception, which, however, a few empirical studies can provide evidence for and support scientifically. In a study by Bone and Ellen (1999), the effects of the sense of smell on mood or psychological arousal were examined using a meta study. The researchers went through 22 empirical studies on scents, which were found to contain 206 texts about the effects of the sense of smell, but only 16.1 percent of the studies showed that the results were significant. Subsequently, a number of empirical studies have been conducted on the effect of scents in marketing with similar results.

In a study by Chebat and Michon (2003), the effects of ambient scents on customers' perceptions and mood were investigated in a shopping mall environment. The researchers used a so-called two-factor experiment, where the data collection took place in two rounds.

In the first round, which addressed the control group, the ambient scent atmosphere did not change, which, however, took place in the second round, that is, for the experimental group. Then a faint, pleasant citrus scent, which in this case was a combination of orange, lemon, and grapefruit, was used. This was sprayed out in the mall corridors, by means of some scent sprayers, every ten minutes for three seconds. The customers belonging to the experimental group were asked to answer a questionnaire, and 145 respondents answered the questions.

The study's results showed that ambient scents help to build a favorable perception of the shopping center environment and indirectly the quality of various products and services. The researchers believed that ambient scents could help increase customers' perceptions, as opposed to product-related scents, which could increase the sales of a particular product.

The main conclusion from Chebat and Michon's experiments was that the ambient scent that is present among other ambient stimuli directly proved to influence customers' perceptions, which in itself had a significant influence on customers' mood. However, marketers should be aware that a deviant or too powerful aroma indirectly influences customers' perceptions of products and services, which in itself can affect sales in perhaps a negative direction. On the other hand, a powerful aroma can enhance customers' perceptions and experiences at the shopping center perhaps in a stronger way, which may have a greater influence on customers' positive and negative emotions.

Another conclusion of the study was that the introduction of a pleasant scent increased shoppers' propensity to buy but only for those shoppers who were relaxed. For those customers who shopped on impulse, it emerged that they were more prone to buy when pleasant music was playing in the background. Furthermore, it appeared that shoppers were at least prone to buying when both the music and the scent were present, which informs marketers to not over stimulate customers with too many stimuli in the service environment.

Research suggests that in the empirical studies in which both mood and excitement have been investigated, it reveals contradictory results. Some researchers claim that ambient scents have a calming effect, whereas other researchers argue that scents have a psychologically arousing effect on people. Therefore, there is need for further research when it comes to scientific mapping and determining the conditions under which ambient scents may have verifiable and reliable effects on mood and arousal in the context of scent perception.

On the other hand, research has shown that the emotional state of people can interact with ambient scents, which, in turn, has been shown to have a significant influence on memory. It has been found that scents, as stimuli, are more effective if respondents are in an anxious mood in comparison with a normal mood when perception is studied. But in general, the scientific evidence shows that ambient scents have a weak influence on people's mood.

A general notion is that scents evoke an appreciative mood and behavioral response, which is considered to be a result of the emotional associations that are made in relation to the actual scents. But it is not possible to determine how these associations over time can be related to a previous episodic event. In contrast, there appears to be times when both a connection to and a memory of a scent can be linked to a scent experience.

> *At Florida Hospital's Seaside Center, they have created environments in the hospital that will contribute to patients' well-being and health. The company has done this through the use of scent machines, which spread scents of the ocean, coconut oil, and vanilla in a hospital environment. The scent of vanilla is used, for example, in the MRI room, where the scent is said to help people feel less claustrophobic.*

Finally, it must be added that the intensity of a scent, i.e., the extent to which a scent is strong or weak, also affects people's affections and actual behaviors. It is considered that even weak scents, which are barely noticeable, have an influence on an individual's scent perception and mood.

Scent Symbolism

It is generally considered in the literature that different scents in a service environment can help to raise the individual's scent experience and act as a symbol of memorable scent experiences. When it comes to scents such as basil, citrus, cinnamon, and lavender, these are considered to help people feel relaxed, whereas scents such as peppermint, rosemary, and thyme are thought to contribute to a more refreshing feeling. Furthermore, smells such as chocolate, cardamom, and licorice are deemed to create a sense of romance in individuals, whereas a scent of roses is considered to be able to fight depression.

> Today, vanilla is a dominant scent ingredient in many perfumes, and Body Shop has recently launched a pure vanilla scent. Many attempts have been made to explain the popularity of vanilla-based scents, which are often regarded as having to do with beautiful childhood memories linked to the smell of vanilla. In this way, vanilla, as a scent symbol, has become associated with warmth, softness, and kindness but also has connotations of simplicity and purity.

The term "pure vanilla," often used by graphic designers and typesetters, means that a text is untouched in the sense that it consists of its natural, original character before being adjusted in various ways. It also occurs that the term is used in other contexts, such as in the perfume industry and symbolizes the pure, the honest, and the unadulterated.

Research has shown that vanilla scented products influence infants already at the age of one. In an experiment with non-scented and scented toys, babies moved their hands when toys with the vanilla scent were placed near their heads. Such was not the case when the same toys were presented without the vanilla scent. Furthermore, a study has shown that the vanilla scent in a clothes store—as gender-like ambient scent—has significant effects on consumers' approach/avoidance behavior as well as how much money they spend and the number of products that are purchased (Spangenberg et al., 2006).

It is also been shown that the vanilla scent at the doctors and psychologists office had a proven positive and beneficial effect in terms of reducing stress and fear. In experiments, the vanilla scent has often appeared as the expression of a universal scent that is considered to be comfortable for people, which has nothing to do with today's fashion or the new scent values. Even in animals, the calming effects have been observed with the help of the vanilla aromas that seem to depend on some important aroma characteristic rather than positive childhood memories, which apply to people. It should also be noted that these effects were incurred in connection with experiments with the pure vanilla scent and does not refer to a combination of vanilla with other scents.

The literature reveals that the scent classification of Western nature assumes that cultivated fields, forests, gardens, and other natural environments that are similar have a pleasant, refreshing smell. In contrast, it has been suggested that the wild nature should be associated with either stinky or spicy, or strong or sweet odors. It is believed that these odors may be considered as overwhelming for many people and can stimulate increased brutality among some.

> *In conjunction with magnetic resonance imaging, six out of ten patients experienced less fear when a vanilla scent appeared in connection with the investigation.*

Furthermore, it is believed that the classification of the wild nature has other symbolic meanings through rotten odors or overly sweet scents. These odors are often associated with more "wild women" as mistresses or prostitutes, who are often characterized as bad or scented people. Also, many people from the Middle East, India, and Asia in the Western world have been regarded in the same way during the past decades, because they use perfumes to smell good. For many of these people, this has come to be a natural way to use the spices and aromas that existed in the regions or countries they come from.

In view of the ongoing climate change, Jackson (2011) discussed how the scent experience of a nature reserve in Ontario, Canada, is affected by the pollution and the contamination that exists there. In the study, attention was especially paid to air pollution and how residents reacted to the smells that arose as a result of this. One of the conclusions was that the local scent landscape that once existed with a positive feeling for the reserve now slowly gives residents a deep sense of alienation from the landscape, which Jackson chooses to call displacement. In this way, the new scents can be regarded as symbols of the transformation that is going on in the landscape and the nature reserve.

In an empirical study on Poland's post-socialist transformation, it was shown how scents, as symbols, are used by individuals to express social class and social participation and to create boundaries between spaces, places, and different social groupings. One of the conclusions was that it is important to understand the dimension of scents in social change, because it expresses the social meaning and significance relating to the particular objects and places. The researchers believed that scents create positive associations for many individuals and that they will become scent socialized so that the presence of synthetic fragrances along with the changing social principles degrades body odors to being completely unacceptable.

Some researchers, with a postmodern starting point, believe that organizational researchers should take the sense of smell seriously to be able to explore how invisible, sensual aspects of organizational behavior in companies and organizations could contribute to new explanations through scent experiences. It is not enough with just visible or visual experiences, which traditionally have received much attention. Scents influence on human interaction and social identity creates new opportunities.

BRAND

When it comes to a brand, whether it is a product, a good, or a service, scent's influence through the sense of smell is of significance to the individual's perceptions and experiences. This section describes and analyzes how different aspects of scents can lead consumers to have a scent experience of a brand.

It is common for companies and organizations to use scents to express their brand identity and create emotional connections with their customers. As previously discussed, this can be done by incorporating mood scents in a service environment or by connecting the product scent directly to a specific brand and its products.

> *In five of Kraft Foods's advertisements in People Magazine in the United States, readers could lightly rub with their hands to experience the scent of Philadelphia Cream Cheese.*

In literature, the term scent marketing refers to how companies and organizations can make use of scents in marketing to create a positive mood and image of a brand name for an individual. One of the reasons that scent marketing has come to be developed is scent's strong influence on consumers' affections, cognitions, and purchasing behaviors.

It is apparent from a study that freshly baked cinnamon buns induced sexual arousal in male students. Another study showed that women who got to sniff T-shirts that men had worn for two days were more attracted by the smells that were more genetically similar to their own in comparison with those that were less equal. One of the conclusions was that people are predisposed to selecting compatible partners, which the sense of smell could help with, among other things.

With the help of the knowledge that exists today, companies can influence an individual's emotions with emotional scent associations through so-called scent manipulation. These are thought to be able to affect the individual's perception of the brand and the actual purchase behavior. It shall also be added that factors, which deal with cognitive or psychological aspects of the sense of smell, should be considered more closely before companies choose to implement scent marketing (Herz, 2010).

Scent Stimuli

Research suggests that companies in recent decades have chosen to incorporate product scents in an increasing number of brands, which is thought to enhance the brand value (consumer-based brand equity). Furthermore, it appears that companies have strived to have scent-based brands for products such as cars, thread, and tennis balls, to name a few. The main reason for this appears to be consumers' ability to easily remember this sensory information over time.

When it comes to the influence of product scents on consumers' affections, cognitions, and purchasing behaviors, research has mostly focused on product evaluation (Bosmans, 2006), timing (Spangenberg et al., 1996), and variety-seeking behavior (Mitchell et al., 1995). Furthermore, recently started research has focused on understanding the effects of scents on the human memory, primarily regarding mood scents rather than product scents.

Concerning product scents, these can be applied in different ways: 1) a primary product attribute or 2) a secondary product attribute, as well as by 3) advertising and sales promotion measures. The primary purpose of these applications is considered to be to create awareness among consumers for a specific good or service.

A product scent as the primary product attribute will lead to consumers paying attention and buying the product just because of the actual scents properties. Often this applies to hygiene products, air fresheners, or perfumes, which will be used in contexts where consumers either want to smell good or control their environment with a pleasant smell.

On the other hand, a product scent as a secondary product attribute to the product's function does not have anything to do with the scent. Even if the product itself is odorless, a company can choose to develop a specific product scent. Then the possibility of creating a strong scent association with the brand is emphasized, which is about developing a sensory scent strategy for consumers. For example, a new car can be the very reason to buy the car, but the secondary product attribute, such as a scent, may later cause an individual to remember the scent and associate it with the brand.

Advertisements and Commercials

A general notion in the literature is that advertisements and commercials can visually be associated with different scents by using pictures and illustrations from past experiences. This is explained by emotional reactions, which are about good or bad emotions being related to the experience of the different scents. This could be assumed to explain why many companies choose to explore the link between product scents, memories, and moods in their marketing.

In connection with advertising and promotional activities, product scents exist to create a buzz around a specific product. It is common that companies use product scents in these contexts, and there are today everything from scented billboards to scented magazines and signs, as the following example illustrates.

> The coffee chain Starbucks and the Omni Hotel cooperated by giving Omni Hotel guests so-called "scratch-and-sniff" tags, which were present in the USA Today newspaper. Hotel guests got the newspaper with a tag that smelled like blueberry muffins to encourage them to buy muffins inside Starbucks, which was adjacent to the Omni Hotel.

As a sensory marketer, one should not believe that scent strategies can always lead to the desired results, which the California Milk Processor Board with the "Got Milk?" campaign got to experience. The company had created a cake scented advertising campaign that was used in five of the bus stops in San Francisco. They were forced to take down the outdoor advertising because there were a lot of consumers who complained about the smell. The basic idea was to capture pedestrians' attention by getting them to think of cookies, which in turn would provoke fantasies about dipping cookies in milk. Unfortunately, the company did not get all viewers to have the same experience, and the side effects of the campaign were that they instead managed to convey a message of anti-odor and antiallergy, simultaneously.

Product Evaluation

Research suggests that scents belong to the sensory stimuli that have the greatest ability to stimulate an individual's memory. It also turns out that the scent stimuli tend to evoke memories that are by nature more emotional than the memories evoked by other sensory stimuli. This means that scent's ability to evoke strong emotional memories through direct association offers the opportunity to develop sensory strategies for product scents and brands.

One study showed that people's ability to recognize a scent depends on the memory of an earlier scent experience. When respondents were asked directly after being exposed to a specific scent, it was found that 70 percent of the respondents could remember the scent and after a year the number was 65 percent. In order to understand scent's effect on memory more clearly, it can be compared with another study, which showed that individuals remember a visual image 99 percent of the time right after they had seen the picture, but they only remember the picture 58 percent of the time after barely four months.

Laird (1932) conducted one of the first studies to examine the influence of product scents on consumers' product evaluation. It appeared that when the silk stockings, which usually had a mildly unpleasant odor during that time, were scented with at a floral scent, they were evaluated more positively by housewives in a door-to-door survey.

Ellen and Bone (1998) found in a study that "scratch-and-sniff" tags, which were glued onto printed ads, had no positive effect on consumers' product evaluation. Rather, there was a negative effect when the scent was not perceived as being consistent with the product being advertised.

Another study by Morrin and Ratneshwar (2003) found that consumers take more time to study product packages on a computer screen when there is a pleasant scent in the room. This reinforces scent's ability to help consumers to remember a brand and recognize it because of its scent. Other studies have also shown that scents improve memory, and there is new scientific evidence that scents really can enhance consumers' memory.

When it comes to product scents and mood scents in connection with product evaluation, there are several studies that deal with this. Spangenberg et al. (1996) found in a study that the effects of mood scents in a simulated retail context generally increased both the store and the product evaluation by the consumers. In this study, 26 different scents were tested, but it turned out that the particular kind of scent did not significantly affect the results.

In a later study by Spangenberg et al. (2006), it was shown that the pleasant mood scents improved the store and product evaluation when the scents were consistent with the background music, which, in this case, was Christmas music in combination with a Christmas scent.

One result of this research was that both the product scents and the mood scents were generally considered to help increase consumers' product evaluation. However, it was required that the actual scent be consistent with the product/the environment for such an effect to be achieved.

Product Resemblance

Scent congruence, or product resemblance, turns out to be a significant factor; therefore, consideration should be given to how good or bad a scent is consistent with the actual product or service. Because scents, to a particularly large extent, can affect consumers' affective responses, this means that the reaction is also indirectly transferred to the product and contributes to the brand experience.

Research suggests that how well a scent matches the environment or the product it relates to has an impact on consumers' affections and purchasing behaviors. Consumers react to scents either by liking or disliking them, which also means that an individual approaches a scent that is pleasant and avoids a scent that is unpleasant. Then the question arises as to how a scent consistent with a certain brand is of importance for the experience of the actual product.

It is clear from several studies that scent congruence, i.e., product resemblance, has an influence on consumers' purchasing behaviors with respect to the number of products sold, products sold by gender, and degree of arousal. One of the conclusions was that the product evaluations seem to be more positive among consumers when there was scent congruence.

Scents as an Additional Service

In the literature, it is considered that it is relatively easy to connect a scent to a physical product, but the question is whether service companies can apply the same reasoning. It is generally considered that services are characterized by not being able to touch, as it is physically possible to do of a product. However, it is suggested that service companies may also apply scents, and thus make their services more visible and clearer for customers. This is shown by a survey of the studies done on scent's application in stores, which includes how scents can be applied to services.

The authors discuss in more detail how the service companies, by adding a scent as part of their product offering, can create a greater competitive advantage. When a scent is to be applied to a service, there are four aspects to consider when designing the scent, namely 1) the scent's presence or absence, 2) the scent's pleasantness or unpleasantness, 3) the scent's congruence with the actual service that is provided, as well as 4) the relationship between the scent and the individual's memory.

Finally, it should be said that in the literature it is also considered that scents can act as "signature scents" for a brand, both in terms of physical goods and services, with the aim of achieving a differentiation of a brand in relation to both consumers as well as competitors.

Scent Perception

Generally, it is believed that it is often enough with a sensation of a previously perceived scent for a person to be able to associate the scent with memories and past experiences. There does not even have to be an awareness of the scent when it was first put into the memory. Furthermore, it is thought that scents trigger strong emotions by evoking memories and creating soothing feelings by, for example, relieving stress, as previously discussed.

> A global survey shows that 80 percent of men and 90 percent of women associate an individual scent to specific memories and experiences.

In the study, "The Smell of Virtue," which was published in the journal Psychological Science in 2010, it was evident that "clean" scents made people more moral and generous. A subtle scent was enough for the ethical behavior to improve drastically. For example, participants who (without knowing it) were subjected to a weak "clean" scent of lemon had greater willingness to volunteer and donate money than participants who were not exposed to the scent.

Effects of Product Scents

In a study by Krishna et al. (2009), the effects of specific product scents—as opposed to mood scents—on the individuals' memories of consumer goods such as facial tissue and pencils were investigated. The researchers chose to focus their study on product scents as secondary product attributes and basic attributes were of a different nature, such as the softness of the facial tissue or the writing ability of the pencils. The reason for this was that the majority of research in psychology has traditionally focused on the relationship between smell and memory, where people's ability to recognize scents have been studied rather than their ability to remember product information related to scents.

Two separate studies were performed, wherein the first component had to do with comparing the memory image of a scented and non-scented pencil. To make the results more secure, the non-scented pencil type was compared with two types of scented pencils, one with less and the other with higher scent congruence; in other words, an ordinary pencil scent.

The results of the first study were in accordance with the researchers' expectations, namely that the actual product scent would improve the memory image of product information and that this would stand the test of time. An important observation was that the effects that arose from a product scent in the memory were not just considered as a function of a contextual repetition. Instead, it was shown that the effects of the scent-based information arose during the exposure time, which in turn improved the memory image of the actual products.

One conclusion from the first study was that the usual pencil scent was effective in both the short- and long-term to enhance the memory image of the pencil. However, it was found that over time, for example two weeks, both of the scent types were equally effective.

The second study focused on replicating the effects obtained from the first study and comparing the effects between the product scent and the mood scent in order to enhance the memory image of product information. The respondents got to experience non-scented/scented facial tissues in both a non-scented room and a scented room with respect to both the product scent as well as the mood scent.

The results of the second study found that 5 percent of the participants felt that the room had a mood scent when it was not the case. This should be compared with 27 percent of the participants who felt that the room had a mood scent when that was the case. It showed that the participants were actually more likely to report that the room had a mood scent when this was the case, but at the same time, the overall awareness of this was relatively low.

The researchers also examined more closely whether the participants' awareness of the mood scent was influenced by the product scent, but it turned out to not be the case. It was evident that awareness of this scent was present regardless of whether or not the facial tissues smelled. Furthermore, the study indicated that most participants were more likely to talk about the product scents when they actually smelled than when they did not smell.

One conclusion from the second study was that the product scents were more effective than the mood scents when it came to reinforcing the memory image of product-related information. It also turned out that the product scents provided long-lasting, strong association possibilities between the scent and other product attributes, which in this case was present up to two weeks after the moment of exposure. With this conclusion, product scents should be considered to be very effective in strengthening the memory image of a single product.

This study clearly shows how a product scent can be remembered by an individual and linked to the data that is stored in the memory when the scent is related to a specific product. If consumers remember the product attributes of a product several weeks after the exposure using a scent, it means that they can look for the product in connection with their purchase and shopping. But in real life, scent stimuli is required to help evoke the memory image for this to work when someone picks up a product and its packaging smells or its smell oozes out of the package.

Finally, the researchers maintain that there are relatively few established scent-based brands in practice. One of the reasons is that the vast majority of marketers have not yet understood the importance of scent and its ability to contribute to product information. In view of this, it is suggested that further research may help to increase knowledge about why scents should be considered for different brands.

Scent Perception, Mood, and Behavior

There is considerable evidence in research that the hedonic experience of scents can be shaped and influenced through memory associations. It is believed that scents, in comparison with other sensory stimuli, elicit more emotional and mood-rich memories, regardless of whether it has to do with a mood scent or a product scent with a connection to a brand. Furthermore, it is considered that scents, through associations with emotional experiences, can influence special emotions, which directly affect a person's mood and behavior.

Several studies show that pleasant scents, such as baby powder and perfumes, which were used in both the field and in laboratory experiments, had an impact on a person's mood and could even relieve some symptoms associated with unpleasant physical conditions. In contrast, we found that unpleasant smells, such as rotten fish, caused individuals to experience a worse mood.

It is an accepted notion in research that there is a sequential transition from perception to mood, which means that mood in general influences the affective and emotional states in humans. Studies have shown that mood influences creativity, which is manifested as individuals with positive moods being more creative than people with negative moods. Similar cognitive effects exist when a mood scent, such as walnut, is introduced into the environment, resulting in an increased ability to problem solve in comparison with an unpleasant scent.

Furthermore, it is found in the psychological literature that the mood in turn affects human behavior. It is believed that a positive mood increases willingness to help others and increases productivity at the individual level. If, on the other hand, a negative mood is present, this appears to reduce both the desire to assist others as well as productivity. But as soon as a product scent, alternatively a mood scent, is introduced in a social context, it strengthens willingness and productivity.

> *Pleasant scents, such as baby powder, perfumes, or walnut, affect people's mood, which increases both an individual's will and his/her productivity.*

In summary, scent perception contributes to appreciation, mood, and actual behavior in individuals, which is considered to be a function of the emotional associations that are present in connection with both product and mood scents. For most people, these associations are general, and it is not possible to accurately link them to a specific event in the past. But there are times where both the associations and the memories can be directly linked to a scent experience by a specific brand.

Symbolism of Scents

Using scents to clarify and symbolize a product or a service, as a brand, is common for many companies. This may occur in connection with both goods and services, which a scent is supposed to symbolize. When it comes to scents as symbols, it gives companies the opportunity to create associations and memories of the brand, which makes it easier for consumers to experience and later remember the brand.

Because scents do not contain information per se, when an individual experiences them, it turns out that the verbal and visual stimuli are more influential in the context of how a scent is perceived. Furthermore, scents are invisible and often cannot be pinpointed in the physical space, which a sensory marketer can use in brand building and product labeling, as the following example illustrates (Herz, 2010)

> *In 2004, Procter & Gamble introduced Febreze Air—products that were supposed to appeal to 20-year-olds by getting them to think that air scent products seemed to be trendy and cool. P & G designed one of their products, Scentstories, as a CD player, complete with stop and play buttons, which radiated scents rather than music.*

It is widely believed that scents that are thematically and emotionally associated to a product should be able to contribute to changing the consumer's cognition, perception, and behavior regarding the brand. It should be mentioned that the scent of sweet oranges is considered to reduce stress and be calming, whereas the scent of grapefruit is considered to provide more energy, to name a few examples of how scents, as sensory stimuli, can affect an individual's reactions.

Olfactory Brand

It is possible to register a scent as a brand in the form of an olfactory brand in the legal sense. An olfactory brand can be compared to a visual logo and can be said to be the symbol of how a certain brand smells and should be perceived. The big difference between a visual logo and an olfactory brand lies in the fact that the olfactory brand is abstract and invisible.

> *The first known scent brand was registered in the United States in the early 1990s and was for a knitting yarn that smelled of oleanders.*

Legally, there are some difficulties with registering an olfactory brand, because this shall be represented graphically in order to avoid subjective elements related to how it can be perceived and interpreted. In addition, an olfactory brand shall also be able to show the differences between other products and brands, which may not always be so simple.

When it comes to products that naturally contain scents, it is often not possible to register an olfactory brand. For example, this is not permissible for a manufacturer of a coffee brand, and the motive for this is thought to be the difficulty in distinguishing the product from the brand, which is considered to be due to the smell of coffee being a natural part of the product.

However, when it comes to products that do not contain scents in a natural way, it is easier to register an olfactory brand. Then there is not a natural association with the product, which can be created by a suitable scent that can be associated with the brand. An example of this is the Dutch company Senta, which registered an olfactory brand for tennis balls and protected the scent of "the smell of fresh, cut grass." In this case, it was considered that the scent could be protected, as it was considered sufficiently distinctive and clear from an objective point of view.

It should also be said that there are examples of olfactory brands where the smell does not have a natural association with the brand. In these cases, it is about further differentiating and distinguishing a brand with a scent experience. This requires that the scent regularly belong to the actual product for it to be able to contribute to the scent experience in different individuals.

Finally, it must be added that Swedish companies are able to get exclusive rights to an olfactory brand, even if a graphical representation is lacking.

Signature Scent
If a company fails to register an olfactory brand, it does not mean that the scents cannot be used as symbols. Signature scent refers to the scent that can be associated with a specific brand and used to differentiate and distinguish this in sensory marketing. One of the main reasons for using signature scents is considered to be to enhance the brand identity and create awareness around the brand, as the following example shows.

> *The brand Westin Hotels uses a signature scent in their hotels that is based on white tea. The scent experience is considered to highlight the brand's personality and lifestyle feeling that the brand wants to convey to guests. After a stay at the hotel, customers are offered the opportunity to purchase "The White Tea Collection by Westin," which includes scented candles and oils. In this way, customers can take the feel of the brand with them.*

This shows the importance a signature scent can have for a brand in creating associations, in the same manner as a color, a logo, a texture, or a font can provide desired associations. Furthermore, it should be said that a signature scent does not need to be unique in its kind; it can be a commonly known scent, which can be linked to the brand in an innovative way.

In a comparison between an olfactory brand and a signature scent, it is easier to use the latter, because it does not require a graphical representation. It also means that a signature scent, as a symbol, is not legally protected and can be used by anyone. It should also be noted that if a signature scent is artificially produced and deviates significantly from known scents, it could be difficult for an individual to be able to associate this scent to past memories and scent experiences. On the other hand, this can offer companies an opportunity to develop and apply their "own" signature scent, which could reinforce the importance of the scent as a symbol of the brand.

By making use of olfactory brands or signature scents, as symbols, it is possible for a company to create emotional bonds and position a brand on a deeper level for an individual.

REFERENCES

Axel, R. (1995), "The molecular logic of smell," *Scientific American*, 273:154–159.
Bone, B.F. and Ellen, P.S. (1999), "Scents in the marketplace: explaining a fraction of olfaction," *Journal of Retailing*, 75, 2:243–262.
Bosmans, A.M.M. (2006), "Scents and sensibility: when do (in)congruent ambient scents influence product evaluations?" *Journal of Marketing*, 70, 3:32–43.
Buck, L. (2004), "The search for odorant receptors," *Cell*, 116:117–119.
Chebat, J.-C. and Michon, R. (2003), "Impact of ambient odors on mall shoppers' emotions, cognition, and spending: a test of competitive causal theories," *Journal of Business Research*, 56:529–539.
Chebat, J.-C., Morrin, M. and Chebat, D.R. (2009), "Does age attenuate the impact of pleasant ambient scent?" *Environment and Behavior*, 42, 2:258–267.
Ellen, P.S. and Bone, P.F. (1998), "Does it matter if it smells? Olfactory stimuli as advertising executional cues," *Journal of Advertising*, 27, 4:29–39.
Engen, T. (1988), "The acquisition of odour hedonics." I: van Toller, S. and Dodd, G.H. (ed.) *Perfumery—the psychology and biology of fragrance*, London: Chapman and Hall, p. 79–90.
Gulas, C.S. and Bloch, P.H. (1995), "Right under our noses: ambient scent and consumer responses," *Journal of Business and Psychology*, 10, 1:87–98.
Herz, R.S. (2007), *The scent of desire: discovering our enigmatic sense of smell*, New York: Harper Collins.
Herz, R.S. (2010), "The emotional, cognitive, and biological basics of olfaction: implications and considerations for scent marketing." I: Krishna, A. (ed.) *Sensory marketing: research on the sensuality of products*, New York: Routledge, p. 87–107.
Herz, R.S., Beland, S.L. and Hellerstein, M. (2004), "Changing odor hedonic perception through emotional associations in humans," *International Journal of Comparative Psychology*, 17:315–339.
Jackson, D.D. (2011), "Scents of place: the dysplacement of a first nations community in Canada," *American Anthropologist*, 113, 4:606–618.
Kirk-Smith, M.D. and Booth, D.A. (1987), "Chemoreception in human behavior: experimental analysis of the social effects of fragrance," *Chemical Senses*, 12, 1:159–166.
Krishna, A., Lwin, M.O. and Morrin, M. (2009), *Beyond the proustian phenomenon: the effect of product-embedded scent on memory for product information*, Working paper, University of Michigan.
Laird, D.A. (1932), "How the consumers estimate quality by subconscious sensory impressions: with special reference to the role of smell," *Journal of Applied Psychology*, 16:241–246.
Lwin, M.O. and Wijaya, M. (2010), "Do scents evoke the same feelings across cultures? Exploring the role of emotions." I: Krishna, A. (ed.) *Sensory marketing: research on the sensuality of products*, New York: Routledge, p. 109–121.
Mehrabian, A. and Russell, J.A. (1974), *An approach to environmental psychology*, Cambridge, MA: MIT Press.
Mitchell, D.J., Kahn, B.E. and Knasko, S.C. (1995), "There's something in the air: effects of congruent or incongruent ambient odor on consumer decision making," *Journal of Consumer Research*, 22, September:229–238.

Morrin, M. (2010), "Scent marketing: an overview." I: Krishna, A. (ed.) *Sensory marketing: research on the sensuality of products*, New York: Routledge, p. 75–86.
Morrin, M. and Chebat, J.C. (2005), "Person-place congruency: the interactive effects of shopper style and atmospherics on consumer expenditures," *Journal of Service Research*, 8, 2:181–191.
Morrin, M. and Ratneshwar, S. (2003), "Does it make sense to use scents to enhance brand memory?" *Journal of Marketing Research*, 40, 1:10–25.
Parson, A.G. (2009), "Use of scent in a naturally odourless store," *International Journal of Retail & Distribution Management*, 37, 5:440–452.
Spangenberg, E.R., Crowley, A.E. and Henderson, P.W. (1996), "Improving the store environment: do olfactory cues affect evaluations and behaviours?" *Journal of Marketing*, 60, April:67–80.
Spangenberg, E.R., Sprott, D.E., Grohmann, B. and Tracy, D.L. (2006), "Gender-congruent ambient scent influences on approach and avoidance behaviours in a retail store," *Journal of Business Research*, 59, 1281–1287.

8 The Sense of Touch

This chapter analyzes and discusses the sense of touch, which is considered to be strongly associated with both emotional and cognitive reactions in a person. The scientific notions about the fundamental role of the sense of touch are addressed initially with respect to both physiological characteristics and psychological aspects, as well as the importance of touch and feeling.

Thereafter, three categories of influential factors for the sense of touch, which relate to the importance of the societal cultural, the service environment, and the brand are presented. Considering this background, it is discussed how various factors affect individuals' affections, cognitions, as well as their actual behaviors in different buying and consumption processes.

THE TACTILE SENSE

There is a general notion in the literature that the tactile sense—or the sense of touch—enables an individual to experience both physical and psychological interaction with a product. When an individual touches a thing or a product, as an expression of a brand, information is transmitted that gives him/her a feeling for precisely that actual brand. For many people, it is natural to pick up a loaf of bread in the shop to form an opinion as to whether it is fresh or a few days old. It is often said that the tactile sense is equivalent to a three-dimensional sense, because the feeling by touch, beyond sight, adds information such as firmness, shape, and texture.

Research on the role of the sense of touch has shown that touch and feeling are important both for consumers' physical and mental interaction with the products in the different service environments and for its influence on the relationships between consumers and the store personnel (Krishna, 2010). In my opinion, the role of the sense of touch in marketing has been underestimated for a long time both in marketing literature as well as in research and practice, which is why it is time to pay serious attention to its role for both businesses and consumers.

> *In tactile marketing, products and brands are made available for physical and mental interaction, both real and virtual.*

Research has shown early on that feeling, along with vision, is one of the most active human senses. Furthermore, feeling has been highlighted as an important tool for consumers to obtain information about products and brands, but despite this there is sparse knowledge about the role that the tactile sense has in consumer's decision-making (Peck and Childers, 2003).

This is particularly unsatisfactory considering that most consumers should be satisfied with their product choices and have positive experiences of their buying and consumption processes. Further knowledge about the importance of the sense of touch for a service environment or a brand that can contribute to individuals' sensory experiences has been highlighted, strengthening relationships to a brand and the image that arises.

Touch is viewed as one of the most important tools when it comes to identifying and categorizing various objects, which is why it can be considered as a processing information system. It is believed that a person discovers an object in two steps: first, one finds the object (the physical thing) and then he/she picks it up to make more detailed investigations. Then different hand movements are used, with the fingertips as the primary tool, to explore the various properties of a physical thing.

Using an example taken from an American study at Yale University, it is illustrated how touch and feel can affect a person's behavior, not only in relation to the physical item and store personnel but also in relation to fellow human beings (Williams and Bargh, 2008).

> *A person's contact with physical things such as objects and furniture influences the behavior of other people. This means that a warm cup of coffee or tea in their hands makes people friendlier toward the environment.*

When it comes to interaction through touch and feeling, consumers prefer to interact with the physical things in store environments that allow physical inspection. Furthermore, consumers are more likely to pick up, touch, and select material products in a retail environment. It also turns out that if there is an opportunity to touch a physical product in the store environment, it increases the consumer's confidence in the brand, because potential sensory information is obtained. In a study by Hulten (2012), it was also shown how touch and feeling could be stimulated by scent and visual experiences, which shows that different senses interact and can help to create a multi-sensory brand- experience.

When it comes to the relationship between consumers and the store personnel, it appears that if the personnel at some point touch the consumer, his/her perception of the retail store and the service level as well as what they think about the personnel is influenced. This can take place, for example, by the personnel putting a hand on the customer's arm or when their hands touch each other when the product is inspected. It also appears that touch itself can lead to consumers remaining longer in the store and that they are more receptive and open to the store/chain's marketing.

It turns out that the ability to touch and feel physical things creates positive emotions, which in itself can lead to positive attitudes toward and experiences of a product. For that reason, it is believed that the tactile sense is of great importance in creating positive effects associated with the different purchasing decision situations, which is also reflected in the possibility that impulse purchases can often arise.

Furthermore, digital technology today is an important communication channel—where, among other things, the Internet provides a platform—that has opened up new opportunities for businesses and consumers to interact with each other. The lack of tactile sense for information and product evaluation on companies' websites may be of negative significance and is a major challenge for many companies to pay attention to. Unless customers' sense of touch is stimulated, the chances that consumers will choose to shop via the Internet are decreased.

THE FUNDAMENTAL ROLE OF THE SENSE OF TOUCH

Physiological Properties

When it comes to the development of the human senses, it is considered that tactile sense was developed first, followed by the senses of smell, taste, hearing, and, finally, sight. As early as the seventh week, the fetus reacts to touch and information and feelings are transmitted through the skin already in the embryonic stage. The skin is the body's largest organ and accounts for about 10–25 percent of the body's weight, equivalent to about two square meters.

> *The skin is the largest human organ and corresponds to an area of about two square meters.*

When it comes to touch, a human being is particularly sensitive to this around the mouth and on the hands. This is attributed to the tactile receptors located so close to each other, with barely a millimeter distance, so that the sensory cortex perceives the slightest touch. This differs from the back where the receptors are located farther apart by about 70–90 millimeters. Figure 8.1 shows the skin's structure.

From a physiological point of view, the sense of touch works by the touch receptors reacting to the touch and transmitting signals to the sensory cortex. There, signals are received and stored on the basis of the number of receptors in the different parts of the body. This means that a finger, e.g., the little finger, takes up more space in the cortex than the entire back, which shows how sensitive our hands and fingers are with the sense of touch.

The tactile sense (or sense of touch), also known as the haptic system, is the sense that is activated when we touch something with our skin or hands. A person's hands, which explore different items or objects, can therefore be said to constitute the brain's link to the outside world. This can be related to physical contact with an object or a person, as well as coming in contact with an object and its temperature, texture, or other properties. The distinguishing feature is that the touch that occurs leads to both physical and

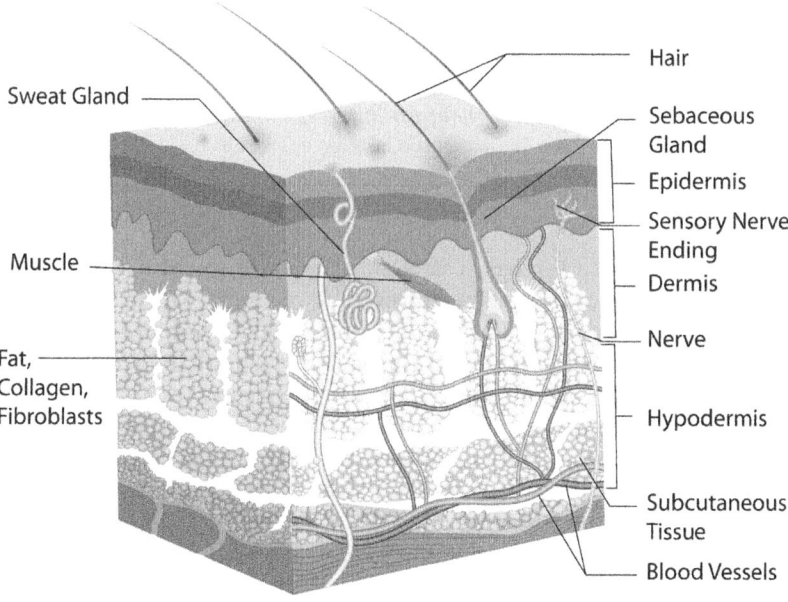

Figure 8.1 The Structure of the Skin
Source: Shutterstock

mental interaction with the object or the person. When compared to the sense of sight, it can be concluded that an object's surface can be registered with the sight from the front, whereas feeling can register an object's surface both from the front and the back at the same time.

The Haptic System

Researchers such as Gibson argued already in the mid-1960s that it was legitimate to regard the tactile sense as a tool for us humans to obtain information from the environment (Gibson, 1966). It is through the haptic system that a person receives this information about both the immediate environment and one's own body. The haptic system includes the entire human body with its various parts and the total body surface area. The following example illustrates how an individual uses the tactile sense.

> *An individual can feel an object that is hidden behind a curtain (or when blindfolded), and this usually happens the following way:*
> *The fingers of the individual are wrapped around the object, and all the fingers are used.*
> *The fingers move "in an explorative manner" on and around the object with movements that are not repetitive or stereotyped.*
> *The fingers are used throughout for different things, such as to follow the object's shapes and lines or rub on the object.*

When it comes to the haptic system in relation to the surface layer, it should be pointed out that temperature, for example, can be divided into two categories, namely, contact temperature on the one hand and air temperature on the other. Examples of this include "Your hand feels cold" and "It's cold out there today," which illustrate the importance of temperature for an individual in the different contexts.

The literature reveals that tactile sense and active touching are considered more as an explanatory sense than a receptive sense. This is explained in that an individual who touches or picks up an object using his/her hands and fingers induces stimulation as it actually is in reality. It is, therefore, important to distinguish between active touch, which is expressed through *touching*, and passive touch, which is expressed by *being touched*.

Active touch is all about the impressions from the skin resulting from an individual actually experiencing a touch, and passive touch is induced by someone else. It is further believed that the fingertips are more sensitive than the palms and how the experience of touch is perceived is determined, to a large extent, by the finger movements of the person in question.

The hand's sensory ability to absorb information about an object or a person plays a critical role in the dexterity that a person exhibits. It turns out, among other things, that it is harder to pick up small objects with cold hands, because their sensory abilities will be fewer because of the cold. A general conclusion is that the best way for an individual to get to know an object, such as a product of a well-known brand, is to feel it, pick it up, and closely explore its contours with the help of the fingertips.

To find out the properties of a product, most people use 1) circular movements to explore the structure, 2) pressure to identify the degree of hardness, 3) static contact to feel the temperature, 4) just keep the object in their hand to identify its weight, and in addition 5) follow the object's shape and contour to identify its exact shape.

But it should also be said that the sensory mechanisms are found in a person's joints, muscles, and tendons, which help to provide information on everything, for example, a surface's roughness to its complacency with regard to comfort and tactile experience.

> The tactile sense is often regarded as the three-dimensional sense of a human being.

The tactile sense can often also increase an individual's experience, especially when the other senses cannot be fully utilized to obtain the sensory information. This may include, for example, in the dark, when the eyes and visual system do not provide sufficient information about the nearby surroundings. Then the tactile sense can broaden the eyes stenography so that it is possible for an individual to perceive the contours, depth, and three-dimensional objects, making the tactile sense unique.

Research also suggests that the hormone oxytocin is released in the body when an individual is exposed to touch, which is thought to contribute to an increase a person's well-being. This applies to both men and women, who are positively affected by touch, and results in many people becoming more relaxed and achieving lower levels of stress, particularly upon multiple touches.

Psychological Aspects

A general notion in the literature is that the skin is not only linked to the development of a person's physical functions, but also to the development of our affections and cognitions. From childhood, there is a need for physical contact, and that affects a person's emotional and intellectual development.

It is believed that the tactile sense has the ability to be received and expressed and can convey and communicate empathy. Furthermore, it is believed that the sense has the ability to awaken a person, unlike the other senses. Many people, therefore, are affected by the hands of doctors, hairdressers, and chiropractors or massage therapists and become more satisfied and feel better.

For a person to be able to identify and recognize an object as a brand, there must be a link between the knowledge of the category that the object relates to and the sensory information that is obtained in the brain and the memory. This means that it requires an understanding of how an object's stimuli is encoded and then is represented in the memory of an individual in connection with touching and feeling.

It is generally believed in research that people are good at being able to identify and recognize an object with the help of touch only. At the same time, it has been pointed out that the tactile sense, with the help of touch, can be seen as a tool to categorize different items, which products and brands represent; thus touch is used as a sensory processing information system in a human.

It is therefore considered that tactile sense helps to create a "sense of form" in an individual, which indicates if a golf ball is round, a knife is sharp, or a stone is hard. In this way, one can remember and reexperience a feeling of touch if one thinks about or gets to see the object.

Instrumental and Hedonic Touch

A taxonomy has been suggested for touch, which assumes that there are two different types of touch, namely, *instrumental touch* and *hedonic touch*. Instrumental touch is related to "touch to purchase," "touch to get non-haptic product information," as well as "touch to get haptic product information," where touch is considered as an end in itself, which can lead to a possible purchase (Peck and Childers, 2010).

In this regard, to touch or to feel a product means that an individual gets more knowledge about a product and its properties, such as hardness, texture, or weight. It is generally considered that sight is not adequate in the context where product evaluation is in focus, which generally omits important information about the material's texture and weight.

On the other hand, it is believed that people who are committed to touching and feeling products because it is fun, pleasurable, or interesting have a more hedonic need. In such cases, it is thought that an individual is more focused on the sensory aspects and therefore has a need to use touch with a more exploratory approach. In itself, this does not mean that he or she intends to make a purchase—but the process is more related to a desire to feel the product and touch it (Peck and Wiggins, 2006).

> *Allowing customers to feel and compare unwrapped toilet rolls can be a way to create a tactile emotional response.*

Studies have also shown that positive affective reactions to the feel and the touch of a product influence people's attitudes and buying behaviors. This is especially true when consumers do not have access to the useful product-related information. It is therefore suggested that companies should engage in and encourage customers to touch various products by coming into physical and psychological contact with them. Making use of touch can have a positive, affective reaction, possibly resulting in more positive attitudes toward a product or a brand.

The researchers Spence and Gallace (2008) assert that through touch, the hedonic attributes of a product can elicit the individual's assessment of the quality and how enjoyable the product is perceived as. They also allege that how a product feels when touched for a long time has been considered to have an influence on whether the product will eventually be bought, as the following quote from Spence and Gallace illustrates:

> *After the eye, the hand is the first censor to pass on acceptance, and if the hand's judgment is unfavorable, the most attractive object will not gain the popularity it deserves. On the other hand, merchandise designed to be pleasing to the hand wins an approval that may never register in the mind, but which will determine additional purchases . . . Make it snuggle in the palm.*

It is further believed that most people probably will not buy a product if it does not comply with their thoughts about how it will feel, for example, in the hand or the upper body. This is particularly evident for products that a person comes close to, that is, has intimate contact with the skin, such as clothing, pillows, shoes, or bed linens. For that reason, many people often rub the materials or the products they are considering buying against parts of their body with high tactile sensitivity, such as the face, legs, or hands, to evaluate the quality, softness, and warmth.

Spence and Gallace (2008) further state that it is possible to manipulate a consumer's tactile experience of a product, for example, by changing its shape or the feeling created by the product surface or surface layer. In this context, it is also pointed out that the fact that a product has a specific shape or a certain look does not mean that it dominates in the consumer's consciousness because of its tactile qualities. Rather, it appears that it is the "vision" of the unique shape of a product, i.e., the visual experience, which leads to the brand image.

> *One out of three buyers of mobile phones believes that it is more important to evaluate how the product feels in one's hand than how it looks.*

This does not mean that there are no tactile products where the tactile qualities often predominate over the visual properties, as is the case with respect to temperature or surface layer. A rule of thumb is that the tactile stimuli has to do with the microstructural characteristics of a product, such as the surface or weight, which then dominate consumers' perceptions of the actual product. However, when it comes to visual stimuli, it seems that these dominate when it comes to characteristics such as shape or size.

Research suggests that humans, with respect to tactile properties, such as the surface, seem to like a product more if they have held it in their hands before, which means that the instrumental and hedonic touch can create appreciation for a product. It is therefore important to pay attention to which tactile properties are affected by the hand or the skin and not confuse these with the visual experiences that shape or appearance may give rise to. Then there is the risk that the tactile experience is rather a visual experience, which is not conducive to a tactile differentiation of a brand, which can be done with the help of stimuli such as temperature, texture, surface, or weight.

INFLUENTIAL FACTORS FOR THE SENSE OF TOUCH

When it comes to the tactile sense, or the sense of touch, the importance of touch and feeling was late to attract attention in retail trade and marketing research. Based on the previously presented SEB model, the factors that may be linked to the sense of touch's influence on an individual's affections, cognitions, and actual behaviors in the buying and consumption processes are presented (Figure 8.2).

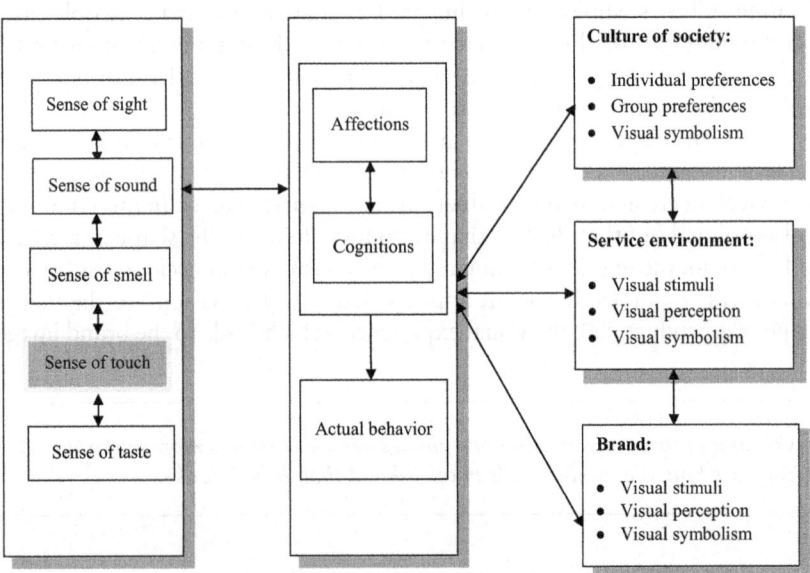

Figure 8.2   The Sense of Touch and the SEB-Model

First, the societal culture, as an influential factor, is addressed in relation to various touch and feeling preferences on the individual and group level, as well as the importance of tactile symbolism. Second, the service environment (or the surrounding), as an influential factor, is addressed in relation to tactile stimuli and tactile perception. Third, the brand, as an influential factor, is addressed in relation to tactile stimuli and tactile perception as well as tactile symbolism. Products, as brands, have different attributes and tactile properties in them, which differ when it comes to influencing individuals' cognitions, affections, and actual behaviors.

SOCIETAL CULTURE

In research, the question as to whether there are cultural similarities or differences between both individuals and groups in terms of touch and tactile preferences is discussed. This is considered to be of great significance in order to understand and explain how people interpret and perceive their surroundings through various sensory impressions, which occur in both personal relationships and in relation to products and brands.

As examples of culture's influence, it can be mentioned that touch and feeling have been linked to human reproduction and survival for thousands of years. As early as the fourth century BC, the Greek philosopher Aristotle, in his theories, suggested that the five human senses have a hierarchical order with *touch* as the first, where feeling is the starting point. This is followed by the other senses based on how they can receive and perceive touch.

> *Because sexual touching has to do with the sense of touch, it was considered for millennia to be the most important human sense.*

According to Aristotle, the true image of an object was shown by touch, which was illustrated with a kitten's smooth and soft fur, expressing the cat's innate soft character. Furthermore, touch and feel through sexual stimulation were also the prerequisites for the human race to survive and develop. Thus it was considered that there was a connection between the cosmos, the universe, and touch, which made the tactile sense the number one of all the senses.

Individual Preferences

Research suggests that people use their ability to examine and touch things in a very individual way, which also applies to how people react to touching. Feeling can take place either by 1) an individual touching an object or a person or 2) an individual being touched by an object or a person, which will now be discussed and presented in more detail.

Furthermore, it is believed that this behavior is context-dependent, which means that it can differ from one situation to another. It has been shown that for some people the effect of touch on their behavior and experience of a product is stronger than for other people.

It is also thought that the need to get to know the products is more or less irresistible and is present in both children and adults. Although feeling has been highlighted as an important tool for obtaining information about products, today there is sparse knowledge about the role of the tactile sense and the possibility to feel a product when evaluating a product as well as in the decision-making as to whether or not a product should be purchased or not.

To Touch Something or Someone

Researchers such as Peck and Childers (2003) have identified differences in people's individual needs for touch, which means that individuals have different preferences in terms of obtaining information about a product by touching it and examining it. It has emerged that there are differences between individuals and how they react with the sense of touch, and an important factor is considered to be a person's motivation or preference for touch, where the term *need for touch* (NFT) was proposed.

Those individuals who have a greater need for touch/getting to know the products become more frustrated when they are not offered the chance to examine the product, whereas customers who have a lower NFT can still evaluate the product by examining it by means of sight, among others.

The researchers believe that further information about the product can compensate for the inability to examine the product and create one's own opinion. A written description, for example, where the weight is indicated can be a good way to elicit a prior experience in an individual, thereby contributing information so that she or he can gain an impression of the product through memory.

However, it is emphasized that for highly motivated customers who want to feel the products, nothing can compensate for being able to touch and feel, because that is part of their experience. On the other hand, it has been presented that for those customers who have less need to examine and touch a product, an image can be enough to activate a previous memory and thus reduce the need for a direct evaluation of the product by touch. Given that there are consumers who have a strong need to examine and touch products, it may also be important for shop owners or manufacturers to rethink packaging, because even these must allow for touch.

Individual Differences

One study examined the interplay regarding individual differences in NFT and compensation for touch (Klatzky and Lederman, 1993). In a laboratory, the participants evaluated a sweater and a cell phone individually, and they had options to touch and feel the product or look at it under plexiglass, which did not offer the option to touch. After the evaluation, the participants got to fill out a form where attitudes, confidence, frustration, and NFT were measured.

It was found that individuals with the highest NFT had more confidence in the products and were less frustrated when they could touch and feel the products in connection with the evaluation. For individuals with low NFT, it showed that their attitudes did not change, considering that they could touch the products. Furthermore, one of the results of the performed study was that written information came to serve as compensation for individuals with high NFT, when they could not evaluate the products by touching them. Similarly, for individuals with low NFT, confidence in the products increased and frustration decreased by not being able to touch the products when written information was available.

Research also shows that not only do individual differences exist when it comes to touch and whether a person likes the product or not, but it has also been highlighted that different situations can motivate individuals to touch a product prior to purchase. A few studies also show that there are individual differences in how touch and the amount of touch may influence the individual in question. Some consumers only examine the product when they move it from the shelf into their basket or cart, whereas others want to spend time exploring the product and feeling it before they decide whether or not to purchase it.

> *Some individuals always want to touch a product prior to purchase, unlike many others.*

Previous studies have shown that many people use touch to evaluate products and become frustrated when they are denied the opportunity to do so. It has, therefore, been suggested that the need to touch and feel a product shall be divided into two different dimensions: the *instrumental* touch, which is necessary to experience the quality of a product, and *auto telic* touch, which is emotional and creates a feel for the product (Citrin et al., 2003).

It is further proposed that people with a high need for instrumental touch "use touch to gather information about a product to help them make judgments" (Peck and Wiggins, 2006, p. 57). An example of this is when an individual feels a shirt to determine the quality of the material.

It is widely believed that customer confidence in a product may be affected by whether or not one can touch a product and possibly experience any sensory feedback. Furthermore, it is believed that the desire to investigate products can be described as problem solving at the same time as it can be seen as fun, imaginative, exciting, something one enjoys, and a sensory stimulation. In other words, shopping can be viewed as an adventure through touch.

The literature also suggests situations of engagement where it can be beneficial for a customer to touch a product. One such situation is when a customer is exposed to a product and by being able to touch the product, the possibility that the customer will make a purchase increases.

To Be Touched by Something or Someone

An American study at Yale University shows that people's physical contact with objects, such as furniture, influences the way a person behaves toward his/her fellow human beings but also how a person feels (Ackerman et al., 2010). In the study, a number of people got to sit on different types of chairs, while at the same time holding smooth and rough puzzle pieces as well as light and heavy clipboards.

> *To sit on something soft or hard in a negotiation can affect willingness to compromise.*

The results showed that if a person sits on a hard chair in comparison with a soft pillow, the person in question would be less willing to compromise in a negotiation. The researchers claim that this can be explained in that physical concepts such as hardness, roughness, and heat belong to the concepts that infants develop early on. One conclusion was that people thereafter develop more abstract images by using expressions such as "a warm smile" or "a hard heart" to describe people and relationships.

It has also been shown that the unconscious touch, such as what a person is exposed to by another person, can lead to greater satisfaction and well-being, which the following example shows:

> *In a study at the University of Perdue, the effects of being touched by another person were investigated in an experiment. The female librarian was asked to lightly touch the students' hands as they returned a library card. When the students left the library, they got to talk about their experiences in the library that particular day. Among other things, they got to answer if the librarian smiled or touched the students when they returned the library card. The result was that the students stated that the librarian smiled, which she actually did not do, and that the librarian did not touch the students, which she did. It turned out that those students who were touched, albeit unnoticed, in general enjoyed life more and the library compared to those students who were not touched.*

Group Preferences

In literature, people are often described using tactile qualities, such as someone is hot or cold. It is generally considered that the importance of contact between people and products is of great importance in daily life and cannot be overestimated. In this concept, there is also an implicit assumption that both tactile touch and haptic touch symbolize deeper emotional and human values.

A person's skin is often regarded as the boundary between the self and the world outside. It is not uncommon that people do not want to be physically touched by other people who they do not have confidence in or trust. But often a handshake or a hug between two people, where physical contact occurs, symbolizes trust and friendship.

In Muslim countries, the handshake, perhaps the most common greeting touch in the Western world, is not a given among men. In countries such as Afghanistan, Pakistan, and Saudi Arabia, an embrace is more common as a symbol of trust and friendship. Furthermore, a man most unwillingly takes a woman's hand and even less often kisses her on the hand. There are also unwritten rules in these countries; for example, a subordinate can show his/her respect and to some extent surrender to a superior by putting his/her cheek on one shoulder. In this way, it is common for tactile touch to symbolize different emotional and human values in the different cultures.

Male and Female

It is widely believed that the way a person reacts when the sense of touch is used can also be linked to whether the individual is a woman or a man. Women are often considered to have a greater need to use touch and feeling when a product is to be evaluated.

When it comes to communicating emotions through touch, it has been shown by an American study that this is a common occurrence (Hertenstein and Keltner, 2011). It appeared that men communicated anger, which should not be attributed to chance, when at least one member of a communication group was a man. Similarly, women communicated sympathy when at least one member of the group was a woman. It is worth noting that when there were only women in the group, happiness was communicated among the members. One of the study's conclusions was that the analysis showed how the communication of emotions through touch is asymmetrical in nature between men and women.

In another study, participants, who were both men and women, took notes and wrote down their physical contacts with the others over a number of days. It was clear that both men and women touched the opposite sex more than their own sex, and women initiated more contact with the opposite sex in comparison with men. The persons who touched the women also had more contacts from women, and it was also found that the women who communicated more also initiated more touching.

Research suggests that when it comes to fashion products, such as clothes and shoes, fashion designers and women have greater need for touch (NFT) in comparison with fashion followers and men regarding the instrumental and appropriate dimensions (Workman, 2009). Both men and fashion followers, however, showed a greater need for touch regarding instrumental dimensions only, which can be seen as an expression that it is necessary only to perceive the quality but not to create an emotional feeling.

Finally, it should be said that when it comes to virtual touch, such as haptic interaction between people, a study of both sexes showed that digital representatives, like humans, were not touched with the same force as non-human objects. It also appeared that both men and women touched male digital representatives more strongly in comparison with female digital representatives.

SERVICE ENVIRONMENT

As indicated in the previous chapter, touch and feeling are attributed to the background stimuli that can help to create an attractive and pleasing atmosphere in a service environment in terms of air, materials, temperature, or texture. It is also considered that this type of stimuli creates various psychological sensations in individuals, which lead to both cognitive and affective reactions in the experience of a service environment.

Tactile stimuli or other sensory stimuli for touch and feeling in shops, restaurants, or shopping centers, therefore, are common occurrences that influence the atmosphere and create a positive sensory experience. In recent years, marketing research has increasingly begun to draw attention to the importance of the tactile sense through touch and feeling in different buying and consumption processes, which historically has been one of the least studied areas.

Tactile Stimuli

Human touch, in the form of input through the tactile sense, has proven to be an important element in product evaluation in the store and the department store contexts. The touching of products has been shown to have a positive influence on shopper's attitudes and buying behaviors as well as on purchase intentions and has also been linked to product placement in stores.

> *To touch a brand leads to physical and mental interaction, which might become an impulse purchase.*

It has also been pointed out that touch may have important implications for store design and signs, which may mean that these can, in different ways, encourage touch and result in a physical interaction with products that customers would otherwise have ignored. This may, in itself, lead to increased impulse buying and unplanned purchases.

It should be noted that the Internet's emergence raises the question of how visual descriptions of products, using images and/or text can complement the importance of feeling/touch. It is considered difficult today to create a sensory experience in a streamlined online environment, which a website on the Internet represents.

To Touch and Feel the Products

The research emphasizes that consumers love to interact with products as tangible objects, which allows for a physical inspection in a service environment. It means to touch and feel the physical goods such as bread, a glass, or a shirt in connection with the purchase and before deciding whether to buy the product in question. The main reason that consumers want to interact with a brand is to form an understanding of the product's characteristics, such as shape, hardness, or texture.

Researchers such as Peck and Wiggins (2006) believe that the customer's confidence in a brand is affected by whether sensory information can be obtained by touching or feeling the actual product. An observational study examined how shoppers in a grocery store were affected by a sign at the point of purchase (POP), where the text "feel the freshness" encouraged customers to touch and feel the actual product. The aim was to find out if this would lead customers to be more impulsive or conduct unplanned purchases.

The results showed that many customers acted more impulsively when the sign "feel the freshness" was present at the point of purchase than if the sign was missing. This applied to those individuals who had a high need for touch (NFT) as well as those who had a low need, which shows the effect of reminding and encouraging customers to touch and feel the products.

The study's findings show that if a customer can be involved and encouraged to touch, feel, or pick up a product, this can, in turn, have the effect that positive attitudes are created for the brand. Therefore, it is argued that it is important to make use of sensory stimuli in marketing if a company wants to create positive experiences of a brand.

In this context, it has also been presented that the very atmosphere and design of a service environment, such as a store or a supermarket, should help to create opportunities for customers to touch and feel the products. The study showed that signs should be placed in a service environment encouraging customers to touch and pick up the products, which of course has been shown to lead to impulse purchases. Researchers believe that this demonstrates the link between feeling and impulses, which illustrate the importance that the sense of touch has in consumers' behaviors in purchasing and consumption processes.

To Be Touched by People

Research suggests that the need for *interpersonal* contact can be regarded as equal to a person's need for food. Different types of interpersonal contact play a crucial role in the development and maintenance of relationships between parents and their children. It has been found that this type of contact has a positive effect on children when it comes to reducing stress and anxiety. Furthermore, it is thought that the need for interpersonal contact is present throughout one's life and that the need for this contact increases with age.

The literature emphasizes the importance of being touched by another person, which is believed to contribute to creating a positive image of the person who does the touch. It is further assumed that touch in itself can help to strengthen the commitment between two people, which in turn can lead to a sense of belonging. This can also lead to the transfer of a sense of confidence and trust between two people, which influences the feelings and thoughts that arise for the person who responds to the touch.

> *If the personnel touch the customer unconsciously, it creates a positive response to the brand.*

The touch that can occur between the personnel and the customers in a service environment is found to affect customers' perceptions of a brand. It appears that if the personnel at some point touch a customer, for example, by letting his/her hands touch the customer's hand or putting a hand on his/her arm, this creates a positive reaction through the tactile sense. The individual's image of the brand is influenced most of all in terms of the retail and service experience, as well as how the personnel are perceived.

In a study by Hornik (1992), three field experiments were conducted to investigate how touch could affect the consumer's behavior and perceptions in service environments, such as shops and restaurants. The first experiment involved 286 shoppers, who were met by three men and three women when they came into the bookstore where the experiment took place. Every shopper then received a four-page catalog with information about products, prices, and discounts, as well as other information.

In this context, the man or woman who gave the catalog to the shopper lightly touched the upper arm of some of the customers. When shoppers came to the register area after their visit to the bookstore, they were asked about their time in the store and how much they had spent. Each customer also had to fill out an evaluation form, which gave the opportunity to win in a lottery.

The results showed that the length of time spent in the store was significantly higher for those who had been lightly touched as they entered the bookstore than for those who had not been touched. The actual time spent was 22 minutes for those who were touched and 14 minutes for those who were not touched. An interesting observation was that the touch influenced the female shoppers more than the male shoppers. Furthermore, those shoppers who were touched were friendlier toward the store and bought more than the untouched shoppers.

One conclusion of the first experiment was that touch not only affects the amount of time spent and purchase behavior in a store but also how customers evaluate the shop. These findings formed the basis for the next two experiments with respect to customers' perceptions of the person who touched them.

In the second experiment, 248 male and female guests, as couples, were tested in conjunction with a restaurant visit with the aim of investigating the effects of touch. They were met by four male and four female waiters/waitresses, who were selected on the basis of their physical attractiveness, where four were considered to have high attractiveness and four were considered to have low attractiveness.

The experiment was conducted for a number of hours during the weekday evenings, and in half of the cases, the waiter/waitress touched either the man or the woman's arm for one second at the end of the meal, while asking if everything was fine.

The significant findings showed that female guests who had been touched by an attractive waiter gave the highest tips on average, whereas male guests gave the lowest gratuity, on average. The male guests had not been touched by a waitress with low physical attractiveness. It also turned out that both male and female guests who had been touched gave more tips, between 2–4 percent, compared with those guests who had not been touched.

Furthermore, the results showed that the guests who had been touched also gave higher evaluations of the waiters/waitresses, where female guests were highest in their evaluations of the male waiters. When it came to the evaluation of the restaurant visit, it also appeared that the male and female guests who had been touched left the highest evaluations.

One conclusion of the second experiment was that there is a clear correlation between touching of customers and their positive evaluations of the waiters/waitresses and the restaurant visit as well as their willingness to tip.

In the third experiment, a number of solitary shoppers at a supermarket were observed, and the purpose was to examine their reactions to a demonstration of taste samples. During the demonstration, the demonstrator touched the shopper when he/she asked if the tastes were good and if the shopper was willing to buy the item in question.

Of the significant results, it was evident that nearly nine out of ten shoppers who were touched physically by the demonstrator agreed that the samples tasted good, whereas only six in ten shoppers who had not been physically touched by the demonstrator agreed with this. Furthermore, it appeared that female shoppers who were physically touched were more willing to buy the product than the male shoppers.

The main conclusion of the study was that consumers' behaviors were influenced by touch and that women seemed to react more positively than men in connection with being touched by another person.

Touch in the Online Environment

The question about how retail businesses should act on the Internet when consumers are not able to touch and feel the products in connection with their shopping has been posed in research. There is a consensus that this fact is considered to have a negative impact on the human sensory experience and thus hampers consumers' product evaluation and purchasing decisions for certain products and brands. It is clear from previous research that tactile stimulation is of importance in the shopping context.

> The Internet complicates the decision to purchase, because touch cannot take place in a virtual environment.

Researchers such as Phillips et al. (1997) believe that the products and brands that require multi-sensory information from multiple senses are probably bought to a lesser extent via the Internet. This is thought to be one of the reasons that many consumers are discouraged from buying online, because the sensory information one can get by being able to touch and feel products, such as fresh produce, is missing.

Therefore, it is argued that products that require multi-sensory information, such as clothing, are more difficult for a retailer to sell online. This is particularly true in relation to the individuals who prefer to use the sense of touch when a garment, such as a skirt, shirt, or sweater that requires physical contact, is to be evaluated.

In a study by Citrin et al. (2003), consumers' need to touch and feel products and its impact on the likelihood that they buy products online was investigated. The survey was conducted using a questionnaire, and 272 students at an American university, of which 51 percent were men, participated in the study. In the questionnaire, there were 69 statements concerning consumers' evaluation of the different brands in a buying situation.

Furthermore, a seven-point scale was used to examine the role of tactile input with statements such as: "I need to touch a product to evaluate its quality," "I need to touch and feel a product in order to evaluate whether I will like the product," "I believe that it is necessary to touch a product to evaluate its physical properties," "I believe it is necessary to touch a product to evaluate its quality," and "I need to touch a product in order to make a general evaluation of it."

The researchers were interested in getting answers to a number of hypotheses concerning the importance of tactile touch in connection with purchases over the Internet. One of the hypotheses was that a greater need for tactile input would result in reduced use of the Internet for product purchases. The results indicated that the hypothesis was confirmed and that there is a negative relationship between the need for tactile input and the use of the Internet.

Another hypothesis was that a greater need for tactile input would result in reduced use of the Internet for products requiring a quality evaluation based on other sensory stimuli than sight and sound. The results showed that the hypothesis was only partially confirmed by the existence of a significant negative effect on clothes shopping, whereas the purchase of flowers was only marginally affected by the need for tactile input. It should also be said that no significant effect, in terms of the need for tactile input, has been observed for other product categories, namely, books, CDs, electronics, or video.

Another hypothesis was that women would exhibit a greater need for tactile input to make a product evaluation than men. The results indicated that the hypothesis was confirmed and that gender has a significant effect in terms of the need for tactile input in product evaluation. It turns out that women exhibit a higher need for tactile input in comparison with men.

One of the study's conclusions was that consumers with a high need for tactile input, to a certain extent, seemed to be discouraged from buying products on the Internet. This may be deemed to apply in particular to products where there is a high element of tactile stimuli or scent and taste stimuli. It is therefore proposed that retail companies with experience-based products should shift the focus from experience stimuli, such as smell and touch, to shopping stimuli, such as product quality and price. One of the reasons is that it might be difficult to succeed in selling on the Internet is that customers' sense of touch, sight, sound, smell, and taste cannot be stimulated sufficiently.

Tactile Perception

To Touch and Feel the Products

The literature reveals that tactile stimuli can contribute in that consumers touch and feel products and brands. However, there are few studies that have studied what other types of sensory stimuli for sight, sound, smell, or taste lead to consumers' touching and feeling a product in a service environment.

One question that research still needs to answer is whether tactile stimuli per se, such as shape, material, temperature, texture, or weight, lead to a personal touching and feeling of a product or if it can take place under the influence of other sensory stimuli, which unconsciously affect the individual's behavior. Furthermore, it is deemed to be important to identify other types of sensory stimuli for sight, sound, smell, or taste, which can be considered to have an influence on consumers' tactile perception in connection with various buying and consumption processes.

To examine what types of stimuli other than tactile stimuli influence consumers' tactile perception, the influence of visual and auditory sensory stimuli for sight and sound on consumers' behaviors with respect to both approaching the computers on a store shelf and touching and feeling the computers was studied (Hultén, 2013). This was done regardless of whether it was deemed a high or low need for touch (NFT) among the respondents.

The survey was conducted in the form of a field experiment in the computer section of a department store at a home electronics chain. Because there was an interest in studying tactile perception for other types of products than soft goods such as home furnishings and clothing where touch is a natural part of the product evaluation, hard goods such as PCs were selected. There was also an interest by the management to evaluate how to get their customers to approach the computers and touch them, which was perceived as a problem, as most just walked past the shelves without touching the computers or even stopping.

The experiment included a control group (n = 319), an experimental group 1 (n = 342), and an experimental group 2 (n = 323) for a total of 984 customers, who visited the computer section during a period of five weeks. The selection included both men and women aged 10-years-old up to 70 years. The relevant observations were made from Friday to Sunday between the hours of 12:00 and 4:00 p.m. when there was the most customers in the store.

In the first experiment, a visual stimulus in the form of a red sign that stated "Touch me" on one of the computers on the shelf was introduced to encourage and stimulate a closer look and touching of the actual laptop. One hypothesis was that the sign would elicit a positive effect on consumers closer to the point of sale (POS), which also proved to be the case. The hypothesis was confirmed, and a significant result with an increase of about 50 percent more customers could be established when it came to consumers approaching the product.

Furthermore, another hypothesis was that the red signpost would have a positive impact on consumers' tactile behavior in terms of increased touching of the actual computer at the point of sale. It turned out that this hypothesis was also confirmed, and there was also a significant increase of 78 percent in the number of customers who touched and felt the computer.

> *A red sign, as a visual stimulus, leads to more shoppers touching a computer.*

A third hypothesis was that the red sign, as sensory stimulus, would also have a positive effect on how long customers touched and felt the computer. Even this hypothesis was confirmed, and it turned out that the length of time touching the computer significantly increased from 1 second to 2.2 seconds.

In the second experiment, an auditory stimulus in the form of a human voice was introduced. The reason for this was to study the impact of voice on consumers' approach to the shelf and touching of the computer, which can be considered to be a rare occurrence in research. The personal voice was played close to the point of sale for approximately ten seconds every minute, and the following message was conveyed to customers: "Hey there, have you missed what I have to offer you? Do you know that you are allowed to touch me, test me, and handle me to better experience me and my possibilities?"

One hypothesis was that the combination of the red sign and the personal voice would elicit a positive effect on consumers' approach to the computer at the point of sale. It turned out that this hypothesis was also confirmed, and with regard to customers coming closer to the computer on the shelf, there was a significant increase of 64 percent.

The manipulation check carried out in connection with the experiments, when the 200 respondents were asked whether they had noticed the red sign or the personal voice, revealed some interesting results. The vast majority of the customers who approached the computer stated that they had not been affected by the red sign, which indicates that the influence occurs in an unconscious way. When it came to touching the computer, only a third of the customers maintained that they were stimulated to touch and feel the computer under the influence of the red sign. For the remaining customers, who did not state that they were influenced, this also indicated that there is an unconscious influence on the sense of touch through the sense of sight.

The conclusions that can be drawn from this study are that sensory stimuli, either by itself or in combination, have an influence on consumers who are closer to the point of purchase (POP) and their tactile behavior. Furthermore, the combination of the visual and auditory stimuli stimulated consumers to both approach and to touch and feel the products in a service environment. This shows the unconscious impact that sensory stimuli can have on consumers' physical and emotional behavior even in connection with hard products, as opposed to soft products, where there is a natural need for touch to evaluate the product in question.

For retailers, this means that sensory stimuli can attract consumers' attention to a product or a product category in an unconscious way. Furthermore, this means unprecedented opportunities for practitioners to design and develop a service landscape where multi-sensory brand-experiences can help to create an attractive and appealing store atmosphere at the point of purchase area.

To Be Touched by People

As previously stated, most people have the need for interpersonal contact by touch for most of their lives, and this need increases with age. It is widely believed that this type of contact has a positive influence by improving the relationships between people and reducing anxiety and stress. In this context, a handshake between two people has been regarded for centuries as a socially acceptable form of ritualistic touch, as a form of greeting upon arrival and departure. Furthermore, a handshake is viewed as being of importance in providing a positive first impression and can be seen as a formal gesture in human interaction.

> A handshake between two people reduces anxiety and stress in the relationship.

In a study by Johansson and Krnjajic (2012), the effects of interpersonal touch by a handshake between an employee and a number of customers were examined. With the help of a field experiment at the retail chain Teknikmagasinet, customers' experiences with the shopping experience in a store were studied. The experiment was conducted during two Fridays between 10:00 a.m. and 7:00 p.m. and two Saturdays between 11:00 a.m. and 5:00 p.m. when many customers visited the store. In the control and the experimental group, 50 respondents participated, and the total sample comprised 100 respondents.

During the investigation, an employee was present in the customer areas. In connection with customer relations, the employee was to shake hands with the customers as a welcoming gesture in the service process. After the customer left the shop, an interview took place concerning the shopping experience, where a number of questions were asked about how the handshake was viewed, if the employee's level of service was evaluated more positively, if the store environment was evaluated more positively, if the customer's mood was positively affected, and if the men perceived the handshake as being more pleasant than the women.

The conclusions indicated that nine out of ten respondents in the experimental group perceived the handshake as pleasant, which was also statistically significant ($p < 0.000$). Nearly nine out of ten respondents in the experimental group perceived the handshake as positive, which can confirm that a handshake, as a physical contact form in a service landscape, is socially accepted among customers. Among other things, the respondents made statements like "You felt welcome" and "It felt like he knew me and I was happy." It should be noted that one in ten customers did not perceive the handshake as positive, which is partly justified by the risk of infection.

When it comes to the question of if the handshake influenced the evaluation of the employee's service level, the retail environment, and the client's state of mind, no significant results could be shown. In contrast, it was found that men perceived the handshake as being more pleasant than women at a statistically significant ($p < 0.036$) level.

The researchers believed that an explanation for this might be that women perceive a handshake as a more dominant gesture from an employee, which they view as negative. Also, the fact that the handshake historically has been a common courtesy between men was cited as a possible explanation for men perceiving the handshake as more pleasant than women.

BRAND

There is a common perception in the literature that products differ with respect to tactile stimuli such as shape, hardness, material, softness, texture, or weight, which directly affect many people's need to touch and feel the actual brand. It is believed that a person's touch with the hands is the optimal way to identify and determine the tactile properties that best benefit the personal sensory experience. The more tactile qualities a product has, the more likely that the individual will be motivated to touch and feel the brand before making a purchase decision.

Tactile Stimuli

Already in 1983, the American consumer researcher Morris B. Holbrook drew attention to the great significance that tactile stimuli have in connection with product evaluation. In a study of consumers' evaluation of real sweaters design, results were compared with those of a previous study with virtual sweaters design, where descriptions and images were used for the evaluation. It turned out that both touch and feeling were crucial for the perception of tactile stimuli, such as texture and weight.

> *In evaluating a sweater's design, the sensory experience of texture and weight are of great importance.*

The conclusions of the study were that in a comparison between the real and the artificial sweaters, it was apparent that tactile stimuli such as the sweater's weight, materials, and knitting play a major role in the sensory experience. In this regard, the real sweaters were superior to the virtual sweaters, as assumed from the images and the verbal descriptions. Given that this study was done before the Internet's breakthrough, it can be noted that the conclusions even today are of high relevance given how difficult it is to evaluate a product without the use of tactile stimuli.

In a study, Peck and Childers (2004) investigated whether consumers' verbal evaluation of products were consistent with their tactile behavior in product evaluation. To find out, participants' hand movements were videotaped while participants spoke about the actual product.

The results showed that there was an agreement between what people said and what they did, when it came to touching and feeling the different brands. It turned out that products with various tactile stimuli, such as tennis racquets and sweaters, were touched longer in comparison with products such as calculators and mobile phones, with a smaller number of tactile stimuli. On the other hand, the latter items were touched longer in comparison with products such as cereals and toothpaste, which lack material characteristics in the form of tactile stimuli.

Another study showed that there are differences when it comes to touching with respect to products with material properties on the one hand and with geometric properties on the other hand. The researchers examined how consumers made purchase decisions in respect to these, in both the traditional stores and the online environment, relating to the significance that touching and feeling the products are deemed to have (Brown McCabe and Nowlis, 2003).

The study was conducted in the form of two experiments with American marketing students. The first experiment concerned the degree to which students touch and feel products with material properties, such as bath towels and rugs, compared to products with geometrical properties, such as rolls of film and videotape.

The respondents had to answer questions about whether they touched the product, from "I did not feel the product" (0) and "I felt the product to a very small degree" (1) to "I felt the product very much" (7), and if touching helped them make their buying decisions, from "I did not feel the product" (0) and "Feeling the product helped me to a small extent" (1) to "Feeling the product helped me to a large extent" (7).

Among the significant findings, it was evident that consumers were more likely to touch, feel, and choose products with material properties in a retail environment, compared with an online environment. In contrast, it appeared that there was no significant difference between the retail environment and the online environment for products with geometric properties. In this respect, the visual experience instead played a crucial role and consumers relied entirely on the ability of sight to make a purchasing decision.

> *In an online environment, the eyes are not enough to get information about a brand's material properties.*

The researchers concluded that the difference, which exists between the stores and the online environment, was due to the additional sensory information that was obtained through the sense of touch when an individual picks up and feels the products physically. The feeling conveyed by physical contact, regarding, for example, softness or hardness, provides an emotional experience of the actual product that not only the sense of sight can convey.

This led researchers to the conclusion that consumers prefer to receive information through different sensory attributes in the store environment rather than simply relying on market information in verbal or written form, as is the case in the online environment. It follows from this reasoning that the researchers believe that written descriptions of product features can be considered more or less important depending on how these interact with other sensory attributes of a product. It is therefore proposed that the written descriptions should be most useful in cases where a product cannot be touched or felt physically.

The second experiment concerned the degree to which the students (n = 419) preferred to buy four products based on five different options, namely, 1) be able to touch and feel, 2) get a description of the touch attributes, 3) the product could not be touched, 4) have just a picture of the product, and 5) get a picture of the product and a list of the various product advantages. Each respondent was given the task to make a purchasing decision in seven different product categories, such as bath towels, rugs, socks, and T-shirts with material properties as well as soaps, motor oil, and video with geometric properties. Furthermore, before making the buying decision, respondents were asked to evaluate each product category and indicate how likely it was that they would purchase the product on a scale of 1 "very unlikely to buy" to 7 "Very likely to buy" with regard to the possible options.

Among the significant findings, it showed that respondents reported a probability of 4.95 to buy the four products with material properties when these could be touched and felt according to the first option. When the same products were investigated using an image and a list of product attributes, according to the fourth option, the likelihood ratio decreased to 3.56. This probability decreased to 3.55 when only a picture of the product was shown to the respondents.

One conclusion was that consumers have greater preferences for products with material properties in a retail environment, compared with the online environment, thereby also increasing the likelihood of a purchase. On the other hand, the preferences increased for these types of products in the online environment when actual product benefits were described in terms of tactile attributes such as softness or hardness.

In practice, this means that products with material properties, such as home furnishings, clothing, and footwear, should be more successful in retail environments where consumers can physically touch and feel the products. When it comes to products with geometric properties, such as prepackaged consumer goods, the difference between the retail environment and the online environment should not be so large, because the sense of sight has a prominent place at the moment of purchase. On the other hand, a retailer can describe different tactile attributes of a product with material properties and thus contribute so that the sense of touch is the focus in both the retail environment and the online environment.

Tactile Perception

Initially, the haptic system was mentioned as an expression for the tactile sense as a tool to get information from the environment, such as various service environments and products. The human body is found within the framework of this system, with its various parts and its total body surface area, which is used for touch and tactile experiences.

In everyday speech, when we speak of feeling, it generally refers to the skin, but that is not enough to understand how a sensory experience shall be perceived. This system is often called skin sense, whereas haptic perception, which includes the joints, muscles, and tendons, lays the foundation for the so-called kinesthetic sense, whereby a person gets information about his/her own movements (Klatzky, 2010).

> *When we use fingers, muscles, or tendons, we get information about our own movements, which is called haptic perception.*

The combination of touch and the kinesthetic sense is expressed by the term haptic or the haptic sense, derived from the Greek word to touch. When a person gets information from this sense, it is called *haptic perception*, which will be discussed in more detail with respect to various products. When it comes to haptic perception, it is usually about using fingertips or the palm to investigate a product or obtain information via the Internet on a computer.

In an Indian study, the need to touch products in the physical store environment associated with shopping was investigated in detail (Abhishek et al., 2013). The purpose of this study was to propose a categorization of products based on low, moderate, or high degree of haptic touch based on Indian consumers' sensitivity and preferences.

The study was conducted in three stages, where the first stage covered the observations of the products that could be applicable. The second step meant that consumers and their degree of contact with various products were observed in the shopping environment; thereafter, in the third step, they were asked to answer a questionnaire in which the responses would make it possible to classify the products on the basis of low, moderate, or high degree of touch.

The results showed that six products, clothes, bed linens, soft toys, cell phones, sofas, and apples, were classified as the highest rated and therefore required a high degree of touch. Thereafter followed products such as oranges, digital cameras, cushions, rugs, and tomatoes, which were the next highest, that is, required a moderate degree of touch. When it came to the lowest grade of touch, it included products such as electrical appliances, glassware, household products, pens, and other kinds of accessories.

One of the study's conclusions was that consumers want to touch both soft and hard products, whether it is an orange or a mobile phone, because other product attributes do not provide enough information about the quality of the product. This can apply to properties like brand name or price, where the haptic touch can provide the information that consumers' want and which are available by feeling or handling the actual product. This is probably the main reason why product categories such as fruits and vegetables are classified as products that require a high or moderate degree of touch

> Mobiles, clothing, sofas, and apples are examples of products that require a high degree of touch.

An experimental study examined how three-dimensional virtual touch via a computer and its software, by means of haptic interfaces and force feedback, in the interactive marketing of a car would affect consumers' haptic perception (Jin, 2011). Particularly in the computer context, haptic perception is all about using your hands and fingers for interaction between computers and humans. The haptic perception includes how a computer user experiences the shape and the structure that is felt when one virtually "touches" the digital object, which in this case was a three-dimensional model of a car.

During the experiment, the haptic interface together with the force feedback was introduced; and when respondents used the handle, which could be controlled in three directions—left-right, forward-backward, and up-down—the car's engine responded and gave a force feedback in the handle, which respondents could feel through the hands and fingers. Furthermore, the force feedback gave a number of other effects, which meant that respondents perceived the structure of the highway through jolts and bumps.

The results showed that respondents with a high *need for touch* (*NFT*) experienced a more positive product evaluation and showed a stronger brand connection when force feedback through the handle was introduced, as a stimulus, as opposed to when it was not present in the experiment. Similarly, respondents with a low need for touch experienced a more positive product evaluation and showed a stronger brand connection when force feedback through the handle did not occur. It shows that the individual differences that exist between individuals regarding the need for touch has significant effects on how a product can be perceived and therefore also practical implications for marketers in terms of sensory experiences in virtual shopping environments online.

It is increasingly common to use the so-called haptic displays to touch digital objects using the hands and fingers, which then take place with the help of something like a pen. When a user makes movements with the pen and the tip touches an object, the pen registers a resistance to the movement, as the corresponding real objects would do.

These displays provide the opportunity to orient oneself in a virtual environment, obtain information, and perform the acts required. Today, it is possible to explore the shape, location, and size of different objects, as well as characteristics such as friction, hardness, weight, and surface structure. But often the haptic perception is not enough, which is why this is often supplemented with visual information on a screen.

The Interaction between Vision and Touch

Research shows that the interaction between different senses has an impact on human perception and the experience of an object or a product. Some researchers believe that when the senses such as vision and touch interact with each other, different stimuli are received, to a greater degree, by one of the senses in comparison with the other. Furthermore, it is widely believed that the visual system may be considered as a stronger sense than the tactile sense when it comes to receiving sensory information.

In a study with glass and its volume, Krishna (2006) examined whether the sense of sight or the tactile sense was more dominant when it came to comparing two different types of glasses. The study used a lower and wider glass and a higher and narrower glass, but both contained the same volume. The first study examined only sight in order to determine which glass could be considered to have the greatest volume, and it appeared that the higher and narrower glass was considered to have the largest volume.

In the second study, where both sight and touch were examined, it was found that the higher and narrower glass was considered to have the largest volume. In the third study, in which only the sense of touch was examined and the participants wore a blindfold, the result was the opposite, namely, that the lower and wider glass was considered to have the largest volume.

Subsequently, an additional substudy was conducted to study the significance of vision and touch in connection with a cinema visit, which included ordering popcorn. It turns out that during the film screening, the sense of sight is completely preoccupied with watching the movie while the tactile sense is used to hold the popcorn. The results showed that many moviegoers felt that a lower but wider package contained more popcorn in comparison with a taller and thinner package.

One conclusion was that movie theaters should choose a shorter and wider package, because such is perceived as providing more popcorn and will increase customer satisfaction and increase the value of the cinema experience.

In research, it is believed that sight and touch together often dominate consumers' perceptions and experiences of various products in real life. Furthermore, it is deemed that sight and touch together provide the most detailed information about different products, especially in terms of consumer fashion choices. It is thought that consumers typically rely more on tactile stimuli when a blazer is to be evaluated, taking into account material characteristics, such as structure, temperature, and weight. For that reason, it is generally assumed that the conscious or unconscious feelings that arise by touching and feeling clothing with the hands and fingers play a prominent role in creating an impression of the products.

> When it comes to consumers' choice of dress, most people rely on more tactile stimuli than visual stimuli, for example, when a blazer is to be evaluated.

A Canadian study looked at the importance of visual and tactile stimuli upon the purchase of denim jeans and its impact on consumers' perceptions of the products (Rahman, 2012). One of the arguments for the study was that previously there was a lack of studies that analyzed the significance of the visual and tactile stimuli when buying clothes. The aim of the study was to identify both cognitive and sensory feedback based on product-specific stimuli, such as color and fabric. The respondents included 42 female students aged 18 to 27 years from the university and college in Ontario.

The study was conducted through in-depth interviews, and each interview lasted between 45 minutes and an hour and a half. During the interview, the respondents were given the opportunity to see and feel seven different pairs of jeans. To avoid bias, the brand names and the price tags were removed from the jeans and other recognizable identifiers were covered with tape.

Then the survey was conducted in three steps, where the first step was to assess the quality and value of the jeans merely on the basis of visual characteristics. Thereafter, in the second stage, the tactile properties were assessed based on touch and interaction with the jeans through the hands and fingers. Finally, the product quality and price were assessed based on past experiences and knowledge of the respondents.

The results indicated that a tactile assessment, that is, how the jeans are perceived, was based on the structure, which was judged to be the most important stimulus. This means that the structure is considered to be an important indicator of quality when it comes to evaluating these products. Furthermore, it appeared that many respondents used their hands and fingers to feel or investigate the structure and thereby assess, for example, thermophysiological (heat) or sensory comfort (softness) and sustainability (thickness, robustness, or weight) of the jeans.

One of the study's conclusions was that before a final product choice is made by consumers, it is considered important to feel and touch the texture of the jeans. This is regardless of whether there is a consistency between the tactile and visual assessments that are done of the quality of the product before the final product choice.

With regard to the interaction between vision and touch, an Indian study showed that sensory information via touch was more important than visual information when it came to product evaluation and selection of the product (Balaji et al., 2011). This applied particularly to the impact on consumer attitudes and purchase intentions, where a tactile evaluation of the tangible products, such as tissue, led to a more positive evaluation. In this case, the respondents preferred touch to obtain relevant information on product characteristics, which was expected because the products were considered to be "haptic" products that required contact with the hands and fingers.

Unlike previous studies, the researchers argued that the results of their study did not support the previously stated hypothesis that only the individual differences when it came to the need to touch products (need for touch) influenced the sensory information that consumers are asking for.

The researchers argued instead that it is the product's/object's properties and characteristics that are crucial, especially when the products can be said to be haptic in nature, which can be considered to apply to many tangible products, such as home furnishings, apparel, paper, chairs, fabrics, etc., where the surface structure is a prominent feature.

One of the conclusions of the study was that the object's or product's characteristics might be more important than the individual differences between individuals in connection with the product evaluation. As an argument for this, it has been presented that tangible products are mainly evaluated using tactile information and then most individuals use touch with the hands and fingers to get the relevant sensory information in connection with a purchase decision.

As previously stated, research shows that consumers' product evaluation is positively influenced by tactile interaction with different products. But whether the same applies to products that consumers touch over shorter periods of time is not clear. In a study by Marlow and Jansson-Boyd (2011), this relationship was examined in more detail in respect to fast moving consumer goods.

The researchers chose to use the visual and tactile stimuli for products such as biscuits and soap by manipulating the surface structure of the actual packaging. Three types of structure were used on the outside of either a biscuit or a soapbox, and three different samples were tested during the experiment. The three biscuits or soapboxes were presented visually to the respondents, followed by a blind tactile evaluation of the three structures. Next, the respondents were asked to make a combined tactile and visual evaluation of the three different boxes, each with its own structure.

The results showed that consumers' perceptions of the packaging of the fast moving consumer goods were influenced, to a greater extent, visually as opposed to tactile. It appears that tactile sensory information can be part of a consumer's product evaluation, but it cannot be considered to be as significant as visual information. Rather, it appears that when it comes to fast moving consumer goods, which are found in grocery stores, consumers do not normally spend any length of time feeling the products but rely more on the visual information available at the point of purchase.

It was also clear from the results that tactile information mostly influences the overall attractiveness of the package concerning biscuits or soap. Furthermore, support cannot be found for the general notion that tactile information may be more influential than the visual information, but rather it shows that the visual experience is more prominent.

One conclusion of the study was that the importance of tactile touch probably varies with the type of product, which also had to do with the amount of time consumers spent on product evaluation. When it comes to touch, this often occurs for longer periods for products such as clothing, home furnishings, or furniture, as previously discussed.

Tactile Symbolism

It is believed in research that skin is to be considered as a powerful tool in marketing with a strong symbolic representation. In this context, the body or skin is viewed as an essential strategic element to emphasize the emotional aspects of a large number of products, services, or websites. Often the body and the self are combined to produce the image of the good life, where pleasure and sexuality are included as natural ingredients.

Furthermore, three metaphors for the skin are mentioned, namely, the skin as a container, the skin as a projection surface, and the skin as the sender. In the case of the skin as a container, this is about how a person, for example, with tattoos, communicates his/her innermost self with the surroundings in the form of different messages, as symbols of the self. In advertising, the skin is often used to express body standards, shaping an appropriate image, or taking responsibility for one's own body (Patterson and Schroeder, 2010).

> To use the skin as a symbol of the tactile sense is increasingly common in advertising.

When it comes to skin as a projection surface, this is about how a person's skin can present itself from a visual perspective. In this context, the body and the skin are seen as a communicative and unifying element in a social culture rather than as an isolated event, such as youth and beauty as symbols of the individual self. This applies to both women's and men's bodies, which have increasingly come to be seen as ideals according to shape, size, and weight.

The naked body has been used for many years in advertising, where male nudity symbolizes masculine strength. But there are also examples of how a male body can symbolize the well-being of the ideal body, as the following example from a Swedish grocery retailer, ICA, showed in 2013.

> The now famous ICA- Stig was depicted in an advertisement for the food chain's "Take a green year" campaign, completely naked except for a rhubarb leaf that hid his privates. According to Håkan Sjöstrand, marketing director, the purpose of the campaign was to highlight and increase the interest in the link between fruits and vegetables and a healthy body. It was not a matter of striving for the ideal well-exercised body, but rather to point to the importance of fruits and vegetables for all people.

When it comes to male nudity, it has been interpreted in different ways during different decades. In the early 1900s, for example, male muscles symbolized the raw strength that was tied to the working class, whereas intellectual manhood was symbolized by a thin ascetic body. When it comes to female nudity, during recent decades, this has automatically been associated with sexism but also with objectification.

Finally, when it comes to skin as the sender, this is about how a person's skin can be seen as something valuable, which in turn can be converted into economic, cultural, or social capital. In this context, the body or skin is seen as something that can be recreated to, in turn, give expression to a certain desired appearance, such as through facial surgeries, diets, or personal style. In this way, the body can also be seen not only as an object but also as an event within the framework of a sensory experience.

REFERENCES

Abhishek, A., Sinha, P.K. and Vohra, N. (2013), "Role of haptic touch in shopping," *Decision*, 40, 3:153.

Ackerman, J.M., Nocera, C.C. and Bargh, J.A. (2010), "Incidental haptic sensations influence social judgments and decisions," *Science*, 328:1712–1715.

Balaji, M.S., Raghavan, S. and Subhash, J. (2011), "Role of tactile and visual inputs in product evaluation: a multisensory perspective," *Asia Pacific Journal of Marketing and Logistics*, 23, 4:513–530.

Brown McCabe, D. and Nowlis, S. (2003), "The effect of examining actual products or product descriptions on consumer preference," *Journal of Consumer Psychology*, 13, 4:431–439.

Citrin, A.V., Stern, D.E., Spangenberg, E.R. and Clark, M.J. (2003), "Consumer need for tactile input: an internet retail challenge," *Journal of Business Research*, 56, 11:915–922.

Gibson, J.J. (1966), *The senses as perceptual systems*, Boston: Harvard Business School.

Hertenstein, M.J. and Keltner, D. (2011), "Gender and the communication of emotion via touch," *Sex Roles*, 64:70–80.

Holbrook, M.B. (1983), "On the importance of using real products in research on merchandising strategy," *Journal of Retailing*, 59, 1:4–20.

Hornik, J. (1992), "Tactile stimulation and consumer response," *Journal of Consumer Research*, 19, December:449–458.

Hultén, B. (2012), "Sensory cues and shopper's touching behavior: the case of IKEA," *International Journal of Retail & Distribution Management*, 40, 4:273–289.

Hultén, B. (2013), "Sensory cues as in-store innovations: their impact on shopper approaches and touch behaviour," *Journal of Innovation Management*, 1, 1:17–37.

Jin, S.-A.A. (2011), "The impact of 3D virtual haptics in marketing," *Psychology and Marketing*, 28, 3:240–255.

Johansson, R. and Krnjajic, A. (2012), *Touched......seduced? A study of interpersonal touching in the retail environment*, Bachelor Thesis, Kalmar: Linneaus University, School of Business and Economics.

Klatzky, R.L. (2010), "Touch: a gentle tutorial with implications for marketing." I: Krishna, A. (ed.) *Sensory marketing: research on the sensuality of products*, New York: Routledge, p. 33–47.

Klatzky, R.L. and Lederman, S.J. (1993), *Toward a computational model of constraint-driven exploration and haptic object identification*, London: Perception.

Krishna, A. (2006), "Interaction of senses: the effect of vision versus touch on the elongation bias," *Journal of Consumer Research*, 32, March:557–566.

Krishna, A. (2010), *Sensory marketing: research on the sensuality of products*, New York, NY: Routledge Academic.

Marlow, N. and Jansson-Boyd, C.V. (2011), "To touch or not to touch; that is the question. Should consumers always be encouraged to touch products, and does it always alter product perception?" *Psychology & Marketing*, 28, 3:256–266.

Pattersson, M. and Schroeder, J. (2010), "Borderlines: skin, tattoos and consumer culture theory," *Marketing Theory*, 10, 3:253–267.

Peck, J. and Childers, T.L. (2003), "To have and to hold: the influence of haptic information on product judgments," *Journal of Marketing*, 67, April:35–48.

Peck, J. and Childers, T.L. (2004), *Self-report and behavioral measures in product evaluation and haptic information: is what I say how I feel? Association for Consumer Research*, Working Paper Track.

Peck, J. and Childers T.L. (2010), "Effects of sensory factors on consumer behaviour: if it tastes, smells, sounds and feels like a duck, then it must be a ..." I: Haugtvedt, C.P., Herr, P.M. and Kardes, F.R. (ed.) *Handbook of consumer psychology*, New York: Taylor and Francis Group, p. 193–219.

Peck, J. and Wiggins, J. (2006), "It just feels good: customers' affective response to touch and its influence on persuasion," *Journal of Marketing*, 70, October:56–69.

Phillips, F., Donoho, A., Keep, W.W., Mayberry, W., McCann, J.M., Shapiro, K. and Smith, D. (1997), "Electronically connecting retailers and customers: interim summary of an expert roundtable." I: Peterson, R.A. (ed.) *Electronic marketing and the consumer*, Thousand Oaks: Sage Publications, p. 101–122.

Rahman, O. (2012), "The influence of visual and tactile inputs on denim jeans evaluation," *International Journal of Design*, 6, 1:11–25.

Spence, C. and Gallace, A. (2008), "Making sense of touch." I: Chatterjee, E. (ed.) *Touch in museums: policy and practice in object handling*, Oxford: Berg, p. 21–40.

Williams, E.W. and Bargh, J.A. (2008), "Experiencing physical warmth promotes interpersonal warmth," *Science*, 322:606–607.

Workman, J.E. (2009), "Fashion consumer groups, gender, and need for touch," *Clothing and Textiles Research Journal*, 28, 2:126–139.

9 The Sense of Taste

This chapter analyzes and discusses the sense of taste, which is considered to be one of the strongest senses of the human's five senses. The scientific notions about the fundamental role of the sense of taste are addressed initially with respect to both physiological characteristics and psychological aspects.

Thereafter, three categories of influential factors for the sense of taste, which relate to the importance of the societal culture, the service environment, and the brands, are presented. Considering this background, it is discussed how various factors affect individuals' affections, cognitions, and their actual behaviors in the different buying and consumption processes.

THE TASTE CONCEPT

The Two-Parted Taste

Taste as a concept has long fascinated scientists in different disciplines, such as philosophy, psychology, and sociology, when it comes to understanding the importance of the sense of taste to a person's feelings, thoughts, and behaviors. In today's global consumer culture, where a high degree of individualization dominates many consumers' behaviors, often with strong hedonic elements, the need for aesthetic aspects in marketing is of increasing importance.

Hedonic products refer to goods and services that give consumers a more aesthetic and experience-based value in comparison with everyday products, which essentially offer a more functional and instrumental value. When it comes to experience-based consumption, this means that hedonic products are more related to factors such as shape, color, appearance, style, and texture, even if most products contain more or less hedonic as well as functional elements.

> In connection with taste, it is natural to speak of aesthetic values, as opposed to just functional values of products such as cars, home furnishings, food, and fashion. The aesthetic values have to do with the product dimensions that can

> be attributed to joy, appearance, and enjoyment and can be related to good taste. Studies have shown that individuals prefer aesthetic values before functional values, which is why aesthetic aspects are more relevant than ever for consumers' choice of products.

This means that both internal and external taste have prominent roles in people's consumption when it comes to satisfying the self and achieving quality of life. With internal taste, it is meant gastronomic or physical taste, and with external, it is meant aesthetic taste (Figure 9.1).

Already early in the classical humanistic tradition of philosophical aesthetics there was a strong link between aesthetics and the physical sense of taste. The latter was regarded early as the model of good judgment and together with aesthetics it was considered as a universal and obvious prerequisite for people's actions. A virtuous person, therefore, showed a sense of taste both in his/her behavior and appearance, which meant to show good taste when it came to food or clothing. But gradually, the sense of taste lost its privileged place in a purely aesthetic context. Especially in comparison

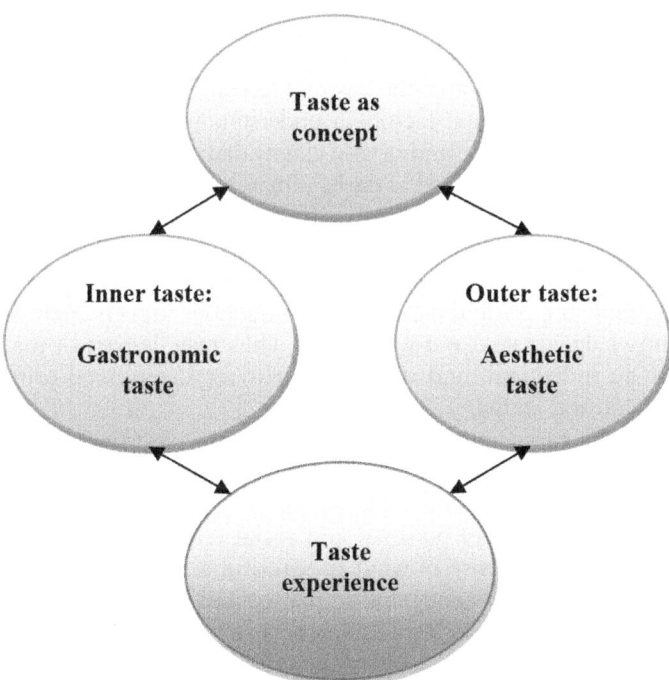

Figure 9.1 The Concept of Taste

with the senses such as sight and hearing, which were considered to be cleaner as senses when it came to being able to convey a nobler, aesthetic well-being to humans (Kant, 1790).

The old saying that one cannot argue about taste did not emanate from the beginning from the fact that taste was regarded as an individual, private affair (Gronow, 1997). Instead, it was thought that taste—or good taste—was obvious to everyone and did not need to be discussed. Instead, one assumed that what felt or tasted good was also both good and beautiful for every human being. In this way, a person cannot fail to distinguish the ugly or beautiful or what could be regarded as right or wrong.

Furthermore, it was considered that taste could not be seen as rational (or logical), which is why it was not possible to formulate some maxims or rules regarding taste. In this way, tradition ensured that every person had at his/her disposal good taste, which was expressed by one's conduct and decisions. Taste, therefore, came to be regarded as a great factor to identify social differences in the societal culture.

> *Good taste is determined by each person according to personal taste, and every individual can develop his/her own taste.*

In the French philosopher Bourdieu's theory of social differences, taste and legitimate good taste constitute the basic concepts. Both food preferences and table manners are important factors in understanding the lifestyle and tastes related to social classes. The author also claims that the taste of the ruling class in a society is generally regarded as the legitimate taste. But against this is raised the objection that this does not represent genuine good taste, because there cannot just exist one genuine good taste in a societal culture (Bourdieu, 1984).

Furthermore, Bourdieu believes that every person, in addition to financial resources, also has cultural capital, which includes aspects such as experiences, knowledge, tastes, and worldview. Thus taste is part of the cultural capital of an individual, and it is thought to be determined primarily by social and cultural status.

In a person's consumption of different products and brands, it is believed that cultural capital becomes objectified by the choices made and that taste is deemed to contribute to the understanding of peer pressure and contributes to the construction of personal and social relationships. "Good taste" in fashion indicates a sense of what is beautiful and appropriate, and people with good taste also understand quality and simplicity. According to DiMaggio (1987), taste can be considered as an "identity marker that facilitates interactions" in personal and social contexts.

Other researchers have argued that taste could be likened to a cultural concept and stands as ideals of human emancipation and education.

According to this view, taste would not be predetermined by birth or social origin but could be embraced through learning without being dependent on each person's social status.

Anyone who can demonstrate good taste when it comes to behavior or conduct is then to be considered as a gentleman or a "gentle woman."

Therefore, that which has come to be known as good taste has gradually increasingly come to be associated with the aesthetics of everyday life and popular culture for the vast majority of people and less on high culture in contemporary society. The sense of taste has two important dimensions when it comes to conveying the flavor and sensory experiences of a brand, namely, the aesthetic taste and the gastronomic (or physical) taste.

The Gastronomic Flavor

In everyday conversations, the inner or gastronomic taste is intimately connected with the taste experiences that a dish or a restaurant visit can give rise to. It is considered that taste sensations, like different physiological and psychological reactions to food and food products, have great importance in people's everyday lives. Not only do they affect our well-being when it comes to the possibility for physical survival, but they also give rise to emotional and social satisfaction (Krishna and Elder, 2010). Considering this background, it is not surprising that in Sweden billions of dollars are spent each year on the consumption of perishables—the biggest cost in an annual household budget—to create dining experiences.

In the dining experience, it is considered that taste, sound, smell, and feel (haptic) of the food constitute the most important elements. It turns out that the meal is the third most time-consuming activity, which also includes cooking, and the single most important economic activity for many people. This means that research on taste should be of greater interest in marketing research than has been the case.

> *Humans are the only creatures that actually flavor their food with the help of different kinds of spices and herbs.*

The physical taste is developed in interaction with the olfactory and tactile senses. When one drinks a glass of wine, how the wine tastes is perceived both through the feeling in the mouth and on the tongue as well as the aroma of the wine through the nose, which means that taste interacts with the sense of smell in this case. Tastes can have both a positive and a negative valence, which refers to how attractive (expressed through positive valence) or repulsive (as expressed by negative valence) the actual taste is for an individual. The term is used to characterize the emotions and feelings an individual may have, depending on how attractive or unattractive the actual taste is.

The Aesthetic Taste

In experience-based consumption, where hedonic elements are crucial to an individual's total sensory experience, aesthetics and taste are leading concepts. Hirschman and Holbrook (1982) drew attention early on to how fantasies, emotions, and multi-sensory aspects are the basis for an individual's consumption experience.

Furthermore, researchers such as Schmitt and Simonson (1997) pointed out that everyone's personal taste influences our decisions when it comes to choosing good friends, decorating the house, or selecting which restaurant to visit. Despite this, research in consumer behavior and marketing has put little emphasis on how the hedonic elements and especially taste can help to increase the understanding of human emotions, cognitions, and behaviors (Hoyer and Stokburger-Sauer, 2012).

Taste is often defined in popular science contexts as a person's personal attitude or reaction to a social context or an aesthetic phenomenon based on what is considered to be good or bad. Moreover, taste is also defined as what might be suitable or beautiful in different contexts within film, art, literature, or fashion. Within consumer behavior, by contrast, good taste has often come to be defined by what is decided by professional experts in the areas mentioned.

This has led some researchers to question whether ordinary consumers in the masses really have "good taste." On the other hand, it is argued that a consumer's good taste can contribute to the creation of a hedonic value for a product or a brand. When it comes to assessing a sofa at Ikea, two people can have completely opposite assessments. But neither of the two can be considered right or wrong, and both are entitled to their own taste.

In the academic literature, the term aesthetics is generally used in two ways, namely to link a theory of beauty and an individual's sense of beauty. In the latter case, this has to do with the individual's aesthetic sensibility and is seen as closely linked to the individual's good taste. It may be noted that in the mid-1700s, taste as a concept came to replace beauty as a concept, as the most prominent term in aesthetics.

One conclusion from the research is that aesthetic taste is neither entirely subjective nor entirely objective, but contains elements of both subjectivity and objectivity. Furthermore, one conclusion is that the role of the sense of taste in marketing, regarding both aesthetic and gastronomic taste, has been overlooked for a long time. This may be considered as a glaring lack when it comes to understanding and increasing the understanding of how companies can create taste sensations of a brand.

THE FUNDAMENTAL ROLE OF THE SENSE OF TASTE

Physiological Properties

It is the tongue, with its many taste buds, that conveys the taste sensations that an individual perceives and experiences in his/her consumption (Figure 9.2). However, there are also the taste buds in the throat and the palate that contribute to this, and an adult is estimated to have about ten thousand taste buds on the tongue. It has been shown that the best taste ability is found in infants, who even have taste buds on the insides of their cheeks.

Taste buds, in and of themselves, have a structure similar to an onion or a volcano, with between 50 to 100 individual cells in each taste bud. These cells send information to the brain, based on, for example, the food's chemical qualities and composition, which form the basis for the sense of taste. In a comparison between men and women, it was evident that women have more taste buds and are more sensitive to taste than men. This could indicate that women can actually be said to have better taste than men, just based on the fact that they have more taste buds in the mouth.

A person's taste buds are exposed daily to a heavy load and quickly become worn out. It is believed that they are worn down in a week, after

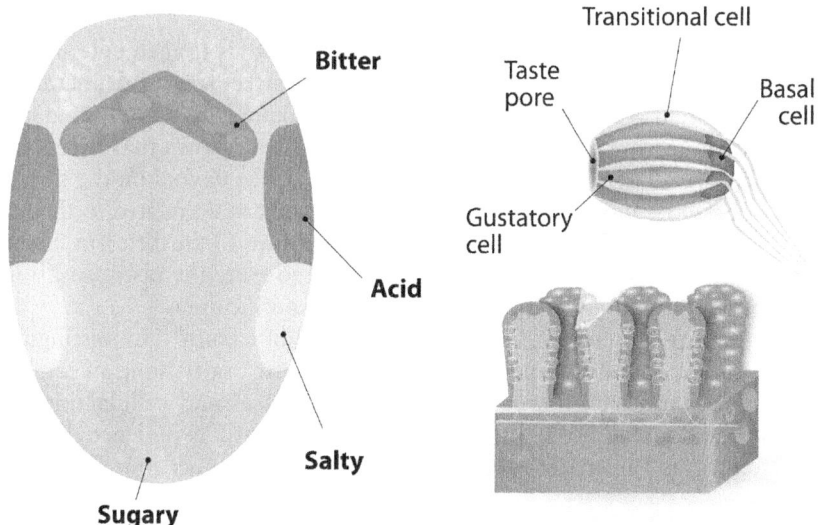

Figure 9.2 The Structure of the Tongue
Source: Shutterstock

which new ones replace them. This process is ongoing throughout life but decreases during five- to ten-years of age, which means that the taste ability deteriorates. This means that each person then needs to feel an intense taste in the mouth in order to reach the same high experience level as before for a brand, for example.

This phenomenon may help explain why older people appreciate the strong flavors of drinks like cognac, whiskey, or beer, which often younger people, such as children and teenagers, perceive as too flavorful. The opposite can be considered valid for candy and other sweets, which older people do not feel are equally tasty as a child would, because a child's tongue has not yet become desensitized after years of taking sugar. But it can also happen that a person can lose his/her flavor abilities for a long time, not only due to increased age, but also because of disease, as the following example shows:

> *In 2010, Diana Appleyard in the United Kingdom had a bad cold with a runny nose, itchy eyes, and constant coughing. When the cold was gone, she discovered that she had a severe side effect, which meant that she had lost the sense of smell and taste. After two months, they still had not come back, and Diana began to get desperate. She visited her family doctor, who gave her an antihistamine and nasal spray and asked her to start smelling and sniffing at everything even though she could not smell anything, to train the receptors in the nose. After two years, Diana could smell and taste again and eventually became healthy again.*

It is widely believed that certain parts of a person's tongue take up different flavors of bitterness, saltiness, sourness, sweetness, and umami. It is also apparent from the illustrations of the tongue where the boundaries are located; however, from neuroscientific studies, it shows that this is not the case. Instead, it seems that the distribution of the flavors on the tongue occurs in a more uniform manner, which is thought to be related to the fact that the nerve fibers in the taste buds seem to capture all the different flavors at the same time. For this reason, it is possible to trace the taste sensations to all parts of the tongue and not just to some specific areas.

It is further assumed in research that a person cannot fully distinguish five clean flavors (or taste perceptions) such as bitter, salty, sour, sweet, and umami, because five different biochemical processes and cellular interactions in the body do not exist. Umami relates to a taste experience that can be described as "aromatic" or "delicious," unlike the other four flavors.

> *A cup of coffee never tastes as good as it smells, because 80 percent of what we think we physically taste reaches us through the olfactory receptors in the nose!*

It is believed that it is the combination of these five pure flavors that is the basis for a taste experience of everything from chocolate and milk to ciabatta and wine. The fact that a person can discern a sophisticated taste is deemed to have to do with the sensory input coming through the other senses besides taste. This is reflected by how a dish smells (sense of smell), how spicy or hot a dish is as well as its texture (sense of touch), how the meal is presented on the plate (sense of sight), and how the dish sounds when chewed (sense of sound).

In research, this is explained by the concept of *synesthesia*, which describes how a person's senses cooperate with each other and work together. In a person, each sense has its own connection to the brain and they run parallel to each other. This means that in some situations, a connection can be crossed by another, which happens when, for example, the eyes see a green color and the smell of freshly cut grass is elicited. Likewise, the sight of a yellow lemon can elicit a sour taste sensation.

Most people have some form of synesthesia, more or less prominent. It is believed that people with strong synesthesia are different from others in that they can express, for example, that "a color can taste," "food can be heard," or "the sound feels." Sensory information from other senses may therefore influence the taste experience of an individual, which means that taste may also have to do with how it smells, sounds, or looks when a dish is to be consumed.

Psychological Aspects

In research, the sense of taste is considered to be one of man's strongest emotional senses, which often finds expression in everyday life. Then verbal expressions are used to illustrate the good taste, as "it is a matter of taste," "it can become a bitter history," or that someone is "sweet" or "sour." It is further believed that every person's mood and frame of mind are affected by the natural taste of what one eats and the needs that exist at the moment. In both work and daily life, much-needed coffee breaks are taken during which various beverages and foods help to reduce stress and improve well-being. But there are also situations where an increased intake, for example, of water and soft drinks can lead to decreased well-being, as the following example illustrates.

> *Some experts claim that the recent trend among young people to carry a water bottle in hand in order to constantly drink is a form of collective panic. There is no scientific evidence that a young person must constantly drink, if he she does not feel thirsty. Both elite athletes and amateurs do not drink as the advertising agencies and sports beverage manufacturer's ads command, but rather they allow the brain to control their thirst. Then the problem with the kidneys and spending time for constant drink-and-pee breaks is also avoided.*

In marketing, where taste plays a crucial role in the perception of a brand, it turns out that the difference between perceived and remembered joy has great significance for the consumer's decision-making (Rozin and Hormes, 2010). Most people consult their long-term memory or the sensory memory when they make decisions about what type of food to choose when they stand in a store or what dish to choose when they are at a restaurant. This is because a person does not have direct access to the latest experience with the food or the dish. This makes daily decisions generally based on the recollections of the previous experiences.

In this research, the relationship between remembered and perceived joy is analyzed based on how consumers perceive and experience hedonic experiences. With hedonic experience in this context, it means a pleasurable experience, which generally can be considered to characterize the taste experience of food and beverages. Three basic principles have been identified, which show the distortion of the experience that occurs when an individual is to remember the actual experience.

The high point of the enjoyment experience is the most positive point in the experience, and the experience's endpoint has been the dominant influence on the recollection of the experience. It turns out that the endpoint is often noticeable if it takes too long to get the bill after an hour of an enjoyable restaurant visit, which then affects the recollection. Within the framework of the experience, it also appears that the recollection does not take into account how long the experience lasts, that is, its duration, which is why one seems to remember the events but not their duration. This is thought to be able to explain why repetitive or continuous experiences appear to be remembered as isolated events.

Rode et al. (2007) studied remembered joy when it has applied to culinary experiences. One of their conclusions was that there was strong support that an experience's duration is neglected. This was illustrated in that even if an individual took twice as much of his/her favorite dish, which in itself probably increases the perceived pleasure, it had no detectable effect on the remembered joy.

> *An individual remembers a delicious wine regardless of whether it is sipped two or eight times by the taste experience.*

It was further assumed that an individual who prefers his/her favorite dish before any other actually probably already has a higher expectation because the recollection is already in place. This means that the recollection does not help the individual to eat the same favorite dish twice, which would be tantamount to only eating it once. But if a new dish would be preferred, before the favorite dish, even if both the expectation and the experience were less positive, a new positive recollection of the experience would be created.

The Interaction with Other Senses

Research has highlighted the importance of the interaction of the sense of taste with the other senses, which is mainly reflected in the influence this has on the consumer's taste perception and taste experience.

When it comes to scent, this sense is considered to be one of the most prominent with regard to understanding and perceiving taste. The reason that scent plays an important role for the taste experience is the proximate placement of the nose to the mouth. A person smells the food when it is outside the mouth and does it again when he or she chews the food. It is considered that the combination of taste and smell gives rise to the concept of aroma.

In the interaction between the sense of taste and the sense of sight, research has highlighted the importance of colors, which turns out to have a significant influence on the taste experience. In a study by DuBose et al. (1980), it was evident that the fruit drink that participants got to taste could be identified by the aroma by just one of the five participants. But when the participants saw the color of the drink, all the participants could recognize the sort. There is a general understanding that increased flavor intensity is due to increased color intensity, which suggests that the sense of sight interacts with the sense of taste.

In a recent study, it was shown that in consumers' evaluation of orange juice, it was the color that was important to distinguish the flavors, whereas the brand name was primarily used to determine the individual preferences for the orange juice in question. This study showed how the exterior, aesthetic stimuli had a direct impact on consumers' taste experience.

Even when it comes to the sense of sound, there is interplay with the sense of taste, which Zampini and Spence (2004) demonstrated in a study. In the study, they changed the frequency and the volume of the sound that a potato chip emits when one chews, and it was found that participants felt that the higher the sound, the fresher the potato chips. The study was conducted as an experiment in which participants sat in a sound safe booth in front of a microphone, and at the same time they wore headphones so they could listen to their own crunching. In this way, the researchers were able to change the frequency and sound level during the experiment, which came to influence the participants' perceptions of the potato chip's quality.

Finally, the interaction of the sense of touch with the sense of taste should be mentioned, which proved to influence taste perception. In a series of experiments, Krishna and Morrin (2008) demonstrated how the shape of a disposable glass, i.e., the haptic design, could have an impact on consumers' taste perception of the water to be drunk. The study compared a solid, hard disposable glass with a delicate, weak glass, which resulted in the water drunk from the solid, hard disposable glass tasting better than the water from the other glass.

Thus various studies show that a positive taste experience of eating and drinking is about interaction and symbiosis with the other senses. Even how the food and drink are presented is of importance for a taste experience, in the same way that the environment can play a crucial role.

INFLUENTIAL FACTORS FOR THE SENSE OF TASTE

In research, three main categories have been studied as influential factors when it comes to the sense of taste. It must be added that taste is undoubtedly the stimuli that has been studied the least, especially in retail and marketing research. Figure 9.3 sets out the factors following the SEB-model that may be linked to the influence that taste has on an individual's affections, cognitions, and actual behaviors in the buying and consumption processes.

First, the societal culture, as an influential factor, is addressed in relation to the different preferences on the individual and group level, as well as taste symbolism. Second, the service environment (or the surrounding), as an influential factor, is addressed in relation to the taste stimuli, taste perception, and taste as aesthetics. Third, the brand, as an influential factor, is addressed in relation to taste stimuli, taste perception, and taste symbolism.

SOCIETAL CULTURE

Individual Preferences

In each society's culture, gastronomic (or physical) and aesthetic taste are individual and personal, which means that there is no universal taste. Instead, the sense of taste is an expression of the diversity and uniqueness

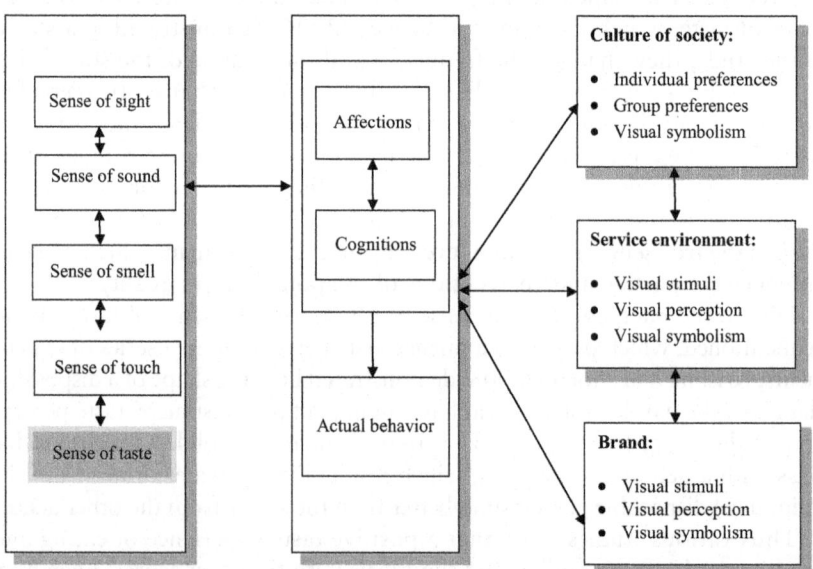

Figure 9.3 The Sense of Smell and the SEB-model

that characterizes different societal cultures, emphasizing the importance of individual preferences in order to create a positive taste experience of a brand.

The sense of taste is often called the *intimate sense*, because it is not possible to physically try on something that is outside the human body or outside the mouth. Research suggests that a person's taste is totally individual, just like our fingerprints, and already in the womb, a child's future tastes are developed. These depend on the composition of the saliva, which in turn is based on genes and heredity, along with the diet a person has. This is expressed in that individuals who prefer salty foods have salty saliva, compared with other individuals, and they are more accustomed to higher sodium content in the mouth.

> People develop individual tastes, something that is often called personal style.

In a study at the London University College, the extent to which taste preferences are due to hereditary factors was examined using five thousand British twins aged between 8- to 11-years-old. The results showed that nearly 80 percent of the preferences could be attributed to heredity and genes. It was also found that genetic factors also played a crucial role in explaining people's reluctance to try or eat different kinds of food. When it comes to trying and eating protein-rich foods, such as beans and fish, this was influenced almost 80 percent by the genes of a person. Similarly, the genes influenced whether a person tried to eat fruit (50 percent) and vegetables (nearly 40 percent). Finally, it should be mentioned that the influence of genetics does not amount to more than 20 percent in terms of trying to eat desserts.

It was also found that the food that children have the opportunity to eat while growing up creates the food preferences that have importance later in life. One of the conclusions of the study was that the results apply to girls and boys and that food preferences could be explained to one-fifth with the help of learning and the environment, whereas four-fifths could be explained with the help of genes.

It is generally accepted in research that a person's sensory properties determine the choice between two brands X and Z, because X is preferred to Z. When it comes to taste, with respect to both aesthetic and gastronomic taste, a person's sensory qualities play a decisive role in the choices made. But the same relationship is also deemed to be valid for the sense of sound and the choice, for example, of the music genre or the sense of sight and the choice between, for example, two garments, where design plays a prominent role in an individual's final choice. This issue is of great importance in daily life and is of interest to both economists and marketers when it comes to understanding how consumer choice is influenced by various sensory properties.

It also turns out that there are differences between individuals with regard to the time spent—and the importance given to—to experience the moment, recollection memory, and being able to create expectations. It is considered that individuals generally make a choice between increasing expectations for an upcoming event at the price of having less time to "consume" the memory of the event or reducing the expectations to have more time to remember the event. This can be illustrated with examples where "A fine meal can take two hours, but the memory of the meal may remain for dozens of hours in the coming years" or "The second visit for the lovely meal can create expectations for many hours."

Some researchers believe that individuals differ in this respect and that favoritism of expectations or memory seems to be related to certain, specific areas and cannot be considered as generally occurring. This can be illustrated with an example where some individuals, when they are served three different platters with, for example, vegetables, meat, and potatoes, generally choose to eat their favorite dish first, while others choose to eat their favorite food last. There are also some individuals who do neither. It is widely believed that people have a very open attitude toward food and that most individuals who like or dislike foods or dishes do so because of the prevailing societal culture. There seems not to be some general, innate smell preferences toward food or dishes in societal cultures, but extreme temperatures in the mouth, bitter tastes, and relatively salty or sour tastes create annoyances and aversion to certain foods and certain dishes.

> *The societal culture that people belong to has a strong impact on the individual's taste preferences.*

For some individuals, sweetness is associated with a positive taste experience at a certain level, whereas others associate it to a higher level. Furthermore, it is believed that most individuals dislike sweets through their experiences as they age, unlike the innate negative traits that already exist for some tastes. Examples of the latter are bitter food or bitter coffee as well as ice-cold drinks or dishes flavored with chilies.

But it is also true that many individuals learn to enjoy food and tastes, like those just mentioned, despite the fact that they have some innate sensory properties that are negative toward them. How can this be explained?

Rozin and Hormes (2010) believe that the transformation from aversion to foods and tastes to positive taste preferences is influenced by two special mechanisms. One mechanism is the shift that may occur and that leads to individuals coming to prefer icy drinks, bitter, salty, or very acidic tastes and other irritations in the mouth. From a sensory point of view, it seems that individuals like the experience of the negative, which is regarded as a taste experience in itself. This can be compared to the experience of fear when riding a roller coaster or the experience of sadness when listening to a piece of music.

The second mechanism is considered masochism, that is, a person's enjoyment of a negative experience, which the brain does not regard as threatening. For many individuals, it is a question of the brain controlling the body when we enjoy a vile experience or irritating taste, precisely because it is a question of negative experiences. When it comes to the experience of chili peppers, it shows that for many individuals, the favorite level of burning in the mouth is just below the level when it becomes too painful. There is no doubt that many people experience a joy in pushing themselves to test their limits of what is possible to accomplish and endure.

When it comes to the consumption of food, research discusses how consumers' emotional ability and mood, used to interpret their own emotions by understanding how they affect the consumption of food, influences the choice of food and meals. It may be, for example, impulse eating and calorie intake, which occur precisely because the individual is not consciously aware of the emotional effect and confidence during the actual moment.

This could explain why some individuals eat more when they are depressed, whereas others eat more when they are happy, as well as how special foods can be consumed more in the context of a particular mood. One conclusion is that there is an increased need for studies to elucidate the relationships that can exist when it comes to explaining how emotional ability, mood, and emotional confidence influence the consumption of food.

Male and Female

A limited number of studies in the research on gastronomic taste have analyzed whether there are gender differences between men and women in the experience of tastes, aromas, and textures. In a study of children's perceptions of tastes such as citric acid, caffeine, sodium, and sugar, among children two years old and the age of nine, it was revealed that there were no significant differences between the girls' and the boys' perceptions.

On the other hand, another study showed that women perceived a higher level of sugar in soft drinks, compared with men, who instead perceived a higher level of salt in soups, compared with women. One conclusion that can be drawn is that the few studies that have been done have produced conflicting results, and more research is needed to clarify whether there are any differences.

In a recent study by Michon et al. (2009), women's and men's sensitivity to food was closely investigated. The survey included 274 respondents, including 187 women and 87 men, and the purpose was to demonstrate whether there were differences between the sexes. The researchers were interested in finding out the sensitivity of taste, smell, texture, hardness, and identifying objects in the mouth.

The results showed that there were several significant differences between the sexes in terms of sensitivity. Women were found to have a higher degree of sensitivity to identify bitter tastes ($p = 0.04$); evaluate bitter, sweet, or sour intensity ($p = 0.001$, $p = 0.01$, and $p = 0.03$); identifying scents ($p = 0.001$); and by means of the tongue recognizing an object in the mouth ($p = 0.02$). The men were found to have a higher degree of sensitivity in chewing ability ($p = 0.05$), which women do not have to the same degree. There were no significant differences between the men and women when it comes to perceiving hardness and irritations in the mouth.

> *Women seem to be more sensitive than men when it comes to identifying different types of flavors.*

When it came to the ability to identify scents, it may be noted that gender differences were between 20 percent and 40 percent for each scent. The researchers explained this in that women are typically more involved than men in cooking and therefore can more easily identify and name the right scent.

The conclusion from this study was that women are better than men in identifying different tastes and identifying different objects in their mouths. In this way, the study showed that there are significant differences between the sexes, pointing to the significance of the fact that women and men can perceive taste and scent experiences in completely different ways.

Group Preferences

As a social sense, the sense of taste is unique, and it should be shared with other people and not in solitude. This is reflected both in everyday life and business life, where food and meals are important social elements that contribute to creating interactions and exchanges between people. The natural meeting place in the home has long been the dining room table, where all the family members can gather to share experiences and thoughts about everyday life's joys and problems. In the business world, the business lunch is considered as a way to get to know the other party to build or maintain a relationship.

To regard food and meals as a social activity has long been a general perception in the literature. It appears from the relevant research that the presence of other people at a meal can both decrease and increase the amount of food that is consumed. Furthermore, it appears that the length of the meal increases when eating with others, which also leads to one drinking and eating more. But it turns out in fact that many people eat just as much or just as little when they eat with strangers. Another important aspect, which is discussed in addition to increased consumption, is what joy a social context could possibly convey.

Krishna and Elder (2010) assert that research to date has not examined the influence that the presence of other people may have on the taste experience. The researchers state that a social context should create a positive influence on a person's mood, which in turn could be transferred to the meal. In this way, a meal and to eat together with other persons could lead to increased taste sensations, which could conceivably lead to a food or a dish being prepared as a social product, enhancing its flavor.

Advertisements are mentioned as examples of this, where food products such as frozen products, which are often consumed on their own, could be present in a social context, such as a party. If consumers retained this notion, it might be possible to change the taste perception of the product, as opposed to if you announced it in an individual manner, without any connection to a social context. In many social cultures, food and meals are commonly consumed as a reward for something or in connection with a celebration, related to cultural or religious traditions. This occurs, for example, in connection with the Christian Christmas, the Muslim holiday of Ramadan, and the American Independence Day on July 4. But despite these occurrences, there is still very little known in research about why food and meals play such a crucial role in our celebrations and various social events.

> *Meals, as a social phenomenon for personal socializing, are allowed to take time to be an enjoyable experience.*

One possible explanation is that food and meals are the basis for a person's nutrition, which is one of the most important functions. But beyond the physical function, food and meals have also historically come to stand for other functions. In this context, the aesthetic function is one of the most significant, for example, when one considers a beautiful buffet that is presented on the dinner table.

In addition, there are numerous social functions, such as a chocolate box in a romantic encounter between two people or on a date with a newfound love across a restaurant table. In this way, since ancient times, food and meals have come to be regarded as special occasions for social interaction. During a French dinner, which easily takes an hour of time, it is obvious that it does not take long to consume the meal. Instead, the food shall be tasted and savored, interesting issues shall be discussed, and general sociability shall prevail during the hour.

It occurs in some Western cultures also that food and meals are considered more as physical refills, but in the vast majority, it is more a question of the expected joy. However, for many Western women today, this is a question of calorie intake, which gives an ambivalent taste experience, where the pleasure perhaps is replaced with a guilty conscience.

Food and meals, therefore, have also come to be associated with ethical and moral dimensions, which are related to the issue of obesity, and caloric foods are examples of that in the Western culture. In some religions, certain foods are not accepted and allowed, such as pork among Muslims, and food must be cooked in a certain way.

The Chinese cuisine, which has rice as a staple, uses the wok technique to maintain consistency and taste as well as having a taste principle that is based on soy sauce, ginger, and red wine. With this taste principle, even potatoes taste like Chinese food, although it is rarely present in Chinese cuisine.

Researchers have also analyzed the kitchen as a cultural phenomenon based on three different components, namely, staple goods, preparation techniques, and flavoring principles. But beyond that, there are a number of other components in different contexts in the actual culture's kitchen, namely, components such as table manners, pans and utensils, how the eating is organized, and the order of the dishes.

The influence that culture has on the importance of food and its sensory properties has been described using the term "kitchen," corresponding to the French word *cuisine*. Often when different food cultures are described, it is done by terms such as "French cuisine" or "Chinese cuisine," which then aim to describe the components that may be included in the kitchen.

The seasoning of food is handed down for generations, and it is relatively easy to discern seasoning traditions including among other places from China, Southeast Asia, Africa, India, Mediterranean, as well as Central and South America. The seasoning methods can vary from simply using one spice at the meal, such as coconut in the islands of the South Pacific, to making use of complex mixtures of spices as in Indian cuisine.

Taste Symbolism

Initially, it was emphasized that taste preferences can be regarded as a cultural and social phenomenon regarding aesthetic taste, whereas it is usually regarded as a biological concept relating to the physical taste. When it comes to understanding and interpreting items or objects such as art, consumer goods, ways, and styles, good taste is about showing the differences. In a social context, gastronomic and aesthetic taste is about a person's ability to judge what is good, fitting, and beautiful.

Social relationships and dynamics between people are closely linked to the taste for different social and cultural phenomenon. Many of the phenomena around us, which are reflected in the interactions between people, would not be possible to understand without understanding taste. For that reason, the aesthetic taste is not possible to separate from its accompanying sociological concepts, which points to its importance as a symbol for various cultural and social phenomena.

There is a consensus among researchers that there is not just one single idea of taste, which is shared by everyone in a societal culture. In contrast, it seems that there are some estimates, in terms of aesthetic taste, that are more legitimate than others. Aristotle, Plato, or Jonathan Swift would never contemplate "good" or "bad" taste as a way to assess their classic works.

It turns out that social origin and education are closely associated with certain aesthetic preferences and attendance at cultural events. Furthermore, it appears that there are different tastes present in different socioeconomic groups in a society, which has meant that social class is considered to be one of the most important factors to explain taste.

Furthermore, there seems to be some agreement that taste and consumption are closely linked. It turns out that taste is regarded as a preference for certain foods, clothing, and other basic goods, which would then directly have an impact on the choices consumers make in a market. But the causal link between taste and consumption is more complicated than that, which is why it is not possible to conclude that taste creates a demand, which in turn creates an offering. In economics and psychology as well as sociology there are several different scientific approaches to understanding the importance that taste has as a cultural and social phenomenon.

As opposed to good taste, bad taste is about a phenomenon, an idea, or an object that cannot be said to fall within the framework of social norms that are established and exist in a social culture. Usually, bad taste has negative connotations regarding a phenomenon or an object, which may differ from one society to another and from one period to another.

> *It is common for artists and comedians to use bad taste to shock their environment and challenge established norms of a social culture.*

It occurs also that retailers, despite the economic risk, consciously design and sell challenging or vulgar products. They rely on the inflated prices to help to introduce an "Emperor's New Clothes effect" among the customers.

Finally, it should be said that taste is an activity—not an attribute, an object, or a person—and a person must do something, like drink wine or listen to music, to evaluate this and be able to assess taste. In this way, taste is not predetermined or given, and not an item that is measured but rather taste arises in an interaction between people and is the object in an often unpredictable way, which makes the sense of taste dynamic, individual, and mysterious at the same time.

SERVICE ENVIRONMENT

In a service environment, such as a store, a mall, or a restaurant, both physical and aesthetic tastes are used to influence consumers' affections, cognitions, and actual behaviors. It can be done, for example, by the tasting of a new juice or a well-known type of cheese or by offering drinks and food in direct connection to a service environment. It has become increasingly common to enhance the experience of a service environment, and it often occurs at gas stations, in bookstores, and home furnishings stores, to name a few examples.

Furthermore, aesthetic taste can give an expression for the design, the style, and the behavior, which a service environment is meant to convey to consumers, as the following example illustrates.

> Today's cinemas have virtually looked the same for a long time, and popcorn began to be sold to visitors already in 1912. Even today, popcorn is the most common taste offering at the cinema, but American cinema chains such as Alamo Drafthouse and National Amusements in the United States now offer food and alcohol service during their screenings. In Sweden, SF Bio, which is basically a monopoly, has started by hiring restaurateurs in some places, including in Gothenburg, to enhance the cinematic experience.

Taste Stimuli

Research has shown that many consumers physically taste the products when different products are displayed or demonstrated in a shop or in a department store. It is not just about tasting with the tongue, often consumers feel and touch the product with their hands to feel how the product feels, which points to the importance of the sense of touch in interaction with the sense of taste.

In one study, customers' behaviors were observed discretely as they shopped for snacks in bulk containers in supermarkets. It turned out that behaviors were characterized by consumers using their hands to pick up snacks. Furthermore, many consumers picked up snacks out of the boxes to taste and chew on. In the large grocery stores, tasting the goods was not allowed, and this behavior came to be regarded as a problem because it was not sanctioned by the supermarkets.

It has also been found that obese and non-obese shoppers behave differently when samples are offered in the supermarket stores. One study examined how obese and non-obese shoppers behaved based on how hungry they were and the sales effect that occurred when they were offered a sample like a donut from the bakery.

The results showed that for the non-obese shoppers, who were hungry, the sample satisfied their hunger and they did not purchase any additional donuts. But for the obese shoppers, the sample meant that they bought more donuts, which could be explained to a lesser degree by the fact that they were hungry. Researchers guess that the obese shoppers were more susceptible to a sample because this further reinforced the importance of food for them, and for this reason they also purchased more.

The research assumed that consumers' taste experiences were due to two components, namely, an *affective* component and an *informative* component. These two components appear to be the basis for the pleasure that consumers experience when they taste, for example, chocolate or cheese, which leads to their subsequent preferences for the products in question. When it comes to the affective component, it is thought to comprise the emotional reactions that taste experiences may give rise to and generally refers to delight, satisfaction, and pleasure. This is unlike the informative component, which is thought to consist of the sensory properties of the taste experience, such as hardness and sweetness. In addition to these properties, other component properties are also included, which are health related, quality aspects, packaging, and brand name.

> *A taste experience is considered to have the greatest pleasure for an individual as an emotional reaction.*

A general notion in the literature is that the pleasure that a person finally experiences is assumed to depend on the affective and informative components. This means the greater the influence of the informative (affective) component, the lower (higher) the degree of pleasure is considered to be for the taste experience that a person has. This leads us to also assume that the person's preference for the selected taste option is weaker (stronger).

When it comes to consumer tasting, a study by Nowlis and Shiv (2005) showed that by distracting or interfering with consumer tastes at a particular moment, it influenced the subsequent choice of the sample product. It was explained that the pleasure a shopper experienced by tasting the sample could be attributed to both the informative component and the affective component. When it came to the latter, it was about an emotional response from the shopper, as a result of the tasting. The informative component was considered to be more objective in relation to the taste experience and was attributed to aspects such as quality.

One of the conclusions of the study was that distracting consumers in the moment of tasting had an influence on the affective component, which resulted in an impact on the subsequent choice that the consumer made. But the researchers also discussed some other possible implications for marketing, which are of interest. First, it was asserted that a consumer who tastes a product that he/she knows has some product benefits does not seem to be affected by distractions. Instead, it was assumed that the knowledge of the product benefits increased the value of the informative component.

Second, it was found that distractions did not seem to have any positive effects on the subsequent choice of product when the affective component had been negatively impacted. Consequently, it was assumed that distractions might have had the greatest impact on tasting where the affective component was not changed by the consumer having tasted or eaten before.

Taste Perception

The literature reveals that everyday positive events have a positive influence on people's social interactions and thought processes. These events give rise to positive emotions, which make a person feel good; examples of such events include succeeding with a simple task, listening to music, or getting a free sample. It is further proposed that as a result of this, people can have more flexible and creative thought processes and notice several aspects of different things, as long as these are neutral or positive to their valence.

Through experiments in a study, researchers found a significant interaction between the influence of a positive effect and variety-seeking behavior. The positive effects arose through a gift, which consisted of a small bag of candy or sugar-free gum, and were studied in three different categories: sandwich crackers, soup, and gourmet cuisine.

It turned out that the taste experience led to more variety-seeking behavior in the manipulated group of shoppers, compared with the control group. But when a negative advantage, such as a bad tasting product, was introduced in the experiment for any of the product categories, there was no difference in the variety-seeking behavior among the shoppers who had received a gift and the control group. One of the conclusions of the study was that the shoppers who were exposed to the gift showed more variety in their search behaviors, compared with those who received no gift.

In two different empirical studies, Sprott and Shimp (2004) examined, in the form of experiments, the ability of the tasting product to enhance a store brand's perceived quality among consumers and whether this was dependent on the level of quality. The first study involved two different food products, and it was shown that the perceived quality of the store brand benefited significantly from the samples when the participants tested products to assess their quality. In the second study, it was revealed that taste samples reinforced the participants' quality perceptions of the store brand, but only when the brand was high (versus low) quality.

Taste as Aesthetics

It is generally accepted in research that consumers use different consumption items, such as drinks, food, or clothing, to express their social belonging and their cultural capital, which shows the actual taste. In this way, aesthetic taste is manifested as an expression of personal attitudes and preferences and is objectified by selecting different service environments.

> *The event A Taste of Stockholm in the month of June in Kungsträdgården attracts hundreds of thousands of visitors for culinary sensations and performances by known artists.*

This is due largely to its immediacy and proximity to the human senses, which has led researchers to suggest that taste, as an aesthetic experience, should be its own sense and be added to the generally accepted five senses. One objection to this could be that aesthetic taste is represented in each of the five senses, namely, sight, sound, smell, touch, and gastronomic tastes. Furthermore, it is a common belief in research on hedonic consumption that a person's five senses interact with each other to create a multi-sensory experience of products and brands, which I will return to in the next chapter.

It is widely believed in research that many people have more knowledge of some products than others; and in this context, it is often the hedonic side of consumption that is ignored in order to explain this. It turns out that both taste and aesthetics can help to explain this relationship more closely.

Researchers such as Hoyer and Stokburger-Sauer (2012) believe that a person who has knowledge of, for example, the product domain "music" by either knowing different music theories or being able to play different instruments does not necessarily have a good sense of taste regarding music. It is therefore important to distinguish whether a person has good knowledge or good taste. For a person may have very good taste in music but have very little knowledge of music theory and other theoretical aspects. In this case, customers' expertise and taste are different from each other, because the person in question has a high level of aesthetic taste but a low level of knowledge. The opposite situation means that a person has a high level of knowledge but a low level of aesthetic taste. At the same time, there are people who may have both aesthetic taste and knowledge of music.

This emphasizes the importance of both knowledge, as a cognitive dimension, and taste, as an emotional dimension, when it comes to understanding the attitudes and preferences that arise at the individual level. For many products of a hedonic character, which are characterized by prominent aesthetic elements, it is important to identify and examine the importance of knowledge and taste in order to achieve a broader and deeper understanding of the customer's behavior.

There is thought to be two reasons for consumers' purchase of goods and services and their consumption behavior, namely, *consumption affective* (hedonic) motive mainly through sensory attributes, and *instrumental* (functional) motive. These premises are consistent with the research that closely studies the importance of hedonism and hedonic dimensions in the consumption of different products and brands (Homburg et al., 2006).

Hoyer and Stokburger-Sauer (2012) proposed a classification that is based on the importance of both emotions (affective or feeling) and cognitions (wisdom) in the evaluation of taste in the purchase and consumption processes. They identified three categories, which were placed in sequence from high usage of cognition to high usage of emotions. In the first category, cognition represented the decision parameter, and in the third category, emotions and feeling represented the most important decision parameters for an individual. In between, there were elements of both cognition and feeling that were the decision parameters.

One of the fundamental ideas of classification is that the various categories are assumed to reflect an individual's interaction with a certain type of product, where the categories are assumed to vary depending on the product and its attributes and characteristics and the individual's degree of commitment to the product in question. The interaction between cognition and emotion for a certain individual is affected by the extent to which the products or brand names are considered to be more functional or more emotional. In that regard, the products or brands that are considered to be more hedonic or sensory are considered to belong to the third category, which emphasizes the individual's dependence on his/her "gut feelings" or different sensory aspects in decision-making and consumption.

> *Think of what happens when you stand at the point of purchase in a grocery store or a fast food restaurant. You usually consult your memory and think about what you thought of the food or the dishes you see in front of you. You cannot directly relate to the past experience and what it meant in terms of less good or very good, but you have a recollection that you can use, and it will therefore affect the purchase decision.*

Whether an aesthetic taste is considered as an objective or subjective phenomenon is discussed extensively in the research. On the one hand, it is argued that aesthetic taste is to be seen as something individual or personal, which means that an aesthetic experience can lead to an emotional response in an individual.

It is thought to be mainly due to how a product, a service environment, or a brand is perceived and what feels good or bad for an individual. With this approach, there are no universal reference points to work from, but taste is regarded as a subjective, individual phenomenon. In other words, as the old saying goes, "Every man to his taste," and it doesn't work to question a person's taste.

On the other hand, it is argued that there are uniform principles in terms of aesthetic taste or aesthetic pleasure. If it did not exist, people would not be able to perceive the same beautiful objects, such as a painting or a building, which previous generations have also done. It is generally accepted that different taste standards have developed over time, allowing aesthetic taste to come to be regarded also as an objective phenomenon. Several studies have been conducted where respondents were asked to evaluate the aesthetic value of common visual aesthetic stimuli and to state which stimulus was preferred. It turns out that there are individuals with a higher aesthetic sensitivity who perceive a higher aesthetic value, in comparison with other individuals.

> *Car designers think of taste not only when it comes to the sense of sight but also the sound of the engine, how comfortable the seats are, and how the interior smells.*

BRAND

The research on taste and physical taste has been mainly focused on understanding the significance of taste in various retail and product contexts. In practice, the sense of taste, by the physical flavor, is rarely present in marketing more than in connection with the demonstration of goods and tastings in various service environments. But there are companies that offer customers coffee and snacks to strengthen their brand image and give them a "taste" of the brand or, as the following example illustrates, offer a taste experience of a brand on a higher plane.

> *The Scandinavian airline company, SAS, has developed a new airplane food, taking into consideration that it is often consumed by passengers at high altitudes. It is the dry air that makes the food taste different in the air, compared with on the ground. For the sake of the foods experience, therefore, salty, sour, and sweet are adapted to how the tastes can be experienced in the air, which led to the bread being given an extra pinch of salt and the salad variety chosen specifically to stay crisp and fresh during the temperature changes that occur during a flight.*

There is extensive research on how different taste stimuli, such as product attributes, create a taste sensation for individual products. In this context, various flavors have a crucial role, and these can be either natural or a mixture of chemical compounds that are formed or added to food as well as to cooking. The characteristic feature of a flavoring agent is that it should be tasty and fragrant to appeal to gastronomic taste in the best way.

Taste Stimuli

Research has shown that product quality, as taste stimuli, has long been studied mainly in terms of a cognitive evaluation of inner product features, such as the quality of raw materials, effectiveness or tolerance, or external product characteristics, such as warranty, price, and service. These characteristics have together come to represent the concept of quality, which then proceeds from factors such as reliability, durability, and craftsmanship. However, emotional factors and their influence on the quality of the experience for a consumer have been studied to a lesser extent.

When it comes to differentiating a brand based on its taste characteristics, a study was already done during the 1960s that investigated the ability of American beer drinkers. The experiment was about letting a number of randomly selected respondents taste the beer from a number of selected brands and then rate the beers' quality with regard to a number of different factors.

The results showed that the respondents could not distinguish a particular brand from another on the basis of the beers' taste, because the bottle labels were removed. It was also revealed that respondents could not rank their favorite brand higher than anything else, because they did not know which beer belonged to which brand and its label wasn't on the bottle. One of the study's conclusions was that the taste alone could not decide which beer was in question but that the assessment took place through interaction with the other senses.

Another study looked at how emotional reactions, in addition to cognitive evaluation, influenced consumers' product evaluation of ice cream. With the help of three experiments, how different sensory stimuli elicited emotional responses was studied.

In one of the experiments, strawberry flavor and coffee flavor were tested to investigate whether there was a negative or positive influence on the emotional reaction. It was shown that consumers who already had a positive emotional attitude toward the actual taste also showed a significantly greater emotional response and showed a significantly higher perception of quality regarding the ice cream.

Overall, the study showed that both past emotional attitudes and emotional responses, which were now recorded in the three experiments, affected consumers' perceptions of quality. It was further noted that a previous positive emotional attitude led to more positive thoughts and less negative thoughts about the actual ice cream. One conclusion of the study was that the emotional response was not only an important factor in consumers' subjective product evaluation, but it also seemed to be that it affected the cognitive responses that occurred, which in turn was the basis for the overall perception of quality.

Taste Goods

Since the 1970s, the different possibilities to distinguish the different product categories from each other for product evaluation have been discussed in research. It is common to distinguish between *search goods*, which consumers look for and where the product quality is known in advance, and *experience goods*, where the product quality will be known only after the purchase and use.

Phillips and McQuarrie (2011) proposed a third category, *taste goods*, which are represented by fashion products. The two main advantages of taste goods are that 1) the individual's preference is based on the subjective taste and that there is no way to objectively measure the product quality and 2) it may be considered possible that the product delivers an experience before the actual purchase.

The researchers believed that every product where the aesthetic component was the main focus could be said to be a taste good. They also claimed that the product category taste goods should be characterized by sensory stimuli such as design or style, making it possible to differentiate the products from each other. This led to a subjective differentiation in the different individuals, where one found the product appealing, whereas others experienced the opposite. An example of this is advertisements in famous fashion magazines where only images are present without verbal arguments.

This also means that the taste goods can be regarded as visual phenomenon and thus fall within the visual experience, which in turn involves visual taste. If so, no verbal arguments in the advertising can help to maybe strengthen the individual's perception of the product quality of fashion products in advance. On the other hand, functional differentiation of a product cannot be done, because verbal arguments are often absent in advertising.

Taste Perception

When it comes to evaluating gastronomic taste in connection with product evaluation, one of the most important questions is to find out if there are, for example, clear taste differences that a consumer can distinguish from actual tastes. For a food manufacturer, it may be important to investigate, for example, whether two alternative product designs are similar in order to evaluate their taste consistency from one production batch compared with another. Generally, most food manufacturers use their own experts to perform these taste tests.

Taste tests can also be used to identify those consumers who are most able to distinguish between the products thanks to taste. The so-called triangle test is used to determine if an individual can identify the sample, out of three presented samples, which are different from each other. One question raised in this context is whether individuals are guessing or really can distinguish between the three samples, which is why statistical techniques are proposed to make the results and the quality of these tests better.

> *In a blind test of 12 leading ice cream brands in Germany, it was shown that the most famous brands had mediocre taste, but when the brand name became known, it was the best judged.*

Taste tests have also been developed in order to get consumers to discriminate between tastes that are compared in pairs. This method is based on an individual receiving three tastings, where one differs from the other two. Individuals are asked to rank the taste that is most preferred to that which is least preferred.

If the deviant taste is ranked as the most preferred or the least preferred, it is deemed that the individual made a correct choice, regardless of what preference one has. If, however, the deviant taste was ranked between the two identical taste tests, then the individual has not succeeded in discriminating the taste samples from each other. In this context, it should be said that researchers have investigated the method of paired comparisons and come to the conclusion that it is the most sensitive method to discriminate between the tastes.

In the research on the sense of taste, the issue of how sensory stimuli (often aesthetic) other than physical taste, in and of itself, can affect consumers' perceptions has been studied more closely. Researchers such as Hoegg and Alba (2007) have examined how perceptual discrimination is attributed to consumers' ability to recognize differences, when these do not exist, among gastronomic stimuli.

In their study, the interest was in studying discrimination by individual attributes of a product, rather than to study the overall use of the product in question. Furthermore, the study assumed that discrimination is considered to have a significant role and precede decision-making, which means that it is not the same thing as the decision itself. Another important theoretical basis was also to present alternatives in the study, which not only described the benefits verbally but also offered sensory stimuli, which previous research largely disregarded.

The study was conducted using three experiments, and the product category orange juice was present in all three experiments. Orange juice was chosen as the product because it was considered easy to manipulate with respect to external product characteristics that do not affect the gastronomic taste. Furthermore, the researchers made use of appropriate color differences (e.g., shades similar to orange) and variations in sweetness.

The first experiment examined consumers' perceptions of color differences. It was revealed that the manipulation of the orange juice led to the consumers perceiving the differences and being able to discriminate, which met the minimum criterion for a color effect. An important finding was that the conflict between color, as an expression of aesthetic taste, and taste, as an expression of gastronomic taste, was resolved due to the color advantage. The researchers concluded that when color differences were subtle (or fine) and offset each other, it was considered unlikely that perception (i.e., ability to perceive) was driven by expectations of exquisite taste.

The second experiment examined consumers' perceptions of differences in etiquette. It was revealed that the manipulation did not lead to consumers being able to perceive differences and thereby discriminate, so the results were almost identical. In a comparison between experiments 1 and 2, it was concluded that the color effect, as an expression of aesthetic taste, led to the ability to discriminate, even though the gastronomic taste was the same. The researchers concluded that a subtle (fine) color manipulation gave a great effect with regard to discrimination, which in turn knocked out the effects of less subtle brands and price information.

In a number of experiments, Biswas et al. (2014) studied how oral haptic regarding hardness/softness or roughness/smoothness could be related to how food is perceived in terms of chewing and obesity. It was also assumed that this would affect calorie estimation, dietary habits, and consumption volume. According to the theories of chewing and mouth perception, the results showed that the food's softness and smoothness led to higher calorie estimates. One of the conclusions was that marketing, by changing the haptic properties of food, could easily affect consumers' calorie estimates, consumption volume, and food choices.

Taste Symbolism

Research has also drawn attention to how different socio-cultural elements affect consumers' perceptions of a brand. Here, the socio-cultural elements are viewed as symbols of consumption and taste, which is meant by the term "taste symbolism." Especially in the area of food and groceries, it seems that a person's knowledge, beliefs, and values about different products and brands play a major role in the purchasing decision that is made.

> *Prior knowledge of a brand leads to the same conclusion at a later date.*

Generally, it is believed that each person makes his/her own objective assessment of the actual food or beverage on the basis of the taste receptors in the mouth. This objective assessment, which in reality is subjective, is controlled by the chemical composition that each individual is equipped with and which leads to a taste perception. This is then evaluated in terms of whether the beverage or food tastes good or not.

But it is not only an objective assessment that enables people to form an opinion about a product or a brand. Research has shown that many individuals also tend to make their assessments in accordance with previously acquired knowledge. This is thought to lead to people's previous perceptions about a product or brand rubbing off on their subsequent assessments.

This can be illustrated with a scientific experiment, where respondents came to prefer the brand Perrier over Old Fashioned Saltzer when they were offered these two products with the label visible. But when the products were offered without the labels, it showed that the respondents did not have any preferences regarding their product choice. It was assumed that the assimilation effect that arises because of a person's earlier knowledge and experience, like the brand Perrier tastes better, was activated by the information that the brand represented. This was assumed to lead to a taste perception, which was consistent with previous knowledge and experience.

But there is no consensus in research that this effect is consistent on both the social and individual levels through various demographic groups of the population. Some researchers therefore claim that the assimilation effects in taste evaluations arise from the interplay of processes at both levels, which are linked to the current societal culture. It is further assumed that the societal culture's influence activates the symbolic content with food and drink, which the individual is assumed to have as a starting point and adapts to in an often-unconscious way.

The human values that food and drink symbolize in the current societal culture are thereby transferred to the individual's own taste perception when there is a match between values and symbolism, which reinforces the positive taste. If such compliance is not considered, it is assumed to lead to a negative taste perception, that is, bad taste.

In a study by Allen et al. (2008), the everyday culture's influence on the perception of taste was studied in an experiment. A survey was conducted using taste tests, where products that objectively tasted the same were provided different symbolic content and values. The questionnaire was designed to measure the human values, attitudes, purchase intentions, and taste evaluation. The respondents got to taste a "sausage roll made of beef" or an "alternative vegetarian roll," and a "Pepsi" drink or a "Woolworth Homebrand Cola."

In a previous pilot study, it was noted that the "beef roll," as red meat, symbolized values such as social power, whereas the "alternative vegetarian roll" symbolized rejection of these values. As for the "Pepsi" drink, it was noted that it symbolized the values of an exciting life, enjoyment of life, social power, and social acknowledgments, whereas "Woolworth Homebrand Cola" instead symbolized a rejection of these values.

In the latter main study, it was revealed that those respondents who distanced themselves from social power had a more positive taste evaluation, attitude, and purchase intention when they thought they had tasted the "alternative vegetarian roll" than when they thought they had tasted the "beef roll." Those respondents who had the same human values as the "Pepsi" drink had a more positive taste evaluation, attitude, and purchase intention when they found out that they tasted this drink than when they thought they had tasted the "Woolworth Homebrand Cola."

One of the study's conclusions was that human values and cultural symbols influence people's attitudes and taste evaluations relating to products and brands. It should be added that there is a general consensus in the research on red meat symbolizing social power and those values related to it, whereas fruits, vegetables, and grains symbolize the rejection of (or distance from) social power.

REFERENCES

Allen, M.W., Gupta, R. and Monnier, A. (2008), "The interactive effect of cultural symbols and human values on taste evaluation," *Journal of Consumer Research*, 35, 2:294–398.
Biswas, D., Szocs, C., Krishna, A. and Lehmann, D. (2014), "Something to chew on: the effects of oral haptics on mastication, orosensory perception, and calorie estimation," *Journal of Consumer Research*, 41, August. doi:10.1086/675739.
Bourdieu, P. (1984), *Distinction: a social critique of the judgment of taste*, Cambridge: Harvard University Press, p. 56.
DiMaggio, P. (1987), "Classification in art." *American Sociological Review*, 52:440–455.
DuBose, C.N., Cardello, A.V. and Maller, O. (1980), "Effects of colorants and flavorants on identification, perceived flavor intensity, and hedonic quality of fruit-flavored beverages and cake," *Journal of Food Science*, 45, 5:1393–1399.
Gronow, J. (1997), *The sociology of taste*, London: Routledge.
Hirschmann, E.C. and Holbrook, M.B. (1982), "Hedonic consumption: emerging concepts, methods and propositions," *Journal of Marketing*, 46, Summer:92–101.
Hoegg, J. and Alba, J.W. (2007), "Linguistic framing of sensory experience: there is some accounting for taste." I: Lowrey, T.M. (ed.) *Psycholinguistic phenomena in marketing communications*, Mahwah, NJ: Erlbuam, p. 3–21.
Homburg, C., Koschate, N. and Hoyer, W.D. (2006), "The role of cognition and affect in the formation of customer satisfaction—a dynamic perspective," *Journal of Marketing*, 70:21–31.
Hoyer, W.D. and Stokburger-Sauer, N.E. (2012), "The role of aesthetic taste in consumer behaviour," *Journal of the Academy of Marketing Science*, 40, 1:167–180.
Kant, I. (1790), *The critique of judgment*, trans. by J. H. Bernard, 2nd edition revised. London: Macmillan, 1914.
Krishna, A. and Elder, R.S. (2010), "The gist of gustation: an exploration of taste, food, and consumption." I: Krishna, A. (ed.) *Sensory marketing: research on the sensuality of products*, New York: Routledge, p. 281.
Krishna, A. and Morrin, M. (2008), "Does touch affect taste? The perceptual transfer of product container haptic cues," *Journal of Consumer Research*, 34:807–818.
Michon, C., O'Sullivan, M.G., Delahunty, C.M. and Kerry, J.P. (2009), "The investigation of gender-related sensitivity differences in food perception," *Journal of Sensory Studies*, 24:922–937.
Nowlis, S.M. and Shiv, B. (2005), "The influence of consumer distractions on the effectiveness of food-sampling programs," *Journal of Marketing Research*, 42, 2:157–168.
Phillips, B.J. and McQuarrie, E.F. (2011), "Contesting the social impact of marketing: a re-characterization of women's fashion advertising," *Marketing Theory*, 11, 2:99–126.
Rode, E., Rozin, P. and Durlach, P. (2007), "Experienced and remembered pleasure for meals: duration neglect but minimal peak-end effects," *Appetite*, 49:18–29.

Rozin, P. and Hormes, J.M. (2010), "Psychology and sensory marketing, with a focus on food." I: Krishna, A. (ed.) *Sensory marketing: research on the sensuality of products*, New York: Routledge, p. 303.

Schmitt, B. and Simonson, A. (1997), *Marketing aesthetics*, New York: Free Press.

Sprott, D.E. and Shimp, T.A. (2004), "Using product sampling to augment the perceived quality of store brands," *Journal of Retailing*, 80, 4:305–315.

Zampini, M. and Spence, C. (2004), "The role of auditory cues in modulating the perceived crispness and staleness of potato chips," *Journal of Sensory Science*, 19:347–363.

10 Multi-Sensory Brand-Experience

This chapter analyzes and discusses the interaction between two or more senses for the individual's perception and sensory experience of goods and services. The scientific notions about the importance of the multi-sensory interactions are highlighted.

Furthermore, various types of multi-sensory interactions and how these contribute to creating a multi-sensory brand-experience for individuals are presented. In this context, factors that are attributed to the multi-sensory experiences such as phenomenon, service environment, and brand are discussed. Finally, how multi-sensory brand-experiences can be created and be expressed in different buying and consumption processes is presented.

Introduction

It is generally believed that people use their five senses to experience their surroundings, retail or service environment, various products, and brands. This points to the importance of the human senses for the perception and sensory experience of items, persons, or objects in the world around us. This is called using the five senses *externally*, which occurs when this text is read with the help of sight.

However, a person may also make use of the five senses when he or she fantasizes and thinks. This may include, for example, how the freshly cut grass smells, how wishful music sounds, or how a cup of hot chocolate tastes. For a human, it is natural to use the five senses to think and it is believed that a person has a mind as the main system, which controls one's perception of how the world looks. This is called using the five senses *internally*.

A human can therefore use all five senses to think. This means that an individual has an internal dialogue with him/herself and can imagine how something feels or looks. When it comes to using the senses internally, some people prefer to use sight, some talk to themselves (sound), whereas others feel their way. However, smell and taste are rarely used as the main senses.

> Mercedes-Benz uses interactive movies and integrates multiple senses through the use of games where customers can click-through, hear the music, and see.

In this way, the external senses play a prominent role in the perception and experience of the external world. But internal senses determine how a person creates fantasies, ideas, and thoughts and how these are embodied and lead to a certain behavior. In this context, a special mind-set can lead an individual to create a positive self-image, shape an image of her/himself, and achieve a higher degree of self-fulfillment in the external and internal interactions between the five senses as the basis for the multi-sensory experience (Figure 10.1).

A multi-sensory experience assumes that the assessments an individual makes of a store, its products, and its personnel are largely influenced by how it looks (the visual system), how it sounds (the auditory system), how it smells (the olfactory system), how it feels to touch (the tactile system), and, finally, how it tastes (the gastronomic/aesthetic system). The information that an individual gains from the environment is handled and processed through the perceptual system, where different stimuli and signals are organized

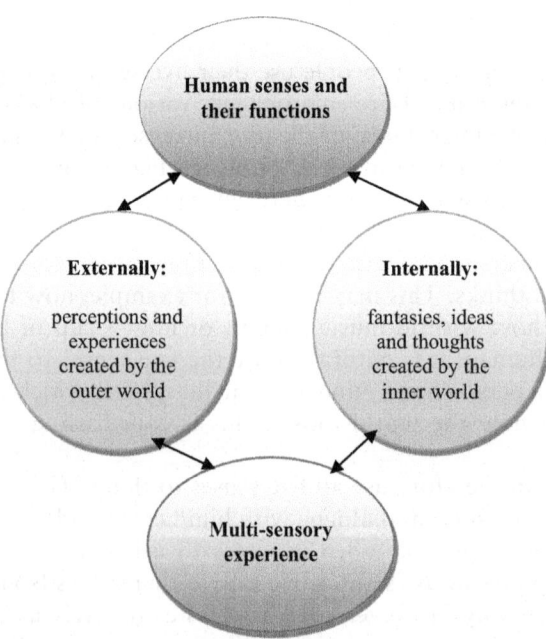

Figure 10.1 The Function of the Human Senses Externally and Internally

according to the five senses. It is this system—as visual experiences—that has traditionally received the most attention in the research.

But for some individuals, the interaction between the senses is experienced as more confusing, which the concept of synesthesia refers to. Unlike most of us who can clearly distinguish between sensory input from sight, sound, smell, touch, and taste, for those with synesthesia, different impressions from the senses from two or more of the senses are mixed together. It turns out that a person can see colors while he or she listens to sounds; loud noise is associated with bright colors, whereas low noises are associated with dark colors. Furthermore, an individual can also "taste" words, which is called lexical gustatory synesthesia.

> *It appears that some people may associate a certain color to a certain sound or a "taste" of words, which synesthesia is about.*

Within psychology and cognitive sciences, the perceptual system, with an emphasis on how an individual perceives his/her environment (i.e., perception), as well as the process of acquiring, interpreting, selecting, and organizing the sensory information has been studied for a long time. In light of this, perception, as a research field, has been regarded as being one of the oldest in scientific psychology.

It is generally accepted that an individual can change his/her perception of an object, an item, or a person with respect to new relevant information that is relative to the knowledge an individual has from past experiences. For experience-based products, such as chocolate, drinks, food, and perfumes, there is a higher degree of sensory stimuli related to sight, sound, smell, touch, and taste (Troye and Supphellen, 2012). This helps our judgments and purchasing decisions of a particular brand in which information using multiple senses can be obtained and made possible by a multi-sensory brand-experience.

Interaction of the Senses

In the literature, *sensory integration*, or interaction of the senses, is considered to be the neurological processes in the brain that take care of the different sensations from the body and the surroundings. Here, sensations refer to the biochemical and neurological processes that occur when the stimulus reaches the receptors of a sense organ, such as sight, sound, smell, taste, or touch. Then the fundamental properties of the various stimuli are discovered, which lead to perception, that is, an individual receives information from the environment and can express, for example, "I see that the wall is freshly painted." Using these processes, various sensory stimuli are managed, first as sensations but then moving on to sensory information, which makes it possible for a person to use the body as effectively as possible with respect to the environment.

It is believed that sensory integration is important for an individual and the activities that are carried out, as these are often a combination of several categories of sensory stimulations, as input, for the individual to understand the surroundings. Among these categories are the five classical senses of sight, sound, smell, touch, and taste, and other sensory categories, for example, balance and movement (*vestibular sense*) and body movement (*proprioception*). Sensory integration occurs by means of electrical signals in various neurological contexts, and it is thanks to the interaction of the senses that the human brain can create an understanding of how interaction with the environment should be conducted.

> *In a virtual environment, the sense of presence can increase if the number of stimuli increases.*

There are a number of different specialized areas of the brain, and a communication takes place within and between these areas, which is called *functional integration*. Recent research shows that these areas are not only responsible in isolation for a single sensory stimulus, but they can also use several sensory stimuli, as input, to feel what your body reacts to. Figure 10.2 shows how the reception, processing, and integration of the sensory stimuli occur in the human brain.

Research suggests that by increasing the number of sensory stimuli in a virtual environment, people can increase their sense of presence and remember the objects in the virtual environment in a better way. In one experiment, the effects of sensory stimuli, such as sight, sound, smell, and touch, were studied regarding presence and memory, which was shown to have a major impact. In this context, it should be mentioned that an increase in the level of detail for vision did not result in such an impact (Dinh et al., 1999).

From an evolutionary perspective, it appears that the senses of smell and taste were developed early in humans and that interaction was necessary for survival. It was important to get adequate nutrients through food and to make sure not to consume poisonous berries or mushrooms. Furthermore, the interaction between vision and hearing was necessary for mapping out the spatial environment and also gradually developed a person's fine motor skills, through sight and touch, to achieve better hand-eye coordination in connection with the production of various goods, such as clothing, furniture, and bags. For people to be transient creatures, it was also necessary to have interaction between the eyes and balance and posture, which led to

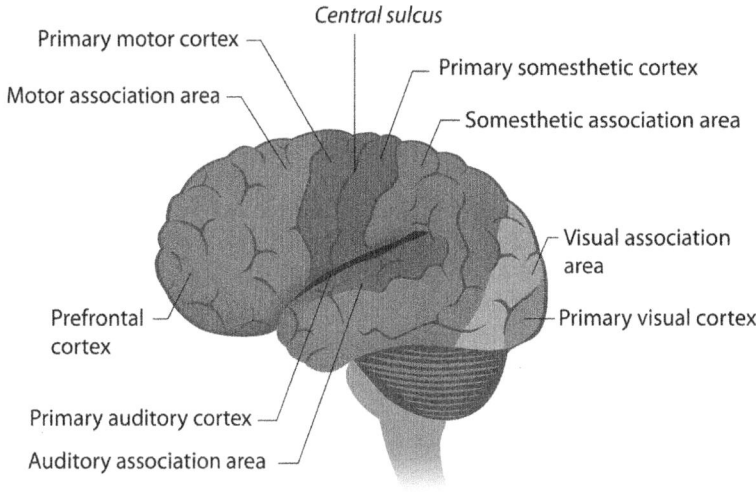

Figure 10.2 Sensory Reception, Processing, and Integration
Source: *Shutterstock*

even the senses of balance and movement being regarded as important for different sensory impressions.

Visual and Auditory Stimuli

When it comes to the interaction of the senses, it is apparent that the relationship between sight and sound is one of the most studied fields. This is because the two senses perceive the same object or environment in completely different ways; but by combining the two, an individual can better understand the sensory information obtained through these. It is considered that vision dominates our perception of the object and the environment, which is attributed to the fact that visual-spatial information is one of the most credible sensory inputs.

> *When visual and auditory stimuli interact, it increases an individual's understanding of sensory information.*

Visual stimuli are recorded immediately on the retina, and it is believed that there are no external (outer) distortions that can give false information to the brain about an actual room or the actual location of a place. In other words, there is no other spatial information that is as reliable as visual-spatial information. With auditory-spatial input, which can provide information about an object's location through sound, the sensory information can easily be changed or modified, which does not provide an equally reliable picture of where an object is located. But in the interaction between visual and auditory stimuli, an individual can obtain a clearer identification of where an object is actually located.

Various studies show that there is a dynamic neural mechanism in the brain that is responsible for matching different visual and auditory inputs that come from an activity or event, aiming to stimulate multiple senses at once. It turns out that the brain can compensate for the distance to the object when one talks to someone or looks at something, because the visual and auditory signals are not processed at the same time but are experienced simultaneously by an individual.

Visual and Tactile Stimuli

Another example of interaction is the hand and eye coordination in the brain, based on what we perceive visually of an object and what we experience by touch of the same object. It is believed that hand-eye coordination is tactile sensation in the visual context, and if the two senses were not combined, then a person would have less ability to handle a particular item or object. It turns out that the visual system is completely static and not able to move to any great extent, whereas the hands and other parts of the body can move freely to gather tactile sensory information. If hand movements did not exist, a person would not be able to visually understand what he or she looked at or touched.

Multi-Sensory as a Phenomenon

The concept of multi-sensory refers to how two or more of the five senses interact when it comes to an individual to perceive and receive sensory information in connection with the service environment and the brand. Furthermore, it should be mentioned that sensory, emotional, and cognitive processes are treated in different parts of the human brain, as previously discussed. One of the fundamental starting points in neuromarketing then is that individuals react unconsciously and instinctively to sensory stimuli as opposed to learned stimuli, such as a logo or a brand like Apple, Nike, or Volvo.

> *A person's perception of the environment is based on multi-sensory stimulation with multiple senses involved at the same time.*

The research has long been mainly focused on the effects of individual sensory stimuli on consumer behavior and product evaluation, which earlier chapters discussed, with respect to sight, sound, smell, taste, and touch. When it comes to studying emotional, cognitive, and sensory processes in the human brain, empirical studies, for example, show that vision can interact with other senses, such as sound, smell, and touch (Thesen et al., 2004). Another study has shown that it is possible to identify multi-sensory convergence zones in the brain, which may mean that "a sense can be influenced by relationships with the other senses" (Driver and Noesselt, 2008).

Regarding the question about learning and how individuals perceive things, the different sensory stimuli are of importance. For a long time, it was assumed that learning was based on just one sensory stimulus, but a person's perception of the outside world is based on continuous multi-sensory stimulation, where several stimuli are present at the same time. It is believed that sensory information from sight and hearing are integrated when it comes to the human brain, for example, to identify and locate moving objects, and the brain has developed to learn to act in a multi-sensory environment. Thus the multi-sensory functions and mechanisms of the human brain are studied when it comes to learning regarding objects or products (Shams and Seitz, 2008).

A common view among scientists is that vision and touch are the most prominent senses through which service environments and brands are perceived in terms of sensory experiences of consumers. In a study by Schifferstein and Cleiren (2005), it was revealed that these sensory experiences make it possible for an individual to become more confident about his/her assessments of a product, especially considering the degree of detail. Furthermore, the researchers assert that tactile and visual sensory information dominates over other sensory information from scent and sound stimuli.

Even other studies of multi-sensory interaction have evaluated the relationship between vision and touch in the consumer's decision-making. It has been found that when tactile and visual information are presented at the same time, visual information is inferior to tactile information. But when it comes to assessing an item or an object's position, size, or shape, visual information is often superior, as it allows more credible assessments (Ernst and Banks, 2002).

One conclusion from these studies is that individual genetic traits determine the extent to which sight or feeling dominates when it comes to an individual evaluating an item or an object. On the other hand, there is research showing that individuals make use of multiple-sensory experiences, which results in a synergistic effect on behavior, evaluation, and memory (Bresciani et al., 2006).

> *Most consumers use multiple senses when buying products, which is quite natural.*

It is thus more than obvious that during the purchase of products, consumers are subject to more than one stimulus, which normally gives rise to a multi-sensory interaction. When it comes to buying a computer, a cell phone, or a pen, sensory information is obtained from both the tactile sense, if how the pen feels is tested with the hands, and from the visual sense, if the pen looks attractive.

Researchers such as Calvert et al. (2004, p. xi) expressed this as follows:

> There is no doubt that our senses are designed to work together and that our brains are organized to use the information we obtain from various sensory channels together to enhance the probability that objects and events are detected quickly, correctly identified, and with a suitable response.

I believe that a multi-sensory brand-experience supports individual value creation and is related to how individuals react when a company interacts with them and supports their purchase and consumption processes by involving the five senses to generate customer value, experiences, and the brand as an image. In this context, it is important to point out that the sensory stimuli that are expressed through the various senses differ from learned stimuli, which marketers often use and which many individuals have learned to recognize.

Multi-Sensory Perception of a Service Environment

When it comes to perceiving a service environment, such as a store, a restaurant, or a department store, various atmospheric stimuli (*retail atmospherics*) are deemed to play a major role in consumers' affections, cognitions, and behaviors (Spence et al., 2014). For that reason, surroundings in a service environment generally consist of many different elements (or stimuli) for sight, sound, smell, taste, and touch, each of which can convey sensory information to the five senses.

In retail research, it is considered that these atmospheric stimuli are interrelated and work together to create synergies with the aim to influence consumers. It is further assumed that consumers regard these elements, such as design, music, scent, aesthetics, and texture, from a holistic perspective and not each one individually (Babin et al., 2004). When it comes to studying the interaction between these atmospheric stimuli as sensory stimuli and sensory information, it has been considered to a lesser extent in retail research for a long time

---

Marketers use sensory stimuli to create a sensory "signature" of a brand, such as the "scent" of Singapore Airlines.

The Interplay between the Auditory and Atmospheric Stimuli

In a field study by Mattila and Wirtz (2001), the researchers studied in a shop experiment the interaction between atmospheric stimuli, such as scent and music, and consumers' perceptions of the store environment. The set hypothesis meant to test how the correlation between scent and music would enhance consumers' evaluation with respect to joy, approach, perceived positive environment, impulse purchase, and satisfaction. The aim of the study was to investigate whether the match, i.e., a high conformity, between these two stimuli would lead to a higher evaluation of the store environment, a more positive behavior, and greater satisfaction among consumers from a holistic perspective.

The study was conducted in a gift shop in the mornings, afternoons, and evenings over a two-week period with a respondent selection of about 343 customers. It should be stated that the majority of the customers (75 percent) were women, and of these, two out of three customers were under 20 years of age. It was considered that this customer selection corresponded well with the store's main target group, and nearly two out of three customers had made a purchase during their visit to the store.

During the experiment, a scent was introduced in the store with the help of four ceramic sprayers, and the music was played simultaneously on the store's sound system using CD players. As stimuli, scent was manipulated as no aroma, pleasant, and arousing and background music as no music, low speed, and high speed.

The results showed that the interaction between scent and music is significant with respect to an approach, an impulse purchase, and satisfaction. It appears that consumers valued the retail environment higher when the smell (in this case lavender) was pleasant and experienced together with music in slow tempo in comparison with high.

One of the study's main conclusions was that sensory stimuli should not be considered individually, but it is the multi-sensory interactions that influence the consumer's response. It should be added that a high correlation between scent and music was necessary to achieve this.

In another experimental field study by Morrison et al. (2011), the effects of music (low or high) and vanilla (absent or present) were examined in a fashion shop with 263 customers, aged 18 to 35 years. The aim of the study was to find out about the positive effects of music and scent pertaining to dependent variables such as customer delight, excitement, approach, time spent, money spent, and overall satisfaction with their shopping experience, based on a number of established hypotheses.

The study was conducted over four weeks, and the two independent variables, music and fragrance, were manipulated separately during the time the experiment was in progress. The music came from a playlist, which the shop already used previously as part of its atmosphere. Furthermore, dance music was played either on high volume, as foreground music, or low volume, as background music for a number of hours together with the data collection. The vanilla scent was chosen because it is considered to be a more feminine fragrance and previous research has shown its impact, particularly on women, which often gives memory associations with childhood.

During the time that the experiment was conducted, customers who visited the store received a questionnaire, which examined the dependent variables. These were measured using a number of seven-point scales, which were taken from previously conducted studies on emotions, approach, and satisfaction. A manipulation control was also conducted in the questionnaire in that respondents were asked to answer whether the music was very low to very high. Regarding scent, they got to answer if they could smell the scent of vanilla.

The results showed that both the music and the vanilla scent, in themselves, had significant effects on customers' excitement. But it turned out that it required an interaction between the music and the vanilla scent to produce significant effects on happiness. This meant that joy was strengthened only in the case when music and scent were simultaneously present in the store. It was also shown that the interaction between music and scent not only affected joy but also customers' behaviors in the form of approach, time spent, and how much money was being spent in the store.

The main conclusion from the study was that the right combination of sensory stimuli, such as scent and music together, not only reinforces consumers' emotions in the form of joy, but also gets consumers to stay in the store longer.

Congruence between Scent and Music in Interaction

Spangenberg et al. (2005) conducted an experiment to investigate the interaction between sensory stimuli for scent and music in connection with retailers' Christmas season. The study aimed to investigate whether consumers' evaluations of a store, its environment, and its product range would be positively influenced by the interaction between an added scent and music, taking into consideration the existence of a congruent musical stimulus in relation to a Christmas scent. It was assumed that consumers' evaluations would be adversely affected if an added fragrance were to be associated with an incongruent musical stimulus.

The experiment was conducted in a laboratory, where both images of a store as well as scent and music could be exposed and controlled. The survey involved 130 American female and male students between 20 and 55 years old, who also received course credit for their participation. Initially, in a pilot study, the participants got to decide on an appropriate scent, which would be associated with the American holiday season. The choice fell on a fragrance called Enchanted Christmas in spray form, which came to be applied in the experiment. When it came to Christmas music, Amy Grant's song "Home for Christmas" was selected, and for non-Christmas music the same singer was chosen with the song "Heart in Motion." After the experiment was carried out, each participant received a questionnaire to complete, which included measuring instruments, manipulation control, and demographic variables.

The results showed that the multi-sensory interaction between scent and music was significant and had a positive effect on consumers' evaluations of the store, the store's environment, and its product range. The most favorable evaluations were given for the added Christmas scent when the Christmas music was played, which did not apply when the non-Christmas music played correspondingly. This came to be expressed through positive attitudes toward the store, stronger intentions to visit the store, more joy, and excitement as well as a better evaluation of the store environment.

> *When Christmas music is played in a department store along with a Christmas scent, positive attitudes arise toward the store.*

It is noteworthy that there appeared to be fewer positive attitudes toward the store in connection with an added Christmas scent being present together with the non-Christmas music. This was also manifested by weaker intentions to visit the store and fewer positive attitudes toward the product range.

The study's main conclusion was that the correlation between a pleasurable Christmas scent and Christmas music seemed to lead to more positive evaluations of a store, its environment, and its product range. Even consumer behavior was positively influenced by the congruence that existed between these two sensory stimuli. But this also shows that all combinations of scent and music that are not congruent can affect consumers negatively, which retailers should pay attention to.

It might even be that using only one single stimulus might be more successful than introducing more stimuli without internal consistency. I will return to this issue later in the chapter.

To Overstimulate the Senses

The researchers Morrin and Chebat (2005) conducted a field study with four different experiments to investigate how sensory stimuli such as background music and lemon scent could positively influence consumers' shopping behaviors in a Canadian shopping mall. This meant to more closely analyze how the correlation between these two stimuli could help explain individual differences in behavior relating to planned purchases or impulse purchases.

The study involved 774 adult shoppers out of which 230 respondents were included in the control group, 145 respondents in the experimental group for the lemon scent, 144 respondents in the experimental group for the background music, and 255 respondents in the experimental group for the background music and the lemon scent. In the latter case, it was about investigating the effects of the multi-sensory interaction between the background music and the lemon scent, which was of interest to discuss and report in detail here. The study lasted four weeks, and the data collection took place during all days of the week from morning to night.

The hypothesis that was tested assumed that shoppers who conducted impulse purchases would be more positive to emotional, atmospheric stimuli, such as background music, and have a more emotionally oriented shopping style. Similarly, shoppers who conducted the planned purchases would be more positive to atmospheric stimuli such as pleasant fragrance, which would strengthen their more cognitively oriented shopping style.

The significant results showed that for the shoppers who made impulse purchases, more money was spent on purchases when only the background music was present. Then the amount was equal to $96.89, compared with $64 for the control group. As for the shoppers who made planned purchases, more money was spent on purchases when only the lemon scent was present. Then the amount was equal to $46.50, compared with $40.79 for the control group. These results meant that the hypothesis was confirmed.

But the most interesting result was that for both groups of shoppers, the presence of multiple stimuli, i.e., background music and lemon scent in interaction, had a negative impact on how much money was spent on the purchase. For those who made impulse purchases, the amount was equal to $36.70, compared with $64 for the control group, and for those who made planned purchases, the amount was equal to $28.29, compared with $40.79 for the control group. How can this be explained?

The researchers concluded that it could be explained with the optimal stimulation theory, which means that individuals desire a certain optimum stimulation level to be satisfied and comfortable with the actual environment. On the one hand, it is believed in theory that when the environment does not offer sufficient stimulus, individuals look for other, more complex or unusual stimuli. On the other hand, it is assumed in theory that when individuals get too much stimulus in the environment, they seek to reduce the level of stimulation that occurred (Steenkamp and Baumgartner, 1992).

> *Customers spend less money on purchases if they become over stimulated at the point of purchase.*

The theory assumes that in order to get away from too many stimuli, consumers change their behavior rather than visit fewer stores, examine fewer products, or buy fewer products, which this study had shown. In this study, there may be a plausible explanation as to why the interaction between the background music and the lemon scent was not appreciated.

Multi-Sensory Perception of a Brand

In the literature, it is assumed that a product or a brand is perceived and experienced by people through several (*multiple*) senses. The sensory information that is sent from a product regarding the color of the product, how the product is heard, how the product feels in your hand, or how it smells influences the whole experience of the product.

When it comes to brand packaging, sensory information is of greater importance today than ever before to create a multi-sensory experience. Various types of packaging have the task of communicating a brand, enhancing the image of the brand, and educating consumers about the brand. For a consumer product that requires packaging, such as food, beer and wine, home electronics, skin care products, and many other products, the old adage that "You cannot judge a book by its cover," does not apply, but rather the opposite applies.

When it comes to wine and beer, sensory information is created, for example, through sound that is associated with how a bottle sounds when it is opened or when the wine cork pops off, or tactile elements, such as a temperature indicator on a bottle, which all give significant emotional connections to the brand.

In most cases, the packages are also sealed, preventing consumers from being able to see, touch, smell, and taste what's inside. This means that packaging must take on the role of conveying a product experience to be able to convince consumers to buy the product in the package. It turns out that most consumers also take into account the packaging design, shape, sound, or hardness in their perception and see these properties as part of the overall product experience.

Research suggests that the perception of a package can change consumers' taste perception of a particular brand. As an example, it can be mentioned that the sound of a flexible, crinkling packaging or the feel of a cardboard structure can affect consumers' perceptions of the care that the brand shows about the product.

It is common that the sound of a product says something to a person about its quality, in the same way as a scent can be perceived as more or less pleasant or the color of the product affects the impression one gets. How a product is perceived and experienced depends on the sensory information that the product in question projects (Schifferstein, 2006). The questions that many researchers have asked themselves include how does the interaction of the sensory information work and how do the different senses combine to create a multi-sensory experience of products?

> *Consumers often believe that "If the company cares about the packaging having high quality, they care also about the product having high quality, which means that they care about me and my family."*

In research, experimental studies have been conducted that have examined both the interaction generally between the senses and the interaction between two specific senses, such as vision and touch, sight and sound, sight and scent, or sound and touch. This research attempts to answer the question of how sensory information from a stimulus affects the information from a different stimulus and how individuals evaluate the item or object that is perceived and experienced. I will return later to the question of what happens when sensory information from two different stimuli of a product is perceived as noncongruent, i.e., that they are not in agreement with each other.

Multi-Sensory Product Evaluation

Research suggests that there are a few studies that study how the evaluation of tangible products is influenced by visual information in connection with a tactile evaluation, in terms of consumer preferences for the actual products. So far, touch, as tactile evaluation, has been most prominent when it comes to individuals being able to obtain relevant information.

However, at the same time, it is generally accepted that goods and services appeal to a variety of human senses; for example, visually pleasing colors of clothes can result in consumers perceiving such products as being softer. This means that it is an important task for marketers to understand how consumers evaluate and process multi-sensory information in order to be able to design and offer brands that lead to the desired response from consumers.

> *The interaction between visual and tactile stimuli is common when it comes to most tangible products.*

In a study, improved results were shown in terms of product evaluation when both visual and tactile sensory information were obtained. One conclusion was that this improvement was due to visual information supporting the resulting tactile information in connection with the evaluation. It was further claimed that visual information created expectations of a tactile experience, and a mismatch between visual and tactile stimuli led to individuals exploring the tangible products more, which in itself created greater surprise and fondness for the product.

Other studies show that there is support for multi-sensory evaluation, and it appears that tactile exploration of a product is made so that an individual shall be able to distinguish between the different stimuli with visual evaluation. For familiar products, touch and sight together give an individual the opportunity to perceive different aspects of a product's structure, which is done by two independent senses that complement each other (Whitaker et al., 2008).

The Interaction between Visual and Tactile Stimuli

It is clear from the research that relatively few studies have been carried out on the multi-sensory interaction of vision and touch in terms of product evaluation. In an experimental study, Balaji et al. (2011) examined closely the multi-sensory interaction between vision and touch. The researchers were interested in testing whether tactile information predominates over visual information as well as if multi-sensory tactile and visual information increases attitudes and purchase intentions compared with single sensory information.

In the study, 126 men and 67 women at an Indian university participated in three different experimental assignments on the experience of tissue paper from the same brand. Three different parts of the soft paper were used, and on the front there was the same identical structure and the same visual design. Specifically, it was a floral design in colors such as pink, green, and blue. Moreover, all three parts of the paper were equally light and thick with regard to weight. The surface of the paper had a soft and smooth feeling when it was touched.

When it came to the visual assignment, the paper was presented only visually to the participants, and they could look at the paper as long as they wished. Participants were not allowed to touch the paper and could only make a visual evaluation of the stimuli. When the participants were done, they were to write their answers in a questionnaire. Thereafter, when it came to the tactile assignment, participants could only touch and feel the paper, but not visually experience it. The paper was placed in an opaque plastic bag and participants were asked to touch the paper on the inside of the plastic bag. They were not allowed to touch the paper more than once to assess the actual stimulus. Finally, when it came to the multi-sensory assignment, participants got to both see and touch the paper at the same time. Each participant had access to the three colored pieces of paper and had the task of evaluating them.

The results showed that the tactile evaluation dominated significantly over the visual evaluation. In the same way, it turned out that there were more positive attitudes toward the brand through the tactile evaluation in comparison with the visual. It also appeared that the multi-sensory evaluation created more positive attitudes toward the brand in comparison with the single sensory evaluation, which also resulted in higher purchase intentions.

The study's conclusions were that tactile sensory information made it easier for consumers to make assessments of products in a purchase decision. It should also be said that the respondents expressed unfavorable feelings about the brand when the opportunity to touch the product did not exist. Furthermore, another conclusion was that the multi-sensory stimulation positively affected both consumers' attitudes as well as their purchase intentions.

The Interaction between Visual and Atmospheric Stimuli

In a field study experiment, Hulten (2012) identified the effects of atmospheric stimuli when purchasing wine glasses at an IKEA store. The purpose of this study was to investigate whether a positive impact on shoppers' purchasing behavior could be established in terms of time spent on the purchase, the time spent touching the glasses, and the number of purchased glasses.

> *When purchasing wine glasses at IKEA, customers stay longer in the point of purchase if the visual and atmospheric stimuli interact.*

The experiment involved 886 shoppers, of which 564 were women and 322 were men of different ages, spread over 451 individuals in the control group and 435 people in the experimental group. During two weekends, from Friday to Sunday, the experiments were conducted in the glass department, and it meant that the place of purchase was made more emotionally appealing.

For the experimental group, visual stimuli were introduced in the form of red and brown table mats with a glass carafe and glasses on a tray, and the lighting was reduced by turning off a number of rows of lights. Furthermore, a scent stimulus, in the form of a vanilla fragrance, was introduced, which was presented in the form of a number of scented candles placed close to the point of purchase.

The results showed that the combination of atmospheric stimuli has a significant effect on the time shoppers spend at the point of purchase. It turned out that the experimental group spent 106 seconds at the point of purchase in comparison with the control group, which spent 75 seconds. Furthermore, it appeared that shoppers who bought wine glasses stayed longer at the point of purchase than the non-buyers, which for the control group corresponded to 68 seconds and for the experimental group 146 seconds.

When it came to the impact of the sensory behavior in terms of the increased touch time, there was a significant increase of 50 percent, which for the control group corresponded to 15 seconds and for the experimental group 23 seconds. Furthermore, it appeared that the more time shoppers spent touching the wine glasses, the greater the likelihood of a purchase, as evidenced by non-buyers touching the wine glasses for 10 seconds, whereas buyers of wine glasses touched the glasses for 40 seconds. It turned out that there was a significant increase and a positive correlation between the time spent on touching the glasses and intention to purchase the wine glasses at the point of purchase.

It also appeared from this study that there was a significant effect on the total sales of wine glasses and the probability of selling more exclusive glasses. The sales of exclusive glasses increased by 217 percent for the experimental group as compared with the control group.

The conclusions of the study were that the combination of sight and smell, as atmospheric stimuli, affected consumer's sensory behavior and purchasing behavior. There were several significant differences after the introduction of new designs and changes in the lighting and a vanilla scent at the purchasing site, leading shoppers to stay longer at the point of purchase and spending more time touching the glasses. This in turn resulted in shoppers buying more glasses, primarily exclusive glasses. How the influence occurs on the shopper's behavior depending on the reduced lighting, the introduction of vanilla scent, or the combination of these is difficult to determine (Spence et al., 2014).

Multiple-Sensory Stimuli

In the research on sensory marketing, a number of studies have recently examined in detail the importance of multi-sensory interaction of different sensory experiences. In a study by Krishna et al. (2010), interactions between smell and touch were studied in which participants were instructed to rate a scented paper based on their experiences of scent and texture. It turned out that the results revealed a significant interaction between the two sensory experiences, where female participants had a more positive haptic perception of a plain paper in comparison with men. The men had, instead, a similar positive experience to a rough paper, which led to a significant sensory experience. One conclusion of the study was that multi-sensory congruence between touch and smell could result in a more positive tactile experience.

It is widely believed in psychological research that multiple-sensory stimuli promote each other when it comes to influencing consumers' perceptions, as shown in the following example (Zampini and Spence, 2004).

> *British researchers have shown that there are common effects of sensory stimuli, where one's own sound experience of the potato chips an individual is chewing affects the perception of the crispness of the potato chips.*

Another study showed how different colors of orange juice, as visual information, could affect the taste discrimination. It appeared that visual information dominated over the actual flavor of the orange juice when it came to influencing the consumer's preferences, whereas verbal stimuli did not dominate the discrimination of taste in the same way.

Consumer's choice of brand samples for products with high sensory elements, such as chocolate, music, perfume, and beer, with similar sensory stimuli regarding sight, sound, smell, and taste has been studied in a number of experiments (Biswas et al., 2014). It often occurs that fragrance samples for perfumes and taste samples of chocolate are used in shops or department stores.

The results showed that consumers chose the first product sample in a sequence of samples when similar sensory stimuli were present. This was explained by the existence of *primacy effects* by the theory of sensory habituation, which means that consumers have a greater preference for the first sample. On the other hand, consumers chose the last product sample when various sensory stimuli were present. This was explained by *actuality effects* by the theory on sensory slowdown, which means that there is a greater preference for the last product samples in comparison with the earlier samples.

Inconsistency between Sensory Stimuli

The sensory information obtained from a product can sometimes be perceived as noncongruent and create conflicts between the different senses. Usually a person has a certain expectation of how a product should sound, smell, or feel just by looking at it. If an individual then perceives and experiences that there is an inconsistency between the different stimuli and the sensory information obtained, it generally leads to a reaction of surprise, which can result in either positive or negative feelings. It is further assumed that inconsistencies have an impact on the product evaluation that an individual makes of an actual product and especially the aesthetic evaluation (Ludden et al., 2006).

In an experimental study with three detailed experiments, the effect of inconsistencies between the sensory stimuli for sight-touch, sight-sound, and sight-scent were studied. The study assumed that the senses could be divided into two groups, namely, the *distance senses*, such as sight, sound, and smell, and the *proximity senses*, such as touch and taste, on the basis that people can see, hear, and smell the items or objects from a distance, but to be able to feel and taste, it requires physical contact. For this reason, it was assumed that it was more likely that an individual first perceives an item or an object with the help of sight, hearing, or smell and that sight gives the most detailed information about a product in the shortest time.

When it came to measuring the impact of inconsistencies, the study was based on sight and relating it to sound, smell, and touch. There was an assumption that inconsistencies between vision and touch were related in that the same product attributes could be perceived by both senses, because an individual could both see and feel a shape or texture. But for sight-sound and sight-scent it was always assumed that inconsistencies were about two different product attributes, because an individual could not see a smell or a sound. Furthermore, it was assumed that when an individual saw a small item or object, he/she could expect a soft sound and when someone saw a pink object, he/she could expect that it smelled sweet.

Inconsistencies between vision, on the one hand, and sound or scent, on the other hand, were probably due to cognitive associations rather than direct perception, i.e., how the product was perceived and experienced. This probably also affected how individuals perceived an inconsistency with respect to various stimuli and sensory information.

The study's findings showed that participants in the three experiments were surprised by the inconsistencies regarding vision-touch but not in terms of sight-sound and sight-scent. One of the explanations when it came to vision-touch could be considered to be that many individuals were likely to experience this because this interaction itself contained noncongruent sensory information about the product attributes. When it came to sight-sound and sight-scent, however, the information was obtained from two different attributes, which in themselves do not need to be consistent.

Furthermore, one of the conclusions was that many individuals were not surprised over inconsistencies, because they did not expect various product attributes to provide sensory information based on congruence. This could be illustrated with an example from one of the three experiments in which a sound that was not congruent with the appearance of the product only moderately affected the perception of the product. Instead, it turned out that the participants placed more importance on the appearance of the product than the sound. Similarly, the effect of scents on the product experience could be considered negligible in comparison with the effect of the appearance of the product.

Finally, it was pointed out that for certain products or product categories, inconsistencies between the different sensory stimuli could be a suitable strategy to create more entertaining and interesting products. This might relate to products that people use, for example, in public events or waiting rooms where inconsistencies could create astonishment and surprise. For this reason, it was proposed that inconsistencies between the sensory information for sight-touch could be an effective strategy in design and product development.

Influence of Multi-Sensory Experiences on the Buying and Consumption Processes

In the context of what has come to be known as *sensory branding*, a multi-sensory experience of products, services, and brands is one of the main starting points for individuals/customers' experience. It appears to be particularly important in industries such as retail, tourism, and service where the total experience of a product or brand is often based on the interaction between several senses.

Kotler (1973) drew attention early on to the importance of different sensory channels and their atmospheric stimuli, especially in retail. For a long time, few empirical studies had examined in detail the importance of the interplay between the five senses; therefore, there is a need to study this interaction. Furthermore, the literature has not dealt extensively with the question of its relevance to consumer affections, cognitions, or actual behaviors in the buying and consumption processes.

SERVICE ENVIRONMENT

In terms of multi-sensory brand-experiences of service environments, there are a number of studies that address this. One explanation for this may be that a service environment for obvious reasons covers several different senses and sensory dimensions, which can contribute to strengthening the atmosphere a company seeks to achieve. In this context, the stimuli that are also linked to the sense of sight traditionally have the greatest importance, as previously discussed based on the importance of different atmospheric stimuli, whereas stimuli related to sound, smell, touch, and taste have had a secondary importance.

> *Sensory components related to sound, smell, touch, and taste should have a more prominent place to create a multi-sensory experience.*

Krishna (2013) mentions casinos as role models for a multi-sensory brand-experience with respect to how the sensory dimensions of sight, sound, smell, touch, and taste can be expressed. It is argued that casinos can be regarded as a perfect example of how a service environment is designed to stimulate each of the five senses. Each sensory dimension is deliberately designed to attract and encourage visitors, to make the casino visit a memorable experience regardless of whether one wins or loses.

In an American study, the relationships between ambient sensory components of sight, sound, smell, and touch in relation to consumers' emotions and behavioral intentions were studied in a spa context (Kang et al., 2011). The researchers were interested in further investigating how different sensory components, through sensory stimulation, could potentially influence customers' emotions and behaviors associated with the experience of a spa.

The survey was conducted by an American spa chain in eleven different locations in Texas, which offered some limited spa services. The respondents consisted of a convenience sample and amounted to 887 customers, who were asked to answer a questionnaire after their spa experience at the specific location. When it came to vision, the importance of components such as design, color, layout, and cleanliness were studied and for audio, components such as classical music, pleasant music, slow music, and quiet music were studied. When it came to smell, the importance of components such as pleasant fragrance and fresh scent were studied and for tactile, components such as silky fabrics, soft equipment, temperature, and humidity were studied.

The significant results showed that vision and touch positively influenced customers' enjoyment in conjunction with the experience and that sound had a direct impact on customers' behavior intentions. In the latter case, it turned out that this did not influence customers' emotions.

The study's conclusions were that the sensory components, such as smoothness, softness, suitable temperature, and humidity, were the most important sensory components to stimulate customer's enjoyment of the spa. Furthermore, it appeared that the visual components such as a well-organized layout, cleanliness, elegant design, and warm colors were other sensory components that appealed to spa goers. It also turned out that the visual and tactile components did not in and of themselves have a significant impact on customers' behavior intentions but it turned out that enjoyment was crucial for it.

Finally, it should be mentioned that the study's results also indicated that each sensory component might have an impact on the other sensory components either in a positive or a negative way. This means that to achieve a positive multi-sensory brand-experience, there should be a balance between the different sensory components through an appropriate combination of the senses. If not, then there is a risk that the multi-sensory experience will be more negative than positive.

In tourism research, studies in recent years have come to emphasize the importance of multi-sensory brand-experiences and how these affect the tourist experience of places and cities. It no longer suffices to only offer tourists products or services without being able to allow meaningful experiences that are not only based on visual stimuli, but also include smells, sounds, and tastes (Pan and Ryan, 2009).

> *Within tourism, the five senses play a crucial role in the experience of a place or a city.*

Furthermore, it is thought to be not possible to rely on visual images (or photos) to convey a sensory impression of a town or a place, which has been the most common in practice over the past century. Within the mass marketing that has dominated the global tourism industry in trying to generate attention and interest to a tourist or a tourist country, the use of visual images are now seriously questioned. Against this background, research has recently become increasingly focused on understanding the importance and the role that several senses may have in the tourist's brand experience of a city or a place.

In a Portuguese study, the importance of sight, sound, smell, taste, and touch of a multi-sensory brand experience of a nature park in southwestern Portugal was closely analyzed. The aim of the study was to identify the importance of the five senses for a tourist experience. This study referred to other studies in anthropology, geography, and history, which theoretically assumed that all perception is physical (*body*) and contained a number of interactions with the environment/surroundings (*place*) during a particular period (*time*), leading to a learned behavior (*culture*). In this context, it was assumed that there was an integration of mind and body, but at the same time the importance of the so-called place paradigm was emphasized, which emphasizes the different sensory relationships between the senses, the body, and the environment/surroundings.

Furthermore, the study assumed that different senses could be place-related, for which the term *sensory landscape* refers to in terms of visual connotations to a landscape. Similarly, other senses could be place-related and expressed as *soundscape, scentscape, tastescape,* or *geography of touch*. Hereby, it is assumed that there are multiple-sensory experiences in geographic meetings, which is considered to be the case in tourism. The survey was conducted in the form of a questionnaire, which was answered by 195 tourists in the nature park, who spent at least one night in the area as visitors. Among the questions asked were five open-ended questions to capture how the five senses affected the tourists' overall experience of the destination.

Furthermore, a number of statements were made about each of the five senses, which were answered by using the five-point Likert scale. The analysis of the data was done using textual analysis for the open-ended questions and chi-square test and descriptive statistics for the statements.

The results showed that each of the five senses contributed positively to the strength of tourists' overall experience. Regarding the significance of the various senses, it was believed that visual pleasure played the greatest role (58percent), followed by sound experiences (41.4percent), taste experiences (39.2percent), scent experiences (35.9percent), and, finally, tactile experiences (28.7percent). It turned out that the five senses together contributed to the strength of the overall experience for at least eight out of the ten tourists. The conclusion from this study was that the five senses together formed the basis of a multi-sensory brand experience.

BRAND

An attempt has been made by Lindstrom (2005) to further discuss and propose a model called Sensogram that illustrates how the five senses may interact with each other when it comes to influencing consumers' image and brand loyalty to a particular brand. Furthermore, Lindstrom tries to show that although some sensory components are interrelated, each component has a distinctive effect in order to be able to explain the relationships between sensory components on the one hand and brand features, brand identity, and brand experience on the other.

> *There is little knowledge about the interaction between the different senses and more research is needed going forward.*

In both marketing research and consumer psychology research, studies of multi-sensory brand-experiences, which include the interaction between the five senses, are very rare. Krishna (2013, p. 163) believes that "One of the main areas of research is the interaction between the senses, where there are unlimited opportunities for multi-sensory stimuli whose effects are not yet known." It requires more research on how the interaction between the different senses affects consumers' affections, cognitions, and actual behaviors in the form of, for example, time spent and purchase.

One of the reasons that this has not been so studied is the focus that has long existed on just the sense of sight, as in traditional advertising and promotions, which is emphasized as the main stimulus at the expense of stimuli such as sound, smell, touch, and taste.

The following example taken from the American coffee chain Starbucks illustrates how a multi-sensory brand-experience can be expressed in practice:

> *Starbucks is the world's largest coffee chain and has about 40 million visitors daily in its cafes. Through a strategic and deliberate work with sensory marketing ever since the 1980s, the company creates a deeper and more personal relationship with their customers.*
>
> *The inviting and stimulating service environment lends itself to read a good book in a soft and comfortable armchair as well as having a cozy chat with good friends. The green and yellow colors of the interior, together with pleasant lighting, create a calm and soothing visual experience. The soothing background music that is played is selected with precision and accuracy by Starbucks's "Content Team" of about 30 people to find the right "sound" for Starbucks.*
>
> *This, together with the flavors and aromas of the freshly ground coffee, along with the comfortable armchair's texture, firmness, and shape, enables the visitor's senses to interact and create a multi-sensory experience of the brand. In this way, Starbucks wants to create an atmosphere in their service environment where positive brand experiences can occur, emotions are expressed, and memories are created.*

In neuromarketing, it is thought that individuals who are stimulated through multiple senses, through a multi-sensory experience from either a service environment or a brand, are more likely to keep this experience in their memory. This is believed to be due to the subconscious processes that select the signals that are conveyed by the senses and which are most relevant for each individual on a personal level.

With regard to the individual's ability to make use of the five senses to create an experience, the brain receives the signals that are conveyed through different stimuli and which are considered to be the most important and worth remembering. This is particularly true in the case of long-term memory where the most valuable signals are preserved, as opposed to the short-term memory, which only takes care of some signals over a shorter time.

REFERENCES

Babin, B.J., Chebat, J. and Michon, R. (2004), "Perceived appropriateness and its effect on quality, affect and behaviour," *Journal of Retailing and Consumer Services*, 11:287–298.

Balaji, M.S., Raghavan, S. and Jha, S. (2011), "Role of tactile and visual inputs in product evaluation: a multisensory perspective," *Asia Pacific Journal of Marketing and Logistics*, 23, 4:513–530.

Biswas, D., Labrecque, L.I., Lehmann, D.R. and Markos, E. (2014), "Making choices while smelling, tasting, and listening: the role of sensory (dis)similarity when sequentially sampling products," *Journal of Marketing*, 78, January:112–126.

Bresciani, J.P., Dammeier, F. and Ernst, M.O. (2006), "Vision and touch are automatically integrated for the perception of sequences of events," *Journal of Vision*, 6, 5:554–564.

Calvert, G., Spence, C. and Stein, B.E. (2004), *The handbook of multisensory processes*, Cambridge, MA: MIT Press.

Driver, J. and Noesselt, T. (2008), "Multisensory interplay reveals cross modal influences on 'sensory specific' brain regions, neural responses, and judgements," *Neuron*, 57, 1:11–23.

Ernst, M.O. and Banks, M.S. (2002), "Humans integrate visual and haptic information in a statistically optimal fashion," *Nature*, 415, 6 870:429–433.

Hultén, B. (2012), "Sensory cues and shoppers' touching behaviour: the case of IKEA," *International Journal of Retail and Distribution Management*, 40, 4:273–289.

Kang, E., Boger, C.A., Back, K.-J. and Madera, J. (2011), *The impact of sensory environments on spagoers' emotion and behavioral intention*, http://scholarworks.umass.edu/gradconf_hospitality/2011/

Kotler, P. (1973), "Atmospherics as a marketing tool," *Journal of Retailing*, 49, 4:48 ff.

Krishna, A. (2013), *Customer sense—how the 5 senses influence buying behaviour*, New York: Palgrave Macmillan, p. 163.

Krishna, A., Elder, R.S. and Caldara, C. (2010), "Feminine to smell but masculine to touch? Multisensory congruence and its effect on the aesthetic experience," *Journal of Consumer Psychology*, 20, 4:410–418.

Lindström, M. (2005), *Brand sense: build powerful brands through touch, taste, smell, sight, and sound*, New York: Free Press.

Ludden, G.D.S., Schifferstein, H.N.J. and Hekkert, P. (2006), *Sensory incongruity: comparing vision to touch, audition and olfaction*, Conference Paper, Department of Industrial Design, Delft University of Technology.

Mattila, A.S. and Wirtz, J. (2001), "Congruency of scent and music as a driver of in-store evaluations and behaviour," *Journal of Retailing*, 77:273–289.

Morrin, M. and Chebat, J.-C. (2005), "Person-place congruency: the interactive effects of shopper style and atmospherics on consumer expenditures," *Journal of Service Research*, 8:181–191.

Morrison, M., Gan, S., Dubelaar, C. and Oppewal, H. (2011), "In-store music and aroma influences on shopper behavior and satisfaction," *Journal of Business Research*, 64:558–564.

Pan, S. and Ryan, C. (2009), "Tourism sense-making: the role of the senses and travel journalism," *Journal of Travel and Tourism Marketing*, 26, 7:625–639.

Schifferstein, H.N.J. (2006), "The relative importance of sensory modalities in product usage: a study of self-reports," *Acta Psychologica*, 121:41–64.

Schifferstein, H.N.J. and Cleiren, M. (2005), "Capturing product experiences: a split-modality approach," *Acta Psychologica*, 118, 3:293–318.

Shams, L. and Seitz, A.R. (2008), "Benefits of multisensory learning," *Trends in Cognitive Science*, 12, 11:411–417.

Spangenberg, E.R., Grohmann, B. and Sprott, D.E. (2005), "It's beginning to smell (and sound) a lot like Christmas: the interactive effects of ambient scent and music in a retail setting," *Journal of Business Research*, 58:1583–1589.

Spence, C., Puccinelli, N.M., Grewal, D. and Roggeveen, A.L. (2014), "Store atmospherics: a multisensory perspective," *Psychology and Marketing*, 31, 7:472–488.

Steenkamp, J.E. and Baumgartner, H. (1992), "The role of optimum stimulation level in exploratory consumer behaviour," *Journal of Consumer Research*, 19:434–448.

Thesen, T., Vibell, J., Calvert, G. and Osterbauer, A. (2004), "Neuroimaging of multisensory processing in vision, audition, touch and olfaction." *Cognitive Processing*, 5, 2:84–93.

Troye, S.V. and Supphellen, M. (2012), "Consumer participation in coproduction: 'I made it myself' effects on consumers sensory perceptions and evaluations of outcome and input product," *Journal of Marketing*, 76, March:33–46.

Whitaker, T.A., Simoes-Franklin, C. and Newell, F.N. (2008), "Vision and touch: independent or integrated systems for the perception of texture?" *Brain Research*, 1, 242:59–72.

Zampini, M. and Spence, C. (2004), "The role of auditory cues in modulating the perceived crispness and staleness of potato chips," *Journal of Sensory Studies*, 19, 5:347–363.

11 Sensory Marketing in the Future

This chapter discusses sensory marketing as a new emerging marketing paradigm. The features that distinguish sensory marketing from transaction marketing and relationship marketing are highlighted. The focus is on the importance of the five senses and a multi-sensory brand-experience.

Thereafter, the new concepts and models needed to develop sensory marketing in theory and practice are discussed. In this context, the main implications of a new approach are discussed. Finally, some personal reflections on the development of future sensory marketing are shared.

AN EMERGING PARADIGM

In a global marketing environment and consumer culture, which may be deemed to characterize the early 2000s, established truths in consumer marketing and brand building are facing major challenges. It is no longer possible to explain and understand corporate and consumer behavior based solely on the traditional concepts and models, but new thinking is required.

Over the past ten years, more and more researchers have started to pay attention to sensory marketing (SM) as a new emerging paradigm (Hulten et al., 2009; Hultén, 2011, 2012; Krishna, 2010, 2011, 2013; Achrol and Kotler, 2012; Krishna and Schwartz, 2014; Spence et al., 2014; Hultén, 2015). The importance of the five senses and the human brain to be able to position and differentiate a brand on a deeper level has grown stronger in respect to both goods and services. This means that transaction marketing (TM) and relationship marketing (RM) are no longer considered as adequate explanatory models when it comes to understanding how consumers engage in identity creation, self-fulfillment, and sensory experiences in the buying and consumption processes.

In my opinion, sensory marketing should been seen as a complement to TM and RM, from a brand perspective, by focusing on the emotional, symbolic content, rather than the functional, rational content of a brand or service offering. As the ultimate goal, SM shall help to create a multi-sensory brand-experience for consumers, which leads to a positive consumer value and a positive brand image. In this context, a company's mission is to create and deliver a service process where the sensory experiences and sensory strategies are the focus of sensory marketing.

In practice, this is already a paradigm shift for many companies based on both the new values and the new digital behavior that characterizes generations X, Y, and Z, with individualization as the lifestyle (Hultén et al., 2009). Previously, several examples of how companies chose to adapt to both the cultural value shift and digital technology have been presented demonstrating marketing's dynamics and the changes that are going on in business. What has been lacking so far, to analyze and explain the causes of these dynamics, has been appropriate concepts, theories, and models conveyed by a language, which sensory marketing is intending to do in a theoretical context.

CONCEPT AND MODEL DEVELOPMENT

As a researcher, I argue that it is entirely possible to validate sensory marketing as a new emerging paradigm, both theoretically and practically. When it comes to sensory marketing as a theoretical field, it takes as its starting point in a number of different scientific disciplines, which together allow for the integration and development of concepts and models other than the traditional ones within the marketing discipline.

For me, as an eclectic, it means an opportunity to combine and integrate various concepts, models, and theories from disciplines such as consumer behavior, consumer psychology, branding, consumer marketing, and sociology. If it should be possible to understand today's global marketing environment and the consumer culture, which consumer marketing should be based on, it is no longer enough with a traditional marketing perspective. Instead, concepts and theories should be derived from other related disciplines so that one can develop a framework for sensory marketing from a branding perspective, as opposed to exchange or relationship perspectives, as previously discussed in the context of the TM and RM framework.

Based on the five senses, therefore, I have focused on concepts such as consumer values, consumer experiences, stimuli, sensations, sensors, sensory strategies, sensory experiences, brand image, and multi-sensory brand-experience as an expression of what is included in sensory marketing as an emerging paradigm. Some of these concepts are established in disciplines such as consumer behavior, marketing, and branding and other disciplines such as consumer psychology and sociology, whereas others have been added to show a relevant framework. These concepts were previously illustrated and discussed in the model of sensory marketing (Figure 3.5).

It has been important for me to be able to validate sensory marketing as an emerging paradigm, based on existing research and literature, when it comes to influential factors such as societal culture, service environment, and brand. The effects that sensory stimuli, sensory perception, and sensory symbolism have on consumers' affections, cognitions, and actual behaviors in the context of sensory marketing are clear from the SEB model (Figure 11.1).

It has been presented in previous chapters that for the societal culture and the service environment as well as the brand, there is scientific evidence that sensory stimuli, sensory perception, and sensory symbolism have positive, significant effects on consumers' affections, cognitions, and actual behaviors.

When it comes to the service environment, which is usually associated with stores, shopping centers, and department stores, for a long time, the atmospheric stimuli has been regarded as natural features to help contribute to consumers' satisfaction and well-being. This is evident from research with respect to the five senses, especially regarding vision, but also in terms of sound and smell (Spence et al., 2014). In contrast, touch and taste are addressed to a lesser extent, indicating the need for further research.

When it comes to a brand, which is usually associated with goods, services, or products, marketing stimuli such as advertising and commercials within the framework of influence have traditionally been regarded as natural features to attract consumers' attention. This is particularly true for the sense of sight, because the eyes are regarded as being dominant for an individual when it comes to assimilating sensory information from the environment in connection with product selection and purchasing decisions.

Research suggests that the other senses have been studied empirically to a lesser extent to identify the impact of sensory stimuli, sensory perception,

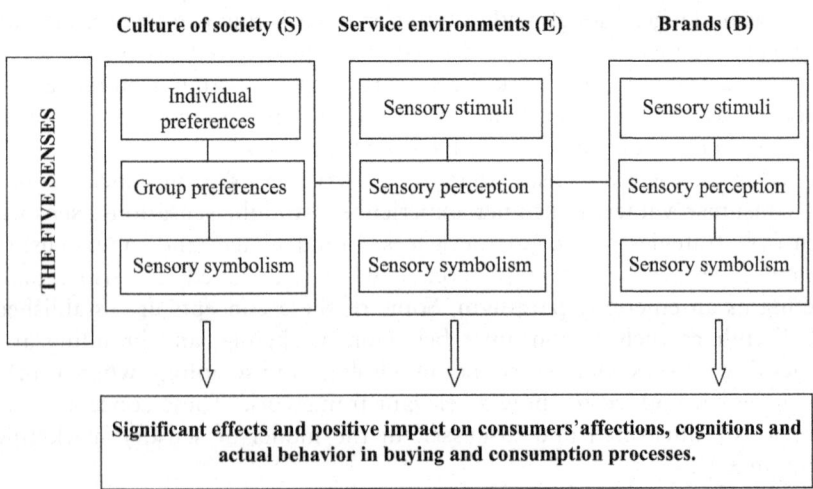

Figure 11.1 The Five Senses and Their Impact Factors

and sensory symbolism for consumers' affections, cognitions, and actual behaviors. Therefore, I assert that sensory marketing, through the presented SEB model, has scientific support in research and literature. This means that SM, in relation to TM and RM, should be considered as a new paradigm, which is based on how sensory stimuli, sensory perception, and sensory symbolism are influenced by societal culture, service environment, and brand.

SENSORY BRANDING

Sensory marketing, as a concept, includes the marketing of goods, services, places, people, companies, organizations, or ideas, which should result in a multi-sensory brand-experience for the consumers. Within the framework of the SEB model, it is possible to identify and define the importance of sensory stimuli, sensory perception, and sensory symbolism in regard to the influential factors such as societal culture, service environment, and brand, for example, of a product, a destination, or an organization.

I mean that there is a lack of theoretical as well as empirical research regarding the importance of the five senses for different brands, i.e., specific goods, services, or products, as opposed to the various service environments. Therefore, there is reason to pay particular attention to *sensory branding*, with a starting point in traditional branding, as a future exciting area of research.

A conceptual framework for sensory branding is proposed, where concepts such as sensory stimuli, sensory perception, and sensory symbolism affect an individual's affections and cognitions, which in turn is the basis for an individual's attitudes, preferences, learning, memory, and actual behavior, resulting in a brand image (Figure 11.2).

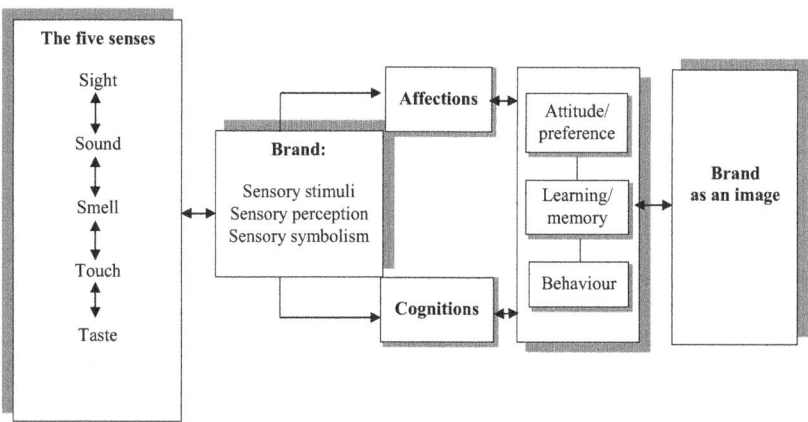

Figure 11.2 A Framework for Sensory Branding

There is a need for new studies of different brands in which the importance of sensory stimuli, sensory perception, and sensory symbolism is made clear to seriously understand the importance of the five senses for the brand image that arises in connection with consumers' purchase and consumption processes.

Today, research in sensory branding is carried out for cars, computers, home decor, food, cell phones, fashion, and hotel and restaurant services, to name a few common examples. But it will take several more years before new scientific results and conclusions can be presented from this research regarding both the physical and the virtual environments.

PERSONAL REFLECTIONS

My interest in sensory marketing began in the early 2000s when I became fascinated by the postmodern notions to explain and understand business and consumer behavior. I found then that neither TM nor RM treated consumers as individuals, which many postmodern proponents suggested. Then I realized the need to renew the established marketing theories to be able to develop a new approach where consumer value, consumer experiences, and brand image came to be in focus.

The basic purpose of developing sensory marketing has been to be able to contribute to a more realistic understanding of consumer marketing through a new approach. In this context, the five senses came to be the center of my interest, because these take into account how a product, a service, or a combination of both can be perceived and experienced in different ways, at a deeper personal level, by an individual. This came to be most clearly expressed through how a product looks, sounds, smells, feels, and tastes, which recognizes the importance of aesthetic and sensory aspects of an individual in the capacity as a consumer.

I found that neither TM nor RM addressed these elements; instead, these theories were focused on explaining and understanding how exchanges and relationships take place in marketing. For me, there was a lack of depth in these theories to understand consumers' affections, cognitions, and the actual behaviors at the individual level, despite the fact that TM and RM were about concepts such as satisfaction of needs, loyalty, and value creation. It grew out of a realization that consumer marketing needed to be reformed and developed with the help of other concepts, theories, and models, which have since taken place through what has become sensory marketing.

It should be mentioned that the year after the book *Sensory Marketing* (Hultén et al., 2009) was published, the book *Sensory Marketing: Research on the Sensuality of Products* (Krishna, 2010) also came to be published. As such, there were two leading perspectives on sensory marketing based on the five senses, which in various ways tried to convey the meaning of sensory marketing from both a marketing and branding perspective and a consumer psychological perspective. Since then, the research on sensory marketing, on the international stage, has taken its starting point from either of these two perspectives, and the area is currently undergoing rapid development.

For me, sensory marketing, as a new paradigm, is a way of trying to explain and understand how consumers through their five senses can create their own identity, self-fulfillment, and sensory experiences. In today's consumer culture, purchasing and consumption of brands thus contribute in that many individuals can create consumer value and consumer experiences on a personal level, containing both aesthetic and functional elements. This is a future challenge for sensory marketers: to develop sensory strategies through different service processes that lead to sensory experiences for tomorrow's consumers.

EPILOGUE

Six years ago, I considered sensory marketing, which had just seen the light, as another springboard for the future. Today, I can say that this proved to be a true assumption, and sensory marketing has been established seriously in both theory and practice. It is now important for both researchers and practitioners to seize the opportunities that a new emerging paradigm can offer. Let the exciting research journey with sensory marketing move full speed ahead!

REFERENCES

Achrol, R.S. and Kotler, P. (2012), "Frontiers of the marketing paradigm in the third millennium." Journal of the Academy of Marketing Science, 40, 35–52.

Hultén, B (2011), "Sensory marketing: the multi-sensory brand experience concept." European Business Review, 23, 3:256–273.

Hultén, B. (2012), "Sensory cues and shopper's touching behaviour: the case of IKEA," International Journal of Retail & Distribution Management, 40, 4:273–289.

Hultén, B. (2015), "The impact of sound experiences on the shopping behaviour of children and their parents." *Marketing Intelligence and Planning*, 33, 2:197–215.

Hultén, B., Broweus, N. and van Dijk, M. (2009), Sensory marketing. Basingstoke: Palgrave Macmillan.

Krishna, A. (ed.) (2010), Sensory marketing: research on the sensuality of products, New York: Taylor and Francis Group.

Krishna, A. (2012), "An integrative review of sensory marketing: engaging the senses to affect perception, judgment and behaviour." Journal of Consumer Psychology, 22, 3:332–351.

Krishna, A. (2013), Customer sense, Basingstoke: Palgrave Macmillan.

Krishna, A. and Schwarz, N. (2014), "Sensory marketing, embodiment and grounded cognition: a review and introduction," Journal of Consumer Psychology, 24, 2:159–168.

Spence, C., Puccinelli, N.M., Grewal, D. and Roggeveen, A.L. (2014), "Store atmospherics: a multisensory perspective," *Psychology and Marketing*, 31, 7:472–488.

Index

active touching 308
actuality effects 386
aesthetic/gastronomic sensations 112, 118
aesthetic taste 358–65
affective reactions 180–3
ambient sound 224
amygdala 136–7
appropriate touching 318, 335
associative learning 267–8, 273, 276
atmospheric sensations 122, 280
atmospheric stimuli 115, 242, 37–7, 380, 384–5, 388, 396
attitude 35–8, 40–1
audio branding 256, 258
auditive communication 232
auditive sensations 122
auditive stimuli 114, 185, 249, 324, 325, 373, 374
awareness 6, 7, 31, 52, 74, 99, 115, 132, 152, 167, 169, 173, 175, 187, 200, 205, 258, 262, 269, 293, 296, 297, 298, 301

background music 377–81
beneficial effects 290
bodily markers 227–8
brain: cerebellum 138; cerebrum 134; conscious processes 131–3; unconscious processes 131–3
brain stem 138
brand 125, 204, 292
brand as an image 100–2
brand building 49
brand experience 169; symbolic content 125
brand identity 49–50
brand image 51–2, 100–1
brand capital 340
brand consciousness 49

brand name 49
brand personality 49–50
brand perspective 92, 102–3, 394–5
brand relations 50
brand song 258
brand sound 256–7
brand voice 258
buying behavior 36–9
buying process 42–4

CCT (consumer culture theory) 46–7
consumer engineering 11
cognition 268
cognitive reactions 178–80
cognitive theories 39
cold cognition 150
color nuances
color preferences 189–90
competitive means approach 21–2, 24
congruence 112, 122, 195, 232, 234, 246, 295, 378–9
consumer behavior 36
consumer culture theory 46–7
consumer marketing 52–5
consumer's sovereignty 2
consumer value 96–7, 128–30
consumption 128–31, 159, 387
consumption culture 46–7
consumption experience 97–100
contour 196–7, 229, 309
convention 229
CRM (customer relationship management) 32, 103
cultural symbolism 219
cultural value shift 65
customer and supplier relationship 31
customer interactions 25
customer orientation 9, 31
customer value 30, 31, 33, 34, 96–7
consumer's sovereignty 2

decision making 38–9, 41–3
design 206
design factors 194–5
digital technology 80–3
distraction 249, 357–8
distribution channels 3, 7, 9–10, 14–15, 18

EEG 163, 164, 165
emotional associations 229, 289, 299
emotional gender differences 158
emotional impressions
emotional preferences 105
emotional quality 229
emotional receptors 115
emotional strategy 111
emotions 226
experience 51–2, 88–9, 95–100, 107–11
experience based consumption 128
experience goods 363
external taste 118, 339
eyes 172, 176
eye-tracking 165, 178, 187, 201

five senses 128; external use of 370; internal use of 370; model 107, 142, 162, 164
fMRI-functional magnetic resonance imaging 164
Fordism model 63
functional approach 14, 41
functional colors 210
functional integration 372

generation X 76–7
generation Y 77–9
generation Z 79–80
Gestalt 175
Gestalt psychology 99, 108, 175, 208
good taste 340

habitual behavior 152–4
habit forming actions 79, 154
haptic perception 330
haptic system 308–9
hedonic attribute 311
hedonic experience 298, 346
hedonic products 338
hedonic touching 310–12
hedonism 251
hippocampus 137
Howard-Sheth model 37–8
Hymns 258
Hypothalamus 137

identity creating 100, 103, 110, 119
Ikea effect 74
impulsive behavior 155–6
impulses 110, 155, 178, 319
individual identity 95
individualization as a lifestyle 92
industrial revolution 4, 9, 10, 11, 45, 60, 61, 62, 279
initial awareness 6, 146
inner taste 117
institutional approach 14, 18
instrumental music 224, 232
instrumental touching 310–12
integrative business processes 32
intermediary values 7,14
intimate sense 221, 349

jingle 49, 52, 114, 225, 257

learning 39–40
left brain hemisphere 142, 159
limbic system 136
logic 32
logo type 212–13
long term memory 145–6

marketing: aesthetics 108; collaboration processes 31; concept 12, 39; concept of usefulness 44–6; economic activity 16; five types of experiences 129; institutions 4; interaction processes 25–7; introduction of the terms 24; leadership approach 16, 18; management 18–19; modern 1, 4, 6, 9, 12; paradigm 32; post-modern approach 74, 91; principles 15–17; program 7, 11; strategy 16, 24
market orientation 7, 9, 12
masochism 351
mass individualization 65
mass marketing 19–21
mass production 65
materialistic values 66–8
MEG 163–4
Memory 128, 142
memory associations 52, 298, 378
men's brain 156
men's voices 253
mobility 63, 75
modern value system 70
mood factors 298
mood music 239–41, 246, 254

Index

mood scents 281–2
motivation 40
multiple sensory experiences 375, 390
multisensory 369
multisensory information 370
multisensory interaction 371–3
multisensory experience 370
multisensory evaluation 382
multisensory brand experience: definition 369
Music 377–9; behavior 228–9; concept 228; sound 221; structure 229, 243; tempo 229
music ear 223–4
music preference 233–4

nanotechnology 53–5
neural activities 54, 164, 169–70
neurophysiology 53–4
neurophysiology methods 54
neuromarketing 54, 161–3
neuroscience 161–2
Network (many pgs)
NFT (need for touch) 314

olfactory cells 263
optimal stimulation theory 380
organizational gender differences 157–8
oxytocin 231, 309

passive touching 308
perception 39
perception ability 130, 176
perception process 44, 130, 140, 200
perception studies 200
perceptual system 370–1
personality 40
physical taste 339, 341, 354
place markers 285–6
pleasant scents 268
post-Fordism model 63
post-materialistic values 66–8
post-modern 69
post-modern value system 70–2
post-modernization 61–2, 65
private consumption 1, 10
producer marketing 5, 7, 9–12
producer oriented approach 7–10
product: definition 2
product based approach
product design 110, 174, 207
product evaluation 294–5
production orientation 7–10
product scents 293–5, 297

product sound 256
Proust phenomena 279
purchaser and seller relations 25–7

rationality 150–2
the real world 70, 81, 85
relationship marketing (RM): as a model 394–6
relationship oriented marketing 25–7
relationship perspective 26–8
reptile brain 137
retail design 194
right brain hemisphere 134–6
RM see relationship marketing

Scent 268; brand 112, 300; congruence 295; experience 115, 252–3, 265; marketing 262–3, 292; perception 296; preferences 267, 274; resemblance 283; signals 279–80; stimuli 280; strategy 115, 293
search goods 363
segmentation 5, 6, 7, 9, 22, 40, 65, 80, 104
selective attention 147
selective perception 44
self-fulfillment 92–3
sensations 51–5, 105, 112, 118, 121, 122
sensogram 390
senses 54, 88–9; collaboration of the senses 97; integration of the senses 371, 372, 395
sensory brand building 397
sensory descriptions 214
sensory gender differences 158–9
sensory experience: definition 107
sensory information 110, 111, 131, 142, 226
sensory input 44, 138, 139, 141, 142
sensory marketing (SM): as an approach 394, 398; definition 394; as a model 395–7
sensory memory 143–4
sensory signals 141, 142
sensory/social colors 210
sensory stimuli 39, 104, 107, 111, 113–15, 121, 376; insufficient agreement
sensory strategy: definition 111

service dominated logic 32
service environment 124–5
service logic 32–5
service marketing 25, 102
service perspective 34–5
signature scent 301
SM (*see* sensory marketing) 88–127
societal culture 124
social differentiation 45
social factors 194, 281
social network 83–4, 86
social sense 352
social waves:-first wave 60–1; second wave 61;-third wave 61
sound design 244, 245, 258
sound experience 221–3
sound icons 258
sound logo types 257, 258
sound stimuli 249–54
sound strategy 113–14
stimulus response theory 37
structure 17, 22, 38, 42, 62, 131–8
sustainable marketing 53
symbol 47–50, 66, 70, 72–4
symbolic self completion theory 216
symbolic innovations 217, 219
symbolic world 58–9
symbolic interaction 46, 47
synesthesia 345, 371
synthetic sense 264

taste 338–68
taste buds 343–4
taste goods 362–3
taste preferences 214, 273, 349, 350, 354
taste sensations 55, 118, 341, 342, 343, 344, 353
taste strategy 118, 122
taste test 363–4, 366
tactile information 195, 334, 335, 375, 382, 383
tactile perception 313, 323, 324, 329
tactile qualities 311, 317, 327
tactile receptors 306
tactile sensations 122
tactile sense 304–6
tactile stimuli 116, 117, 233, 267, 312, 313, 318–23, 327–9, 332, 333, 334, 374, 382, 383

tempo 207, 229, 236, 237, 239, 240, 243, 244, 246, 251, 255, 377
tip-of-the-nose effect 278
touching 216, 308, 310, 313, 314, 315, 317, too many pgs
TM (*see* transaction marketing)
trigeminal stimulation 264

umami 117, 344
unpleasant sound 224, 255
unpleasant smells 272, 298
unconscious touching 316

valence 41, 148, 149, 181, 210, 229, 242, 341, 358
value creating 9, 27, 28, 29, 31, 33, 34, 35, 50, 52, 57, 75, 89, 96, 97, 119, 376, 398
verbal information 178 179, 202
verbal stimuli 179, 186, 193, 250, 280, 287, 386
visual aesthetics 195, 208, 361
visual consumption 172–4
visual element 192, 213
visual information 143, 144, 175, 178, 186, 195, 202, 332, 334, 335, 375, 382, 383, 385
visualization 173, 185, 205
visual marketing 112, 193
visual perception 175, 176, 177, 178, 182, 183, 186, 187, 188, 189, 199–202, 211, 213–16
visual preferences 183, 184, 185, 186, 189
visual sensations 122
visual stimuli 113, 137, 173, 174, 175, 178, 179, 180, 181, 182, 183, 184, 185, 186, 187, 190, 193–9
visual symbolism 183, 184, 190–2, 202–4, 216–19
visual system 112, 113, 176, 177, 309, 332, 370, 374
voices 113, 114, 122, 148, 221, 222, 224, 225, 226, 232, 233, 236, 238, 246, 248, 251–4, 258

wholesale merchant function 7
women's brain 128, 156, 157, 158
women's voices 225, 253, 254
working memory 144–5